EATING DISORDERS

A Clinical Guide to Counseling and Treatment

Monika M. Woolsey, MS, RD

American Dietetic Association
Chicago, Illinois

Library of Congress Cataloging-in-Publication Data

Woolsey, Monika.
    Eating disorders : a clinical guide to counseling and treatment /
    Monika Woolsey.
       p. ; cm.
    Includes bibliographical references and index.
    ISBN 0-88091-179-4
      1. Eating disorders—Diet therapy. I. Title.
    [DNLM: 1. Eating Disorders—diet therapy. 2. Eating Disorders—
    psychology. 3. Counseling. 4. Dietary Services. WM 175 W916e 2001]
    RC552.E18 W66 2001
    616.85'2606—dc21   2001033528

The views expressed in this publication are those of the authors and do not necessarily reflect
policies and/or official positions of the American Dietetic Association. Mention of product names
in this publication does not constitute endorsement by the authors or the American Dietetic
Association. The American Dietetic Association disclaims responsibility for the application of the
information contained herein.

10 9 8 7 6 5 4 3 2 1

CONTENTS

CHAPTER 12

Axis II: Personality Disorders   232

LISA M. VARNER, PH.D, R.D.

CHAPTER 13

Axis III: Medical Complications of Eating Disorders   258

TRUDY ALEXANDER, R.D.

CHAPTER 14

Nutrition and Nervous System Function   269

MONIKA M. WOOLSEY, M.S., R.D.

CHAPTER 15

Outpatient Nutrition Therapy for Eating Disorders   286

DIANE KEDDY, M.S., R.D.

CHAPTER 16

Development of Psychotherapeutic Techniques to Facilitate
Successful Change   312

SONDRA KRONBERG, M.A., R.D.

**SECTION FOUR:
Nutrition Therapy and
Eating Disorders**

This book provides a framework for understanding the relationship between nutrition and neuroendocrinology. The brain is where all our impulses originate — sometimes with split-second timing. The ability to perceive environmental changes and respond to them with appropriate choices is the key to ensuring survival. When those responses are inappropriate the results can be devastating.

Understanding why we eat what we eat and when we choose to eat it is fundamental to planning choices that successfully address eating problems. Whether your specialty is weight management, gastroenterology, cancer, or endocrinology, the brain influences your client's behaviors. Working with the client from the inside out, rather than from the outside in may mean adopting a nontraditional approach. Your outcome measures, treatment plans, and recommendations will be different than those resulting from the outside-in perspective. As dietitians, we have knowledge and skills that can help people live healthier lives. As dietitians who understand neuroendocrinology, we have the potential to bring a greater depth of knowledge and understanding to our practice and to our patients.

Eating Disorders: A Clinical Guide to Counseling and Treatment is designed to help nutrition therapists understand how they can apply the biopsychosocial model in their practices. The first two sections discuss biological, psychological, and social perspectives on the treatment of eating disorders and explore their interconnectedness. Section Three presents the American Psychiatric Association system of diagnosis and classification of mental disorders and nutritional treatment plans based on that diagnostic model. The last section offers additional perspectives on the relationship between nutrition therapy and eating disorders. The Appendix is a collection of additional research and learning resources.

ACKNOWLEDGMENTS

In addition to having a brain that carried me through the writing process, there are some other very important reasons this book exists. ADA was willing to publish my ideas and to be patient with me as I learned many details of publishing. My family was always there to encourage my nontraditional project and career choice. Several colleagues contributed important chapters to this book. Many, many other colleagues encouraged me to see this project through to completion. (And I can't forget the friends at the Arrowhead Starbucks who graciously let me park myself in their store for a year while I wrote and edited and fact-checked!) To all of you, its time to turn the page and see just what you encouraged. I hope the pages to follow enhance your professional work as much as it enhanced my work to put them together.

The author and the American Dietetic Association are grateful for the contributions of Trudy Alexander, R.D., Michael Braun, M.S., Diane Keddy, M.S., R.D., Karin M. Kratina, M.A., R.D., Sondra Kronberg, M.A., R.D., and Lisa M. Varner, Ph.D., R.D. who each wrote a chapter for this book.

"**A**norexia." The very word evokes the image of a wispy teenage girl, hovering over a leaf of lettuce, mentally calculating whether it will throw her daily intake off balance. In certain circles, that behavior has a mysterious, glamorous appeal. More than once, introducing myself and my specialty at social gatherings has brought the response, "Man, I wish *I* could be anorexic!" or "Can you share their secret?"

Bulimia, the cousin of anorexia, has a not-so-pleasant reputation, with less picturesque images of laxatives, self-induced vomiting, secretive behavior, and the lies required to explain so much time spent in the bathroom.

Binge eating empties our pockets. The diet industry grosses $32 billion annually. That's $4,000 per person *per year!* Binge eating. It stares us in the face every time we stand in line at the grocery store and read a magazine headline advertising the newest diet or the latest Hollywood weight loss success. But despite these advances, Americans are heavier than ever (1).

Eating disorders afflict 5–10 million American girls and women a year (2). They affect men, too; 10 percent of all teenagers with eating disorders are boys (3). Once thought to be "rich white women's diseases," they have crept into every culture and social strata, robbing women and men in all walks of life of the opportunity to be productive members of society. Eating disorders kill more of their victims than any other psychiatric disorder (4). They also debilitate. More than just an obsession with calories and fat, they are syndromes often accompanied by depression, fear, isolation, and suicidal thoughts (5).

Eating disorders intimidate. Eating disorders specialists at conferences are often buttonholed by dietitians who asked, "I have this client, and I know she's got an eating disorder, but I've never learned how to work with these disorders. How do I talk to them? How do I help? Am I qualified?"

This book tackles anorexia, bulimia, and binge eating disorder from all of these angles: their origins, pathology, and treatment. Because qualified nutrition professionals are needed to work to eradicate these disorders, this book is designed to introduce those professionals to the basics in the field, and to describe interventions they can incorporate into their own practices. It is the product of the collaborative efforts of eating disorders specialists across the country, and should allow those who want to move into this specialty do so without "reinventing the wheel" that others have so painstakingly created.

Individuals with eating disorders are not mysterious, glamorous, intimidating, or frightening. They are intelligent, thought-provoking, sensitive individuals who deserve to be valued for themselves and not for their size. They deserve to be heard and helped.

A CLOSER LOOK In a world of excess, the person with anorexia is an object of fascination. Seemingly unaffected by television ads, chocolate, and buffet dinners, she appears to cruise through life successfully avoiding fat and calories. She's the first one on the jogging trail in the morning, the only person in her peer group to fit into an enviable "size 2". She can always pass up the birthday cake at the office party, and is a vegetarian to boot. The self-control she exhibits impresses her peers.

In the next room, away from the spotlight, lives the person with bulimia. She starts the day with every intention of following in her friend's fat-free footsteps, but along the way things go wrong. The doughnut shop on the way to work smells a little too good. Then the boss brings bagels and cream cheese to the morning staff meeting. Lunch is OK—a dry green salad with some crackers on the side. But by 4 P.M. all she can think of is the end of work and happy hour. Three beers and a taco bar later, the person with bulimia is at home, waiting for her laxatives to kick in, ashamed and depressed, vowing that tomorrow will be different. It never is.

The person who binge eats has a highly visible eating dysfunction (*Box I.1*). She knows she would lose weight if she followed a diet, but time and time again she makes it through a few weeks of "compliance", only to have old behaviors reemerge and regain control. Despite the disapproval of her peers and the judgments about her intelligence and willpower on the part of her physician and even her nutrition therapist, the person who binge eats cannot break the cycle. Instead, she pulls out the ice cream and a magazine, and dreams about what it would be like to have anorexia.

When questioned by a reporter about speculation that she might have an eating disorder, a popular actress replied, "I don't do the 'throwing up' thing . . . that's disgusting." Yet later she proudly described restrictive eating habits that are red flags for anorexia. Anorexia, bulimia, and binge eating disorder are superficially different. The first presents itself as a disease of control, the second as some type of bizarre self-punishment, while the third would seem to demonstrate a complete lack of control. Under the surface, however, these three disorders are strikingly similar. All revolve around a preoccupation with food. All are dysfunctional responses to stress. All are associated with metabolic disturbances, including amenorrhea and thyroid dysfunction. All frequently coexist with unipolar

Box I.1
About Binge Eating Disorder and Obesity Research

Binge eating disorder (BED) was introduced to the *Diagnostic and Statistical Manual of Psychiatric Disorders* (DSM) in 1993. Currently it is a "research" category, and is being tested for inclusion as a bona fide diagnosis alongside anorexia nervosa and bulimia nervosa. Because BED has been officially classified fairly recently, the use of this term has just begun to appear in eating disorders research.

Obesity, on the other hand, has been well studied and documented for decades. Though not all obesity can be attributed to dysfunctional eating, psychoneuroendocrine studies in the field of obesity have elucidated hormonal profiles that are strikingly similar to those found in anorexia nervosa and bulimia nervosa.

In addition to the physiological similarities, the emotional presentations are also similar. An individual who presents with bulimia often reports that her eating disorder started as obesity, progressed to anorexia, and currently exists in its bulimic form. Clients often relate to periods of time using terminology such as "that was a bulimic phase" or "I got anorexic when that happened," suggesting that the eating disorders are all exacerbations of similar physiological and emotion origin, but present along a continuum of behaviors stretching from severe anorexia to morbid obesity.

At the time of this writing, research specifically addressing binge eating disorders is not plentiful. However, the direction that obesity research appears to be taking suggests that omitting this very important population merely because terminology has not caught up with technology would have been a mistake. For this reason, obesity, and visceral or android obesity in particular, has been included alongside anorexia nervosa and bulimia nervosa as if it were an official DSM-IV category.

depression. And in almost all cases, regardless of the diagnosis, the individuals want desperately to be able to go to the taco bar and eat normally. For all of her control and her small dress size, the person with anorexia, like her counterparts with bulimia and binge eating disorder, is alone and miserable.

Eating disorders have existed for centuries. The Romans routinely induced vomiting as part of their feasts. St. Catherine of Siena reportedly fasted for long periods of time and used twigs of a tree to bring up food she was forced to eat. Cases of both anorexia and bulimia have been described in medical literature for centuries, usually as rare case studies, and from a descriptive rather than an etiological point of view.

However, in the past century, cases of eating disorders have increased in frequency and have attracted the interest of numerous disciplines. Research on the subject appears regularly in psychology, psychiatry, nutrition, medical, and endocrinology journals, to name a few. The American Psychiatric Association now lists four subcategories of eating disorders in its *Diagnostic and Statistical Manual* (see *Boxes I.2-I.5*). Body image therapy is a career that until a decade ago didn't even exist. A popular topic of made-for-television movies is the plight of the young girl with an eating disorder. Yet despite this attention, eating disorders produce a higher mortality rate than any other psychiatric illness, and the number of victims continues to increase (2).

Box I.2
American Psychiatric
Association Diagnostic
Criteria for 307.1
Anorexia Nervosa

A. Refusal to maintain body weight at or above a minimally normal weight for age and height (eg, weight loss leading to maintenance of body weight less than 85% of that expected; or failure to make expected weight gain during period of growth, leading to body weight less than 85% of that expected).

B. Intense fear of gaining weight or becoming fat, even though underweight.

C. Disturbance in the way in which one's body weight or shape is experienced, undue influence of body weight or shape on self-evaluation, or denial of the seriousness of the current low body weight.

D. In postmenarcheal females, amenorrhea, ie, the absence of at least three consecutive menstrual cycles. (A woman is considered to have amenorrhea if her periods occur only following hormone, eg, estrogen, administration.)

Restricting Type: During the current episode of anorexia nervosa, the person has not regularly engaged in binge-eating or purging behavior (ie, self-induced vomiting or the misuse of laxatives, diuretics, or enemas).

Binge-Eating/Purging Type: During the current episode of anorexia nervosa, the person has regularly engaged in binge-eating or purging behavior (ie, self-induced vomiting or the misuse of laxatives, diuretics, or enemas).

Source: American Psychiatric Association. *Diagnostic and Statistical Manual of Psychiatric Disorders.* 5th ed. Washington, DC: American Psychiatric Association; 2000.

Box I.3
American Psychiatric
Association Diagnostic
Criteria for 307.51
Bulimia Nervosa

A. Recurrent episodes of binge eating. An episode of binge eating is characterized by both of the following:

　1. eating, in a discrete period of time (eg, within any 2-hour period), an amount of food that is definitely larger than most people would eat during a similar period of time and under similar circumstances;

　2. a sense of lack of control over eating during the episode (eg, a feeling that one cannot stop eating or control what or how much one is eating).

B. Recurrent inappropriate compensatory behavior in order to prevent weight gain, such as self-induced vomiting; misuse of laxatives, diuretics, enemas, or other medications; fasting; or excessive exercise.

C. The binge eating and inappropriate compensatory behaviors both occur, on average, at least twice a week for 3 months.

D. Self-evaluation is unduly influenced by body shape and weight.

E. The disturbance does not occur exclusively during episodes of anorexia nervosa.

Purging Type: During the current episode of bulimia nervosa, the person has regularly engaged in self-induced vomiting or the misuse of laxatives, diuretics, or enemas.

Nonpurging Type: During the current episode of bulimia nervosa, the person has used other inappropriate compensatory behaviors, such as fasting or excessive exercise, but has not regularly engaged in self-induced vomiting or the misuse of laxatives, diuretics, or enemas.

Source: American Psychiatric Association. *Diagnostic and Statistical Manual of Psychiatric Disorders.* 5th ed. Washington, DC: American Psychiatric Association; 2000.

A. For females, all of the criteria for anorexia nervosa are met except that the individual has regular menses.

B. All of the criteria for anorexia nervosa are met except that, despite significant weight loss, the individual's current weight is in the normal range.

C. All of the criteria for bulimia nervosa are met except that the binge eating and inappropriate compensatory mechanisms occur at a frequency of less than twice a week or for a duration of less than 3 months.

D. The regular use of inappropriate compensatory behavior by an individual of normal body weight after eating small amounts of food (eg, self-induced vomiting after the consumption of two cookies).

E. Repeatedly chewing and spitting out, but not swallowing, large amounts of food.

F. Binge-eating disorder: recurrent episodes of binge eating in the absence of the regular use of inappropriate compensatory behaviors characteristic of bulimia nervosa.

Source: American Psychiatric Association. *Diagnostic and Statistical Manual of Psychiatric Disorders*. 5th ed. Washington, DC: American Psychiatric Association; 2000.

Box I.4
Diagnostic Criteria for 307.50 Eating Disorder Not Otherwise Specified

A. Recurrent episodes of binge eating. An episode of binge eating is characterized by both of the following:
1. eating, in a discrete period of time (eg, within any 2-hour period), an amount of food that is definitely larger than most people would eat in a similar period of time under similar circumstances;
2. a sense of lack of control over eating during the episode (eg, a feeling that one cannot stop eating or control what or how much one is eating).

B. The binge-eating episodes are associated with three (or more) of the following:
1. eating much more rapidly than normal,
2. eating until feeling uncomfortably full,
3. eating large amounts of food when not feeling physically hungry,
4. eating alone because of being embarrassed by how much one is eating,
5. feeling disgusted with oneself, depressed, or very guilty after overeating.

C. Marked distress regarding binge eating is present.

D. The binge eating occurs, on average, at least 2 days a week for 6 months.

   Note: The method of determining frequency differs from that used for bulimia nervosa; future research should address whether the preferred method of setting a frequency threshold is counting the number of days on which binges occur or counting the number of episodes of binge eating.

E. The binge eating is not associated with the regular use of inappropriate compensatory behaviors (eg, purging, fasting, excessive exercise) and does not occur exclusively during the course of anorexia nervosa or bulimia nervosa.

Source: American Psychiatric Association. *Diagnostic and Statistical Manual of Psychiatric Disorders*. 5th ed. Washington, DC: American Psychiatric Association; 2000.

Box I.5
Research Criteria for Binge Eating Disorder

In response, researchers have developed a model for the development of eating disorders that combines the efforts of all of these disciplines, the biopsychosocial perspective. With this multidisciplinary approach, practitioners have learned that pharmacological treatment is more effective when combined with cognitive-behavioral therapy, and that psychological treatment is most effective when conducted on a well-nourished brain. The effects of social messages on the biochemical functioning of the brain have even been questioned (6). The biopsychosocial model has demonstrated how the mind and body are intricately connected.

For all of the research and theory, however, it is important not to forget that each person who suffers from an eating disorder is a human being. The disease disrupts self-esteem, relationships, productivity, and possibly survival. It is a painful, lonely, isolating disease. One young woman recovering from anorexia recorded some of the most significant impacts her disease had on her life in the following journal entry:

I always separated my food, and refrained from putting margarine or fats on my vegetables, salads, etc.

At every opportunity, my mind raced with thoughts of what I'd eaten that day, what I could have, when I could eat next, how I could somehow keep going or get by with skipping or restricting my food.

I would buy different foods that nobody else would eat, or else hide what I had decided was "safe" so no one else could eat it.

Any disappointment, excuse, or interruption would give me an "out" to delay eating or not eat at all.

At restaurants, I told myself that I would "make up" when I get home, then I would order the most "healthy", unbreaded, never-fried, plainest meat on the menu. Any sides (salads, baked potatoes, vegetables, etc), I would order without butter, and with dressing "on the side". Then I would just dribble the dressing on.

I always had a great fear of unknown contents of food, ways of preparation, added sauces, etc, as if I was afraid of eating something "unsafe" without knowing it.

After receiving food orders, I usually would leave at least a bite or two of the meat, and maybe the potato, depending on the size of each.

Many times I would get a serving of something that I knew I'd never eat, just to look like I was planning to eat more; then I'd claim it tasted bad or cover it with my napkin and throw it away.

This client finally entered treatment not for medical reasons, but because she wanted to participate in family gatherings and spend time with her children, regardless of the food involved in these activities. She needed practitioners who could provide state-of-the-art treatments without losing sight of her personal goals. She needed her treatment team to understand her pain, not just her lab reports.

In addition, this young woman needed to trust the nutrition therapist in charge of her care. For her nutrition therapist, nutrition was an important part of the biopsychosocial model. For the client, nutrition was everything. As much as she knew she needed the other components of her treatment, she was not able to trust them if she couldn't trust the person in charge of her food.

The nutrition therapist on the eating disorder treatment team has a unique and important role. In addition to having considerable training in each component of the biopsychosocial model, the nutrition therapist, by virtue of his knowledge of food, has the immediate attention of his clients. In many cases he functions as the liaison between the client and the rest of the treatment team. This focus can intimidate the inexperienced nutrition therapist. (In this book the term "nutrition therapist" is used to identify a dietetics practitioner who also has training in psychology, psychiatry, and counseling. While no professional certification currently distinguishes this advanced level of practice, Chapter 18 describes the training and supervision recommended for nutrition therapists.)

This book is designed to help nutrition therapists understand how they can convert this focus into a treatment style that balances treating, educating, listening, and coaching. The right approach wins over the client as well as the other caregivers, both personal and professional. And it can save lives. The first two sections (Chapters 1 through 8) are devoted to the etiology of eating disorders from the three perspectives of the biopsychosocial model. In each chapter, examples are provided that demonstrate the interconnectedness that makes eating disorders so difficult to treat. Section Three introduces the system for diagnosis and classification of mental disorders developed by the American Psychiatric Association, the current professional standard. It also presents nutritional treatment plans based on this diagnosis system, and explains how the nutrition therapist can facilitate the treatment modalities employed by other team members. The final section includes the perspectives of a variety of nutrition therapists with experience in eating disorders. The concepts, interventions, and handouts offered can serve as resources for nutrition therapists who would like to accept the challenge of treating the eating disordered client.

Numerous case studies are included throughout to show how the textual information might be integrated into the real world. These case studies demonstrate that eating disorder treatment is often an art rather than hard science. However, this does not mean that learning to work with this population requires a God-given talent! Many initially reluctant nutrition therapists have learned to their surprise that they actually have a gift for this very special work.

REFERENCES

1. American Psychiatric Association. *Diagnostic and Statistical Manual of Mental Disorders*. 5th ed. Washington, DC: American Psychiatric Association; 2000.

2. Crowther JH, Wolf EM, Sherwood N. Epidemiology of bulimia nervosa. In: Crowther M, Tannenbaum DL, Hobfoll SE, Stephens MAP, eds. *The Etiology of Bulimia Nervosa: The Individual and Familial Context*. Washington, DC: Taylor & Francis; 1992: 1–26.

Fairburn CG, Hay PJ, Welch, SL. Binge eating and bulimia nervosa: Distribution and determinants. In: Fairburn CG, Wilson GT, eds. *Binge Eating: Nature, Assessment, and Treating*. New York: Guilford; 1993:123–143.

Gordon RA. *Anorexia and Bulimia: Anatomy of a Social Epidemic*. New York: Blackwell; 1990.

Hoek HW. The distribution of eating disorders. In: Brownell KD, Fairburn CG, eds. *Eating Disorders and Obesity: A Comprehensive Handbook*. New York: Guilford; 1995: 207–211.

Shisslak CM, Crago M, Estes LS. The spectrum of eating disturbances. *Int J Eating Disord*. 1995;18(3): 209–219.

Available at: http://www.edap.org/edinfo/stats.html. Accessed March 9, 2001.

3. Too fat? Too thin? How media images of celebrities teach kids to hate their bodies. *People*. June 3, 1996;45(22):64–74.

4. Comer RJ. *Abnorm Psychol*. 2nd ed. New York, NY: WH Freeman Publishing Co; 1995.

5. Brewerton TD. Toward a unified theory of serotonin dysfunction in eating and related disorders. *Psychoneuroendocrinol*. 1995;20(6):561–590.

6. Hoek HW, Bartelds AI, Bosveld JJ, et al. Impact of urbanization on detection rates of eating disorders. *Am J Psychiatry*. 1995 Sep;152(9):1272–1278.

CHAPTER 1

The Neuroendocrine Basis of Eating Disorders

MONIKA M. WOOLSEY, M.S., R.D.

Of the three types of influences on eating behavior—biological, psychological, and social—the biological are the most intimate and intuitive. They are a combination of reflex responses that have evolved over the years to ensure that body temperature, blood pressure, blood glucose level, oxygen intake, and waste removal are all maintained. In other words, they ensure survival. Because eating disorders are usually accompanied with at least a few medical complications, much research into these diseases initially focused on a biological origin.

In recent years the focus of biological influences has narrowed to the neuroendocrine system (1-4), where the control of most organ functions originates. This highly complex system is susceptible to numerous internal and external influences. A basic review of healthy neuroendocrine function will make a discussion of the pathophysiology of the dysfunctional system more meaningful. Throughout this book, we will continuously refer to the basic groundwork laid out in this chapter, as neuroendocrine function affects our thoughts, choices, moods, and behaviors. As the chapter progresses, keep in mind how many biological forces are interacting at any given time to determine whether eating does or does not occur. The intricacy and coordination of multiple processes and environmental changes are mind-boggling; they illustrate what an amazingly complex and truly wonderful machine the body really is.

Neuroendocrinology is the study of glands, the organs that enable an individual to adapt to changes in his or her environment. It is also the study of the neural input that regulates the functions of these glands (5). Within the human brain, the hypothalamus directly coordinates some changes in glandular function while other coordination is delegated to the anterior pituitary.

Each gland in this system monitors information it receives, provides important information about critical changes to the hypothalamus and anterior pituitary, and responds to directions it receives from both these control centers to maintain stability in its portion of the system. In addition, specialized receptors (ie, osmoreceptors, baroreceptors, and taste receptors) are stationed at crucial points throughout the body and apprise the hypothalamus of upcoming situations that will soon need attention. The hypothalamus constantly adjusts its instructions based on the information it receives from glands and receptors. This process is known as a "feedback loop" (*Figure 1.1*) (5).

Figure 1.1
Feedback Loop

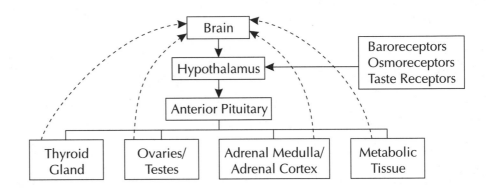

THE FOUR TYPES OF REFLEXES

Four types of instructions are sent from the hypothalamus and anterior pituitary to endocrine organs: neural reflexes, endocrine reflexes, neurohormonal reflexes, and neuroendocrine reflexes. To begin to understand them, imagine a woman hiking through the woods who suddenly hears a large "crack". She stops, looks for the source of the sound, and spots a tree leaning over the trail. As our hiker approaches slowly to investigate the stability of the tree, it creaks again and leans a few inches closer to the ground. She decides to walk around the opposite side of the tree and continue her hike. This seemingly simple response was executed by the brain, based on dozens of messages from the body's endocrine consultants. Together they initiated what is commonly known as a *stress response*.

Neural Reflexes

The initial "creak" supplied audio information to the nervous system, which in turn sent a neural reflex message to the skeletal muscle arterioles: "Strange noise! Send norepinephrine!" Immediately the arterioles dilated to allow more blood flow to the muscle fibers, and began to pull glucose from the bloodstream to fuel the muscles, which were now tensed and ready to respond to the noise.

Since the arterioles are connected to the hypothalamus through direct innervation, this course of events transpired in a fraction of the time it took to read about it. The hiker was probably startled enough to jump and gasp for breath, and might have noticed her heart rate rise temporarily, but otherwise she reacted instinctively to the sound of the falling tree.

As the readied skeletal muscle pulled glucose out of circulation, the adrenal medulla sensed the drop and responded with an endocrine reflex. An urgent message was sent back to the brain: "Low blood glucose!"

Endocrine Reflexes

The brain immediately responded to the accumulating evidence of trouble with an urgent order to the adrenal medulla: "Send epinephrine!" The adrenal medulla, as directed, released this hormone message into the bloodstream. The body reacted with a number of measures. Glycogen was converted to glucose and sent to the bloodstream. The cardiovascular system accelerated its output. Respiration rate increased. Blood flow to nonessential organs was deployed to skeletal muscle. The sensory system was mobilized to further research the sights and sounds of the nearby environment. All systems were notified that a potential enemy was being investigated, and they should be ready to fight the foe or mobilize and run.

These changes enabled the hiker to explore the falling tree while remaining ready to flee at any moment. Her sensory intake was working at maximum output, sending information about the tiniest shadow and faintest noise back to the brain for input. She might have heard her own heartbeat in the silence of the woods. All of this occurred because of an endocrine reflex, a glandular response to a change in chemical concentration.

With the body now poised and ready to fight or flee, the sensory system sent a message back to the brain: "There's a tree leaning over the trail, about ready to fall to the ground, but it's several feet ahead. It's not so urgent." A neural reflex message was sent back to the skeletal muscle arterioles, which responded by constricting slightly. The adrenal medulla communicated back to the hypothalamus that, because of this change in the arterioles, blood sugar was rising. In return, the "Epinephrine!" message was canceled and the hiker chose to walk around the tree and continue the hike.

The rapid speed at which instinctive reactions are triggered is crucial for survival. Had this hiker not been able to stop and change her course, she might have been crushed by the tree. Because she did respond, in a few seconds she was out of imminent danger. However, to be on the safe side, the hypothalamus followed its immediate reflexive measures with reinforcements.

The same neural messages that triggered the adrenal medulla also stimulated the hypothalamus to send corticotropin-releasing hormone (CRH) to the anterior pituitary with the message "Our system needs backup help!" In response, the anterior pituitary, functioning as a special messenger, sent adrenocorticotropic hormone (ACTH) to the adrenal cortex, stating that additional measures needed to be put into action. The adrenal cortex responded to this directive with the message "Send cortisol!" Immediately peripheral tissues converted available proteins and fats to glucose to help restore what the muscles had taken out of circulation (*Figure 1.2*).

Neuroendocrine Reflexes

This communication route combined a neural message and two separate hormone messages, hence the name "neuroendocrine reflex." Neuroendocrine reflexes

Figure 1.2
Neuroendocrine Reflex

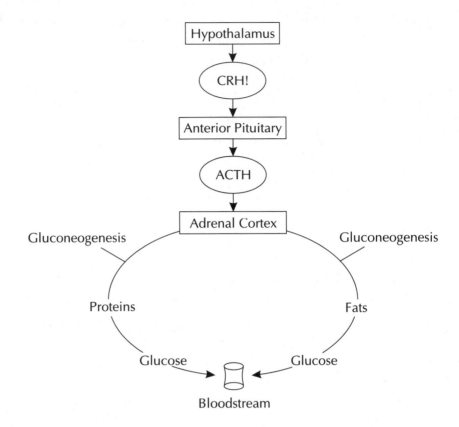

are more complex than neural or endocrine reflexes. Additional steps in the communication chain allow for more subtle adjustments in output messages, so neuroendocrine reflexes generally occur where "fine-tuning" can help maintain physiological balance. However, it will soon become apparent that the additional steps in the communication process leave this system susceptible to multiple errors in the transmission of messages.

Neurohormonal Reflexes

In addition to immediate threats, the endocrine system also monitors subtle changes in the environment that could, over time, be troublesome. In the process of responding to the falling tree, the hiker's respiration rate increased to provide more oxygen to her muscles. Her rapid expirations increased the loss of body water into the atmosphere. By the time the hiker was several miles away from the tree, osmoreceptors and baroreceptors throughout the system had detected increased blood sodium levels and blood pressure had dropped. The hypothalamus responded by sending a "Send vasopressin!" order to the pituitary gland, which in turn told the kidneys to switch from filtering water out of the system to reabsorbing and conserving water *(Figure 1.3)*. Again, because multiple messages need to be sent in this pathway, multiple opportunities exist for the transmission of erroneous messages.

The hiker scenario is an oversimplification of a highly complex system, not a thorough overview of hormone function. It illustrates four important concepts about the neuroendocrine system that will become recurring themes throughout this book:

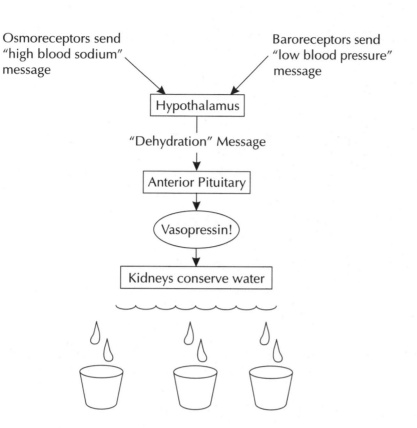

Figure 1.3
Neurohormonal Reflex

- The neuroendocrine system responds to input from a variety of sources, including sensory input, chemical concentrations in the body, levels of other hormones, and the influences of specialized receptors throughout the body.

- A change in input from any of these sources changes the body's reflexive responses, which are programmed to maintain homeostasis and survival.

- Most neuroendocrine systems have been organized into hormone groups, which function within a feedback loop commonly known as an axis. (For example, the hypothalamo-pituitary-ovarian axis is the feedback loop that involves all the hormones in the reproductive system.) Though an axis tends to have most of its influence within its own system, endocrine axes are also interrelated. When stress triggers the hypothalamo-pituitary-adrenal axis, for example, the resulting cortisol increase can affect the hypothalamo-pituitary-ovarian axis and reduce the production of reproductive hormones. Practically, the end result of prolonged stress is often reproductive dysfunction.

- The more complicated the system, the more sources exist from which input can alter the final action of the target organ.

TRANSMISSION OF A NEURAL MESSAGE

Neurons are aligned end to end, originating in the brain and spreading out to locations throughout the body. The brain, hypothalamus, anterior pituitary, and other centers coordinate voluntary and involuntary responses by means of these neurons. Neurons have a shape uniquely designed to facilitate efficient communication. Long and slender, they have both "sending" and "receiving" ends, a design that allows them to quickly and specifically communicate important messages. (See *Figure 1.4.*) The *axonal,* or sending, end is bulb-shaped and contains synaptic vesicles in which neurotransmitters are stored for future use. The *dendritic,* or receiving, end is shaped like a starburst. Its membrane is lined with sites specifically programmed to receive specific messages. Between each axon and its target dendrite is a space known as the *synapse.*

Figure 1.4
Basic Neuron Anatomy

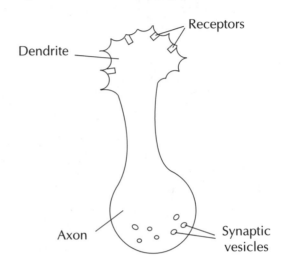

Neural stimulation triggers the synaptic vesicles to move toward the axonal membrane and release neurotransmitters by diffusion through the membrane into the synapse, across the synapse, to receptors on the dendrite of the next neuron in the pathway *(Figure 1.5)*. Once the neurotransmitter binds with the receptor, that neuron is stimulated to send an impulse to its own axon. Transmission continues until the message reaches its target site: another part of the brain, another nerve, a tissue, or an organ. Once the dendrite has received and passed on its neural message, the neurotransmitter molecules are recollected by the axon and recycled into new synaptic vesicles to be used for the next message.

An alteration in any of these steps, by internal feedback or by a change in the external environment, changes the message that is sent. Because so many of the medical complications observed in eating disorders occur along the neuroendocrine pathways, much research has been to devoted to determining steps in the neuroendocrine communication system that may be malfunctioning.

NEUROTRANS- MITTERS —WHERE IT ALL STARTS

Each neurotransmitter communicates a specific message. For example, norepinephrine is programmed to initiate one part of the stress response, skeletal muscle arteriole dilation. Norepinephrine receptors are located in the neurons linking the brain to skeletal muscle arterioles, as well as in the arterioles themselves. The stress response elicits many other changes on organ functions (ie,

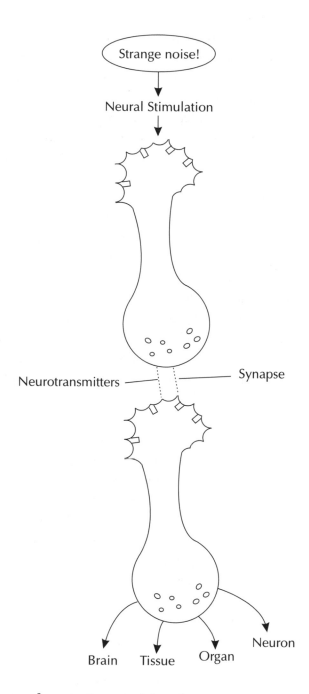

Figure 1.5
Impulse Transmission
in CNS

increased heart and respiration rates), but these are communicated by other neu-rotransmitters specific to those functions, including acetylcholine and dopamine (6).

The synaptic steps in the communication link are crucial for complete message transmission. Because their function originates at such a high level in the neu-roendocrine system and because their influence spans the entire system, under-standing neurotransmitter physiology has been important to understanding numerous disorders, including depression, aggression, seasonal affective disorder, anxiety, suicide, obsessive-compulsive disorders, and eating disorders (7).

Most early neurotransmitter research focused on the origins of depression. This direction was taken because individuals using the antihypertensive drug reserpine were found to have a higher than average incidence of depression. When researchers discovered that reserpine lowered axonal and synaptic norepinephrine levels, they concluded that depression was the result of a norepinephrine deficiency (8). For approximately 30 years this theory prevailed, and pharmacological treatment of depression took mainly two forms: monoamine oxidase (MAO) inhibitors and the tricyclic antidepressants, medications that increase circulating levels of norepinephrine (9).

In the 1980s reserpine was discovered to have the additional effect of lowering axonal/central nervous system (CNS) serotonin levels (10). On the basis of this research, a new class of antidepressants was introduced. Selective serotonin reuptake inhibitors (SSRIs), which function by selectively inhibiting recycling of released serotonin and thus increasing synaptic levels of serotonin, have been used with wide success (11).

An acetylcholine deficiency can also create a depressive state (12), suggesting that numerous neurotransmitters play a part in mood formation. Because there are over 100 neurotransmitters, some researchers believe that attributing the cause of all depression to just three might be premature. Rather, they propose an imbalance in proportions of all the neurotransmitters, not the level of a specific one, is the root biological cause of depression (13,14).

Another research focus is the neurons themselves. Studies have suggested that dendritic receptors in depressed individuals are not efficient at binding with available neurotransmitters (15,16). In other words, under normal conditions, there may be more than enough neurotransmitter molecules available to create a nerve impulse, but because neurotransmitters cannot bind and are left in the synapse, the neurons function as if there is a neurotransmitter deficiency. According to this theory, current antidepressant medications work because they increase the ratio of neurotransmitters to receptor sites and increase the chance that binding will occur. What may become apparent as research continues is that depression is a collection of malfunctions that elicit a set of common symptoms, and that there are actually several routes by which these symptoms manifest. As the brain is more clearly understood, treatment for depression and related disorders may become so refined that the point of dysfunction can be isolated and an intervention specific to the individual's physiological dysfunction prescribed.

DEPRESSION, EATING DISORDERS, AND NEUROTRANSMITTERS

Approximately 50 to 75 percent of all individuals with eating disorders have a lifetime history of major depressive disorders (17). Evaluation of the effects of antidepressant medications on eating disorder symptoms has demonstrated that these drugs lessen the severity of eating disorder behaviors, as well as comorbid conditions (ie, obsessive-compulsive disorder, anxiety disorder, panic disorder, phobic disorder, and seasonal affective disorder) (11). These findings have stimulated speculation that biological influences on these diseases are significant, and research into various aspects of the biology of eating disorders in recent years has exploded. The following summarizes some of the research highlights in the area of influences of neurotransmitter and synaptic function on eating disorders, and factors that affect neurotransmitter function.

Stress

Stress is defined as any physiological or emotional influence that can affect physiological function. A "eustressful" condition is one in which the body manages environmental input at the rate at which it is occurring. When the scales tip and the body is stimulated faster than it can react, the stress reaction occurs. Most of us can identify episodes of stress from our everyday lives: traumatic events, personal conflicts, extreme changes in weather, and serious illnesses. However, positive life events that bring about significant biological, emotional, or behavioral change can also be stressful. Marriage, divorce, a new job, a lost job, the birth of a child, exercise, and even changes in weight are all significant changes which the body responds to as a stress.

A high percentage of eating disorders begin soon after a traumatic event or other significant change (eg, the loss of a loved one, divorce in the immediate family, graduation, or leaving for college). The peak age of onset for anorexia nervosa is 14 to 18 years, a time when many physical, psychological, and social changes are occurring (9). Abuse histories are also common in eating-disordered individuals; 80 percent of individuals treated for eating disorders at the Rader Institute reported a history of sexual abuse (18). Obese individuals tend to have a higher incidence of meaningful life events in the period immediately preceding weight gain (17). These observations suggest that stress is a major factor in the development of eating disorders.

In the 1970s Hans Selye advanced one of the first theories about the physiological impact of stress. He proposed that, when exposed to a stressful situation, the body elicits a three-stage coping response, which he called the "general adaptation syndrome" (9). In the initial stage of this response, the body initiates the "alarm reaction," or a set of neuroendocrine coping mechanisms, in an attempt to maintain homeostasis. If the stress continues, the body enters the "resistance stage," or continued secretion of stress hormones, such as cortisol. Over a prolonged period of time the body's ability to maintain homeostasis wears down, and the "exhaustion stage" is entered. Unchecked, this course of events can lead to death.

Selye's theory suggests that certain crucial physiological functions can literally be worn out by prolonged stress. As the central component of the stress response, the neuroendocrine system is especially vulnerable to wear and tear. When neurons constantly fire, axons release neurotransmitters faster than they can be recaptured, and a deficiency is likely to develop. Eventually the body cannot respond to further input and "shuts down" its sensory intake. Isolation and excessive sleep, classic symptoms of depression, may be attempts by the body to turn off input and "take a breather" to restore neurotransmitter levels. (See *Box 1.1*.) Note that many of these behaviors are also common in the eating-disordered individual.

Box 1.1
Symptoms of
Depression

Depressed mood

Loss of interest in activities

Significant weight loss or gain when not dieting

Decreased or increased appetite

Insomnia OR Hypersomnia

Psychomotor agitation OR Psychomotor retardation

Fatigue or loss of energy

Feelings of worthlessness or guilt

Diminished ability to think, concentrate, or make decisions

Recurrent thoughts of suicide or death

Source: American Psychiatric Association (11). Used with permission.

In some situations stress conditions the nervous system to become hypersensitive and "misfire" at inappropriate times (9). This type of dysfunction wastes neurotransmitter supplies and exacerbates the stress response. It often manifests as panic disorder, anxiety disorder, or post-traumatic stress disorder. Individuals with these diagnoses tend to have difficulties sleeping, are hypervigilant, and have an extra sensitivity to sensory stimuli (11). All three eating disorders have a high incidence of comorbidity with these psychiatric conditions (17). In either type of dysfunction, the end result is a neurotransmitter deficiency that creates significant functional problems throughout the system.

Light Exposure   In many people depression seems to cycle with the seasons, worsening in the fall and improving in the spring. Epidemiologists have noted that incidence of this type of depression (known as seasonal affective disorder, or SAD) tends to increase with latitudinal distance from the equator, and believe that it is due to a lack of adequate exposure to light (17). This disorder also affects appetite; individuals with SAD report increased appetite and carbohydrate cravings during winter months (11).

Evidence suggests that eating disorders and SAD are related to a similar neurotransmitter dysfunction. Eating disorder symptoms, particularly those of bulimia, tend to follow similar seasonal patterns, and individuals with bulimia report more severe SAD symptoms than others (19,20). Eating-disordered individuals with seasonal patterns have also been reported to respond well to light therapy, as do individuals with uncomplicated SAD (21).

Environmental light is believed to have its influence through the pineal gland, part of the neuroendocrine system. This gland, positioned just behind the eyes, responds to changes in detected light by affecting the production and secretion of the hormone melatonin (5,9). Triggered by norepinephrine, melatonin production increases in darkness and decreases with increased exposure to light (22). Since serotonin is a metabolic precursor for melatonin (5), serotonin metabolism is also light dependent; increased production of melatonin may act to deplete serotonin stores *(Figure 1.6)*. The amino acid tryptophan, a precurser to serotonin, is absorbed across the blood-brain barrier, and is converted into melatonin. In the presence of ultraviolet light, serotonin is preferentially used as a neurotransmitter, and is eventually broken down into its metabolite, 5-HIAA (5-hydroxyindole-3-acetic acid). Without ultraviolet light stimulating the pineal gland, serotonin is preferentially converted into melatonin, which prepares the body for sleep.

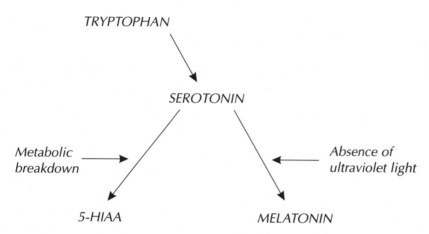

Figure 1.6
Metabolic Pathway for
Formation of Melatonin

Seasonal affective disorder and eating disorders with seasonal components may actually stem from a serotonin deficiency. This deficiency may "jumpstart" an individual into a vicious cycle of behaviors that is difficult to break. As depression increases, so does isolation, which decreases exposure to light, which furthers depression, and so on.

Variations in light exposure are not completely related to latitude. At least one researcher has proposed that the change over the past century from physical to sedentary work has moved humans from outdoor to indoor environments and decreased exposure to natural light (7). Another major lifestyle change affecting exposure to light has been an increase in work around the clock in an effort to increase productivity. The biological impact of these sociological changes is starting to gain attention as partial explanations for why the incidence of depression and eating disorders has increased over the past century.

Sleep

Once thought to be insignificant, sleep is now considered crucial to survival. During sleep, metabolism slows down and body temperature drops, allowing for energy conservation. During certain stages of sleep, particularly rapid eye movement (REM) sleep, brain waves and neurotransmissions increase, leading sleep researchers to propose that sleep is a period not of inactivity, but of highly specialized activity without which function during waking hours begins to deteriorate. Sleep deprivation in volunteers has repeatedly been demonstrated to be a stress in itself, resulting in hallucinations, psychoses, paranoia, and bizarre behavior (23).

Bouts of sleep are made up of two distinct types. Non-REM sleep is thought to be the portion of sleep during which recovery from fatigue occurs, while REM sleep is thought to be when information processing and information storage takes place. While non-REM sleep typically takes place at the beginning of sleep, REM sleep is predominant in the later hours of sleep.

The hypothalamus, in addition to controlling the endocrine system, contains the body's circadian clock, which controls REM and non-REM sleep cycles. Acetylcholine is known to increase REM sleep in humans, while norepinephrine and serotonin secretions "turn off" REM sleep (23). The concept that the ratios of acetylcholine, serotonin, and norepinephrine are important to normal sleep is popular with sleep scientists, just as neuropsychologists believe they influence depression and eating disorders.

Since altered neurotransmitter ratios in the hypothalamus induce changes both in mood and in sleep, it would make sense that sleep and depression are related. It would also make sense that stress would influence sleep patterns, as it does mood state. Since half of all REM sleep occurs in the last third of a normal night's sleep, a voluntary loss of sleep (which is common with stress) deprives one mainly of REM sleep. Lack of REM sleep may serve to deprive the body of its information processing time, and may leave it more susceptible to stresses that occur in the next wake cycle.

Stress affects the quantity and quality of sleep, presumably because it increases the release of norepinephrine and serotonin. In depression, nocturnal sleep is shortened and daytime sleep increases (9). The quantity of sleep may actually exceed that of nondepressed sleep, but the sleep pattern is distinctively different. Depressed individuals experience REM sleep soon after falling asleep, experience longer periods of REM sleep in the early phases of falling asleep, and have less REM sleep at the end of a sleep bout. They also experience more eye movements and less deep sleep than nondepressed individuals (9). Similar sleep patterns have been observed in eating-disordered individuals, especially those with anorexia (24,25).

From a neuroendocrine standpoint, these findings make sense, since an individual whose neurotransmitter ratio is disrupted would more easily "turn on" REM sleep and be less likely to achieve non-REM sleep, where recovery from fatigue appears to occur. This may explain why depressed individuals report less restful sleep than nondepressed individuals. In individuals who are sleeping more, the increased exposure to darkness could be increasing melatonin production and depleting serotonin stores, further enhancing depression and creating another factor that adds to the vicious cycle of behaviors seen in depression and eating disorders (Figure 1.7).

Changes in sleep habits also affect nutritional status. A sleep-deprived animal with normal caloric intake and output will lose weight. As an animal is sleep deprived, it requires more calories to maintain energy balance (25). A change in sleep habits can also decrease dietary intake, as it can interfere with habitual mealtimes and decrease total dietary intake or alter meal timing. As nutritional status is important for the maintenance of neurotransmitter function (see Chap-

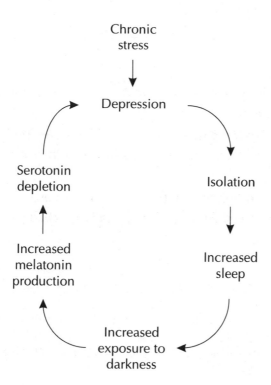

Chronic
stress

Depression

Serotonin
depletion

Isolation

Increased
melatonin
production

Increased
sleep

Increased
exposure to
darkness

Figure 1.7
Cycle of Light
Deprivation Initiated by
Chronic Stress

ter 14), sleep deprivation may contribute to the development of eating disorders by making it difficult to maintain adequate neuronutritional status.

Sleep dysfunction can sometimes be a crucial part of eating disorders. Individuals with bulimia and binge eating often report waking up in the morning and only learning from the food wrappers left on the counter that they binged the night before. This specific behavior occurs frequently enough that several new subcategories have been proposed for inclusion in the DSM-IV (*Box 1.2*) (26). Nutrition assessments should include questions about sleeping habits, particularly when binge eating is reported or being ruled out, and especially in individuals who insist that they are keeping accurate records and cannot understand why they do not seem to be making progress.

Sleepwalking
Periodic limb movement disorder
Triazolam abuse
Obstructive sleep apnea with eating during apnea-induced confusional arousal
Obstructive sleep apnea with periodic limb movement disorder
Familial sleepwalking and sleep-related eating
Sleepwalking and irregular sleep/wake pattern disorder
Familial restless legs syndrome and sleep-related eating
Anorexia nervosa with nocturnal bulimia
Amitryptiline treatment of migraines

Source: Schenck et al (26).

**Box 1.2
Proposed New
Subcategories of Eating
Disorders with Sleep
Disorder Comorbidity**

SUMMARY

- The hypothalamus and anterior pituitary regulate homeostasis with four types of responses: neural, endocrine, neurohormonal, and neuroendocrine.

- The hypothalamus and anterior pituitary send messages through neurons. These messages can be interrupted or altered by changes at numerous locations between their origin and destination.

- Depression is a common comorbid condition with eating disorders. It may be related to a number of predisposing factors, including stress, light exposure, and sleep changes.

REFERENCES

1. Abrams GM, Schipper HM. Neuroendocrine syndromes of the hypothalamus. *Neurol Clin.* 1986;4(4):769–782.

2. Brewerton TD. Toward a unified theory of serotonin dysfunction in eating and related disorders. *Psychoneuroendocrinol.* 1995;20(6):561–590.

3. Logue AW. *The Psychology of Eating and Drinking.* 2nd ed. New York, NY: WH Freeman & Company; 1991.

4. Morley JE, Blundell JE. The neurobiological basis of eating disorders: some formulations. *Biol Psychiatry.* 1988;23(1):53–78.

5. Norris DO. *Vertebrate Endocrinology.* 2nd ed. Philadelphia, Pa: Lea & Febinger; 1985.

6. Brooks GA, Fahey TD. *Exercise Physiology: Human Bioenergetics and Its Applications.* New York, NY: Macmillan Publishing Company; 1985.

7. Norden MJ. *Beyond Prozac: Brain-Toxic Lifestyles, Natural Antidotes, and New Generation Antidepressants.* New York, NY: Regan Books/HarperCollinsPublishers; 1995.

8. Ayd FJ Jr. A clinical evaluation of Frenquel. *J Nerv Ment Disord.* 1956;(124):507-509.

9. Selye H. Forty years of stress research: principal remaining problems and misconceptions. *Can Med Assoc J.* 1976;115(1):53–56.

10. Amsterdam JD, Brunswick DJ, Mendels J. The clinical application of trycyclic antidepressant pharmacokinetics and plasma levels. *Am J Psychiatry.* 1993;137(6); 653–662.

11. American Psychiatric Association. *Diagnostic and Statistical Manual of Mental Disorders.* 5th ed. Washington, DC: American Psychiatric Association; 2000.

12. McNeal ET, Cimbolic P. Antidepressants and biochemical theories of depression. *Psychol Bull.* 1986;99(3):361–374.

13. Risch SC, Janowsky DS. Cholinergic-adrenergic balance in affective illness. In: Post RM, Ballenger JC, eds. *Neurobiology of Mood Disorders.* Vol 1. *Frontiers of Clinical Neuroscience.* Baltimore, Md: Williams and Wilkins Publishers; 1984.

14. Ballenger JC. The clinical use of carbamazepine in affective disorders. *J Clin Psychiatry.* 1988; 49(Suppl):13–19.

15. Newman ME, Lerer B, Shapira B. 5-HT-1A receptor mediated effects of antidepressants. *Prog Neuro-Psychopharmacol Biol Psychiatry.* 1993;17(1):1–19.

16. Singh A, Lucki I. Antidepressant-like activity of compounds with varying efficacy at 5-HT receptors. *Neuropharmacology.* 1993;32(4):331–340.

17. Salmans S. *Depression: Questions You Have . . . Answers You Need.* Allentown, Pa: People's Medical Society; 1995.

18. Cohn L, Schwartz MF, eds. *Sexual Abuse and Eating Disorders.* New York, NY: Brunner Mazel Publishers; 1996.

19. Brewerton TD, Krahn DD, Hardin TA, Wehr TA, Rosenthal NE. Findings from the Seasonal Pattern Assessment Questionnaire in patients with eating disorders and control subjects: effects of diagnosis and location. *Psychiatry Res.* 1994;52(1):71–84.

20. Fornari VM, Braun DL, Sunday SR, Sandberg DE, Matthews M, Chen IL, Mandel FS, Halmi KA, Katz JL. Seasonal patterns in eating disorder subgroups. *Compr Psychiatry.* 1994;35(6):450–456.

21. Gruber NP, Dilsaver SC. Bulimia and anorexia nervosa in winter depression: lifetime rates in a clinical sample. *J Psychiatry Neurosci.* 1996;21(1):9–12.

22. Danilenko KV, Putilov AA, Russkikh GS, Duffy LK, Ebbesson SO. Diurnal and seasonal variations of melatonin and serotonin in women with seasonal affective disorder. *Arctic Med Res.* 1994;53(3):137–145.

23. Hobson JA. *Sleep.* New York, NY: Scientific American Library; 1989.

24. Hicks RA, Rozette E. Habitual sleep duration and eating disorders in college students. *Percept Motor Skills.* 1986;62(1):209–210.

25. Walsh BT, Goetz R, Roose SP, Fingeroth S, Glassman AH. EEG-monitored sleep in anorexia nervosa and bulimia. *Biol Psychiatry.* 1985;20(9):947–956.

26. Schenck CH, Hurwitz TD, O'Connor KA, Mahowald MW. Additional categories of sleep-related eating disorders and the current status of treatment. *Sleep.* 1993;16(5):457–466.

CHAPTER 2

The Impact of the Hypothalamus and Anterior Pituitary on Eating Disorders

MONIKA M. WOOLSEY, M.S., R.D.

Neural, endocrine, neurohormonal, and neuroendocrine responses related to appetite, mood, stress, and reproduction tend to be clustered in the hypothalamus and anterior pituitary. This arrangement makes evolutionary sense, as stress and changes in reproductive state affect nutritional needs, and moods influence responses to environmental stress.

The anterior pituitary sits just below the hypothalamus and stores the hormones that trigger the release of endpoint hormones that trigger responses from target tissues. The relationship between the anterior pituitary and the hypothalamus has a crucial effect on the release. The anterior pituitary responds to hypothalamic stimulation by secreting releasing- hormones into the circulation. Under homeostatic conditions, the anterior pituitary acts independently by changing its secretion of hormones based on feedback it receives from the target tissues and can initiate basic directions based on its knowledge of the internal system. However, when outside information mandates a more complex response, it defers to the hypothalamus. In such a case, the hypothalamus sends a releasing hormone to the anterior pituitary with the message that a target tissue effect is needed. While the hormones influenced by the anterior pituitary may also be influenced by other metabolic processes, this chapter will focus on the anterior pituitary and hypothalamus and their impact on eating disorders.

Four major organs or organ systems are controlled by the hypothalamus with additional input from the anterior pituitary: the adrenal medulla, the reproductive organs, the thyroid gland, the liver, and muscle and fat tissue, each with specific target effects. *Figure 2.1* shows the systems influenced by anterior pituitary activity and the end results of anterior pituitary influence on these systems.

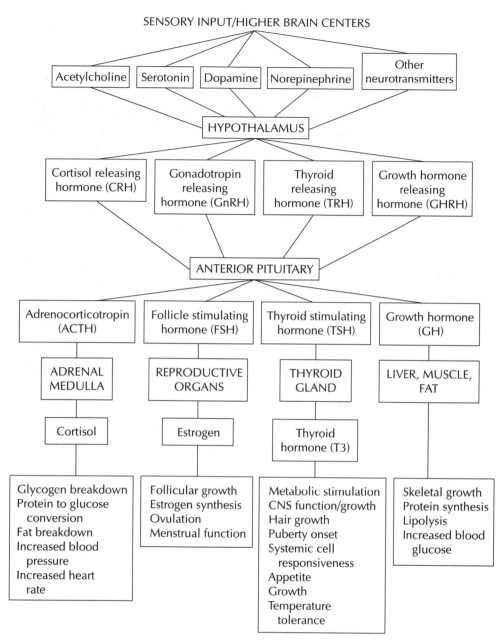

Figure 2.1
Effects of Neurotransmitter Stimulation at Organ Endpoints of Four Major Organ Systems

Each neurotransmitter important for maintaining healthy mood response to environmental stimuli is also important for anterior pituitary stimulation of these pathways or axes (1). Because the path through the anterior pituitary creates an additional step in the communication process, secretion and function of these hormones can be more finely tuned to meet physiological needs. However, this extra step also provides an addition site of vulnerability in a system when an imbalance exists.

Table 2.1 illustrates the complexity of neurotransmitter balance in endocrine regulation. The neurotransmitters cannot easily be categorized as "stimulants" or "depressants". For example, while acetylcholine stimulates the reproductive axis, it both stimulates and depresses the adrenal axis. Dopamine is a depressant in

**Table 2.1
Anterior Pituitary
Hormone Axes**

Axis	Releasing Hormone	Stimulating Neurotransmitters	Suppressing/ Depressing Neurotransmitters
Hypothalamic-Pituitary-Adrenal (HPA)	Adrenocorticotropin (ACTH)	Serotonin Acetylcholine Norepinephrine	Acetylcholine Dopamine Endorphins
Hypothalamic-Pituitary Ovarian/Testes (HPO/T)	Gonadotropin releasing hormone (GnRH)	Acetylcholine	Norepinephrine Dopamine Serotonin Endorphins
Hypothalamic-Pituitary-Thyroid (HPT)	Thyroid releasing hormone (TRH)	Norepinephrine Serotonin	Dopamine Endorphins
Hypothalamic-Pituitary Somototropic (HPS) (Growth Hormone System)	Growth hormone releasing hormone (GHRH)	Norepinephrine Dopamine Serotonin Endorphins	

two axes, yet it stimulates liver metabolic processes. Norepinephrine stimulates the adrenal system, which specializes in the breakdown and usage of energy, and depresses any system functions that would oppose this function during times of crisis. Endorphins are included in this table because many eating disordered behaviors increase endorphin secretion, and they are known to function as neurotransmitters. (See *Box 2.1.*) Rather than have specific "on-off" duties, the system responds to finely tuned balances, or neurotransmitter ratios.

All of the releasing hormones for the four pituitary axes also function as neurotransmitters. The effects of neurotransmitter imbalances on nervous system function have not yet been a major focus of research. However, the importance of other neurotransmitters and the abnormalities along these four axes suggest that the releasing hormones might some day be found to have more influence than is now understood.

Since the hormones of the hypothalamus stimulate anterior pituitary to release hormones and are both organs are responsive to neurotransmitters, they respond to environmental changes in a similar fashion. Under normal circumstances, the physical closeness of these organs tends to amplify the messages sent to the rest of the body (1). However, if an imbalance disrupts the message, the disruption is also amplified. The organ systems most seriously affected by individuals with eating disorders and individuals with major affective disorders are the adrenal system (hypothalamic-pituitary-adrenal axis), the reproductive system (hypothalamic-pituitary-ovarian/testes axis), the thyroid (hypothalamic-pituitary-thyroid axis), and growth hormone system (hypothalamic-pituitary-somatotropic axis).

It is important to remember that these four axes do not function independently of each other. The hypothalamus and anterior pituitary prioritize their orders to each axis based on the needs of the moment. An imbalance in one system easily creates an imbalance in the others. For example, detection of a stressful influ-

**Box 2.1
Endorphins:
Neurotransmitters as
Well as Mood Enhancers**

Though they are best known for the "runner's high" they produce, the morphine-like substances known as endorphins also have other important physiological functions. Endorphin levels increase anytime the body perceives stress, and exert specific physiological responses such as altering cerebral arteriole wall diameter (2). Endorphins also have a neurotransmitter-like quality that helps to modulate feeding behaviors (3).

In addition to exercise, increased endorphin levels have been observed in other conditions that alter homeostasis and therefore increase physical stress, including diabetes and alcoholism (2). On the psychiatric front, high levels of beta-endorphins are positively correlated with psychic anxiety, phobia, obsessions, and compulsions (4), and negatively correlated with depression (3).

Endorphin levels tend to be decreased in individuals with anorexia (5) and bulimia (3). The well-known endorphin-producing effect of exercise suggests that activity may be an attempt to correct or self-medicate low endorphin levels. It might also explain why compulsive exercise is such a prevalent symptom in these two types of eating disorders. Recent research has even suggested that elevated cerebrospinal fluid levels of endorphins are correlated with dissociative behavior in eating disordered individuals (6).

In contrast, endorphin levels are elevated in obese individuals (7,8). This contrast provokes some interesting questions about the treatment of obesity and binge eating disorder. If endorphin levels are consistently high, could their ability to stimulate feeding be a predominant influence on the individual who is trying to restrict her intake? If endorphins are consistently elevated, is there also a constant endorphin "high"? Perhaps there is an already elevated mood state that would preclude any perceived mood-elevating benefits achieved with exercise in other individuals. This might explain some of the difficulty encountered by many obese individuals in maintaining a regular exercise regimen as part of a healthy lifestyle. Perhaps losing weight reduces endorphin levels and creates a discomfort that encourages resuming previous behaviors and setpoint weight.

This scenario complements the addiction model in that, despite the social stigma and personal sacrifices the addictive behavior creates, physiological withdrawal produces such discomfort that external motivators are not enough to effect behavioral changes. In an addiction, immediate relief of withdrawal becomes the behavioral focus. As these questions are answered and more is learned about the brain and neurotransmitters, nutrition therapy will benefit from a thorough understanding of the neurological influences on feeding behavior.

ence in the outside environment shifts the functional focus from repair and maintenance to survival. Metabolic priorities are shunted to the stress-fighting adrenal axis. Acetylcholine and serotonin are mobilized and stimulate the adrenal medulla to secrete the "fight or flight" hormones necessary for survival. The same serotonin levels that increase adrenal activity function to depress reproductive activity, which is more of a maintenance function. The liver and thyroid gland mobilize metabolic processes that aid in the fight or flight process; they are therefore stimulated to help the adrenal medulla resist potentially harmful environmental changes.

THE PITUITARY AXES

Anterior pituitary axis functions are significantly affected in the eating disorders. Those axes that carry out the stress response (adrenal and somatotropic) tend to be overstimulated and hyperresponsive. In those axes that specialize in maintenance functions (ovarian and thyroid), there is a blunted response to stimulation in anorexia nervosa and a hyperresponsiveness in obesity (*Table 2.2*). Gradations of eating disorders that fall along this continuum appear to have gradations of axis function as well.

A consistent element in all the anterior pituitary axes is that achievement of goal weight does not restore hormonal function. In fact, hormonal aberrations can persist for months after goal weight is achieved (9). These physiological dysfunctions are more deeply rooted, and in understanding the treatment of an eating disorder it is important not to focus on weight change as the most important outcome of treatment. Though weight changes are more tangible and easier to induce, the hypothalamic and anterior pituitary origins of the problem should not be forgotten. Continued significant hormone imbalances are an important marker of a persistent dysfunctional stress response that, if left unchecked, could lead the individual back into relapse.

THE HYPOTHALAMIC-PITUITARY-ADRENAL AXIS

Of all the hypothalamic-pituitary axes, the hypothalamic-pituitary-adrenal (HPA) axis dominates, having the ability to shut down activity across the board when an impending crisis is sensed. The HPA axis is instantaneously aroused and often mobilizes resources before an individual recognizes something is wrong. Without this powerful axis, humans would likely not survive. *Figure 2.2* summarizes the influences that stimulate and depress HPA function.

In modern society, air conditioning regulates environmental temperature and conflicts are less frequently solved with physical aggression than they were long ago. Is the HPA axis system still important? Absolutely. As humans have evolved, so have their stresses. Many are not as heart-stopping as a falling tree, but they are equally effective in mobilizing the HPA axis into action. The Holmes-Rahe Social Adjustment Scale (10) is a popular evaluation of stress in an individual's life. The higher the score, the more likely it is that the HPA axis is dominant, at the expense of other physiological functions. Remember that both positive and negative stresses are listed because stress is not necessarily something "bad". Rather, it is an event that changes the environment significantly enough that one must change her actions to cope with the new stimuli this environment produces.

Whether initiating battle or fleeing, the fight-or-flight response is designed to effect physical activity. This hypothalamic mandate functions to directly confront and eliminate the conflict at hand, and to provide a release of physical energy that the stress has produced. Unfortunately, many of today's stresses and environments do not allow full activation of the fight-or-flight response. During a typical modern day, stress builds up without much opportunity for physical outlet. Office disputes are often best not settled by confrontation, and the most that can be

Axis	Anorexia Nervosa	Bulimia Nervosa	Obesity
HPA Axis			
ACTH response to corticotropin releasing hormone	Blunted		Blunted
24–hour plasma cortisol	Increased	Increased	Increased
Response to dexamethasone suppression test°	Nonsuppression (>90%)	Nonsuppression (~50%)	Normal suppression
Cortisol secretion	Increased		Increased
Urinary free cortisol	Increased		Increased
HPO Axis			
Incidence of amenorrhea°°	100%	Frequent	Frequent
Luteinizing hormone levels	Decreased	Occasionally low, usually normal	Elevated
Follicle stimulating hormone levels	Decreased	Occasionally low, usually normal	Elevated
Luteinizing hormone secretory pattern	Immature		
Luteinizing hormone response to gonadotropin releasing hormone	Blunted, sometimes delayed		
FSH response to gonadotropin releasing hormone	Variable		
HPT Axis			
T4 levels	Normal or low	Normal	Elevated
T3 levels	Decreased	Normal	Decreased
rT3 levels	Increased		
TSH	Normal	Normal	Increased
TSH response	Delayed in ~50% Blunted in ~15%	Blunted	Elevated
HPS Axis			
Growth hormone releasing hormone response	Elevated		Decreased
Growth hormone secretion in response to chemical stimulation	Hypersensitive		Low
Growth hormone secretion in response to a meal	Increased		

Table 2.2
Common Hypothalamic-Pituitary Axis Changes That Occur in Eating Disorders

°A dexamethasone suppression test is a method for measuring plasma cortisol. Nonsuppression is an indication of elevated plasma cortisol secretion.

°°Required for diagnosis.

Sources: Hudson and Hudson (11), Zamboni et al (12), Bernini et al (13), Hautanen and Adlercreutz (14), Hall et all (15), Pijl et al (16), Chomard et al (17), Mota et al (18), Bjorntorp (19), Leibowitz (20).

Figure 2.2
Regulation of HPS Axis
Functions

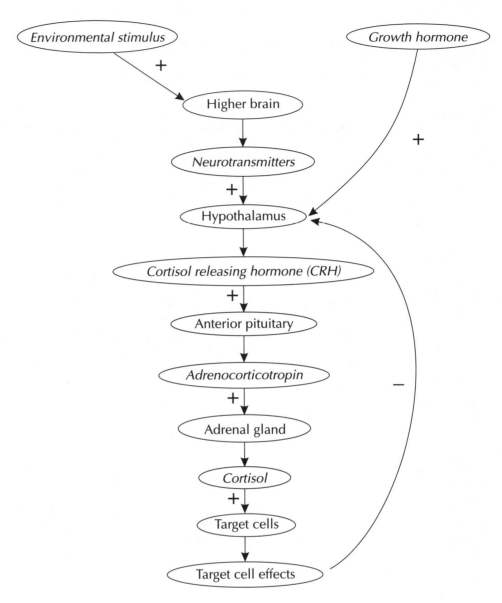

＋ indicates positive feedback or stimulation
－ indicates negative feedback or stimulation

done about rush hour is to wait out the delay. If left unchecked, the HPA axis continues to dominate and stress accumulates. A vicious cycle can evolve, as the built-up stress is interpreted as a stress itself and triggers the HPA axis to further amplify its efforts *(Figure 2.3)*.

It has been proposed that HPA dysfunction is one of the primary biological origins of alterations in eating behavior observed in anorexia, bulimia, and binge eating disorder. When the HPA axis is chronically dominant with no outlet for the energy it creates, aggression is often the end result. Rudeness, short tempers, and physical, verbal, and sexual abuse are some physical outlets of stress. Anxiety and obsessive-compulsive behaviors also function as physical energy releases. Rather than justifying inappropriate outlets of physical energy, this perspective provides an argument for recognizing that inappropriate behaviors often have biological

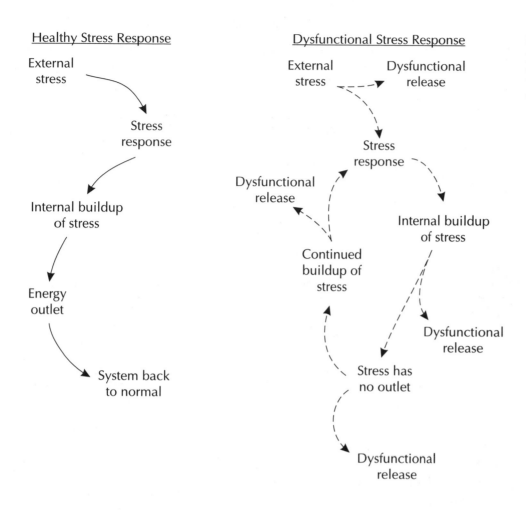

Healthy Stress Response

External stress

Stress response

Internal buildup of stress

Energy outlet

System back to normal

Dysfunctional Stress Response

External stress

Dysfunctional release

Stress response

Dysfunctional release

Internal buildup of stress

Continued buildup of stress

Dysfunctional release

Stress has no outlet

Dysfunctional release

Figure 2.3

Effects of Stress on Hypothalamic-Pituitary-Adrenal Axis

roots, that learning to channel emotional stress into positive physical outlets is a basic need for everyone, and that stress management counseling should be a foundation of eating disorder treatment.

If multiple stresses occur over a short period of time (graduation, moving from home, marriage), a major trauma occurs (unexpected death, rape), or a major stress continues over a prolonged period of time (ongoing family conflict or abuse), chronic stimulation of the HPA axis to respond to these situations drains the body of the neurotransmitters needed for normal impulse communication. Some behaviors may correct neurotransmitter imbalances for awhile (*Table 2.3*), but eventually the body can no longer mobilize its stress defenses, the system shuts down, and depression sets in. End-stage depression occurs when a person is so overstimulated that he seeks activities that reduce stimulation: isolation, sleep, and avoidance (*Box 2.2*).

THE HYPOTHALAMIC-PITUITARY-OVARIAN/TESTES AXIS

The hypothalamic-pituitary-ovarian/testes (HPO/T) axis regulates all aspects of reproductive function, from ovulation and menstruation to pregnancy and lactation (*Figure 2.5*). Input from the HPA axis depresses HPO/T activity. From an evolutionary perspective, this axis is sensitive to any environmental input suggesting that conception and pregnancy could not be supported to completion. It

Table 2.3
Indicators of Stress

Physical	Emotional	Behavioral
Dry mouth	Depression	**Temper**
Perspiration	Helplessness	**Isolation**
Upset stomach	Hopelessness	**Crying**
Headache	Overwhelmed	Insomnia
Backache	Joylessness	**Use of mood modifiers**
Impotence/frigidity	Anxiety	Decreased interest in sex
Chest pain	Tension	**Procrastination**
Rash	Mental block	Forgetfulness
Frequent urination	Sadness	Preoccupation
Diarrhea/constipation	Fear	**Compulsive acts**
Fatigue	Feeling "out of control"	Easily startled
Cold feet/clammy hands	Disjointed thoughts	Stuttering
Butterflies in stomach	Conflict	**Grinding teeth,**
Racing heart	Neuroses	**clenching jaw**
Trembling	Boredom	**Verbal attacks**
Lump in throat	Diminished sense of	**Sleep as an escape**
Temporal mandibular	"quality of life"	**Change in appetite**
Joint syndrome		**Increased smoking**
		Accident proneness
		Migraine headache
		Loss of sense of humor
		Diminished work performance

Boldfaced behaviors may serve to maintain neurotransmitter balances temporarily.

relies on HPA input to decide when stress is too high to attempt pregnancy. The HPO/T axis depresses function until the perceived stress is no longer a threat.

Amenorrhea and oligomenorrhea are common consequences of eating disorders. In fact, amenorrhea must be present for the clinical diagnosis of anorexia nervosa. Since estrogen is manufactured in adipose tissue, a common belief is that low body fat is the primary cause of amenorrhea in anorexia and that menstrual dysfunction does not occur in the other eating disorders. In fact, even when body weight is maintained at or above a desirable level, women with eating disorders often report changes in HPO axis function. Again, restoration of weight and/or body fat does not always restore regular menstrual function. It is more closely related (negatively correlated) with circulating cortisol levels.

Though body fat percentage is an important influence on menstrual function, it appears to be a stronger influence in individuals who experienced irregular menstrual cycles before they lost weight or developed an eating disorder (21–25). An individual who has restored weight and changed dysfunctional eating behaviors but who is still reporting menstrual abnormalities may still be experiencing emotional distress that, if left untreated, might lay the groundwork for future relapse.

In addition to body composition, other environmental influences are important influences on menstrual function. It is no coincidence that these influences are the same that influence the development of depression and eating disorders.

The hormone profile associated with obesity is gaining increasing research attention. The mid-1980s brought the discovery that individuals with elevated waist-to-hip ratios (WHRs) were more likely to have hypertension, diabetes, and hypercholesterolemia than individuals whose fat was primarily in the hip area. Since then, metabolic disturbances in the "android" type of fat distribution have become a popular research topic. Findings common to android obesity include reduced serotonin levels, reduced norepinephrine sensitivity, increased ACTH sensitivity, elevated cortisol levels, low growth hormone secretion, hyperprolactinemia, sex hormone imbalances, hypercholesterolemia, hyperglycemia, insulin resistance, hypertriglyceridemia, low HDL, higher c-peptide levels, and hypersensitive insulin secretion (26).

Psychologically, android individuals have also been found to have more pronounced blood glucose responses to mental and physical stress challenges (9). Pima Indians (who have a particularly high incidence of diabetes and android body types), when given simple math tests to do, have elevated blood pressure, heart rate, and blood glucose levels that take longer than normal to return to baseline than white controls. These findings, combined with the numerous medical dysfunctions, have prompted researchers to suggest that android obesity is actually a complicated maladaptive stress response (metabolic syndrome) that, like anorexia and bulimia, originates in the hypothalamus (27).

An individual with metabolic syndrome tends to overreact to stress. In other words, changes in schedules and daily challenges (eg, squeezing all of one's assigned tasks into a hectic daily schedule) that might be perceived as minor stresses in some produce a major physiological stress reaction in those with metabolic syndrome. As stress accumulates throughout the day, cortisol levels increase.

The major function of cortisol is to liberate glucose for the "fight or flight" response, so as cortisol levels rise and stay elevated, glucose metabolism is altered. Insulin resistance and hyperglycemia result. At the same time that glucose uptake is impaired, lipid metabolism is enhanced; cortisol also promotes liberation of free fatty acids and very-low-density lipoproteins, which are easily stored in the presence of elevated circulating insulin. Receptors in the abdominal cavity have more affinity for these circulating lipids than do receptors in other fat tissues in the body (28). The end result is accumulation of fat around the waist.

As with anorexia and bulimia, this entire chain of events is thought to originate with a serotonin deficiency created by an abnormally frequent elicitation of the stress response *(Figure 2.4)* (12). Binge eating is a learned behavior that may temporarily restore serotonin levels, but unfortunately, in the process, may make large boluses of calories available for storage in abdominal fat.

Until recently, the prevailing attitude toward obesity was that medical problems such as diabetes, cardiovascular disease, and hypertension were the consequences of overweight. The simple solution to these diseases was to follow a low-calorie diet. However, compelling evidence is mounting that suggests a paradigm shift is in order. That is, it appears that these metabolic problems are not consequences of poor eating habits, but the *cause* of overeating.

A common symptom of diabetes, for example, is hyperphagia. Much of the energy eaten by individuals with diabetes never reaches the cells, resulting in a hunger message being sent back to the brain. Despite this commonly known fact, one of the most common treatments for metabolic syndrome is a low-calorie diet. It makes sense that

continued

**Box 2.2
Metabolic Syndrome:
Consequence or Cause
of Obesity?**

Figure 2.4
Metabolic Syndrome

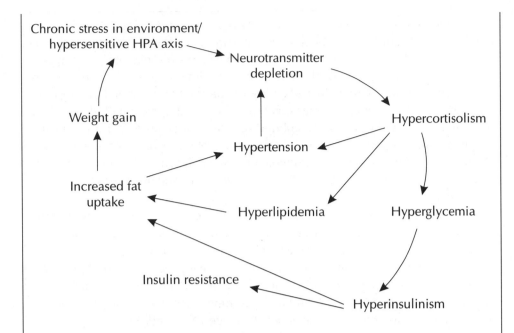

someone who is already chronically hungry would have difficulty following such a regimen, and the low success rate of individuals on these diets supports this hypothesis. If treatment of metabolic syndrome starts and stops with a low-calorie diet, it seems almost guaranteed that the next stressful period in the client's life will elicit a weight gain. Even if weight loss is achieved, it does not always decrease android obesity as well as exercise (29) or hyperactivity (30), and therefore does not seem to be an outcome that accurately measures treatment success. Could it be that the starvation state provoked by calorie reduction creates an additional stress that results in elevated cortisol levels and exacerbates the syndrome? What about rigid meal plans that focus on counting calories and exchange? Do they evoke a stress response similar to that produced with the simple math challenges used in the Pima Indian study?

Creative thinking produced a major shift in thinking about the role of dietary cholesterol in heart disease. Reducing dietary cholesterol initially seemed to be the obvious dietary recommendation. Time proved this paradigm wrong, and an answer was found that went to the root of the problem, liver cholesterol production and degree of fat saturation. The diet concept deserves a similar fresh look. Since metabolic syndrome appears to start with a dysfunctional stress response, lifeskill or cognitive behavioral therapy may be in order. Exercise might be more useful for its stress reduction benefits than for its use of calories. Perhaps the key to weight management is stress hormone reduction, rather than caloric balance. As for measurable indicators of success, plasma cortisol levels or dexamethasone suppression might become the new bottom line. As stress levels decrease (or as management of stressful situations improves), so would the stress response and the compulsive eating. Weight loss would be the natural outcome, but not the only measure of successful treatment.

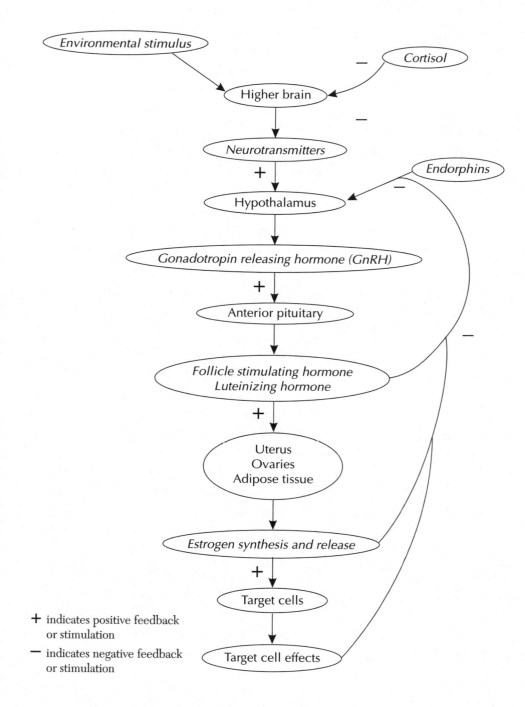

Figure 2.5
Regulation of HPO
Axis Function

Stress

Emotional stress and physical stress both depress the HPO/T axis. Women commonly report this phenomenon, but it has also been formally studied. Female students at Stanford University were found to have more irregular menstrual patterns than those at a less rigorous university (31).

Physical stress is particularly effective in depressing HPO/T function. This effect has been well studied in athletes. Compared to sedentary females, athletes have later menarche (26-30) and higher incidences of both amenorrhea fitting the DSM-IV diagnostic criteria for anorexia (26,29) and cycles that are irregular but occur more frequently than twice a year (26,27). Menstrual irregularities are more common and more severe in athletes of professional or Olympic rank than in those who participate at less elite levels (32).

Physical stress is thought to be a major influence on activity-related menstrual changes because athletic activity elevates stress hormone secretion. For example, even a brief bout of exercise elevates serum concentrations of at least three hormones, including beta endorphins (33,34), catecholamines (35), and cortisol (35,36). Two of the catecholamines, norepinephrine and dopamine, are also neurotransmitters. The effects of excessive neurotransmitter secretion were explained earlier in this chapter.

Reproductive activity is often depressed in binge eating disorder as well. Chronically elevated beta-endorphin levels might be partly responsible for this, having an effect similar to excessive exercise in anorexia and bulimia. In addition, normal reproductive function is dependent on the ratio of testosterone to estrogen (1). As body weight increases, so do free testosterone levels; the disruption commonly affects menstruation (36).

Sleep

A cyclic, pulsatile surge of luteinizing hormone results in menarche. This surge occurs during REM sleep, and if normal sleep patterns are disturbed, this developmental event is delayed (37). Both types of sleep changes observed in eating disorders and depression—nocturnal insomnia and prolonged daytime sleep—have the potential for disturbing this important reproductive event.

Dietary Deficiencies

The same dietary practices that promote depression also suppress menstrual function. These practices include a large increase or reduction in caloric intake (38,39) and reduction in total protein intake (40) or protein quality (eg, an unbalanced vegetarian diet) (41). These dietary practices are discussed in detail in Chapter 17.

Despite the high incidence of menstrual dysfunction in individuals with eating disorders, some women pursue their eating disorders, experience wide fluctuations in weight, and continue to menstruate regularly. Evidence suggests that, as with depression and other physiological responses to stress, in some individuals there is a predisposed vulnerability to dysfunction in the reproductive axis.

THE HYPOTHALAMIC-PITUITARY-THYROID AXIS

The hypothalamic-pituitary-thyroid (HPT) axis is well known to nutrition scientists. Its impacts on metabolism and weight balance are well known, and continue to be studied at all points along the eating disorder spectrum. In addition to its regulation of metabolic rate, thyroid hormone is important for enhancing reproductive function and potentiating cell activity. It is crucial to proper growth and function of the nervous system. It also has a permissive action, which means that though many of its actions are not as specifically measurable as those of other hormones, it enhances the ability of other cells to respond to external, internal, and hormonal stimuli (1).

Two thyroid hormone configurations are commonly measured to assess thyroid activity: T3, the biologically active form, and T4, the biologically inactive storage form. Reverse T3, or rT3, is a degradation product often measured as an evaluation of the body's metabolism of circulating thyroid hormone.

Symptoms of hypothyroidism include hypophagia, coarse voice, reduced growth, rough skin/coarse hair, slow thoughts/actions, and cold sensitivity (1). These are common symptoms of anorexia as well, and thyroid medication is a common prescription to "jumpstart" metabolic processes. In addition, psychiatrists often take advantage of thyroid hormone's permissive effects and prescribe it in tandem with psychiatric medications to achieve a more powerful therapeutic effect.

Interestingly, in obesity there is no thyroid hormone deficiency, as is commonly believed, but rather a decreased ability to convert the stored form of the hormone into its biologically active form (1). The anterior pituitary interprets this malfunction as a need for more thyroid stimulating hormone, and the thyroid secretes more thyroid hormone in an attempt to restore T3 levels. However, since the problem is not a thyroid hormone shortage, a vicious cycle develops, with hyperthyroidism being the result *(Figure 2.6)*.

THE HYPOTHALAMIC-PITUITARY-SOMATOTROPIC (GROWTH HORMONE) AXIS

The hypothalamic-pituitary-somatotropic (HPS) axis is particularly important in the development of muscle (1). In addition to promoting the uptake of nutrients for anabolism, growth hormone generates an increase in blood glucose to provide fuel for muscle building. Growth hormone is different from the other hypothalamic-pituitary hormones in that it is secreted directly by the anterior pituitary. Anabolism and muscle maintenance are apparently hypothalamic priorities; half of the anterior pituitary by weight consists of growth hormone.

Growth hormone liberates energy through the stimulation of cortisol secretion *(Figure 2.7)*. Its anabolic influence is most effective in the presence of thyroid hormone, which increases target cell responsiveness to growth hormone. When thyroid hormone function is altered, as in an eating disorder, it is possible that more growth hormone is available for interaction with the HPA axis. The net result of this shift would be an exacerbation of an already hyperactive stress response.

Growth hormone secretion increases after meals, and aids in the uptake and use of the recently ingested meal. Its secretion is heightened significantly in response to protein ingestion (42). This phenomenon presents an interesting possibility. A cardinal behavior in anorexia and bulimia is the avoidance of meat. Though much of this behavior has psychological origins, a potential biologically rooted influence might be that individuals with heightened growth hormone function might experience a heightened stress response after the ingestion of protein. Could their avoidance of proteins be a subliminal attempt to avoid such

Figure 2.6
Regulation of Thyroid
Axis Function

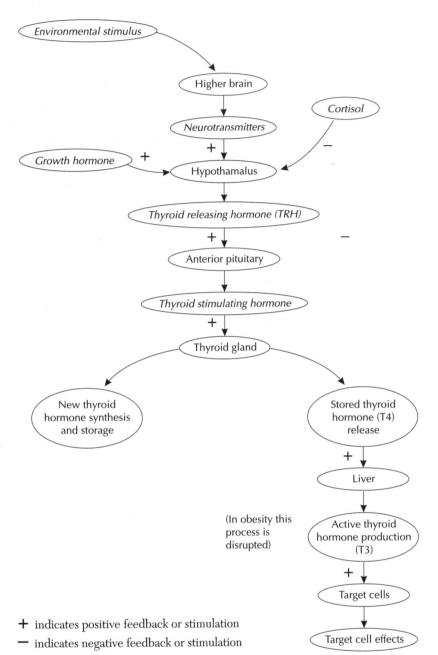

+ indicates positive feedback or stimulation
− indicates negative feedback or stimulation

ADDITIONAL HYPOTHALAMIC INFLUENCES: OXYTOCIN AND VASOPRESSIN

a consequence? The new age of brain research might present some intriguing answers to these and other questions about biological influences on behavior.

In addition to the releasing hormones, the hypothalamus secretes a set of hormones with direct target tissue effects. Release of these hormones, arginine vasopressin (AVP) and oxytocin (OT), is stimulated by neural input (43). In addition to their physiological influence, AVP and OT elicit behavioral responses and are thought to be an important link between physiological function and observed behaviors.

Arginine vasopressin (AVP) is known mainly for its peripheral modulation of fluid balance; its release is triggered by in increase in osmotic pressure. Oxytocin is best known as a peripheral uterotonic hormone, but has several other important functions as well (*Table 2.4*).

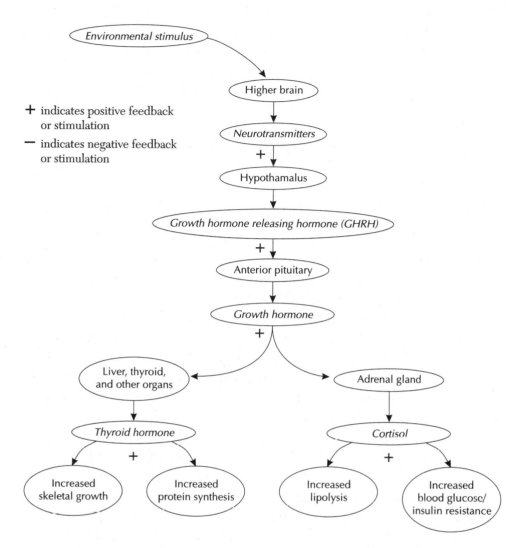

Figure 2.7
Regulation of the Growth Hormone-Pituitary-Somatotropic Axis Function

Centrally, AVP and OT elicit important behavioral responses *(Table 2.5)*. Arginine vasopressin delays the extinction of aversive conditioning (44). In other words, if an individual has a negative experience that results in an aversion to a stimulus (eg, aversion to loud noises because of growing up in a verbally abusive household), this aversion will tend to persevere in the presence of AVP. On the other hand, OT triggers the stress response and impairs aversive conditioning (45). Arginine vasopressin also seems to affect other central functions, as its levels are often low in depressed individuals. In fact, some individuals with depression improve after central administration of AVP (45). Serotonin is the neurotransmitter that appears to mediate AVP and OT release (46). Under normal conditions AVP and OT levels are inversely correlated, and antagonize each other to maintain homeostasis.

Alterations in the levels of these hormones have been found in the eating disorders, and current research suggests that these alterations may have a significant impact on thought processes and behaviors in individuals with these diseases. Arginine vasopressin hypersecretion is common in anorexia, and has been proposed to be a physiological influence on the food avoidance common in this disorder (45). At the same time, OT levels are low and the antagonistic balance of

Table 2.4 **Peripheral Effects of Hypothalamic Neurohormones**	Arginine Vasopressin	Oxytocin
	Increased cell permeability	Uterine contractions (both in labor and in orgasm)
	Water reabsorption	Milk ejection
	Elevated blood glucose	Lowered blood pressure
	Inhibited lipolysis	Elevated blood glucose
	Inhibited GH release	
	Elevated blood glucose	
	Promotion of ACTH release	

Sources: Norris (1), Joja et al (47), Nishita et al (48).

the nondisordered state is lost (46). Thus, aversive conditioning is promoted and is reflected in the food avoidance that accompanies anorexia. As with the hormone imbalances described in the previous chapter, this hypersecretion persists after weight recovery, suggesting that weight loss is not a cause but a consequence of a greater metabolic disorder (49).

Individuals with bulimia have been observed to have a blunted AVP response when actively bingeing and purging (45). An enhanced sense of thirst is also common (44). Since thirst and hunger are not always easily distinguishable, an AVP deficiency might function to enhance hunger in a person who already has a disturbance in these sensations. In active bulimia, OT and AVP levels are low (44). Individuals who have discontinued bingeing and purging have elevated AVP levels (44). This phenomenon may affect behavior in bulimia in some interesting ways. The fluid retention, swelling, and bloating that result from high AVP levels, when seen as weight gain on the scales, can easily be interpreted as fat gain. To complicate matters further, aversive conditioning is intensified under such conditions and may explain some of the intensity of the fear of weight gain that is often demonstrated in the early stages of recovery from bulimia (44). There is a high prevalence of abnormal eating attitudes and behaviors in clients with idiopathic edema (45), suggesting that the influence of AVP in eating disorders is significant.

Under normal conditions, both OT and AVP counteract the natural hyperphagic response to opioids (46). The combination of depressed OT and AVP levels, along with the increased opioid levels seen in obesity, may exacerbate hyperphagia and provide yet another physiological explanation for its occurrence.

Table 2.5 **Central Effects of Hypothalamic Neurohormones**	Arginine Vasopressin	Oxytocin
	Delayed extinction of aversive conditioning	Promotion of aversive conditioning Stimulation of stress response

Sources: Demitrack et al (46,47).

SUMMARY

- The anterior pituitary coordinates day-to-day function in more delicate organ systems and augments important messages from the hypothalamus. However, in crisis it defers to the hypothalamus, which has a more global perspective and coordinates function in times of stress.

- As with the hypothalamus, any disruption in anterior pituitary function also disrupts messages to target organs at the end of the anterior pituitary axis.

- The individual axes do not function independently, but rather respond to orders from the hypothalamus and anterior pituitary, which coordinate changes to provide a collaborative defense against stress or to support repair and maintenance.

- Eating-disordered individuals have a high incidence of functional disruption along the anterior pituitary axes, further supporting the theory that disruption of neurotransmitter production and maintenance is an important first step in the development of anorexia, bulimia, and binge eating disorder.

- Some of the first symptoms of these disorders that are apparent externally are changes in behavior and mood, but treatment of the individual with these diseases requires medical as well as psychological intervention.

- Physiological changes along the hypothalamic-pituitary axes often exist for months after weight gain or stabilization is achieved. Though weight change is an indicator of the direction of progress, it is not the bottom line.

- Understanding the endocrine aspects of the eating disorders and translating the signs and symptoms of how the mind and body are interacting can help to focus the treatment team on important occurrences that still require interventions, and increase the chance of a successful progression through recovery without major relapse.

- The hypothalamic neurohormones OT and AVP regulate several functions that may be important bases for some physiological and psychological phenomena. These phenomena should be considered as a potential basis for some of the fears and dysfunctional behaviors seen in individuals with eating disorders.

REFERENCES

1. Norris DO. *Vertebrate Endocrinology.* 2nd ed. Philadelphia, Pa: Lea & Febinger; 1985.
2. Dalayeun JF, Nores JM, Bergal S. Physiology of beta-endorphins: close-up view and a review of the literature. *Biomed Pharmacother.* 1993;47(8):311–320.
3. Brewerton TD, Lydiard RB, Laraia MT, Shook JE, Ballenger JC. CSF beta-endorphin and dynorphin in bulimia nervosa. *Am J Psychiatry.* 1992;149(8):1086–1090.
4. Darko DF, Risch SC, Gillin JC, Golshan S. Association of beta-endorphin with specific clinical symptoms of depression. *Am J Psychiatry.* 1992;149(9):1162–1167.
5. Wlodarczyk-Bisaga K, Bisaga A. Selected issues of biological aspects of eating disorders. *Psychiatr (Poland).* 1994;28(5):579–591.
6. Demitrack MA, Putnam FW, Rubinow DR, Pigott TA, Altemus M, Krahn DD, Gold PW. Relation of dissociative phenomena to levels of cerebrospinal fluid monoamine

metabolites and beta-endorphin in patients with eating disorders: a pilot study. *J Psychiatry Res.* 1993;49(1):1–10.

7. Balon-Perin S, Kolanowski J, Berbinschi A, Franchimont P, Ketelsbergers JM. The effects of glucose ingestion and fasting on plasma immunoreactive beta-endorphins, adrenocorticotropic hormone and cortisol in obese subjects. *J Endocrinol Invest.* 1991;14(11):919–925.

8. Giovannini C, Ciucci E, Cassetta ME, Cugini P, Facchinetti F. Unresponsiveness of the endorphinergic system to its physiological feedback in obesity. *Appetite.* 1991; 26(1):39–43.

9. Pasquali R, Anconetani B, Chattat R, Biscotti M, Spinucci G, Casimirri F, Vicennati V, Carcello A, Labate AM. Hypothalamic-pituitary-adrenal axis activity and its relationship to the autonomic nervous system. I. Women with visceral and subcutaneous obesity: effect of the corticotropin-releasing factor/arginine-vasopressin test and of stress. *Metabolism.* 1996;45(3):351–356.

10. Holmes TH, Rahe RH. The social readjustment rating scale. *J Psychosomatic Res.* 1967;11:213–218.

11. Hudson JI, Hudson MS. Endocrine dysfunction in anorexia nervosa and bulimia: comparison with abnormalities in other psychiatric disorders and disturbances due to metabolic factors. *Psych Dev.* 1984;4:237–272.

12. Zamboni M, Armellini F, Turcato E, de Pergola G, Todesco T, Bissoli L, Bergamo Andreis IA, Bosello O. Relationship between visceral fat, steroid hormones and insulin sensitivity in premenopausal obese women. *J Intern Med.* 1994;236(5): 521–527.

13. Bernini GP, Argenio GF, Del corso C, Vivaldo MS, Birindelli R, Franchi F. Serotoninergic receptor activation by dextrofenfluramine enhances the blunted pituitary-adrenal responsiveness to corticotropin-releasing hormone in obese subjects. *Metabolism.* 1992;41(1):17–21.

14. Hautanen A, Adlercreutz H. Altered adrenocorticotropin and cortisol secretion in abdominal obesity: implications for the insulin resistance syndrome. *J Intern Med.* 1993;234(5):461–469.

15. Hall RC, Dunap PK, Hall RC, Pacheco CA, Blakely RK, Abraham J. Thyroid disease and abnormal thyroid function tests in women with eating disorders and depression. *J Fla Med Assoc.* 1995;82(3):187–192.

16. Pijl H, Koppeschaar HP, Willekens FL, Frohlich M, Meinders AE. The influence of serotonergic neurotransmission on pituitary hormone release in obese and non-obese females. *Acta Endocrinol Copenh.* 1993;128(4):319–324.

17. Chomard P, Beltramo JL, Ben Cheikh R, Autissier N. Changes in thyroid hormone and thyrotropin in the serum and thyroid glands of developing genetically obese male and female Zucker rats. *J Endocrinol.* 1994;142(2):3317–3324.

18. Mota A, Bento A, Penalva A, Pombo M, Dieguez C. Role of the serotonin receptor subtype 5-HT1D on basal and stimulated growth hormone secretion. *J Clin Endocrinol Metab.* 1995;80(6):1973–1977.

19. Bjorntorp P. Neuroendocrine abnormalities in obesity. *Metabolism.* 1995;44(2;Suppl 2):38–41.

20. Leibowitz SF. The role of serotonin in eating disorders. *Drug.* 1990;39(Suppl 3):33–48.

21. Bullen BA, Skrinar GS, Beitins IZ, von Mering G, Turnbull BA, McArthur JW. Induction of menstrual disorders by strenuous exercise in untrained women. *N Engl J Med.* 1985;312:1349–1353.

22. Carlberg KA, Buckman MT, Peake GT, Riedesel MI. Body composition of oligo/amenorrheic athletes. *Med Sci Sport Exerc.* 1983;15:215–217.

23. Dale E, Gerlach DH, Wilhite MA. Menstrual dysfunction in distance runners. *Obstet Gynecol.* 1979;54;47–53.

24. Sanborn CF, Martin BJ, Wagner WW. Is athletic amenorrhea specific to runners? *Am J Obstet Gynecol.* 1982;143:859–861.

25. Schwartz B, Cumming, Riordan E. Selye M, Yen SSC. Exercise-associated amenorrhea: a distinct entity? *Am J Obstet Gynecol.* 1981;41:662–670.

26. Hollman M, Runnebaum B, Gerhard I. Impact of waist-hip ratio and body mass index in hormonal and metabolic parameters in young, obese women. *Int J Obest Relat Metab Disord.* 1997;21(6):476–483.

27. Brooks CM. The history of thought concerning the hypothalamus and its functions. *Brain Res Bull.* 1988;20(6):657–667.

28. Bjorntorp P. Body fat distribution, insulin resistance, and metabolic diseases. *Nutrition.* 1997;13(9):795–803.

29. Wood PD. Impact of experimental manipulation of energy intake and expenditure on body composition. *Crit Rev Food Sci Nutr.* 1993;33(4–5):369-373.

30. Bjorntorp P. Endocrine abnormalities of obesity. *Metabolism.* 1995;44(9;Suppl 3):21–23.

31. Harris D. Secondary amenorrhea linked to stress. *Phys Sports Med.* 1978;6:24-29.

32. Malina RM, Spirduso WW, Tate C, Baylor AM. Age at menarche and selected menstrual characteristics in athletes at different competetive levels and in different sports. *Med Sci Sport.* 1978;10(3):218–222.

33. Carr DB, Bullen BA, Skrinar GS. Physical conditioning facilitates the exercise-induced secretion of beta-endorphin and beta-lipotropin in women. *N Engl J Med.* 1981;305:560–564.

34. Colte E, Wardlaw SL, Frantz AG. The effect of running on plasma beta-endorphin. *Life Sci.* 1981;28:1637.

35. Fraioli F, Mortti C, Paolucci E, Aliccio E, Crescenzi F, Fartunio G. Physical exercise stimulates marked concomitant release of ß-endorphin and adrenocorticotropic hormone (ACTH) in peripheral blood in man. *Experientia.* 1980;36:987–990.

36. Loucks AV, Horvath SM. Exercise-induced stress responses of amenorrheic and eumenorrheic runners. *J Clin Endocrinol Metab.* 1984;59:1109–1120.

37. Litt IF. Menstrual disorders during adolescence. *Pediatr Rev.* 1983;4:203–207.

38. Calabrese LH, Kirkedall DT. Nutritional and medical considerations in dancers. *Clin Sports Med.* 1983;2:539–542.

39. Carlberg KA, Buckman MT, Peake GT, Riedesel ML. A survey of menstrual function in athletes. *Eur J Appl Physiol.* 1983;51:211–222.

40. Malina RM, Harper AB, Avent HH, Campbell DE. Age at menarche in athletes and non-athletes. *Med Sci Sports.* 1973;5:11–13.

41. Benson J, Gillien K, Bourdet K, Loosli AR. Inadequate nutrition and chronic calorie restriction in adolescent ballerinas. *Phys Sport Med.* 1985;13(10):79–90.

42. Pirke KM, Friess E, Kellner MB, Krieg JC, Fichter MM. Somatostatin in eating disorders. *Int J Eat Disord.* 1994;15(1):99–102.

43. Demitrack MA, Lesem MD, Brandt HA, Pigott TA, Jimerson DC, Altemus M, Gold PW. Neurohypophyseal dysfunction: implications for the pathophysiology of eating disorders. *Psychopharmacol Bull.* 1989;25(3):439–443.

44. Demitrack MA, Kalogeras KT, Altemus M, Pigott tA, Listack SJ, Gold PW. Plasma and cerebrospinal fluid measures of arrginine vasopressin secretion in patients with

bulimia nervosa and in healthy subjects. *J Clin Endocrinol Metab.* 1992;74(6): 1277–1283.

45. Bihun J, McSherry J, and Marciano D. Idiopathic edema in eating disorders: evidence for an association. *Int J Eat Disord.* 1993;14(2):197–201.

46. Gulati K, Ray A, Sharma KK. Effects of acute and chronic morphine on food intake rats: modulation by oxytocin and vasopressin. *Pharmacol Biochem Behav.* 1993; 44(3):749.

47. Joja O, Goldstein R, Popa M. Vasotocin effects in depressive patients with eating disorders. *Rom J Endocrinol.* 1993;31(3–4):171–177.

48. Nishita JK, Ellinwood ED Jr, Rockwell WJ, Kuhn CM, Hoffman GW Jr, McCall WV, Manepalli JN. Abnormalities in the response of plasma arginine vasopressin during hypertonic saline infusion in patients with eating disorders. *Biol Psychiatry.* 1989; 26(1):73–86.

49. Demitrack MA, Kalogeras KT, Altemus M, Pigott TA, Listwack SJ, Gold PW. CSF oxytocin in anorexia nervosa and bulimia nervosa: clinical and pathophysiologic considerations. *Am J Psychiatry.* 1990;147(7):882–886.

CHAPTER 3

Feeding Regulation

MONIKA M. WOOLSEY, M.S., R.D.

W hy do we eat the way we do? This seemingly simple question has puzzled humans for centuries. Journals, books, and scientific societies have been devoted to the topic; in the early 1990s alone several thousand research projects studied various aspects of the phenomenon. Various inputs and metabolic regulatory systems have been elucidated, and specific brain influences have been identified. But despite all of this attention, no conclusive, comprehensive model for feeding regulation has been developed (1).

Individual mechanisms, the relationships between them, and the reaction to environmental changes must all be studied to produce a complete picture of feeding. The research process is slow. Many feeding mechanisms are redundant; that is, they replicate the work of other systems. Redundancy is important for a behavior as important to survival as eating, as it provides numerous backup communications to ensure nourishment, should one or more aspects of the regulatory mechanism fail. However, this complexity makes understanding feeding a challenge because often several mechanisms must be studied in order to understand a single phenomenon, such as carbohydrate ingestion.

Eating disorders further complicate feeding behaviors. The decisions to procure energy and to choose necessary nutrients, normally subconscious and spontaneous, become either overly restrictive or uninhibited. Deviations from the norm can occur in one or more of literally billions of locations in the brain. Our current understanding of the brain's influence on eating disorders is at best rudimentary. Yet that which is understood suggests that biological influences on the eating disorders are significant. A basic understanding of what is currently known is helpful in determining what types of interventions will help the client and which might actually exacerbate his behaviors.

In this and the next chapter, the role of the central nervous system (CNS) and the gastrointestinal tract in feeding will be described to provide an overview of feeding, to develop an appreciation for the complexity of the behavior, and to provide some basic references, should further reading be desired. Psychological, developmental, and cultural influences on feeding will be covered in Section Two so that an appreciation for the complexity of eating can be developed.

Energy procurement involves the behaviors that result in the consumption of calories, including meal onset, duration, size, and termination, rate of ingestion, and any feeding-related processes such as salivation, chewing, and food preparation. Nutrient selection involves the food choices made once a need for calories has been recognized, and includes phenomena such as taste preference, cravings, and taste aversion. A thorough discussion of feeding research is not possible here; however, a basic outline of current paradigms will be presented with the emphasis on their relationship to eating disorders.

The central nervous system (CNS) coordinates the intake and response to various feeding-related stimuli, which can be categorized into four general areas: homeostatic regulation, learning, reward, and neural control (1). Each performs a unique and equally important function in the process of feeding.

HOMEOSTATIC REGULATION

Regulation includes control mechanisms that maintain physiological homeostasis. Biochemical fluctuations, such as in glucose levels and blood pressure, are monitored by chemoreceptors, osmoreceptors, and baroreceptors throughout the body. Significant changes are communicated back to the brain so that body function can be altered to maintain the status quo. This feeding paradigm accounts for instinctive feeding behaviors that ensure survival, and is similar to the regulation of stress and the stress response described in Chapter 1.

In the brain, some biochemical events, such as low blood glucose, facilitate excitatory feeding impulses, while others, such as high serum insulin, facilitate inhibitory processes. Though numerous individual biochemical markers have been shown to be directly correlated with the onset and termination of feeding (*Box 3.1*), regulation is a redundant function, with many feedback systems providing input to the central nervous system. This redundancy provides a system of checks and balances, and ensures that no one receptor mechanism is completely responsible for nutrient intake.

Caloric Regulation

One of the best understood mechanisms of regulation is the counterregulatory relationship between cortisol and insulin (2). The blood-brain barrier separates the CNS from the cardiovascular system (periphery). In the periphery, cortisol promotes blood glucose and fatty acid release, while insulin promotes the uptake and storage of these nutrients. This ensures survival by guaranteeing that glucose is available to cells even when food may not have been recently ingested, and by maintaining the brain's energy supply.

Changes in the following have been associated with changes in feeding:

Body fat stores	Vasopressin concentration
Rate of glucose utilization	Neuropeptide Y concentration
Peripheral insulin concentration	Energy content of food eaten
CNS insulin concentration	Rate of fat oxidation
Peripheral cortisol concentration	High-energy phosphate levels
CNS cortisol concentration	Oxidation of NAD+ → NADH
Aldactone concentration	

Sources: Kissileff (1) and Friedman (3).

Box 3.1
Regulation of
Feeding Behavior

In the CNS, the roles of cortisol and insulin are different. Cortisol promotes feeding behaviors. By notifying the brain that a significant environmental change has depleted peripheral energy stores, cortisol functions as a long-term feeding regulator. The presence of insulin, on the other hand, communicates that energy has been consumed and stored, and there is no further need for food consumption (3).

Under normal conditions, a balance of cortisol and insulin allows for energy eaten to equal energy consumed. Under conditions of chronic stress, the influence of cortisol predominates and insulin resistance develops. In other words, peripheral energy stores are liberated, resulting in hyperglycemia, hyperlipidemia, and eventually storage of some of the excess circulating substrates as triglycerides from abdominal fat. In the CNS, the predominance of cortisol over insulin is interpreted as a "need to feed," and appetite increases (3,4) *(Figure 3.1)*.

Figure 3.1
Impact of Stress on
Energy Regulation

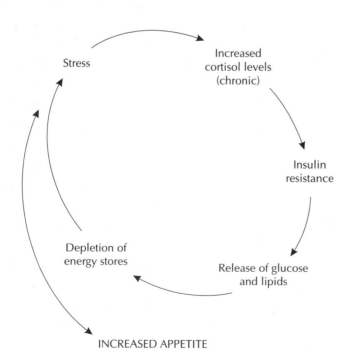

Individuals with metabolic syndrome may have difficulty following low-calorie diets because those diets exacerbate hunger in a condition that the brain already perceives as starvation. Because they limit the total energy supply, they can intensify feeding impulses, possibly even promoting behaviors such as food obsession. For this reason, a treatment plan for obesity should include the evaluation of potentially significant hormonal imbalances. The incorporation of interventions such as meditation, moderate exercise, and massage can increase the effectiveness of nutrition therapy.

Circadian Regulation

An extremely powerful and often overlooked feeding regulator is the circadian clock. This regulator acts as an internal timetable, altering hormone secretion and behavior in a regular, cyclic fashion. Daily circadian rhythms are the best known and studied; however, hormones have weekly, monthly, seasonal and annual fluctuations as well. The menstrual cycle is an example of a monthly hormonal fluctuation that affects feeding. A seasonal shift in carbohydrate preference has been attributed to circadian shifts (5), and even cholesterol levels are susceptible to these rhythms, with a tendency to be higher in the winter than in the summer (6).

The primary circadian clock is located in the suprachiasmic nucleus (SCN) of the hypothalamus (7). The pineal gland transmits information about the quantity of ultraviolet light exposure to this neuron bundle (8). From the SCN, this information is distributed to other hypothalamic centers that coordinate cycles for sleep, appetite, feeding, and even macronutrient intake (9,10). The circadian clock is thought to regulate secretion of feeding-related neuropeptides, including cortisol-releasing hormone (CRH), cortisol, growth hormone-releasing hormone (GHRH), and neuropeptide Y (NPY) (11), and therefore to influence behaviors related to these neuropeptides, including appetite for carbohydrates in the evening (12), shortened mealtimes during active cycles (13), and meal anticipation (14).

A redundant, or backup, system to the SCN circadian clock is the oscillator system. This circadian system is not light-dependent, but appears to be a natural pacemaker with an approximately 22-24-hour cycle that triggers behaviors such as feeding anticipation (15). When both the SCN pacemaker and the oscillator system are functioning normally, a powerful feeding impulse occurs on a regular basis that likely affects the ability of the individual to successfully manipulate her food intake with an externalized feeding regulation system (eg, a restrictive diet).

Cortisol, growth hormone, and insulin secretion fluctuate in response to circadian influences. Cortisol is naturally higher in the morning (16). During the daytime, blood glucose tends to decrease in normal individuals but increase in insulin-resistant individuals (16). During sleep, growth hormone secretion normally decreases and results in a decrease in both blood glucose and insulin, but this does not happen in obese individuals (16,17). This phenomenon might intensify appetite and increase the difficulty of complying with a restrictive eating plan.

Again, this phenomenon has been attributed to stress. Excess cortisol secretion flattens circadian fluctuations and the behaviors they influence (18). The initial stages of stress seem to depress appetite, and inconsistent exposure to stress (requiring more adaptation than consistent, anticipated, or acclimatized stressors) appears to have the most marked influences on circadian rhythms, resulting in acute decreases in feeding (18). This pattern again is consistent with the short- and long-term feeding effects of the stress hormone cortisol, discussed earlier in this section.

The same sociocultural influences on circadian rhythm (19) (eg, longer waking hours in the dark) could affect feeding as well. It is important to evaluate an individual's schedule for potential circadian disruptions (shift work, travel, long hours), and to develop interventions that address feeding disturbances that result from these disruptions whenever possible. *Box 3.2* discusses situations in which a sleep disorder, not an eating disorder, may be the prevailing condition.

**Box 3.2
Impact of Stress on
Energy Regulation**

In addition to the DSM-IV diagnoses of anorexia nervosa, bulimia nervosa, and binge eating disorder, there are feeding variations that might be more intricately tied to circadian disruption. These categories have been proposed for inclusion in the next revision of the *Diagnostic and Statistical Manual,* and include eating during apnea-induced confusional arousal, familial sleepwalking and sleep-related eating, familial restless legs syndrome and sleep-related eating, and anorexia nervosa with nocturnal bulimia (20). All of these variations have been linked with acute stress related to reality-based concerns about family or relationship distress, suggesting that they stem from some type of stress-related circadian disruption.

In one sleep disorder clinic, only 11 percent of clients with nocturnal eating disorders reported similar observable symptoms during the daytime (21). Most of these individuals could trace their nocturnal feeding behaviors to influences affecting neuroendocrine balance, including sleepwalking, triazolam abuse, premenstrual syndrome, nicotine abstinence, and acute stress (22). Of those individuals who woke from sleep to eat, 68 percent binge ate during these episodes (23). In another study individuals with nocturnal eating disorders were observed to have shorter than average periods of REM sleep and to be more easily awakened (22). These incidents were either recorded by a significant other or observed but usually not remembered by the individual (24). In all of these studies, diagnosable psychiatric conditions were found in more than half of the subjects.

A nutrition assessment should include an evaluation of nighttime sleeping habits and feeding patterns so that circadian variations can be evaluated. In addition, clients whose diet diaries do not seem to be consistent with their observed weight trends should not be immediately assumed to be noncompliant or dishonest. Often there are incidents of nighttime eating that the client may not be aware of or may be embarrassed to share. These incidents might provide important clues to prevalent hormonal influences and should be given attention by the treatment team.

LEARNING

The learning paradigm adds to the regulation paradigm the idea that food experiences reinforce and influence future food intake and specific food choices. Foods can be both positive and negative reinforcers. For example, a child who has skipped breakfast and gone hungry is likely to learn that breakfast is an important meal. Likewise, a child who grows up in a household in which cake is served to celebrate good grades might view cake in a more positive context than a child who constantly hears that cake is "bad" or "fattening". An individual's developmental environment is important to explore, as it provides valuable clues to significant learning experiences that affect his feeding behavior.

Much of nutrition education is based on the idea that learning is the predominant feeding paradigm. While nutrition education can help to influence food behavior, knowledge about healthy nutrition does not always result in behavioral change. Every nutrition therapist has experienced the frustration of dealing with a client who has spent hours in nutrition education but cannot implement the low-fat diet she has been prescribed. In eating disorder treatment, the nutrition therapist's role is somewhat different. Rather than create and teach a new set of behaviors based on scientific principles, one of the most important jobs of the eating disorder specialist is to identify what an individual's most important feeding or nonfeeding reinforcers are. These will constitute the basis on which a treatment plan is developed.

Learning occurs in many types of environments. When a client does not implement a recommended food plan, it is helpful to consider that other feeding paradigms may currently be stronger influences for this individual. A client is likely to have stronger reinforcers in his environment that override the dictates of a specific exchange plan. (For example, a client may eat a bowl of ice cream every night because he has learned that this is the only time he has positive socialization with his spouse.) The nutrition therapist's assuming intentional noncompliance suggests to the client that he is personally responsible for his failure. Exploring other physiological and psychological explanations for his difficulties with food is more validating, and opens the door to a supportive relationship in which true problem-solving occurs.

Food aversions are a very specific type of learned behavior. It is perfectly normal to develop food aversions based on negative food experiences. This phenomenon has been repeatedly demonstrated in the laboratory (25–35), and often results from gastrointestinal distress following the ingestion of a specific food. Under normal circumstances, this conditioned learning functions to protect individuals from repeating potentially fatal behaviors. In a dysfunctional individual, food aversions can develop into an avoidance technique that intertwines with the eating disorder. In eating disorders, learning often becomes the dominant feeding influence, at the expense of appropriately nourishing eating.

A stressful situation elicits more than an elevated pulse and blood pressure. Along with these cardiovascular changes, blood flow to the sensory and memory centers (located mainly in the brain's limbic system) increases and allows for more acute evaluation of the sights, sounds, and smells accompanying the unsafe situation (35,36). This increased sensory acuity is useful at the immediate time of crisis, but it also serves another function. Sensory input from environments that elicited the stress response is also stored for future reference. For example, a young child who puts his hand on a heated stove hot plate will burn his hand the first time, but will probably remember the next time that a red coil is to be avoided.

Pleasant sensations can be stored as well. Most people can think of a favorite odor—fresh-cut grass, grandma's perfume, or hot apple pie—that immediately brings back fond memories of childhood. As individuals mature through adulthood, they collect numerous experiences along the way that are categorized into storage as "safe" or "unsafe". For most individuals, safe experiences outnumber unsafe and only a handful of sensations elicit a stress reaction.

Some individuals, however, because of a natural hyperresponsiveness to stress, take in more "unsafe" information than their peers. Other individuals grow up in dysfunctional environments where they do not have the opportunity to express fears and overcome them. This information may be processed in the emotion-memory centers of the limbic system, where it influences food choices. Still others live in outright unsafe situations and become conditioned to always be on alert for a potential trauma and to be hyperresponsive to aversive stimuli.

The trauma memory system is believed to be located in the limbic system of the brain. The limbic system is a primitive system that can elicit instinctive responses based on environmental input. It registers and stores sensations that elicit the stress response. After the initial trauma (eg, food poisoning, accident, or injury), it alerts the individual to potential dangers when similar sensory conditions reoccur.

Teicher and coworkers found that individuals who were subjected to sexual or physical abuse had elevated scores on the Limbic System Checklist-33, an assessment that evaluates symptomatology relating to limbic system function (36). Limbic system function has been found to be abnormal in genetically obese, hypercortisolemic individuals (37). In anorexic individuals the caudate nucleus, another nonlimbic region that has been identified as involved in taste aversions, is hyperactive (38). These findings suggest that there are significant changes in learning and memory that affect feeding behaviors.

Avoidance is a coping mechanism common in anorexia. When an individual reports a food dislike, she may actually dislike the feeling the food provokes and not the food itself. It is important to establish such a distinction in the process of counseling. In some individuals who grew up in households in which arguing and physical violence occurred at the dinner table, "table trauma," or loss of appetite when simply sitting down at a table, is a common reaction.

Often there are no specific trigger foods, but the feeling of fullness is the source of retraumatization. Feeling full can trigger memories of a pregnancy, which can be particularly traumatic to someone who has had an abortion or miscarriage. Fullness can also retraumatize a sexually abused individual, who can equate the presence of *anything* in her stomach with the violation of her physical boundaries.

Nutrition therapists with experience in the field of disordered eating frequently report that clients relate independently that many foods commonly listed as hate or fear foods have textures, appearances, and sounds reminiscent of unwanted sexual experiences *(Box 3.3)*. Some individuals even relate that as they

Box 3.3
Foods That Commonly
Trigger Sexual Memories

Butter/margarine	Mayonnaise
Cherry tomatoes	Melted cheese
Creamy foods	Milk
Hard-boiled eggs	Sausages
Hot dogs	Sour cream

become more aware of traumatic memories, they realize that their vegetarianism was a subconscious avoidance mechanism. Meat tends to be especially provocative for those who have been orally sexually abused; this possibility should be kept in mind when working with the severely eating disordered vegetarian individual. However, there have been no studies to support these theories.

In addition to food fears, in bulimia and binge eating disorder, foods are often chosen that recreate a positive memory. When faced with a difficult feeling, the individuals often seek out a food that they connect with comfort and safety. For example, a child who frequently came home to freshly baked chocolate chip cookies might later seek this food out when he felt lonely as an adult because he remembered feeling taken care of when his mother baked cookies. A child who grew up in a family in which both parents worked might equate pizza with companionship if Friday night family pizza dinners were the one guaranteed family get-together during the week.

Nutrition therapists are traditionally trained to honor intolerances and aversions and to individualize food plans out of respect for the client's personal needs. However, with an eating disorder, these very intolerances can be psychosomatic expressions of the eating disorder. For example, individuals with chronic stress-related syndromes, such as irritable bowel syndrome or migraine headaches, are likely to have a long list of foods they avoid because of a headache or incident of diarrhea that occurred soon after eating. For a person with psychosomatic tendencies, it is easier to blame physical discomfort on a tangible item such as a food. It is also easier to avoid a food than it is to address the stressful incident or situation that is truly the source of the problem.

As eating disordered individuals are prone to psychosomatic ailments (39), they tend to blame negative feeling on recently eaten foods. The "no white flour, no sugar" diet is popular among individuals with eating disorders, and may reflect this tendency (Box 3.4). Well-intended but naive nutrition therapists can be hooked into justifying eating disordered behaviors by prescribing restrictive diets without pursuing whether or not the physical and psychological history of the client warrants their use. Working with the client to honestly evaluate the validity of her perceived intolerance liberates her from a restrictive pattern and allows her to focus on cognitive and behavioral changes that will truly reduce her distress. A team approach, including interventions from a psychologist and psychiatrist, can help the client stay focused in nutrition therapy sessions (Box 3.5).

Andrew had had anorexia for 8 years. As his disease progressed, he became obsessive-compulsive to the point of being completely unable to function independently. When he left college and moved back home with his parents, he continued to deteriorate to the point where he was using the exercycle 7 hours a day and spending the rest of his waking hours doing the family laundry. In the course of one year, he completely wore out two washing machines.

Finally Andrew decided to enter inpatient treatment to break the cycles that were holding him hostage. In his initial medical assessment, he reported allergies to pine trees and crunchy peanut butter. Curious about this interesting combination, his nutrition therapist investigated the alleged allergies and learned that both the smell of pine trees and crunchy peanut butter elicited symptoms similar to an anaphylactic reaction. The two allergies had surfaced simultaneously just a few years before.

Initially Andrew was granted permission to not eat crunchy peanut butter. The initial nutrition counseling sessions focused on building trust and practicing healthy communication skills. In the meantime, the allergy information was passed on to the psychotherapist as a potential discrepancy worth investigating.

Shortly after admission, Andrew began to tell his psychotherapist about a trauma he had experienced a few years before, about which he still had nightmares. He had been walking down a gravel road in a pine grove near his home when he was seized and molested. This incident happened at almost the same time that he reported his food allergies became significant.

Andrew's psychotherapist contacted his nutrition therapist to suggest a joint session to help Andrew understand the connection between his allergies and his past trauma. In the session, Andrew was asked to talk about his allergies, to describe memories of pine trees that were significant to him, and to share his memories about peanut butter. Eventually a connection between Andrew's memories and allergies was established. Andrew realized that the smell of pine trees and the texture of chunky peanut butter were sensory inputs similar to those in the environment of his trauma, and that he might be avoiding these stimuli to avoid retraumatization. In a later session, he discussed his obsessive-compulsive behaviors and began to understand how he used them as an avoidance technique to keep from thinking about extremely painful events.

Andrew's reaction to this treatment was relief. Upon making the initial connection, he asked, "You mean I'm not crazy?" He related that, even though he had wanted to comply with his nutrition program, the crunchy peanut butter had always been a stumbling block. A previous nutrition therapist had told him, "That makes no sense. You can't be allergic to crunchy but not creamy peanut butter." He had entered treatment highly anxious, wanting to comply, fearful that his nutrition therapist would make the same assessment, and ashamed at the thought of "failing" treatment once again. He wanted to be able to eat peanut butter, but didn't know how to take the fear out of the food.

Andrew and his psychotherapist continued to work through his sexual trauma issues. Finally Andrew decided it was time to recondition his responses. When he felt strong enough to challenge himself, he asked to be served half of a crunchy peanut butter sandwich. This challenge was scheduled for a day that was relatively uneventful for him in other therapeutic activities, to allow him to focus on the task at hand and to ensure that his challenge environment would provide positive

continued

Box 3.4
CASE STUDY:
Separating
Psychosomatic and
Physical Symptoms

Box 3.4
(continued)

reinforcement. Andrew succeeded in eating the peanut butter sandwich, excited about overcoming what had seemed to be an insurmountable fear.

Andrew brought a list of other fear foods to his next nutrition therapy session, and asked if there might be memories attached to them as well. Each food was investigated individually; some had memories that needed to be processed, and some were scary for other reasons. Regardless of how they had become fear foods, Andrew was eager to use his new understanding of the ways behavior and memory influence food choices. Though he left inpatient treatment with many food challenges still to conquer, he said he was excited that he now knew how to develop an action plan that would help him over the remaining stumbling blocks.

Box 3.5
Binge Eating:
Addiction to Food or
Compulsive Behavior?

A food plan often used to treat binge eaters is the "no white flour, no sugar" diet. The basis for this diet is the belief that certain individuals have a physical addiction to processed foods and must avoid them the same way recovering drug addicts must avoid alcohol and drugs. This approach seems to work for some individuals, but over the long term may encourage avoidance of foods that provide important clues to what causes bingeing behavior.

Though sugar addiction has not been disproved, it is unlikely that an individual would develop an addiction to a substance on which the brain depends for fuel. A more likely scenario is that some people who binge eat may have a dopamine receptor (DRD2) deficiency/resistance that contributes to intense food cravings that can feel similar to chemical addictions. In addition to the hypersensitive stress reaction that is likely to exist, emotional discomfort may be more easily triggered in someone who binge eats than in other individuals. The binge eater has learned that bingeing calms her physically and emotionally, so she repeatedly engages in the behavior. However, this form of self-medication is a double-edged sword. Though it provides relief, it also creates guilt and shame, which increase emotional discomfort *and* a need for even more emotional relief. Thus, a vicious cycle can exist that is difficult to break *(Figure 3.2)*.

Figure 3.2
The Binge Cycle:
Proposed Mechanism
for Physiological/
Psychological/
Environmental
Influences on
Binge Eating

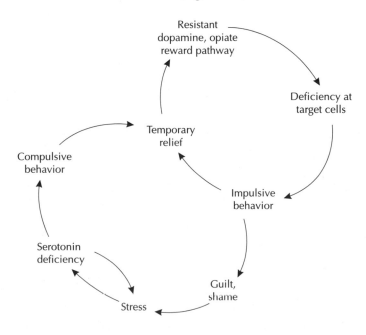

continued

White flour and sugar avoidance might reduce shame and guilt, but without the development of assertiveness skills to manage stress in a more appropriate fashion, the source of the problem may go completely unaddressed. In addition, any food regimen that consists of significant restrictions or elimination of complete food categories automatically requires having to think more about food. Alternatives might have to be requested in restaurants, some social events avoided, and in some situations not eating might be the only alternative. There are ways to decrease both physical and emotional cravings without requiring social and/or food restrictions that could worsen the problem.

For many of these individuals, it may be the behavior and not the food that is addictive. In other words, over time eating as a reaction to perceived stress becomes second nature, rather than addressing the stress at its source or coping differently. Learning to recognize and respond to stressful events in a different manner is the key to overcoming the behavior. A rigid diet may provide structure in the beginning phases of recovery, when the client feels overwhelmed and out of control. As therapy progresses, it is important to explore the meanings certain trigger foods may have. (Why is a Snickers bar the choice when the client feels lonely?) The client is likely to learn that certain food relationships were learned early in childhood, and the connections are ingrained by adulthood.

A model that facilitates avoidance of trigger foods may block the client from complete understanding of his behavior. A craving for a certain food may not necessarily be "bad," but may be an important emotional barometer. ("I know when I want a Snickers bar it often means I am lonely.") Accepting these barometers as important indicators of actions that need to be taken can facilitate true emotional awareness and a response to emotions that does not always involve food.

Figure 3.2
(continued)

REWARD

Reward theory introduces the concept that feeding is a repetition of behaviors that are emotionally or physiologically reinforcing or rewarding. When these behaviors are enacted, a neuron configuration known as the *reward pathway* is stimulated in a way that is physically satisfying, and the need for further stimulation ceases. Rewards come in many forms, including physical satiety, sensory stimulation, praise, and socialization.

In eating disorders and common comorbid conditions, such as polysubstance abuse, gambling, compulsive spending, binge eating, attention deficit-hyperactivity disorder (ADHD), conduct disorder, and post-traumatic stress disorder (PTSD) (40), aberrations in the reward pathway are common and suggest that there is a strong biological basis for the impulsive behaviors often seen in individuals with these conditions. Dopamine is the predominant neurotransmitter involved in the reward pathway. Carbohydrate consumption, addictive behaviors such as drug and alcohol use, and compulsive behaviors such as gambling and shoplifting are thought to satisfy this reward pathway.

Obese individuals have fewer dopamine (DRD2) receptors than nonobese individuals (41). In addition, CSF dopamine levels are greater (42) and hyperresponsive to stimulus, and dopamine receptors are resistant to stimulation (43). This "dopamine resistance" is similar to peripheral insulin resistance, functioning to maintain a deficiency in endpoint cells despite adequate neurotransmitter levels (44). A craving for rewarding behaviors persists, and the addiction cycle persists, much like hunger and feeding persist in type 2 diabetes.

The incidence of DRD2 deficiency in obesity is thought to be great; 45.2 percent of obese subjects in one study had a genetic profile consistent with such a receptor inadequacy (45). Individuals with this profile have an 85 percent chance of developing obesity if at least one parent is obese, obesity developed after adolescence, and it is accompanied by a preference for carbohydrates. In addition, cross-addiction is likely. In one study 82 percent of individuals with a DRD2-deficient genetic configuration were also polysubstance abusers (40).

Both food restriction and food bingeing are neurally rewarding behaviors (41). They increase levels of endogenous opiates such as endorphin and dynorphin, which also satisfies the reward pathway. In addition, food restriction increases opioid receptor sensitivity (45) and therefore potentiates endogenous opiate highs induced by later bingeing, suggesting that a binge after a period of food restriction has the same effect as a mood-altering drug. Weight loss has been shown to induce its own opiate high, which might potentiate the reward provided by food restriction. In anorexia, self-starvation might actually create a physiologically addictive condition. This phenomenon might also explain why some individuals get locked into yo-yo dieting.

In obesity opioid levels are chronically high, and are thought to significantly increase hyperphagia (46). Though some of this elevation is likely due to bingeing, other comorbid conditions may also be responsible. For example, active thyroid hormone, often deficient in obesity (46), inhibits opioid secretion (47), and diabetes elevates opioid levels (48). These factors might trigger hyperactive reward impulses that result in increased cravings and eating.

All of these findings support the idea that, in eating disorders, a simple behavioral approach to treatment might not promote long-term recovery. As our understanding of the physiology of eating improves, it is likely that genetic screening and more complex, individualized pharmacological interventions will be developed to address the neuroendocrine source of many of these conditions.

The principles of reward and learning are integral to the science of disordered eating, and will reappear throughout this book as various aspects of eating disorders and addictions are discussed.

NEURAL CONTROL

The neural control paradigm combines the first three paradigms and explores their neurohormonal origins. All feeding behavior originates from neural impulses, and numerous studies have been devoted to the intricacies of the "under the hood" process that results in food ingestion. Under normal circumstances, most of this process is carried out without conscious thought. Information on the nature and quantity of nutrients ingested and stored is communicated to the brain by sensory nerve fibers throughout the body. This information is integrated by the various brain centers, which then relay messages through the motor nerve fibers back to the various target tissues, coordinating either feeding or its termination (49).

The person with anorexia ignores what her brain is trying to tell her. With bulimia and binge eating, individuals are unable to respond to volume loads and eat past the point of comfortable satiation. The neural origins of these behaviors are important to understand, as treatment planning often involves medication and dietary manipulations that help to restore the imbalances that developed as the disease progressed.

Neural feeding impulses do not originate from any specific brain region, but appear to be located in numerous sections and nuclei (bundles of neurons with specialized functions) *(Figures 3.3, 3.4, Table 3.1)*. In addition to specific tasks, brain regions communicate with each other and respond to feedback from other regions. For example, when a carbohydrate load is sensed by the hypothalamus, this sensation is communicated to the cerebral cortex, which in turn decreases its sensitivity to environmental sights and smells (50). The net result is a lowered sensitivity to food sensations, followed by inhibition of feeding. This feedback helps to explain why the first chocolate chip cookie is usually the best tasting of the batch!

In the process of eating a cracker, from hunger recognition, to walking into the kitchen for the box, to chewing, swallowing, and digesting, numerous brain centers must transmit, receive, and properly execute impulses. Energy and chemicals are liberated, biochemical balances are changed, and sensations are triggered, all of which provide feedback to the brain to determine when feeding should terminate. As with the stress response, the nervous system must be intact from start to finish for all impulses to be properly initiated, transmitted, and received.

For simplicity, neuroendocrine physiology thus far has been condensed to examples using one neuron, one neurotransmitter, and one receptor. In actuality, the complexity is staggering. As Karen Parfitt, PhD, assistant professor of neuroscience at Pomona College, notes: "There are 100 billion neurons, each with at least 1000 synapses, each synapse using a principle neurotransmitter plus who-knows-how-many neuromodulators, each chemical acting at multiple receptor subtypes bringing about a multitude of postsynaptic effects . . . a complexity that will never be mimicked by a manmade machine." This translates into hundreds of billions of daily impulses revolving around the simple task of feeding! The CNS network is vast and not unlike the World Wide Web, with each computer (neuron) linked to every other computer (neuron) in the system and an endless number of possible directions of communication.

Neurochemicals and Feeding

Many neurochemicals involved in feeding are hormones that are already circulating and effecting other changes. Cortisol, insulin, aldosterone, and vasopressin all have their own specific target effects, but they also promote an increased appetite for and intake of carbohydrates, which allows near-immediate feedback to the brain and fine-tuning of feeding. This efficient messenger system uses already circulating hormones to communicate current metabolic needs to the brain.

Neuroanatomy of Eating Behaviors

Lateral cross-section of brain at midline
with some structures in right hemisphere visible

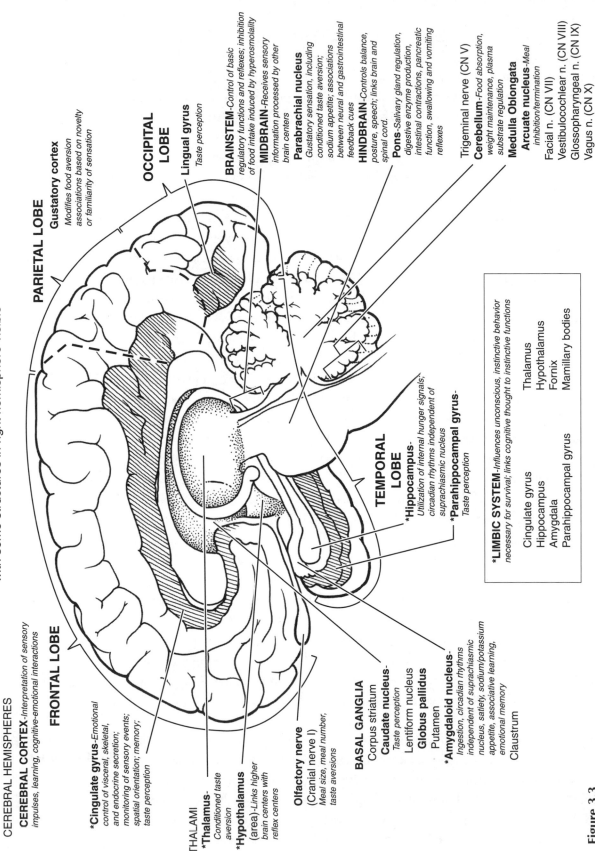

CEREBRAL HEMISPHERES
CEREBRAL CORTEX-*Interpretation of sensory impulses, learning, cognitive-emotional interactions*

FRONTAL LOBE

*Cingulate gyrus-*Emotional control of visceral, skeletal, and endocrine secretion; monitoring of sensory events; spatial orientation; memory; taste perception*

PARIETAL LOBE

Gustatory cortex
Modifies food aversion associations based on novelty or familiarity of sensation

OCCIPITAL LOBE

Lingual gyrus
Taste perception

BRAINSTEM-*Control of basic regulatory functions and reflexes; inhibition of food intake induced by hyperosmolality*
MIDBRAIN-*Receives sensory information processed by other brain centers*
Parabrachial nucleus
Gustatory sensation, including conditioned taste aversion; sodium appetite; associations between neural and gastrointestinal feedback cues
HINDBRAIN-*Controls balance, posture, speech; links brain and spinal cord.*
Pons-*Salivary gland regulation, digestive enzyme production, intestinal contractions, pancreatic function, swallowing and vomiting reflexes*

Trigeminal nerve (CN V)
Cerebellum-*Food absorption, weight maintenance, plasma substrate regulation*
Medulla Oblongata
Arcuate nucleus-*Meal inhibition/termination*
Facial n. (CN VII)
Vestibulocochlear n. (CN VIII)
Glossopharyngeal n. (CN IX)
Vagus n. (CN X)

THALAMI
*Thalamus-
Conditioned taste aversion
*Hypothalamus
(area)-*Links higher brain centers with reflex centers*

Olfactory nerve
(Cranial nerve I)
Meal size, meal number, taste aversions

BASAL GANGLIA
Corpus striatum
Caudate nucleus-
Taste perception
Lentiform nucleus
Globus pallidus
Putamen
*Amygdaloid nucleus-
Ingestion, circadian rhythms independent of suprachiasmic nucleus, satiety; sodium/potassium appetite, associative learning, emotional memory
Claustrum

TEMPORAL LOBE
*Hippocampus-
Utilization of internal hunger signals; circadian rhythms independent of suprachiasmic nucleus
*Parahippocampal gyrus-
Taste perception

*LIMBIC SYSTEM-*Influences unconscious, instinctive behavior necessary for survival; links cognitive thought to instinctive functions*

Cingulate gyrus	Thalamus
Hippocampus	Hypothalamus
Amygdala	Fornix
Parahippocampal gyrus	Mamillary bodies

Figure 3.3
Neuroanatomy of Feeding: Lateral Cross-section of Brain at Midline with Some Structures in Right Hemisphere Visible

Neuroanatomy of Eating Behaviors
Frontal cross-section of brain at optic chiasm

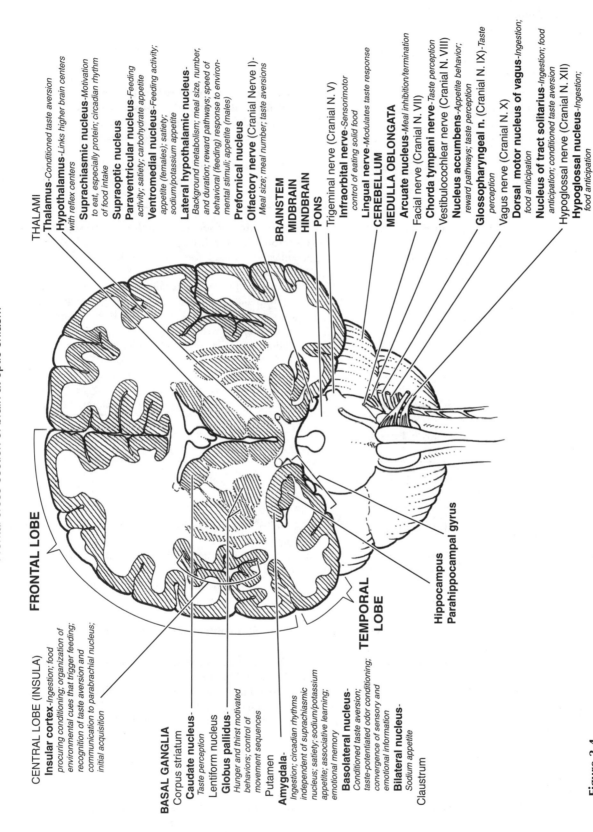

FRONTAL LOBE

CENTRAL LOBE (INSULA)
Insular cortex-*Ingestion; food procuring conditioning; organization of environmental cues that trigger feeding; recognition of taste aversion and communication to parabrachial nucleus; initial acquisition*

BASAL GANGLIA
Corpus striatum
Caudate nucleus-*Taste perception*
Lentiform nucleus
Globus pallidus-*Hunger and thirst motivated behaviors; control of movement sequences*
Putamen
Amygdala-*Ingestion; circadian rhythms independent of suprachiasmic nucleus; satiety; sodium/potassium appetite; associative learning; emotional memory*
Basolateral nucleus-*Conditioned taste aversion; taste-potentiated odor conditioning; convergence of sensory and emotional information*
Bilateral nucleus-*Sodium appetite*
Claustrum

TEMPORAL LOBE

Hippocampus
Parahippocampal gyrus

THALAMI
Thalamus-*Conditioned taste aversion*
Hypothalamus-*Links higher brain centers with reflex centers*
Suprachiasmic nucleus-*Motivation to eat, especially protein; circadian rhythm of food intake*
Supraoptic nucleus
Paraventricular nucleus-*Feeding activity; satiety; carbohydrate appetite*
Ventromedial nucleus-*Feeding activity; appetite (females); satiety; sodium/potassium appetite*
Lateral hypothalamic nucleus-*Background metabolism; meal size, number, and duration; reward pathways; speed of behavioral (feeding) response to environmental stimuli; appetite (males)*
Prefornical nucleus
Olfactory nerve (Cranial Nerve I)-*Meal size; meal number; taste aversions*

BRAINSTEM
MIDBRAIN
HINDBRAIN
PONS
Trigeminal nerve (Cranial N. V)
Infraorbital nerve-*Sensorimotor control of eating solid food*
Lingual nerve-*Modulates taste response*
CEREBELLUM
MEDULLA OBLONGATA
Arcuate nucleus-*Meal inhibition/termination*
Facial nerve (Cranial N. VII)
Chorda tympani nerve-*Taste perception*
Vestibulocochlear nerve (Cranial N. VIII)
Nucleus accumbens-*Appetite behavior; reward pathways; taste perception*
Glossopharyngeal n. (Cranial N. IX)-*Taste perception*
Vagus nerve (Cranial N. X)
Dorsal motor nucleus of vagus-*Ingestion; food anticipation*
Nucleus of tract solitarius-*Ingestion; food anticipation; conditioned taste aversion*
Hypoglossal nerve (Cranial N. XII)
Hypoglossal nucleus-*Ingestion; food anticipation*

Figure 3.4
Neuroanatomy of Feeding: Frontal Cross-section of Brain at Optic Chiasm

Table 3.1
Brain Regions and
Their Known Feeding
Functions

Region	Function
Basal Ganglia	
Caudate nucleus	Taste perception
Globus pallidus	Hunger- and thirst-motivated behaviors; control of movement sequences
Brain Stem	**control of basic regulatory functions and reflexes; inhibition of food intake induced by hypersomolality**
Pons	salivary gland regulation; digestive enzyme production; intestinal contractions; pancreatic function; swallowing and vomiting reflexes
Parabrachial nucleus	gustatory sensation, including conditioned taste aversion; sodium appetite; associations between neural and gastrointestinal feedback cues
Cerebral Cortex	**interpretation of sensory impulses, learning, cognitive-emotional interactions**
Gustatory cortex	modification of food aversion associations based on novelty or familiarity of sensation
Insular cortex	ingestion; food-procuring conditioning; organization of environmental cues that trigger feeding; recognition of taste aversion and communication to parabrachial nucleus; initial acquisition
Nucleus basalis magnocellularis	conditioned taste aversion; integration of feeding behaviors
Lingual gyrus	taste perception
Occipital lobe	interpretation of visual input
Temporal lobe	ingestion; interpretation of pressure sensations; taste perception
Chorda Tympani Nerve	**taste perception**
Glossopharyngeal Nerve	**taste perception**
Hindbrain	**control of balance, posture, speech, link between brain and spinal cord**
Cerebellum	food absorption; weight maintenance; plasma substrate regulation
Dorsal motor nucleus	ingestion; food anticipation
Nucleus of solitary	ingestion; food anticipation; conditioned taste aversion tract
Hypoglossal nucleus	ingestion; food anticipation
Infraorbital Nerve	**sensorimotor control of eating solid food**
Hypothalamus	**link between higher brain centers and reflex centers**
Arcuate nucleus	meal initiation/termination
Lateral area	background metabolism; meal size, number, and duration; reward pathways; speed of behavioral (feeding) response to environ-mental stimuli; appetite (males) Paraventricular nucleus feeding activity;
Perifornical nucleus	satiety, carbohydrate appetite
Posterior nucleus	
Suprachiasmic nucleus	motivation to eat; especially protein; circadian rhythm of food intake
Ventromedial nucleus	feeding activity; appetite (females); satiety; sodium/potassium appetite

continued

Region	Function	**Table 3.1**
		(continued)

Region	Function
Limbic System	**influences unconscious, instinctive behavior necessary for survival; link between cognitive thought and instinctive functions**
Amygdala	ingestion; circadian rhythms independent of suprachiasmic nucleus; satiety; sodium/potassium appetite; associative learning; emotional memory
Basolateral nucleus	conditioned taste aversion, taste-potentiated odor conditioning; convergence of sensory and emotional information
Bilateral nucleus	sodium appetite
Cingulate gyrus	emotional control of visceral, skeletal, and endocrine secretion; monitoring of sensory events; spatial orientation; memory; taste perception
Hippocampus	utilization of internal hunger signals; circadian rhythms independent of suprachiasmic nucleus
Olfactory bulb	meal size and number; taste aversions
Parahippocampal gyrus	taste perception
Lingual Nerve	**modulation of taste response**
Midbrain	**reception of sensory information processed by other brain centers**
Striatum	
Nucleus accumbens	appetitive behavior; reward pathways; taste aversions
Neostriatum	motor hyperactivity; food-procuring movements
Subfornical Organ	**thirst; electrolyte appetite**
Thalamus	
Posteromedial nucleus	conditioned taste aversion
Medial section	conditioned taste aversion

Note: This chart presents a sampling of what is currently known. As neuroscience advances, this list will likely lengthen and include brain regions that have not yet been studied.
Sources: 7, 51–93.

The neurotransmitters important to the stress response, serotonin, dopamine, acetylcholine, and norepinephrine, also have responsibilities in feeding maintenance. Like the hormones, these neurochemicals have dual duties, coordinating both physiological responses and the energy-related behaviors necessary to support these responses.

Serotonin's function is best understood in the hypothalamus. In the paraventricular nucleus and ventromedial nucleus, it regulates energy balance (94,95). Circadian eating patterns, including nocturnal and seasonal increases in carbohydrate preference and a decreased preference for carbohydrate in the morning (97), are serotonin-mediated and originate in the medial hypothalamus and suprachiasmatic nucleus.

Feeding increases central serotonin concentrations, which trigger carbohydrate satiety and switch food preference to protein (96). One of the most significant feeding related neurohormones is neuropeptide Y (NPY). This neuropeptide is produced in the arcuate nucleus of the brain (97) and stimulates carbohydrate and fat feeding and fluid consumption in several brain centers, including the hypothalamus (97–99), the arcuate nucleus (98,100,101), the amygdala (102), and the cortex (103). Synthesis of NPY increases under conditions of food deprivation (either short-term fasting or long-term dieting) (98,100,104) or weight loss (101), and decreases in the fed state (104).

Neuropeptide Y can elicit feeding independently of other neurotransmitters (105,106). Interestingly, the presence of NPY inhibits both the hypothalamic-pituitary-growth hormone and the hypothalamic-pituitary-ovarian axes (107), which may mean it is indirectly responsible for the growth inhibition and amenorrhea seen in anorexia. This relationship makes evolutionary sense; NPY communicates a metabolic state that is not conducive to growth, and to inhibit behaviors that would impair maintenance and reproduction.

Neuropeptide Y metabolism is altered in several conditions related to eating disorders. Obesity, fasting (108), and insulin-deficiency (98) increase NPY levels. Whether this is a result of the restrained eating patterns common to these conditions or a predisposing condition is not currently known. Nevertheless, it provides yet another possible explanation for the difficulty most experience in following low-calorie food plans.

Interestingly, NPY has been observed to have an anxiolytic effect (109). While it is normally the fasting state that is physiologically stressful, this finding may explain the attraction of anorexia. In some individuals fasting may produce a calming effect, making it a desirable behavior under stressful conditions.

Why is there such a physiological emphasis on maintaining carbohydrate intake? Under optimal conditions, the brain uses glucose almost exclusively as an energy source. Without a mechanism to ensure that this fuel is available on a constant basis, humans would never have survived as a species. When carbohydrate-containing foods were not readily available, it was important to have a craving mechanism that promoted behaviors that sought out carbohydrates. Unfortunately, today carbohydrate is too easily available. Human feeding behavior has not evolved as quickly as the food supply; what was once a feeding instinct crucial for survival has become a preference that can increase susceptibility to eating disorders.

Though a carbohydrate preference is natural, it is intensified in eating disorders because of a possible combination of factors including serotonin deficiencies, NPY excesses, environmental/stress-related serotonin depletion, or carbohydrate-restrictive diets that intensify both serotonin- and NPY-related carbohydrate cravings, and likely numerous other influences that remain unidentified. Individuals with these cravings often fear them. Or, because food advertising and nutrition information can label these types of foods as "bad", there is often shame about this preference or a desire to ignore it or eradicate it. With his knowledge of brain physiology and feeding behavior, the eating disorder specialist can help increase the client's understanding of her food preferences, which helps to reduce this shame and allow for a natural response to instinctive feeding impulses. In addition, counseling sessions can be used to develop eating plans that work with, rather than against, the natural desire for carbohydrates.

Acetylcholine is secreted in the limbic system when cortisol levels are elevated (37). Its presence in these memory and learning regions suggests that it is important for learning and conditioning processes. Norepinephrine and to some extent epinephrine have not been identified as having a specific feeding-related impact on the brain. However, their importance in eliciting the stress response suggests that there is probably an indirect influence due to the increased metabolic needs that restoring homeostasis requires.

Other Monoamines

It is interesting that the neurotransmitters involved in the stress response function dually in regulating feeding behavior *(Table 3.2)*. In addition, the neuroendocrine releasing hormones also have feeding effects. The CRH-releasing neurons and NPY-releasing neurons are interconnected in the paraventricular nucleus (110), further suggesting that stress and feeding are interrelated.

In the laboratory, the effect of stress on the brain and on behavior is often studied by inducing various types of stressors, then measuring the hormonal or behavioral response. An acute, unexpected, inescapable stress produces the greatest increase in stress hormones and the most marked variations in food behavior

STRESS, EATING DISORDERS, AND FEEDING

Neurotransmitter/ Region of Brain	Systemic Effect
Dopamine	
Amygdala	Sets reward pathways.
Lateral hypothalamus	Inhibits food intake.
Mesolimbic region	Communicates reward, terminates feeding and drinking, communicates with the lateral hypothalamus for the reinforcement of learning.
Midbrain	Terminates feeding activity
Neostriatum	Triggers motor hyperactivity and food procuring movements.
Nucleus accumbens	Sets reward pathways
Serotonin	
Lateral hypothalamus	Interprets peripheral physiologic and metabolic information, as well as environmental features; regulates circadian clock; initiates behavioral response.
	Inhibits/disinhibits impulses coming from other brain centers.
	Provides overall control of mood, aggression, pain, anxiety, sleep, memory, addictive behavior, temperature control, endocrine regulation, and motor behavior, all of which impact on feeding behavior.
Acetylcholine	
Hippocampus	Controls emotional processing, learning and memory, feeding regulation, taste aversion.
Thalamus	
Hypothalamus	
Norepinephrine	
	Indirectly, through its influence on the sympathetic nervous system and in integrating the stress response, alters metabolic environments, which in turn stimulate feeding.

Table 3.2 Specific Monoamine Neurotransmitter Effects on Brain-Related Energy Procurement Behaviors

Sources: Zhou and Palmiter (111), Feifel and Vaccarino (112), Yakimovskii and Filatova (113), Mark et al (114), Weisinger et al (115), Orosco et al (116), Griffiths et al (117).

(118). With time, rats exposed to these conditions become immobile and experience a significant increase in cortisol levels (119). A short-term stress tends to reduce food consumption and increase food finickiness (116,117). When given an option to escape the stress, rats display active coping behaviors, have lower cortisol increases, and do not decrease their food intake as significantly (117).

On a neural level, acute inescapable stress induces dopamine and norepinephrine increases in the frontal cortex and norepinephrine increases in the nucleus accumbens regions (118). When stress evokes emotional arousal, dopamine and norepinephrine levels increase in the limbic system to a moderate degree as well (119). Serotonin stimulation and neural anxiostimulation reduce active coping behavior and increase feeding behavior. Chronic stress sensitizes the nervous system so that, when subsequent stresses are administered, norepinephrine release is more expedient and significant (119,120).

These findings open some windows into the mechanics of stress and its impact on eating disorders. One of the most common psychological characteristics of depression is that of "learned helplessness," which is the tendency to give up active coping in situations that are perceived to be unresolvable (122). Learned helplessness in humans is a behavior similar to the loss of active coping seen in rats that were exposed to prolonged inescapable stress.

Because each individual develops in a different environment and learns different coping mechanisms for his own stressors, a stress that is imposed in equal amounts to a group of individuals will be perceived as minor to some and major to others. Likewise, the behavioral response to the given stress will vary widely among individuals. The magnitude of the stress depends on the perception of the individual, rather than on any measurable aspect of that stress.

Despite these difficulties in measurement, some commonalities among individuals with eating disorders have been observed. Obese individuals have a much more sensitive stress response, with exaggerated ACTH-mediated cortisol release (121,123,124) and glucose elevations in response to that circulating cortisol (125). A group of Pima Indians (well known for their genetic predisposition to obesity and type 2 diabetes), when given a computer-driven mental task, developed significantly more increased stress hormone levels, heart rate, and blood pressure than a control group of white subjects (126). White subjects with abdominal obesity developed a similar physiological response when asked to perform a mental arithmetic task (127), compared with white controls who did not exhibit this obesity pattern. Women receiving treatment for post-traumatic stress disorder (PTSD) have both significantly elevated norepinephrine, dopamine, and cortisol levels and a tendency toward obesity (128). Obese women report a higher incidence of meaningful life events in the year before a significant weight gain (129), and perceive themselves as having less social support than nonobese individuals (130).

Elevated cortisol can result in weight loss as well as weight gain (131,132). Mental arithmetic tasks given to anorexic and bulimic women elicit a response of "mistaken pessimism," or overestimation of body size, in anorexics and bulimics.

This emotional response may predispose some people to dieting when under duress *(Box 3.6)* (133). Women with a history of sexual assault (to a female, the ultimate inescapable stress) are more likely to experience weight loss of at least 15 pounds, display one or more symptoms of anorexia, or experience a sudden

Box 3.6
Food Intolerance, Food
Aversion, or Disordered
Avoidance?
The Role of the
Nutrition Therapist in
the Discovery Process

Developing a client's food profile is not always a scientific procedure. Nutrition assessment of an eating disorder, unlike that of other diagnoses, occurs throughout the duration of treatment. Information gained in the initial interview is likely to be filtered because of the client's fear, lack of trust, and even shame. At this point, the client is likely to present food preferences and tolerances more out of a desire to maintain current disordered behaviors than out of a desire to cooperate with the nutrition therapist. As trust is built, disclosure normally increases. A client who may initially have perceived the problem as a food intolerance may come to understand the psychosomatic nature of his disorder and express the desire to work such foods back into his food plan.

Though an oral report of symptoms is a good beginning, what happens at the table is often quite different from what is reported in the nutrition therapist's office. Directly observing the client's physical responses to specific foods and/or talking with others who are present at mealtime will provide insight into the origin of the behavior. For example, a client may perceive that red meat makes her nauseous. What she may not have considered is that hamburgers trigger memories of family barbecues that always ended in drunken arguments.

Because the nutrition therapist is trained in both the physiological and psychological bases of gastrointestinal disorders, processing food intolerances for their validity is naturally in his realm of treatment. Because the client has often used her intolerances to justify her disordered eating, the nutrition therapist who questions these behaviors is naturally perceived as the treatment team "bad guy" who threatens to remove an important avoidance and defense mechanism and expose the client's emotional vulnerability. The natural consequence of this mixture is a great potential for misdirected anger, which can intimidate even the most seasoned nutrition therapist.

Though accommodating all food intolerances follows the traditional dietetic teaching of individualizing meal plans, it may also promote the continuation of disordered behavior. Important clues to the source of the disorder may end up being avoided. However, suggesting to a client that apparent food intolerances may actually be food avoidances before a working relationship has been developed can be invalidating.

A good compromise is to focus initial sessions on information gathering without diagnosing, explaining, or validating any food choices. Most clients will respond positively when asked whether they are willing to explore whether their food behaviors are restricting their ability to socialize and enjoy life, and if they have a list of foods they would really like to eat but can't get over the fear of. From there, an action plan can be developed that allows the client to focus his treatment strategy. He should be involved in planning a schedule of foods to try, one at a time, to evaluate their function in his eating disorder. A client who is resistant to this approach may be communicating that fear is still the predominant emotion or that he is more invested in staying sick than in working toward recovery. By asking for permission to eliminate foods from his meal plan, he may be seeking justification

continued

Box 3.6
(continued)

for his behavior (as well as a scapegoat, should someone confront him about his eating habits).

The nutrition therapist's role in this aspect of treatment is to set the expectation that food fears will be addressed and not avoided, and to stress that sufficient support will be provided during this process to make the experience a positive one. He can help the client prioritize her list, identify food relationships she observes, and facilitate a discussion about what is being learned in the process. This process is emotional, but also provides tangible, encouraging markers of progress to the client. For the nutrition therapist, the advancement in the relationship, the change in behaviors, and the confidence in self and food that result are some of the most rewarding aspects of eating disorder treatment.

Not every food or trauma will elicit sensory memories, and not every memory will manifest through food behaviors. Individuals with personality disorders, who may be more invested in staying sick than in working through food fears, frequently use sensory memories as an excuse for their disordered behaviors, rather than looking at the relationships with the motivation to work through and past them. It is not uncommon for memories to be created to distract the treatment team from the central issue or to please a clinician who is focusing too single-mindedly on finding a nonexistent food memory. The nutrition therapist who uses the concepts presented in this section will be most effective if he can set boundaries with these clients and not get talked into justifying behaviors that in the long run keep the client sick.

weight change (134). All of these findings suggest that in eating disorders, regardless of the direction of weight change, there are dysfunctional physiologic, emotional, and behavioral responses to stress, which are exacerbated when the stress is significant and perceived to be inescapable.

The rapidly advancing field of neuroscience and its impact on nutrition may eventually shed some light on why feeding behavior has traditionally been so difficult to modify. Perhaps low-calorie diets are too counterregulatory. Neural mechanisms may be so strongly programmed to protect against starvation that feeding behaviors not supportive of this goal are responded to with the transmission of feeding impulses that eventually restore nutrient procurement. Perhaps food focus and obsession, classic behaviors seen in eating disorders, are part of a defense mechanism enacted to trigger a most crucial survival behavior.

Dietetic education traditionally has not emphasized neuroendocrinology and its impact on nutritional science. However, the advances being made in this discipline add a challenging and exciting twist to dietetics practice *(Box 3.7)*. An understanding of at least the basic principles of the specialty will soon become a prerequisite to the training of the competent eating disorder specialist.

Box 3.7
Noninvasive Brain
Imaging: Unlocking
the Door to the Brain

A full understanding of feeding regulation has remained elusive in part because of the vast number of networks and inputs to this system from all parts of the body. In addition, the brain, where a major portion of feeding regulation originates, is difficult to study. Until recently brain function could be studied only by examining tissue slices or by stimulating various brain regions by means of electrodes.

continued

Because these studies were performed on animals, the results were limited because similar effects in humans could only be speculated upon.

However, recent advances in brain research have accelerated the progress of neurobehavioral science and the study of feeding regulation. Positron emission tomography (PET) scanning measures regional brain activity by measuring regional uptake of glucose radioisotopes. This noninvasive technique produces images of the brain that highlight regions that control thinking, listening to music, and processing color, as well as regions that are active in conditions like attention-deficit disorder and obsessive-compulsive disorder (8), which are often found in eating disorders. Scans of eating disordered brains have identified anatomical differences in functional regions that are likely to affect the behaviors that make these disorders so challenging to treat (135).

Magnetic resonance imaging (MRI) (136) and single-photon emission computed tomography (SPECT) (137) have also been used to evaluate feeding-related brain regions. The SPECT procedure is currently being tested for its potential to visualize the histologically different regions of these organs (137), known to be crucial to both feeding regulation and disordered eating.

The PET scan and the MRI scan have major advantages over animal studies, as they evaluate human function and can be used to map the complexities of *in vivo* function. These techniques will likely unlock some of the doors to the brain that have been closed to neuroscience for generations, and renew hope among neuroscientists that the biological origins of anorexia, bulimia, and binge eating disorder will finally be discovered.

Box 3.7
(*continued*)

SUMMARY

- There are numerous central nervous system regulation mechanisms that are programmed to ensure food intake for survival.

- The body's varied receptors monitor chemical, osmolality, and pressure changes and are responsible for homeostatic regulation of hormones and other substrates.

- Learning incorporates memories of past food experiences that influence the development of food preferences and food aversions.

- Reward pathways may promote food behaviors that physiologically stimulate and satisfy reward neurons in the central nervous system. These neurons may be stimulated by a variety of behavioral influences, and often support the development of addictive/compulsive behaviors.

- Inside the brain there are billions of neurons with even more billions of impulses that coordinate responses to regulatory receptors, learning experiences, and reward neurons. These neurons are located throughout the brain and are involved in every aspect of feeding.

- In nondisordered eating, these four mechanisms are instinctive and coordinated so that a balance of input is achieved. In eating disorders, the balance is tipped; some pathways become dominant, and even certain brain regions may become hyper- or hypoactive.

- Accounting for the influences of the brain on behavior is an important aspect of treatment planning.

REFERENCES

1. Kissileff HR. Chance and necessity in ingestive behavior. *Appetite.* 1991;17(1):1–22.
2. Strack AM, Sebastian RJ, Schwartz MW, Dallman MF. Glucocorticoids and insulin: reciprocal signals for energy balance. *Am J Physiol.* 1995;268(1 Pt 2):R142–R149.
3. Friedman MI. Control of energy intake by energy metabolism. *Am J Clin Nutr.* 1995;62(5)(5 Suppl):1096S-1100S.
4. Dallman MR, Adena SF, Strack AM, Hanson ES, Sebastian RJ. The neural network that regulates energy balance is responsive to glucocorticoids and insulin and also regulates HPA axis responsivity at a site proximal to CNS neurons. *Ann NY Acad Sci.* 1995;771:730–742.
5. Danilenko KV, Putilov AA, Russkikh GS, Duffy LK, Ebbesson SO. Diurnal and seasonal variations of melatonin and serotonin in women with seasonal affective disorder. *Arctic Med Res.* 1994;53(3):137–145.
6. Mustad V, Derr J, Reddy CC, Pearson TA, Kris-Etherton PM. Seasonal variation in parameters related to coronary heart disease risk in young men. *Atherosclerosis.* 1996;126(1):117–129.
7. Proser RA, Edgar DM, Heller KC, Miller JD. A possible glial role in the mammalian circadian clock. *Brain Res.* 1994;643(1–2):296–301.
8. Foulkes NS, Whitmore D, Sassone-Corsi P. Rhythmic transcription: the molecular basis of circadian melatonin synthesis. *Biol Cell.* 1998;89(8):487–494.
9. Norris DO. *Vertebrate Endocrinology.* 2nd ed. Philadelphia, Pa: Lea & Febiger; 1985.
10. Leibowitz SF, Alexander JT, Cheung WK, Weiss GF. Effects of serotonin and the serotonin blocker metergoline on meal patterns and macronutrient selection. *Pharmacol Biochem Behav.* 1993;45(1):185–194.
11. Akabayashi A, Levin N, Paez X, Alexander JT, Leibowitz SF. Hypothalamic neuropeptide Y and its gene expression: relation to light/dark cycle and circulating corticosterone. *Mol Cell Neurosci.* 1994;5(3):210–218.
12. Paez X, Stanley BG, Leibowitz SF. Microdialysis of NE levels in the paraventricular nucleus in association with food intake at dark onset. *Brain Res.* 1993; 606(1): 167–170.
13. Whishaw IQ, Dringenberg HC, Comery TA. Rats *(Ratunorvegicus)* modulate eating speed and vigilance to optimize food consumption: effects of cover, circadian rhythm, food deprivation, and individual differences. *J Comp Psychol.* 1992;106(4):411–419.
14. Yoshihara T. A neuroendocrinological study on the mechanism of feeding-associated circadian rhythm of plasma corticosterone and feeding behaviour in rats: a role of neuropeptide Y in the paraventricular nucleus. *Hokkaido Igaku Zasshi.* 1995;70(1): 113–131.
15. Mistlberger RE, Mumby DG. The limbic system and food-anticipatory circadian rhythms in the rat: ablation and dopamine blocking studies. *Behav Brain Res.* 1992;47(2):159–168.
16. Van Cauter EV, Polonsky KS, Blackman JD, Roland D, Sturis J, Byrne MM, Scheen AJ. Abnormal temporal patterns of glucose tolerance in obesity: relationship to sleep-related growth hormone secretion and circadian cortisol rhythmicity. *J Clin Endocrinol Metab.* 1994;79(6):1797–1805.
17. Vaccarino FJ, Sovran P, Baird JP, Ralph MR. Growth hormone-releasing hormone mediates feeding-specific feedback to the suprachiasmic circadian clock. *Peptides.* 1995;16(4):595–598.
18. Kant GJ, Bauman RA, Pastel RH, Myatt CA, Closser-Gomez E, D'Angelo CP. Effects of controllable vs uncontrollable stress on circadian temperature rhythms. *Physiol Behav.* 1991;49(3):625–630.

19. Norden MJ. *Beyond Prozac: Brain-Toxic Lifestyles, Natural Antidotes, and New Generation Antidepressants.* New York, NY: Regan Books/HarperCollinsPublishers; 1995.

20. Schenk CH, Hurwitz TD, O'Connor KA, Mahowald MW. Additional categories of sleep-related eating disorders and the current status of treatment. *Sleep.* 1993;16(5):457–466.

21. Schenck CH, Hurwitz TD, Bundlie SR, Mahowald MW. Sleep-related eating disorders: polysomnographic correlates of a heterogeneous syndrom distinct from daytime eating disorders. *Sleep.* 1991;14(5):419–431.

22. Schenk CH, Mahowald MW. Review of nocturnal sleep-related eating disorders. *Int J Eat Disord.* 1994;15(4):343–356.

23. Spaggiari MC, Granella F, Parrino L, Marchesi C, Melli I, Terzano MG. Nocturnal eating syndrome in adults. *Sleep.* 1994;17(4):339–344.

24. Sonka K, Spackova N, Marusic P. The nocturnal eating syndrome (2 case reports and polysomnography). *Cesk Psychiatr.* 1993;89(4):227–232.

25. Fernandez-Ruiz J, Miranda MI, Bermudez-Rattoni F, Drucker-Colin R. Effects of catecholaminergic depletion of the amygdala and insular cortex on the potentiation of odor by taste aversions. *Behav Neural Biol.* 1993;60(3):189–191.

26. Aguero A, Arnedo M, Gallo M, Puerto A. The functional relevance of the lateral parabrachial nucleus in lithium chloride-induced aversion learning. *Pharmacol Biochem Behav.* 1993;45(4):973–978.

27. Yamamoto T, Shimura T, Sako N, Yasoshima Y, Sakai N. Some critical factors involved in formation of conditioned taste aversion to sodium chloride in rats. *Chem Senses.* 1994;19(3):209–217.

28. Arzuffi R, Racotta IS, Angeles TP, Racotta R. The role of conditioned taste aversion in the hypophagia induced by intraperitoneal epinephrine and glucose. *Horm Behav.* 1995;29(1):1–11.

29. Mickley GA, Lovelace JD, Farrell ST, Chang KS. The intensity of a fetal taste aversion is modulated by the anesthesia used during conditioning. *Brain Res Dev Brain Res.* 1995;85(1):119–127.

30. Shaw NA. Impairment of the gustatory engram by generalised seizure activity without associated loss of conditioned tate aversion. *Physiol Behav.* 1993;53(5):839–843.

31. Ninomiya Y, Nomura T. Effects of cerebroventricle administration of acidic fibroblast growth factor on conditioned taste aversion learning in rats. *Neurobiol Learn Mem.* 1996;65(3):283–286.

32. Smith P, Inglis IR, Cowan DP, Kerins GM, Bull DS. Symptom-dependent taste aversion induced by an anticoagulant rodenticide in the brown rat *(Rattus norvegicus).* *J Comp Psychol.* 1994;108(3):282–290.

33. Ninomiya Y, Nomura T, Kawamura S. Effects of feeding on conditioned avoidance responses in rats. *Neurobiol Learn Mem.* 1996;65(3):287–290.

34. Weingarten S, Senn M, Langhans W. Does a learned taste aversion contribute to the anorectic effect of bacterial lipopolysaccharide? *Physiol Behav.* 1993;54(5): 961–966.

35. LeDoux JE. Emotional memory systems in the brain. *Behav Brain Res.* 1993;59(1–2):69–79.

36. Teicher MH, Glod DA, Surrey J, Swett C Jr. Early childhood abuse and limbic system ratings in adult psychiatric outpatients. *J Neuropsychiatr Clin Neurosci.* 1993;5(3):301–306.

37. Doyle P, Guillaume-Gentil C, Rohner-Jeanrenaud F, Jeanrenaud B. Effects of corticosterone administration on local cerebral glucose utilization of rats. *Brain Res.* 1994;645(1–2):225–230.

38. Krieg JC, Holthoff V, Schreiber W, Prike KM, Herholz K. Glucose metabolism in the caudate nuclei of patients with eating disorders, measured by PET. *Eur Arch Psychiatry Clin Neurosci.* 1991;240(6):331–333.

39. Zerbe KJ. Whose body is it anyway? Understanding and treating psychosomatic aspects of eating disorders. *Bull Menninger Clin.* 1993;57(2):161–177.

40. Blum K, Sheridan PJ, Wood RC, Braverman ER, Chen TJ, Comings DE. Dopamine D2 receptor gene variants: association and linkage studies in impulsive-addictive-compulsive behavior. *Pharmacogenetics.* 1995;5(3):121–141.

41. Noble EP, Noble RE, Ritchie T, Syndulko K, Bohlman MC, Noble LA, Zhang Y, Sparkes RS, Grandy DK. D2 dopamine receptor gene and obesity. *Int J Eat Disord.* 1994;15(3):205–217.

42. Orosco M, Rouch C, Meile MJ, Nicolaidis S. Spontaneous feeding-related monoamine changes in rostromedial hypothalamus of the obese Zucker rat: a microdialysis study. *Physiol Behav.* 1995;57(6):1103–1106.

43. Comings DE, Flanagan SD, Dietz G, Muhleman D, Knell E, Gysin R. The dopamine D2 receptor (DRD2) as a major gene in obesity and height. *Biochem Med Metab Biol.* 193;50(2):176–185.

44. Hamdi A, Porter J, Prasad C. Decreased striatal D2 dopamine receptors in obese Zucker rats: changes during aging. *Brain Res.* 1992;589(2):338–340.

45. Bodnar RJ, Glass MJ, Ragnauth A, Cooper ML. General, mu and kappa opioid antagonists in the nucleus accumbens alter food intake under deprivation, glucoprivic and palatable conditions. *Brain Res.* 1995;700(1–2):205–212.

46. Katzeff HL, Selgrad C. Impaired peripheral thyroid hormone metabolism in genetic obesity. *Endocrinology.* 1993;132(3):989–995.

47. Giardino L, Ceccatelli S, Hokfelt T, Calza L. Expression of enkephalin and dynorphin precursor mRNAs in brain areas of hypo- and hyperthyroid rat: effect of kainic acid injection. *Brain Res.* 1995;687(1–2):83–93.

48. Berman Y, Devi L, and Carr KD. Effects of streptozotocin-induced diabetes on prodynorphin-derived peptides in rat brain sections. *Brain Res.* 1995;685–(1–2):129–134.

49. Norton P, Falciglia G, Gist D. Physiologic control of food intake by neural and chemical mechanisms. *J Am Diet Assoc.* 1993;93(4):450–454.

50. Blundell JE. Serotonin and the biology of feeding. *Am J Clin Nutr.* 1992;55(1 Suppl): 155S-159S.

51. Clark JM, Clark AJ, Bartle A, Winn P. The regulation of feeding and drinking in rats with lesions of the lateral hypothalamus made by N-methyl-D-aspartate. *Neuroscience.* 1991;45(3):631–640.

52. Davidson TL, Jarrard LE. A role for hippocampus in the utilization of hunger signals. *Behav Neurol Biol.* 1993;59(2):167–171.

53. De Nicola AF, Grillo C, Gonzalez S. Physiological, biochemical and molecular mechanisms of salt appetite control by mineralocorticoid action in brain. *Braz J Med Biol Res.* 1992;25(12):1153–1162.

54. Flynn FW, Curtis KS, Verbalis JG, Stricker EM. Dehydration anorexia in decerebrate rats. *Behav Neurosci.* 1995;109(5):1009–1012.

55. Galaverna OG, Seeley RJ, Berridge KC, Grill HJ, Epstein AN, Schulkin J. Lesions of the central nucleus of the amygdala. I: Effects on taste reactivity, taste aversion learning and sodium appetite. *Behav Brain Res.* 1993;59(1–2):11–17.

56. Hatfield T, Gallagher M. Taste-potentiated odor conditioning: impairment produced by infusion of an N-methyl-D-aspartate antagonist into basolateral amygdala. *Behav Neurosci.* 1995;109(4):663–668.

57. Hernandez L, Parada M, Baptista T, Schwartz D, West HL, Mark GP, Hoebel BG. Hypothalamic serotonin in treatments for feeding disorders and depression as studied by brain microdialysis. *J Clin Psychiatry.* 1991;52(Suppl):32–40.

58. Hillerup S, Hjorting-Hansen E, Reumert T. Repair of the lingual nerve after iatrogenic injury: a follow-up study of return of sensation and taste. *J Oral Maxillofac Surg.* 1994;52(10):1028–1031.

59. Houpt TA, Philopena JM, Wessel TC, Joh TH, Smith GP. Increased c-fos expression in nucleus of the solitary tract correlated with conditioned taste aversion to sucrose in rats. *Neurosci Lett.* 1994;172(1–2):1–5.

60. Kesner RP, Williams JM. Memory for magnitude of reinforcement: dissociation between the amygdala and hippocampus. *Neurobiol Learn Mem.* 1995;64(3):237–244.

61. Klein BG, Duffin JR, Kraje B. Neonatal infraorbital nerve damage and the development of eating behavior in the rat. *Behav Brain Res.* 1994;60(1):25–33.

62. Kravtsov AN, Sudakov SK. The neuronal reaction of the sensorimotor cortex to stimulation of the lateral hypothalamus with a background of the microiontophoretic administration of tetragastrin and bradykinin: the role of food reinforcement. *Ah Vyssh Nerv Deiat Im I P Pavlova.* 1995;45(4):757–764.

63. Lehman DC, Bartoshuk LM, Catalanotto FC, Kveton JF, Lowlicht RA. Effect of anesthesia of the chorda tympani nerve on taste perception in humans. *Physiol Behav.* 1995;57(5):943–951.

64. Lenard L, Sandor P, Hajnal A, Jando G, Karadi Z, Kai Y. Sex-dependent body weight changes after iontophoretic application of kainic acid into the LH or VMH. *Brain Res Bull.* 1991;26(1):141–148.

65. Lopez-Garcia JC, Fernandez-Ruiz J, Escobar ML, Bermudez-Rattoni F, Tapia R. Effects of excitotoxic lesions of the nucleus basalis magnocellularis on conditioned taste aversion and inhibitory avoidance in the rat. *Pharmacol Biochem Behav.* 1993;45(1):147–152.

66. Mahler P, Guastavino JM, Jacquart G, Strazielle C. An unexpected role of the cerebellum: involvement in nutritional organization. *Physiol Behav.* 1993;54(6):1063–1067.

67. Maldonado-Irizarry CS, Swanson CJ, Kelley AE. Glutamate receptors in the nucleus accumbens shell control feeding behavior via the lateral hypothalamus. *J Neurosci.* 1995;15(10):6779–6788.

68. Marfaing-Jallat P, Portha B, Penicaud L. Altered conditioned taste aversion and glucose utilization in related brain nuclei of diabetic GK rats. *Brain Res Bull.* 1995;37(6):639–643.

69. McMahon LR, Morien A, Davies BT, Wellman PJ. Conditioned taste aversion in rats induced by the alpha 1–adrenoreceptor agonist cirazoline. *Pharmacol Biochem Behav.* 1994;48(3):601–604.

70. Meguid MM, Gleason JR, Yang ZJ. Olfactory bulbectomy in rats modulates feeding pattern but not total food intake. *Physiol Behav.* 1993;54(3):471–475.

71. Meguid MM, Yang ZJ, Bellinger LL, Gleason JR, Koseki M, Laviano A, Oler A. *Surgery.* 1996;119(2):202–207.

72. Meiri N, Masos T, Rosenblum K, Miskin R, Dudai Y. Overexpression of urokinase-type plasminogen activator in transgenic mice is correlated with impaired learning. *Proc Natl Acad Sci USA.* 1994;91(8):3196–3200.

73. Parada MA, Puig de Parada M, Hoebel BG. Rats self-inject a dopamine antagonist in the lateral hypothalamus where it acts to increase extracellular dopamine in the nucleus accumbens. *Pharmacol Biochem Behav.* 1995;52(1):179–187.

74. Plamondon H, Merali Z. Push-pull perfusion reveals meal-dependent changes in the release of bombesin-like peptides in the rat paraventricular nucleus. *Brain Res.* 1994; 668(1–2):54–61.

75. Persinger MA, Bureau YR, Peredery O. Dissociation between conditioned taste aversion and radial maze learning following seizure-induced multifocal brain damage: quantitative tests of serial vs parallel circuit models of memory. *Physiol Behav.* 1994;56(2):225–235.

76. Reilly S, Grigson PS, Norgren R. Parabrachial nucleus lesions and conditioned taste aversion: evidence supporting an associative deficit. *Behav Neurosci.* 1993;107(6): 1005–1017.

77. Ruffin MP, Caulliez R, Nicolaidis S. Parallel metabolic and feeding responses to lateral hypothalamic stimulation. *Brain Res.* 1995;700(1–2):121–128.

78. Sahu A, Dube MG, Phelps CP, Sninsky CA, Kalra PS, Kalra SP. Insulin and insulin-like growth factor II suppress neuropeptide Y release from the nerve terminals in the paraventricular nucleus: a putative hypothalamic site for energy homeostasis. *Endocrinology.* 1995;136(12):5718–5724.

79. Sandyk R. L-tryptophan in neuropsychiatric disorders: a review. *Int J Neurosci.* 1992;67(1–4):127–144.

80. Schafe GE, Seeley, RJ, Bernstein IL. Forebrain contribution to the induction of a cellular correlate of conditioned taste aversion in the nucleus of the solitary tract. *J Neurosci.* 1995;15(10):6789–6796.

81. Scalera G, Spector AC, Norgren R. Excitotoxic lesions of the parabrachial nuclei prevent conditioned taste aversions and sodium appetite in rats. *Behav Neurosci.* 1995;109(5):997–1008.

82. Schalomon PM, Robertson AM, Laferriere A. Prefrontal cortex and the relative associability of taste and place cues in rats. *Behav Brain Res.* 1994;65(1):57–65.

83. Schick RR, Schusdziarra V, Yaksh TL, Go VL. Brain regions where cholecystokinin exerts its effect on satiety. *Ann NY Acad Sci.* 1994;713:242–254.

84. Spector AC. Gustatory parabrachial lesions disrupt taste-guided quinine responsiveness in rats. *Behav Neurosci.* 1995;109(1):79–90.

85. Spector AC. Gustatory function in the parabrachial nuclei: implications from lesion studies in rats. *Rev Neurosci.* 1995;6(2):143–175.

86. Swank MW, Bernstein IL. c-Fos induction in response to a conditioned stimulus after single trial taste aversion learning. *Brain Res.* 1994;636(2):202–208. [Published erratum appears in *Brain Res,* 1994;645(1–2):359.]

87. Turton MD, O'Shea D, Gunn I, Beak SA, Edwards CM, Meeran K, et al. A role for glucagon-like peptide-1 in the central regulation of feeding. *Nature.* 1996;379 (6560):69–72.

88. Uwano T, Nishijo H, Ono T, Tamura R. Neuronal responsiveness to various sensory stimuli, and associative learning in the rat amygdala. *Neuroscience.* 1995;68(2): 339–361.

89. Wang Y, Erickson RP, Simon SA. Modulation of rat chorda tympanic nerve activity by lingual nerve stimulation. *J Neurophysiol.* 1995;73(4):1468–1483.

90. Xu B, Li BH, Rowland NE, Kalra SP. Neuropeptide Y injection into the fourth cerebroventricle stiulates c-Fos expression in the paraventricular nucleus and other nuclei in the forebrain: effect of food consumption. *Brain Res.* 1995;698(1–2): 227–231.

91. Yamamoto T, Shimura T, Sako N, Yasoshima Y, Sakai N. Neural substrates for conditioned taste aversion in the rat. *Behav Brain Res.* 1994;65(2):123–137.

92. Yamamoto T, Fujimoto Y, Shimura T, Sakai N. Conditioned taste aversion in rats with excitotoxic brain lesions. *Neurosci Res.* 1995;22(1):31–49.

93. Beck B, Stricker-Krongrad A, Burlet A, Nicolas JP, Burlet C. Specific hypothalamic neuropeptide Y variation with diet parameters in rats with food choice. *Neuroreport*. 1992;3(7):571–574.

94. Barbas H. Anatomic basis of cognitive-emotional interactions in the primate prefrontal cortex. *Neurosci Biobehav Rev*. 1995;19(3):499–510.

95. Stricker-Krongrad A; Barbanel G, Beck B, Burlet A, Nicolas JP, Burlet C. K (+)-stimulated neuropeptide Y release into the paraventricular nucleus and relation to feeding behavior in free-moving rats. *Neuropeptides*. 1993;24(5):307–312.

96. Noach EL. Appetite regulation by serotoninergic mechanisms and effects of d-fenfluramine. *Neth J Med*. 1994;45(3):123–133.

97. Beck B, Burlet A, Nicolas JP, Burlet C. Unexpected regulation of hypothalamic neuropeptide Y by food deprivation and refeeding in the Zucker rat. *Life Sc*. 1992; 50(13):923–930.

98. Corrin SE, McCarthy HD, McKibbin PE, Williams G. Unchanged hypothalamic neuropeptide Y concentrations in hyperphagic, hypoglycemic rats: evidence for specific metabolic regulation of hypothalamic NPY. *Peptides*. 1991;12(3):425–430.

99. Currie PJ, Coscina DV. Dissociated feeding and hypothermic effects of neuropeptide Y in the paraventricular and perifornical hypothalamus. *Peptides*. 1995;16(4): 599–604.

100. O'Shea RD, Gundlach AL. NPY mRNA and peptide immunoreactivity in the arcuate nucleus are increased by osmotic stimuli: correlation with dehydration anorexia. *Peptides*. 1995;16(6):1995.

101. Pesonen U, Huupponen R, Rouru J, Koulu M. Hypothalamic neuropeptide expression after food restriction in Zucker rats: evidence of persistent neuropeptide Y gene activation. *Brain Res Mol Brain Res*. 1992;16(3–4):255–260.

102. Fernandez-Ruiz J, Miranda MI, Bermudez-Rattoni F, Drucker-Colin R. Effects of catecholaminergic depletion of the amygdala and insular cortex on the potentiation of odor by taste aversions. *Behav Neural Biol*. 1993;60(3):189–191.

103. Gasanov GG, Ismailova Khiu, Gromova EA, Semenova TP, Nesterova IV. The role of the catecholaminergic innervation of the neocortical frontal area in regulating the behavior of rats with differing resistance to acoustic stress. *Zh Vyssh Nerv Deiat Im I P Pavlova*. 1995;45(5):1006–1013.

104. Beck B, Stricker-Krongrad A, Burlet A, Max JP, Musse N, Nicolas JP, Burlet C. Macronutrient type independently of energy intake modulates hypothalamic neuropeptide Y in Long-Evans rats. *Brain Res Bull*. 1994;34(2):85–91.

105. Pages N, Orosco M, Rouch C, Yao O, Jacquot C, Bohuon C. Refeeding after 72–hour fasting alters neuropeptide Y and monoamines in various cerebral areas in the rat. *Comp Biochem Physiol Comp Physiol*. 1993;106(4):845–849.

106. Pages N, Orosco M, Rouch C, Yao O, Jacquot C, Bohuon C. Fasting affects more markedly neuropeptide Y than monoamines in the rat brain. *Pharmacol Biochem Behav*. 1993;44(1):71–75.

107. Pierroz DD, Catzeflis C, Aebi AC, Rivier JE, Aubert ML. Chronic administration of neuropeptide Y into the lateral ventricle inhibits both the pituitary-testicular axis and growth hormone and insulin-like growth factor I secretion in intact adult male rats. *Endocrinlogy*. 1996;137(1):3–12.

108. Beck B, Burlet A, Bazin R, Nicolas JP, Burlet C. Elevated neuropeptide Y in the arcuate nucleus of young obese Zucker rats may contribute to the development of their overeating. *J Nutr*. 1993;123(6):1168–1172.

109. Heilig M. Antisense inhibition of neuropeptide Y (NPY)-Y1 receptor expression blocks the anxiolytic-like action of NPY in amygdala and paradoxically increases feeding. *Regul Pept*. 1995;59(2):201–205.

110. Menzaghi F, Heinrichs SC, Pich EM, Tilders FJ, Koob GF. Functional impairment of hypothalamic corticotropin-releasing factor neurons with immunotargeted toxins enhances food intake induced by neuropeptide Y. *Brain Res.* 1993;618(1):76–82.

111. Zhou QY, Palmiter RD. Dopamine-deficient mice are severely hypoactive, adipsic, and aphagic. *Cell.* 1995;83(7):1197–1209.

112. Feifel D, Vaccarino FJ. Growth hormone-regulatory peptides (GHRH and somatostatin) and feeding: a model for the integration of central and peripheral function. *Neurosci Biobehav Rev.* 1994;18(3):421–433.

113. Yakimovskii AF, Filatova EV. Food-procuring behavior of rats under the conditions of chronic activation and blockade of the neostriatal dopanimergic system. *Neurosci Behav Physiol.* 1995;25(5):427–432.

114. Mark GP, Weinberg JB, Rada PV, Hoebel BG. Extracellular acetylcholine is increased in the nucleus accumbens following the presentation of an aversively conditioned taste stimulus. *Brain Res.* 1995;688(1–2):184–188.

115. Weisinger RS, Denton DA, McKinley MJ, Mislis RR, Park RG, Simpson JB. Forebrain lesions that disrupt water homeostasis do not eliminate the sodium appetite of sodium deficiency in sheep. *Brain Res.* 1993;628(1–2):166–178.

116. Orosco M, Rouch C, Meile MJ, Nicolaidis S. Spontaneous feeding-related monoamine changes in rostromedial hypothalamus of the obese Zucker rat: a microdialysis study. *Physiol Behav.* 1995;57(6):1103–1106.

117. Griffiths J, Shanks N, Anisman H. Strain-specific alterations in consumption of a palatable diet following repeated stressor exposure. *Pharmacol Biochem Behav.* 1992;42(2):219–227.

118. Korte SM, Bouws GA, Koolhaas JM, Bohus B. Neuroendocrine and behavioral responses during conditioned active and passive behavior in the defensive burying/probe avoidance paradigm: effects of ipsapirone. *Physiol Behav.* 1992;52(2):355–361.

119. Cenci MA, Kalen P, Mandel RJ, Bjorklund A. Regional differences in the regulation of dopamine and noradrenaline release in medial frontal cortex, nucleus accumbens and caudate-putamen: a microdialysis study in the rat. *Brain Res.* 1992;581(2):217–228.

120. Job RF, Barnes BW. Stress and consumption: inescapable shock, neophobia, and quinine finickiness in rats. *Behav Neurosci.* 1995;109(1):106–116.

121. Balkan B, Strubbe JH, Bruggink JE, Steffens AB. Overfeeding-induced obesity in rats: insulin sensitivity and autonomic regulation of metabolism. *Metabolism.* 1993;42(12):1509–1518.

122. Comer RJ. *Abnormal Psychology.* 2nd ed. New York, NY: WH Freeman Publishing Co; 1995.

123. Weaver JU, Kopelman PG, McLoughlin L, Forsling ML, Grossman A. Hyperactivity of the hypothalamo-pituitary-adrenal axis in obesity: a study of ACTH, AVP, beta-lipotropin and cortisol responses to insulin-induced hypoglycaemia. *Clin Endocrinol Oxf.* 1993;39(3):345–350.

124. Tassava TM, Okuda T, Romsos DR. Insulin secretion from ob/ob mouse pancreatic islets: effects of neurotransmitters. *Am J Physiology.* 1992;262(3 Pt 1):E338–E343.

125. Marin P, Darin N, Amemiya T, Andersson B, Jern S, Bjorntorp P. Cortisol secretion in relation to body fat distribution in obese premenopausal women. *Metabolism.* 1992;41(8):882–886.

126. Esposito Del Puente A, Lillioja S, Bogardus C, McCubbin JA, Feinglos MN, Kuhn CM, Surwit RS. Glycemic response to stress is altered in euglycemic Pima Indians. *Int J Obes Relat Metab Disord.* 1994;18(11):766–770.

127. Pasquali R, Anconetani B, Chattat R, Biscotti M, Spinucci G, Casimirri F, Vicennati V, Carcello A, Labate AM. Hypothalamic-pituitary-adrenal axis activity and its relationship to the autonomic nervous system in women with visceral and subcutaneous obesity: effects of the corticotropin-releasing factor/arginine-vasopressin test and of stress. *Metabolism.* 1996;45(3):351–356.

128. Lemieux AM, Coe CL. Abuse-related posttraumatic stress disorder: evidence for chronic neuroendocrine activation in women. *Psychosom Med.* 1995;57(2): 105–115.

129. Ferreira MF, Sobrinho LG, Pires JS, Silva ME, Santos MA, Sousa MF. Endocrine and psychological evaluation of women with recent weight gain. *Psychoneuroendocrinology.* 1995;20(1):53–63.

130. Wing RR, Matthews KA, Kuller LH, Meilahn EN, Plantinga P. Waist-to-hip ratio in middle-aged women: associations with behavioral and psychosocial factors and with changes in cardiovascular risk factors. *Arterioscler Thromb.* 1991;11(5): 1250–1257.

131. Casper RC, Swann AC, Stokes PE, Chang S, Katz MM, Carver D. Weight loss, cortisol levels, and dexamethasone suppression in major depressive disorder. *Acta Psychiatr Scand.* 1987;75(3): 243–250.

132. Corder R, Castagne V, Rivet JM, Mormede P, Gaillard RC. Central and peripheral effects of repeated stress and high NaCl diet on neuropeptide Y. *Physiol Behav.* 1992;52(2):205–210.

133. Waller G, Hodgson S. Body image distortion in anorexia and bulimia nervosa: the role of perceived and actual control. *J Nerv Ment Dis.* 1996;184(4):213–219.

134. Laws A, Golding JM. Sexual assault history and eating disorder symptoms among white, Hispanic, and African-American women and men. *Am J Public Health.* 1996;86(4):579–582.

135. Nozoe S, Naruo T, Yonekura R, Nakbeppu Y, Soejima Y, Nagai N, Nakajo M, Tanaka H. Comparison of regional cerebral blood flow in patients with eating disorders. *Brain Res Bull.* 1995;36(3): 251–255.

136. Korogi Y, Takahashi M. Current concepts of imaging in patients with pituitary/hypothalamic dysfunction. *Semin Ultrasound CT MR.* 1995;16(4):270–278.

137. Kinomura S, Kawashima R, Yamada K, Ono S, Itoh M, Yoshioka S, Yamaguchi T, Matsue H, Miyazawa H, Itoh H, et al. Functional anatomy of taste perception in the human brain studied with positron emission tomography. *Brain Res.* 1994; 659(1–2):263–266.

CHAPTER 4

Gastrointestinal Influences on Feeding

MONIKA M. WOOLSEY, M.S., R.D.

"I'm hungry."

"I'm so full I could burst."

"I really have a taste for a good piece of cheesecake."

"I just don't like brussels sprouts."

Each of these comments represents a basic aspect of feeding—hunger, satiety, appetite, and aversion—that is inherent in humans and other animals and necessary for survival. Under normal conditions, the impulses that generate responses to these sensations are so subtle that they are not even noticed. The terminal behavior, eating or not eating, is the only indication we have that the feeding process is at work.

As previous chapters described, the neuroendocrine system is the coordinating center for all four feeding functions. However, the influence of this center reaches far beyond the endocrine organs. One of the most important systems in feeding is the gastrointestinal tract. It is here that food is ingested, processed, and absorbed. It is here that fluids are obtained. All of these functions proceed so efficiently and automatically that we take them for granted until their disruption reminds us of their importance for normal feeding.

The gastrointestinal tract is where eating-disordered individuals experience many of the consequences of their dysfunctional feeding. Understanding the contribution of the gastrointestinal tract to hunger and appetite is important, as much of a nutrition therapist's work in eating disorders treatment involves restoring both normal gastrointestinal function and normal responses to the feeding impulses it generates.

The four terms introduced above will be used throughout this book. They are defined as follows:

Hunger	A physiological sensation that drives the ingestion of calories
Satiety	A physiological sensation that inhibits the ingestion of calories
Appetite	A physiological and/or psychological impulse that triggers a desire for a specific food or type of food
Aversion	A physiological and/or psychological sensation that inhibits a desire for a specific food or type of food

Hunger and satiety can be considered oppositional, as can appetite and aversion. When these sensations are equally balanced and communicating efficiently, caloric and nutritional balance is maintained. Hunger and satiety regulate caloric intake, while appetite and aversion pertain more to specific food choices than to food amounts. Even so, appetite and aversion responses can indirectly affect hunger and satiety, and are important to understand.

HUNGER AND SATIETY

Several gastrointestinal feedback mechanisms regulate hunger and satiety. Short-term responses, such as *pressure/stretch reception*, help terminate feeding and determine meal size (1). *Sensory-specific satiety* is an intermediate response. In addition to contributing to meal termination, this mechanism helps to extend the sensation of satiety past the period when food is physically in contact with pressure and stretch receptors. *Chemoreception* is a long-acting mechanism that takes longer to stimulate than stretch/pressure reception or sensory-specific satiety and is longer lasting once activated *(Figure 4.1)*. Each of these systems has been identified as a potential break in the intricate hunger and satiety system that maintains the integrity of food intake. The remainder of this chapter will explain these mechanisms and their contribution to feeding in more detail.

Pressure/Stretch Reception

The physical presence of food in the gut stimulates gastrointestinal pressure, or stretch receptors. These, in turn, transmit a neural message to feeding centers in the brain, and food intake decreases as a consequence. This mechanism is active only as long as there is food in the system. Pressure receptors facilitate the ending of a meal, but their importance fades as the meal passes through the gastrointestinal system (2).

The vagus nerve is the major gastrointestinal nerve (3-5), and is responsible for communicating numerous types of information between the gastrointestinal tract and the brain, including taste sensations, gastrointestinal contractions, and satiety (6,7). The vagus nerve communicates with the brain through the serotoninergic system (8), which makes it a likely location for susceptibility to serotonin imbalance-related disorders such as the eating disorders. The high incidence of delayed gastric emptying and gastrointestinal dysfunction and distress

Figure 4.1

Overview of Feeding Regulation in the GI Tract (Between Meal Interval)

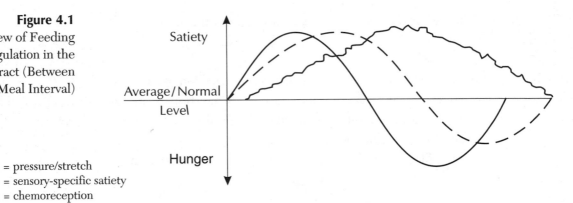

——— = pressure/stretch
- — = sensory-specific satiety
〜〜 = chemoreception

(9-14) in eating disorders supports this hypothesis *(Box 4.1)*, as does the recent finding that administration of the drug ondansetron, a serotonin-3 antagonist, decreases vomiting in bulimics (15).

The hyperactive vagus nerve in bulimia may be yet another manifestation of the neural characteristics of binge eating described earlier, namely, hypersensitivity to environmental stressors and behaviors that result in widely fluctuating neurotransmitter levels. Under acute conditions, gastrointestinal problems such as vomiting, indigestion, nausea, and diarrhea would be more likely to develop in an individual whose vagus nerve was hyperreactive. In many eating-disordered individuals, normal fullness is interpreted as bloating and constipation. Though much of this sensation is psychosomatic, some of it may be physiologically based and reflect hypersensitivity of the vagus nerve.

When eating behaviors have created a malnourished state (ie, anorexia), gas-

Box 4.1
Gastrointestinal Symptoms in Eating Disorders

Proportion of anorexics reporting delayed gastric emptying: 65%–80%

Symptom	Binge eaters reporting (%)
Bloating	74.4
Flatulence	74.4
Constipation	62.8
Decreased appetite	51.2
Abdominal pain	48.8
Borborygmi (rumbling stomach)	48.8
Nausea	46.5

The symptoms reported more often in obese binge eaters than in nonobese controls include:

Abdominal pain	Dyschezia (painful	Irritable bowel syndrome
Bloating	evacuation)	Nausea
Constipation	Flatus	Straining
Diarrhea	Indigestion	Vomiting

Sources: Chami et al (9), Crowell et al (10), Rigaud et al (11), Waldholtz and Andersen (12), Szmukler et al (13).

trointestinal problems are more reflective of a hyporeactive vagus nerve. These problems include delayed gastric emptying, gastric distention, constipation, and, in severe cases, impaction.

Gastrointestinal problems have a strong correlation with depression even in non-eating-disordered individuals (9). This relationship is well documented; in fact, two cardinal symptoms of depression are increased appetite and decreased appetite (16), suggesting that while gastrointestinal problems commonly coexist with eating disordered behaviors, they are symptoms of other important psychological disturbances. While dietary modifications to counter gastrointestinal problems might provide temporary relief, if the root cause of the problems is not addressed, they will persist.

Food manufacturers have capitalized on volume/pressure reception in recent years by adding fillers and gums to foods to discourage excessive caloric intake. This decreases caloric density while increasing volume. Accumulating evidence suggests that these foods may not be appropriate for individuals susceptible to eating disorders. These foods may not provide the other satiety mechanisms with the cues that are needed to create a sense of fullness. In anorexia, a result of unsatiated hunger may be an increase in compulsive behaviors (eg, calorie counting, exercise) to provide a distraction. In bulimia and binge eating disorder, more food may end up being consumed, which in extreme cases may provoke gastrointestinal distress and vomiting.

If a binge eater attempts to follow a structured diet based on calorically diluted foods, a nutritional deficit can develop. Since malnutrition can slow gastrointestinal motility, an important consequence of dieting may be susceptibility to fullness, bloating, and constipation. For an individual conditioned to focus on physical satiety, the sense of fullness that comes with slowed motility may intensify temptations to restrict or purge. The cycle resulting from this series of events can be difficult to break (*Figure 4.2*).

A more suitable technique in eating disorders treatment is to use gastrointestinal problems as a barometer of emotional distress and depression and to investigate the feelings that might be manifesting in a psychosomatic fashion. It is important for the client to understand that gastrointestinal problems can be important indicators of psychological stress. Treating problems at a merely superficial level can prolong overall physical and emotional discomfort. To recognize that these physical problems may point to psychological problems that need resolution, and to confront the psychological problems with healthy problem-solving techniques, is a longer-lasting approach to resolving ongoing physical discomfort.

For example, on a particularly stressful day an individual might eat a slice of pizza, experience nausea, and assume that she does not tolerate pizza or cheese. This reasoning is particularly common in stress-related gastrointestinal disorders such as irritable bowel syndrome, and over time can develop into a food dislike/intolerance list that is longer than the list of foods that are tolerated. Unless

Figure 4.1
Consequence of Eating
Calorically Dilute Foods

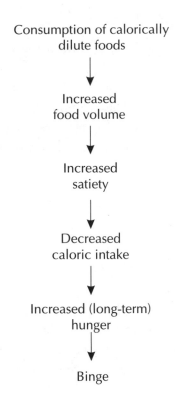

Consumption of calorically
dilute foods

↓

Increased
food volume

↓

Increased
satiety

↓

Decreased
caloric intake

↓

Increased (long-term)
hunger

↓

Binge

a food consistently produces gastrointestinal symptoms or distaste, it should not be eliminated *(Box 4.2)*.

Another important goal in eating disorders treatment is to normalize food choices so that unadulterated foods (foods in which fat and sugar content have not been diluted) are the most frequent food choices. An unadulterated meal plan is likely to be lower in total volume, and allows pressure receptors to have influence on food intake without becoming the dominant mechanism and overly restricting intake or encouraging bingeing in the long run.

Sensory-Specific Satiety

Chemoreceptors that are scattered along the gastrointestinal tract from the tip of the tongue to the end of the small intestine provide feedback about the macronutrient composition of ingested foods (ie, fat, protein, carbohydrate content) (17). They are thought to contribute to the phenomenon of sensory-specific satiety, which decreases the perceived pleasantness of a food as it is eaten and facilitates the termination of feeding (18). At the same time, it makes new foods more appetizing and more likely to be eaten. The satiety mechanism is activated only in the physical presence of food (17). In a functional eater, it promotes survival by encouraging variety in nutrient intake. It also regulates total food intake by inhibiting food ingestion past the point of metabolic need.

Macronutrients vary in their impact on sensory-specific satiety. High-protein foods appear to be the most satiating (18,19) and fats the least, with carbohydrates falling somewhere in between (20). These findings suggest that disordered eating patterns may disrupt normal hunger and satiety cues. Protein, the most satiating

1. *Evaluate the symptomatic history.*

    Does a symptom consistently occur with stress? Or is it unpredictable?

    Does a particular food consistently result in symptoms? Or is the consistency an external stressor?

    Does a specific food cause symptoms only when eaten under conditions of emotional duress?

    Is the food a "comfort" food, commonly eaten when under emotional duress?

2. *Evaluate the symptoms.*

    Are the symptoms truly dysfunctional?

    Would they result in complaints from the nondisordered eater?

    Or are they normal sensations of satiety/variations in gastrointestinal volume due to food content, gastric emptying, and gas production that are interpreted as abnormal in the eating-disordered mind because of psychosomatic tendencies and body image issues?

3. *Process the symptoms for their psychological origin.*

    Ask, "How would you describe this feeling if you couldn't use any weight, food, or symptom-related words?" This question discourages psychosomatic complaints and encourages an exploration of the emotional origins of the problem.

4. *Teach*

    the skills of recognizing gastrointestinal symptoms as important clues to underlying emotional states that are best recognized and confronted, rather than avoided,

    the importance of normalized eating behaviors to maintain healthy hunger, satiety, appetite, and aversion responses, and

    the importance of varied intake to enhance healthy feeding responses.

5. *Special dietary regimens that eliminate foods*

    can be useful for the short-term alleviation of gastrointestinal symptoms,

    should be recommended for long-term use only if a specific food consistently causes the same symptoms, regardless of emotional state,

    should not be encouraged without evaluating possible psychosomatic contributions to the reported symptoms, and

    should be discouraged if they appear to be a way to avoid discussion of important emotional issues.

Box 4.2
Guidelines for Managing Chronic Gastrointestinal Disorders in Eating Disorders

macronutrient, is commonly eliminated from the diet or significantly reduced. Although carbohydrates are not the most satiating foods over the long term, they are fillers in many low-calorie foods and meal plans. In bulimia and binge eating, an overemphasis on carbohydrates may incline the individual toward bingeing. An anorexic individual may adopt compulsive behaviors in an attempt to ignore the food thoughts that result from inadequate caloric intake. Again, an effective treatment might be to balance protein and fat, as well as carbohydrate, and to limit nonnutritive fillers to promote long-term satiety and normalized appetite feedback.

Dieting and restrained eating disrupt the effectiveness of sensory-specific satiety. In the physical presence of a pizza, restrained eaters salivate more profusely than nonrestrained eaters (21), suggesting that sensory-based cues heighten in the face of food restriction. A restrictive eater, therefore, is likely to be more sensitive to external food cues than to internal messages that reflect the current need for food.

Dieters given a caloric preload and then offered a meal at which they can control the volume eaten (a situation that should trigger sensory-specific satiety and reduce the volume of food eaten) eat more food than nondieters (22). When a high-calorie food offered with the meal is labeled as low-calorie, nonpreloaded dieters increase their intake while preloaded dieters decrease their intake. In other words, dieters appear to rely more on external feedback than on internal regulation to determine their food intake. They do not fully utilize internal gastrointestinal feedback mechanisms, and are likely to eat past the point of what would normally be satiation.

In a similar test, anorexic individuals exhibited sensory-specific satiety after a high-calorie preload but not a low-calorie preload. This behavior runs counter to what these individuals commonly report, which is feeling full after small amounts of even low-calorie or noncaloric food, suggesting that this perception also stems from feedback outside of the normal hunger and appetite regulation network (23).

Bulimic individuals demonstrate sensory-specific satiety only after a low-calorie, high-volume preload, again suggesting more of an external than an internal feeding response (23). This observation is consistent with the psychiatric finding that bulimic individuals and binge eaters often dissociate, or become detached from and unaware of their immediate surroundings (24,25). When dissociation is severe, they may be unable to respond to more subtle satiety cues and may be more dependent on physical discomfort as an indicator of satiety.

These studies help explain many of the behaviors seen in individuals with eating disorders. While nondisordered eaters can satiate their senses by consuming food and move to other activities after a meal, disordered eaters remain susceptible to environmental food cues throughout the day. A leftover doughnut at staff meeting, a women's magazine with chocolate recipes, and a vending machine in the hallway all have the potential to trigger food thoughts more strongly in a restrictive eater than a nonrestrictive eater. Some individuals focus this energy on food-related activities such as cooking, reading cookbooks, counting calories, etc, while others eat. These thoughts and actions are frightening to the disordered eater. Compulsive behaviors become a coping mechanism that helps to distract the individual from thoughts and behaviors that produce guilt and shame.

These findings also illustrate the relative importance of pressure/stretch reception and sensory-specific satiety. Under normal circumstances, pressure/stretch reception is a more immediate appetite suppressant, while the caloric content and macronutrient content of food has a longer lasting impact on food intake. When eating patterns are disrupted or internal cues are no longer used to determine satiety, intake is also disrupted.

Chemoreception

Many of the digestive peptides secreted in the gastrointestinal tract function dually as neurotransmitters *(Box 4.3)*. When these hormones enter the circulation and travel to the brain, they trigger a decrease in appetite and food intake. Of these peptides, three have been specifically studied in eating-disordered individuals: cholecystokinin, neurotensin, and galanin.

Cholecystokinin (CCK) is best known for its digestive function of emulsifying fats and facilitating their absorption. As digestion and absorption proceed, CCK enters the bloodstream, eventually crossing the blood-brain barrier. Receptors for CCK have been identified in the supraoptic and paraventricular nuclei of the hypothalamus (34), providing evidence that this digestive peptide is a neurotransmitter as well.

The most direct neural feeding function of CCK is to limit meal size. This function occurs in a dose-dependent manner; the more CCK that is present, the less food is eaten (35). Cholecystokinin inhibits several other eating-related behaviors as well. In laboratory rats that can normally be trained to perform a task in return for food, this incentive value is reduced when CCK is administered (36). When CCK levels increase, microbehaviors (such as licking) decrease, satiety-related behaviors (such as sleeping) increase (33), and insulin secretion increases (37).

The dual functions of CCK create an efficient feedback mechanism that allows the brain to alter behaviors as it receives messages about whether food consumption should continue or terminate. However, this mechanism is functional only as long as food is consumed. If food or fat intake is restricted, CCK secretion is likely not sufficient to provide feedback to the brain.

Cholecystokinin levels have been found to be lower in bulimic individuals than in controls. Meal-related CCK secretion and postprandial satiety are impaired in these individuals (38), which has led some researchers to suggest that this phenomenon is an inherent metabolic characteristic that contributes to bingeing behavior (39). Part of this deficiency might be an inherent predisposition to low CCK levels. In nondisordered eaters as well, depression has been correlated with

Decrease food intake	Increase food intake
Neuropeptide Y	Galanin
Cholecystokinin (CCK)	Peptide YY (PYY)
Amylin	
Bombesin	
Satietin	
Neurotensin	

Box 4.3 Digestive Peptides That Function as Neurotransmitters

Sources: Ballinger et al (26), Lutz et al (27,28), Stratford et al (29), Bellinger et al (30), Bartafi et al (31), Beck et al (32), Kapas et al (33).

high CCK levels, and the levels return to normal with the administration of anti-depressants (39). However, many eating disordered behaviors, including food restriction, fat restriction, purging, laxative use, and chewing and spitting out food, alter or inhibit the exposure of the gut to food and may either purge important peptides along with food or lower peptide secretion, exacerbating an existing condition.

Although a disrupted CCK feedback response has not been identified in binge eating, CCK is an anti-opioid (40), which suggests that it might be deficient in obese binge eaters (who have high circulating opioid levels) as well. CCK metabolism has not been studied in anorexia, but the possibility exists that CCK abnormalities is important in the pathophysiology of this eating disorder as well.

Neurotensin is another peptide that has been found in the hypothalamus and that inhibits food intake. In one study neurotensin levels were 50 percent lower in obese than in lean rats (32). This discrepancy stayed constant even when obese rats were denied food, again providing evidence that some dysfunctional feeding influences are inherent and cannot be changed merely by correcting weight. This peptide has not yet been studied in anorexia or bulimia, but is a compound worthy of future research.

Galanin promotes several feeding-related functions, including food (especially fat) intake and inhibition of insulin release (41,42). Galanin concentrations are decreased in the hypothalamus of obese rats (41). Plasma galanin levels are decreased in anorexic individuals, but brain levels are thought to be a more important indicator of dysfunction (42). For obvious reasons, these relationships have not yet been evaluated in humans, but hopefully will be as neuroscientists develop less invasive ways to evaluate brain function.

The relationship between gastrointestinal and neuroendocrine function is a relatively new focus in eating disorder research. However, preliminary findings thus far provide a strong foundation for the argument that a healthy gastrointestinal tract is crucial to healthy appetite and feeding responses. Restrictive eaters and binge eaters who alter the quality of food presented to the gastrointestinal tract may change the quality of the feedback response and impair feeding. As discussed in *Box 4.4,* a most important strategy in the nutrition therapy of eating disordered individuals is to promote reintroduction of a variety of foods into the system that stimulate and maintain appropriate hunger and satiety responses.

APPETITE AND AVERSION

Survival of any species depends on the ability to choose and eat foods free of toxins that provide adequate nutrition. One of the most highly developed mechanisms designed to carry out this function is the sensory system (43-45). When taste buds on the tongue are triggered through contact with food, specialized nerves in the brain transmit impulses that analyze the nature of this food for its value as nourishment (44). Humans interpret this data analysis as the taste of

A necessary component of nutrition therapy in eating disorders is restoring natural responses to hunger and satiety. For these responses to occur, pressure receptors and the sensory-specific satiety mechanism must both be utilized without pushing either system to extremes as eating disordered behaviors have the potential to do. A nutrition plan should include the following goals in order to restore balance:

- a physiologically intact sensory intake and evaluation system, not impaired by destructive behaviors such as purging
- an adequate caloric intake
- an intake of a variety of foods (including protein, fat, and carbohydrates)
- moderate use (at best) of high-carbohydrate, high-volume, calorically dilute foods
- Helping the client to understand the importance of these systems in restoring natural hunger cues is important. The client also needs to understand that hunger is a natural phenomenon, as important as an itch or a sneeze in signaling that a behavior is needed to restore equilibrium.

Initial work with hunger and satiety cues may be frustrating and frightening for the client. She needs to be reassured that, with time and trust, these cues will return, and that they are to be welcomed rather than feared. Small steps (such as adding a protein at breakfast and noting what happens the rest of the day) are usually best; when a structured diet is provided with the expectation of many dietary changes at once, the opportunity is lost to help the client connect each individual change with the change in hunger/satiety it produces.

Box 4.4
Hunger and
Nutrition Therapy

food. The resulting selection or rejection of foods reflects the phenomena of appetite and aversion.

The sense of taste has evolved as a mechanism for evaluating the relative benefit of or need for a food. Humans taste combinations of four basic sensations: sweet, sour, salty, and bitter. The chemicals that are recognized as these sensations bind with protein molecules in saliva, which then trigger nerve endings to carry the taste message to higher brain centers (44).

Foods crucial to survival have sensory characteristics that the brain interprets as pleasing (43), which encourages continued ingestion. For example, the taste of glucose, a substrate the brain depends on, is pleasant to almost every human. Without its pleasantness, carbohydrate-containing foods might not be consumed in adequate quantities to maintain basic neurological functioning. Early in our evolutionary history, the ability to identify and seek out foods containing sugar was a genetic strength. In recent decades, as sugar-containing foods have become readily available, carbohydrate craving is not as necessary for survival. However, industrial progress has outpaced evolutionary adaptation, and the human strong preference for sweetness persists despite the fact that it is no longer a scarce commodity.

The Evolution
of Taste

Our sweet tooth, once a key to survival, now increases our susceptibility to chronic disease.

Similarly, foods that are potentially dangerous are often distasteful. Humans cannot digest grass; consuming it would be a waste of effort and potentially fatal. It makes evolutionary sense that grass is not as tasty as apple pie or ice cream. Poisonous foods are often aversive as well. Many foods that could contain compounds harmful to the fetus cause nausea in pregnant women (45). This phenomenon appears to be nature's way of protecting the developing child.

Malnutrition and Taste

Through the centuries, our sensory system has evolved so that it rewards us for eating foods that promote survival and steers us away from foods with toxic potential. In a well-nourished individual this mechanism is complex, with many backup systems to ensure intake of appropriate foods and avoidance of inappropriate ones.

However, when nutritional status begins to deteriorate, so does the sense of taste. Dietary components that would normally taste acceptable become distasteful. Two compounds perceived as bitter are the amino acids tryptophan and phenylalanine (46,47), the building blocks for serotonin, dopamine, and norepinephrine, the neurotransmitters integral to healthy mental function. Zinc deficiency, another consequence of malnutrition, is another well-known cause of loss of taste (48,49). All of these compounds are found in most abundance in protein-containing foods, which are often severely limited or avoided in eating disorders. Could this avoidance have neuroendocrine origins? It may be that a vegetarian who does not eat a wide variety of protein sources risks falling into the vicious cycle of depleting nutritional status, which decreases appetite for foods that contain taste-enhancing compounds, which restricts food intake, which further depletes nutritional status (*Figure 4.3*).

Avoidance of meat because of a perceived "lack of taste" is commonly reported by eating disordered individuals. Dietary sources of zinc, tryptophan, and pheny-

Figure 4.3
Proposed Effect of Protein Restriction on Taste and Nutritional Status

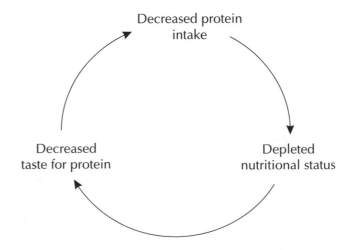

lalanine should always be reviewed in the nutritional assessment, and increased consumption of these foods should be encouraged when possible (see Chapter 15). A word of caution about zinc is in order: though zinc deficiency has been hypothesized to be a significant contributor to the disruption of food intake in anorexia (49), it is but one of numerous influences on taste distortion in eating disorders. It is important to remember that zinc therapy will only correct disrupted taste sensation if its deficiency was the cause of the problem.

Smell and Taste

The sense of smell, or olfaction, is important to the evaluation of taste (50). The importance of olfaction to taste becomes apparent when a cold results in nasal congestion and favorite foods become tasteless. A variety of influences affect the ability to smell, and ultimately to taste. Estrogens promote a healthy sense of smell, and in their absence olfaction is not as acute (51). A severe ear infection (otitis media) can damage taste sensation, as can head trauma (50). Even psychological and psychiatric conditions can adulterate sensations; chemosensory distortion is often present in depression (52,53). All of these conditions are likely to exist in an eating disordered individual. It is therefore important to evaluate both the client's perception of taste and any changes in taste through the progression of the disease.

The senses of taste and smell tend to differ from the norm in eating disorders. In one study, 29 percent of eating disordered individuals had olfactory hallucinations (compared to 19 percent of non-eating disordered depressed individuals and 35 percent of schizophrenics) (53). In individuals with anorexia, this characteristic might translate into perceiving high-fat foods, (generally pleasing to most people) as distasteful. Aversions to foods with a low sugar content are common (54), which is often reflected in the common eating disordered food ritual of using large amounts sugar to flavor beverages, fruits, and carbohydrates. Though possibly a behavioral expression of the brain's need for glucose, this taste preference has been shown to persist even after treatment (55), suggesting that it is an inherent taste preference and not merely a consequence of malnutrition or neurochemical depletion.

Bulimic individuals appear to have a hypersensitivity to flavors, and rate lower-fat and lower-sugar solutions as more intensely flavored than controls do (54). This taste preference normalizes after treatment, suggesting that it reflects a state of sensory overstimulation that responds to psychological management of the prevailing stress or trauma.

Supertasting vs Nontasting

A relatively new area of interest in sensory science may prove to have important implications for eating disorder treatment. Several taste and smell research centers have discovered that different individuals have different tasting "personalities" that affect their food choices. "Supertasters" perceive more bitterness and sweetness in foods than other types of tasters. These individuals perceive the greatest oral burn when exposed to capsaicin, the "hot" compound found in peppers (56), and detect the greatest bitterness when exposed to propothiouracil, a research chemical used to identify genetic taste sensitivity. "Nontasters" do not taste many of the flavors found to be intense by supertasters, and "tasters" have a range of sensations that fall in between these two extremes. Interestingly, nontasters have a stronger preference for fat than supertasters (56). As many flavors are chemically fat-soluble, this preference may be an adjustment made by nontasters to augment the palatability of foods eaten.

These tasting characteristics have been found to be genetically derived (52), a finding that has great implications for nutrition therapists who strive to recommend changes in food intake. There may be a population of supertasters who can easily adhere to food plans with a lower fat content because to them food is still palatable after being adulterated. Nontasters may have more difficulty with such a manipulation because altering fat content reduces the palatability of food.

Some of the food preference characteristics observed in eating disorders may reflect different taste characteristics. Individuals often demonstrate a preference for bland carbohydrates (eg, cereals, pasta, and bread) or report that food "tastes too good" or that "it's easier to eat when I don't have to taste." These behaviors may be attempts to decrease a sensory overstimulation that makes the individual uncomfortable or fearful.

Other individuals attempt to limit fat intake but after a few days consume a high-fat food or binge on a high-fat snack, creating feelings of guilt and shame. These dietary restrictions might not be appropriate for nontasters, as for them they reduce the sensory quality of food, which, as described above, is an important component of satiety.

In eating disorders, such behaviors definitely have psychological issues attached to them, but it is important to understand the possibility that there is a genetically driven component as well. Everyone's perception of taste is individual. General dietary guidelines are good starting points, but at times they are too rigid for individual situations. It is important to accommodate variations in food preferences when designing a long-term treatment plan, and to adjust meal plans if it appears they are not sensitive to an individual's taste personality.

Like other gastrointestinal feedback, taste reception is communicated to the brain through the serotonin receptors (57). Therefore, depression has the potential to decrease and trauma the potential to overstimulate taste sensation. These changes are natural, and often resolve as the underlying issues are addressed. However, because eating disordered individuals are more likely to focus on physical symptoms than to look at their psychological origins, they are also likely to make long-term adjustments in food choices based on the outcome of one negative experience with food. Encouraging the inclusion of new foods and maintaining variety is important, as tastes and aversions often change as treatment progresses.

SUMMARY

- The gastrointestinal tract is an important regulator of hunger, satiety, appetite, and aversion. Without its feedback, the brain does not appropriately implement satiety messages, which has important consequences for individuals susceptible to eating disorders.

- Three hunger mechanisms are especially important in the maintenance of healthy hunger and satiety responses in eating disordered individuals: pressure/stretch reception, sensory-specific satiety, and chemoreception.

- The gastrointestinal tract requires contact with a variety of foods on a regular basis for the efficient functioning of these responses.

- Normalizing food intake with a balanced intake of macronutrients, minimizing the use of calorically diluted foods, and maintaining consistent exposure of the gastrointestinal tract to food should be encouraged. This helps to maintain a spatial relationship with food that allows for changes in gastrointestinal content to be recognized as normal fluctuations, rather than as aberrations requiring dietary intervention.

- Taste and aversion responses vary greatly among individuals, and affect food choices.

- Food avoidance and restriction can alter taste and aversion. Consuming a variety of foods is important to ensure that food preferences are based on a nourished state rather than on nutritional imbalance that could promote further malnutrition.

REFERENCES

1. Read N, French S, Cunningham K. The role of the gut in regulating food intake in man. *Nutr Rev.* 1994;52(1):1–10.
2. Lavin JH, Read NW. The effect on hunger and satiety of slowing the absorption of glucose: relationship with gastric emptying and postprandial blood glucose and insulin responses. *Appetite.* 1995;25(1):89–96.
3. Jiang JC, Gietzen DW. Anorectic response to amino acid imbalance: a selective serotonin3 effect? *Pharmacol Biochem Behav.* 1994;47(1):59–63.
4. Terry-Nathan VR, Gietzen DW, Rogers QR. Serotonin3 antagonists block aversion to saccharin in an amino acid-imbalanced diet. *Am J Physiol.* 1995;268(5 Pt 2): R1203-R1208.
5. Washburn BS, Jiang JC, Cummings SL, Dixon K, Gietzen DW. Anorectic responses to dietary amino acid imbalance: effects of vagotomy and tropisetron. *Am J Physiol.* 1994;266(6 Pt 2): R1922–R1927.
6. Niijima A. Effects of taste stimulation on the efferent activity of the pancreatic vagus nerve in the rat. *Brain Res Bull.* 1991;26(1):161–164.
7. Niijima A. Effects of oral and intestinal stimulation with umami substance on gastric vagus activity. *Physiol Behav.* 1991;49(5):1025–1028.
8. Washburn BS, Jiang JC, Cummings SI, Dixon K, Gietzen DW. Anorectic responses to dietary amino acid imbalance: effects of vagotomy and tropisetron. *Am J Physiol.* 1994;266(6 Pt 2):R1922–R1927.
9. Chami TN, Andersen AE, Crowell MD, Schuster MM, Whitehead WE. Gastrointestinal symptoms in bulimia nervosa: effects of treatment. *Am J Gastroenterol.* 1995;90(1):88–92.

10. Crowell MD, Cheskin LJ, Musial F. Presence of gastrointestinal symptoms in obese and normal weight binge eaters. *Am J Gastroenterol.* 1994;89(3):387–391.

11. Rigaud D, Bedig G, Merrouche M, Vulpillat M, Bonfils S, Apfelbaum M. Delayed gastric emptying in anorexia nervosa is improved by completion of a renutrition program. *Dig Dis Sci.* 1988;33(8):919–925.

12. Waldholtz BD, Andersen AE. Gastrointestinal symptoms in anorexia nervosa: a prospective study. *Gastroenterology.* 1990;98(6):1415–1419.

13. Szmukler GE, Young GP, Lichtenstien M, Andrews JT. A serial study of gastric emptying in anorexia nervosa and bulimia. *Aust N Z J Med.* 1990;20(3):220-225.

14. Pirke KM, Friess E, Kellner MB, Krieg JC, Fichter MM. Somatostatin in eating disorders. *Int J Eat Disord.* 1994;15(1):99–102.

15. Drug reduces binge/purge frequency. *Eating Disord Rev.* 1996;7(4):1.

16. Salmans S. *Depression: Questions You Have . . . Answers You Need.* Allentown, Pa: People's Medical Society; 1995.

17. Smith GP. The direct and indirect controls of meal size. *Neurosci Biobehav Rev.* 1996;20(1):41–46.

18. Hetherington MM. Sensory-specific satiety and its importance in meal termination. *Neurosci Biobehav Rev.* 1996;20(1):113–117.

19. Johnson J, Vickers Z. Factors influencing sensory-specific satiety. *Appetite.* 1992; 19(1):15–31.

20. Porrini M, Crovetti R, Testolin G, Silva S. Evaluation of satiety sensations and food intake after different preloads. *Appetite.* 1995;25(1):17–30.

21. Tepper BJ. Dietary restraint and responsiveness to sensory-based food cues as measured by cephalic phase salivation and sensory-specific satiety. *Physiol Behav.* 1992;52(2):305–311.

22. Lowe MR. Restrained eating and dieting: replication of their divergent effects on eating regulation. *Appetite.* 1995;25(2):115–118.

23. Rolls BJ, Andersen AE, Moran TH, McNelis AL, Baier HC, Fedoroff IC. Food intake, hunger, and satiety after preloads in women with eating disorders. *Am J Clin Nutr.* 1992;55(6):1093–1103.

24. Demitrack MA, Putnam FW, Brewerton TD, Brandt HA, Gold PW. Relation of clinical variables to dissociative phenomena in eating disorders. *Am J Psychiatry.* 1990;147(9):1184–1188.

25. Everill J, Waller G, Macdonald W. Dissociation in bulimic and non-eating disordered women. *Int J Eat Disord.* 1995;17(2):127–134.

26. Bellinger A, McLoughlin L, Medbak S, Clark M. Cholecystokinin is a satiety hormone in humans at physiological post-prandial plasma concentrations. *Clin Sci Colch.* 1995;89(4):375–381.

27. Lutz TA, Del Prete E, Szabady MM, Scharrer E. Circadian anorectic effects of peripherally administered amylin in rats. *Z Ernahrungswiss.* 1995;34(3):214–219.

28. Lutz TA, Geary N, Szabady MM, Del Prete E, Scharrer E. Amylin decreases meal size in rats. *Physiol Behav.* 1995;58(6):1197–1202.

29. Stratford TR, Gibbs J, Smith GP. Microstructural analysis of licking behavior following peripheral adminstration of bombesin or gastrin-releasing peptide. *Peptides.* 1995;16(5):903–909.

30. Bellinger LL, Nagy J, Hamilton J. HPLC-purified bovine satietin suppresses food intake and weight without causing conditioned taste aversion. *Pharmacol Biochem Behav.* 1994;47(3):659–666.

31. Bartfai T, Hokfelt T, Langel U. Galanin—a neuroendocrine peptide. *Crit Rev Neurobiol.* 1993;7(3–4):229–274.

32. Beck B, Nicolas JP, Burlet C. Neurotensin decresases with fasting in the ventrome-dial nucleus of obese Zucker rats. *Metabolism.* 1995;44(8):972–975.

33. Kapas L Obal F Jr, Alfoldi P, Rubicsek G, Penke B, Obal F. Effects of nocturnal peri-toneal administration of cholecystokinin in rats: simultaneous increase in sleep, increase in EEG slow-wave activity, reduction of motor activity, suppression of eat-ing, and decrease in brain temperature. *Brain Res.* 1988;438(1–2):155–164.

34. O'Shea RD, Gundlach AL. Regulation of cholecystokinin receptors in the hypothal-amus of the rat: reciprocal changes in magnocellular nuclei induced by food depri-vation and dehydration. *J Neuroendocrinol.* 1993;5(6):697–704.

35. Corp ES, Curcio M, Gibbs J, Smith GP. The effect of centrally administered CCK-receptor antagonists on food intake in rats. *Physiol Behav.* 1997;61(6):823–827.

36. Balleine B, Davies A, Dickinson A. Cholecystokinin attenuates incentive learning in rats. *Behav Neurosci.* 1995;108(2):312–319.

37. Malm D, Giaever A, Vonen B, Florholmen J. Cholecystokinin and somatostatin mod-ulate the glucose-induced insulin secretion by different mechanisms in pancreatic islets: a study on phospolipase C activity and calcium requirement. *Scan J Clin Lab Invest.* 1993;53(7):671–676.

38. Geriacioti TD Jr, Kling MA, Vanderpool JR, Kanayama S, Rosenthal NE, Gold PW, Liddle RA. Meal-related cholecystokinin secretion in eating and affective disorders. *Psychopharmacol Bull.* 1989;25(3):444–449.

39. Woods SC, Gibbs J. The regulation of food intake by peptides. *Ann NY Acad Sci.* 1989;575:236–243.

40. Cesselin F. Opioid and anti-opioid peptides. *Fundam Clin Pharmacol.* 1995; 9(5):409–433.

41. Beck B, Burlet A, Nicolas JP, Burlet C. Neurotensin in microdissected brain nuclei and in the pituitary of the lean and obese Zucker rats. *Neuropeptides.* 1989;13(1):1–7.

42. Invitti C, Brunani A, Pasqualinotto L, Dubini A, Bendinelli P, Maroni P, Cavagnini F. Plasma galanin concentrations in obese, normal weight and anorectic women. *Int J Obes Relat Metab Disord.* 1995;19(5):347–349.

43. Astback J, Arvidson K, Johansson O. Neurochemical markers of human fungiform papillae and taste buds. *Regul Pept.* 1995;59(3):389–398.

44. Li XJ, Snyder SH. Molecular cloning of Ebnerin, a von Ebner's gland protein asso-ciated with taste buds. *J Biol Chem.* 1995;270(30):17674–17679.

45. Ackerman D. *A Natural History of the Senses.* New York: Random House; 1990.

46. Plata-Salaman CR, Scott TR, Smith-Swintosky VL. Gustatory neural coding in the monkey cortex: L-amino acids. *J Neurophysiol.* 1992;67(6):1552–1561.

47. Gietzen DW, Duke CM, Hammer VA. Amino acid imbalance, a nutritional model: serotonin3 mediation of aversive responses. *Physiol Behav.* 1991;49(5):981–985.

48. Huttenbrink KB. Disorders of the sense of smell and taste. *Ther Unsch.* 1995;52(11):732–737.

49. Lask B, Fosson A, Rolfe U, Thomas S. Zinc deficiency and childhood-onset anorexia nervosa. *J Clin Psychiatry.* 1993;54(2):63–66.

50. Bartoshuk LM, Duffy VB, Reed D, Williams A. Supertasting, earaches and head injury: genetics and pathology alter our taste worlds. *Neurosci Biobehav Rev.* 1996;20(1):79–87.

51. Ehret G, Buckenmaier J. Estrogen-receptor occurrence in the female mouse brain: effects of maternal experience, ovariectomy, estrogen, and anosmia. *J Physiol Paris.* 1994;88(5):315–329.

52. Deems DA, Doty RL, Settle RG, Moore-Gillon V, Shaman P, Mester AF, Kimmel-man CP, Brightman VJ, Snow JB Jr. Smell and taste disorders, a study of 750 patients

from the University of Pennsylvania Smell and Taste Center. *Arch Otolaryngol Head Neck Surg.* 1991;117(5):519–528.

53. Kopala LC, Good KP, Honer WG. Olfactory hallucinations and olfactory identification ability in patients with schizophrenia and other psychiatric disorders. *Schizophr Res.* 1994;12(3):205–211.

54. Sunday SR, Halmi KA. Taste perceptions and hedonics in eating disorders. *Physiol Behav.* 1990;48(5):587–594.

55. Simon Y, Bellisle F, Monneuse MO, Samuel-Lajeunesse B, Drewnowski A. Taste responsiveness in anorexia nervosa. *Br J Psychiatry.* 1993;162:244–246.

56. Tepper BJ, Nurse RJ. Fat perception is related to PROP taster status. *Physiol Behav.* 1997;61(6):949–954.

57. Yamamoto T, Nagai T, Shimura T, Yasoshima Y. Roles of chemical mediators in the taste system. *Jpn J Pharmacol.* 1998;76(4):325–348.

CHAPTER 5

Development and Learning:
A Psychological Perspective

MONIKA M. WOOLSEY, M.S., R.D.

The preceding chapters described the many and varied physiological influences on eating behaviors. Eating disordered behaviors can also frequently be traced back to a dysfunctional reaction to acute or chronic stress or trauma. Stress management and behavior modification are not new concepts, but the constructive problem solving, moderate exercise, balanced diet, meditation, social interactions, and spiritual pursuits that all contribute to a healthier state of mind and body can be difficult behaviors to adopt. Why do we repeatedly choose old, destructive behaviors? Why do we struggle with addictions, compulsions, and impulsive behaviors when we know there is a better way to live?

The answers to these questions are found outside the medical model. Medicine can measure, calibrate, and calculate, but it cannot motivate. Medicine can diagnose an eating disorder, but it has limited success in producing a cure. Medicine can help explain the consequences of responses and behaviors, but not why those behaviors were chosen in the first place. The science of psychology can provide an understanding of this aspect of eating disorders.

Psychological treatment explores an individual's past experiences and seeks to determine which of those influence current behavior. Quantitative medical measures are used to determine whether an environmental stressor is or is not being adequately handled. Rather than prescribing a quick "fix", psychological treatment addresses why dysfunctional behaviors occur and how they can be modified or coped with in a fashion that does not cause physical distress. Combined with the medical model, the psychological model provides a comprehensive picture of how the mind and body interact to promote survival, despite exposure to a variety of environmental changes.

This chapter and the next two describe psychological concepts as they relate to eating disorders: healthy learning and development, unhealthy or dysfunctional learning and development, and the impact of trauma on learning and development. These concepts, when combined with the physiological concepts presented in the first four chapters, help explain the mind-body connection that drives addictive behaviors such as eating disorders.

LEARNING: BUILDING THE BEHAVIORAL HIGHWAY

Information that is processed by the brain must navigate through billions of neurons before a response to that information is generated. As the hiking example in Chapter 1 illustrated, these responses can occur in a split second, and they can be multisystemic. In addition to generating responses to stimuli, the nervous system functions as an information storage and processing system. Each time a similar situation arises, experiences stored in the "data bank" are called on to facilitate faster, more judicious decision making (1). The more quickly a response to a stimulus can be generated, the greater the chance that the individual will survive the stimulus.

As situations are encountered again and again, certain neuronal/behavioral pathways are used more frequently than others. Because of their frequent use, these pathways become preferred over others when decisions must be made. The process is much like the creation of a well-traveled road. Several different routes might take one to a destination, but the one that is used the most frequently is generally the most worn. Regular use "paves" this road and makes it the preferred behavioral pathway.

For example, the hiker in Chapter 1 would probably always walk through the forest "on alert" if she encountered a falling tree every time she ventured in. If the falling tree were just an isolated incident, she would not be quite so guarded. She would base her behavior on information stored from past experiences in the woods. This information storage and retrieval mechanism is usually referred to as *learning*.

When a highway is being built, several conditions must be met for process to be successful:

- there must be sufficient building materials to complete the project,
- there must be an agreed-on route and destination,
- the highway must be well maintained.

Problems with any of these conditions will result in an unnavigable highway. In that case, alternative routes will develop. Some of those may go in undesirable directions, some may circle round and round, some may be impassable, and some may be dead ends (*Figure 5.1*). Psychology is the study of how behavioral highways are designed, built, and maintained, what happens when undesirable behavioral routes impair decision making, and how new highways can be constructed

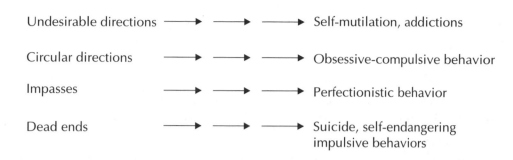

Figure 5.1
Examples of Unhealthy Decision-Making Pathways

when they are needed. Understanding these processes is crucial to developing treatment plans that put the client in control of her behavior and life.

Construction Materials: A Neuropsychological Perspective

A baby's brain is like a clean slate. Its billions of neurons are fresh and susceptible to stimulation, with an infinite number of response pathways that can be triggered in response to a stimulus. Initially nature provides infants with some neural "defaults", or instinctive transmission pathways generating behaviors that are necessary for immediate survival. An example of a nutritional default is the rooting and sucking reflex (2), which allows the infant to turn toward the nipple and feed; without it, the infant would starve.

As the infant is held by his mother and nurses, he is exposed to one of his first external environmental stimuli—physical touch. Being held positively stimulates neurons and is perceived as pleasurable. Every time this scenario is recreated, the neural pathway that creates this pleasurable sensation is restimulated, or "paved". Eventually, the infant learns that he can generate pleasure with behaviors (crying, reaching for his mother) that result in his being held (*Figure 5.2*).

Figure 5.2
A Pleasure-Seeking Decision Pathway

As the baby develops and his world expands past his mother, he experiences thousands of sensations each day. Some, such as being tickled by his father or sitting in his swing, create sensory pleasure. The infant's data collection system stores the pleasant sensations these experiences produce. When Daddy comes home, the infant smiles, knowing he is someone who generates pleasant experiences. Other experiences, such as sitting too long in a dirty diaper or being separated from Mommy and Daddy, are not so pleasant. Negative stimulation induces the child to change his behavior so he can avoid unpleasant sensations. For example, he might cry to indicate his diaper is dirty; eventually, he will become potty trained. The child's repetitive choices end up paving these behavior pathways so that frequently enacted behaviors occur almost without conscious thought.

Throughout this process, the child's parents function as guides who facilitate a healthy learning process. Rather than leave the infant to his own devices, with hundreds of behavioral options for each decision that arises, the parents guide the child to a limited selection of behavioral choices. At times they may provide the negative input (time-outs, stern voice) that discourages the child from repeating a bad decision. With time, as situations and decisions are repeated, those neural pathways that are frequently used become the brain's "superhighways", or preferred decision-making pathways. Though other pathways could be accessed and other behaviors chosen, these established routes transmit the desired information most efficiently.

After a time, frequently used behaviors become almost reflexive, and can occur before the individual realizes she has done something. For example, an individual who routinely comes home and has a snack before checking the mail or the answering machine may walk into the kitchen, open the refrigerator door, and pull out a piece of cake without consciously making a decision to eat. This behavior may have its roots in childhood, when a snack was on the kitchen table every day after school. Or sweets may have been the family's mechanism of rewarding good behavior or providing consolation for a bad day. Each of the behaviors necessary to implement this sequence has been enacted so many times that the visual stimulus of entering the front door is enough to start the series of actions that result in eating a piece of cake, while the initial rationale for the behavior has long been forgotten. In many cases, an important part of nutrition therapy is looking backward and uncovering some of these sequences.

In addition to behavioral changes, the neural "paving" that occurs during learning creates some physically evident changes. Neural pathways that are frequently used develop a series of membrane connections that serve to contain nerve transmission along the paved route (3). Construction of these membranes, like any other biological synthesis, requires building materials and energy. An anorexic or a restrained eater who is unable to eat a varied diet is likely not able to provide her nervous system with the materials it needs to construct the new behavioral pathways that are the goal of therapy. A bulimic or binge eater consistently reinforces dysfunctional behavioral pathways with compulsive/excessive use.

These neurophysiological inputs to behavior can create frustration for both the client and the nutrition therapist. If a behavior has been identified as needing change, the client may honestly commit to making a change between appointments, only to return the following session reporting that no progress has been made. The client is likely to feel guilt and shame about his lack of success; the nutrition therapist is likely to feel as if she has not been effective or helpful. These feelings can impede progress in treatment. The key to successfully managing these impasses is to identify where the "off-ramps" to alternative behaviors lie.

Finding "Off-Ramps" to Alternative Behaviors

Any stimulus that results in a response progresses through an impulse, or stimulus-response, curve (Figure 5.3) (4). A behavior is first identified when it has already occurred. One of the first steps toward eliminating a behavior is developing an awareness of the environment, events, and emotions that lead up to it. As awareness of these triggers increases, alternative thinking can be implemented

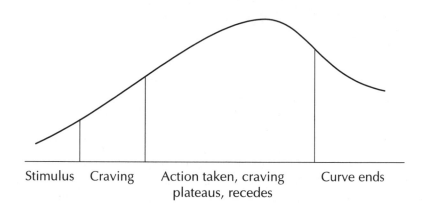

Figure 5.3
The Stimulus-Response Curve

| Stimulus | Craving | Action taken, craving plateaus, recedes | Curve ends |

and new behavioral routes can be chosen. The earlier into an impulse that awareness occurs, the greater the chance that an alternative behavior can be employed. (Chapter 16 details techniques for developing awareness in nutrition therapy.) This concept forms the basis for behavior modification therapy (5).

In some individuals, behavior modification may be an effective method of changing undesirable behaviors. For example, an individual starting an exercise program who is reluctant to regularly walk may be conditioned to a sedentary life merely out of habit. Breaking the desired new behavior into small, achievable steps (eg, 5 minutes of walking a day to start with, gradually increasing to 30 minutes a day) may provide an opportunity to experience the benefit of the new behavior before the final goal is achieved.

Often, however, the motivation for the behavior being targeted for change is much more deeply rooted. "Unconstructive" behaviors have been developed as coping mechanisms. To remove them without understanding their purpose and without providing an acceptable replacement coping tool leaves the client vulnerable. Many individuals who genuinely attempt to stop a behavior such as bingeing, drinking, or living a sedentary life are unable to do so because the change creates unbearable anxiety or depression. Though the behavior they wish to change is not desirable to them, the cost of discontinuing it is greater. These behaviors may create a state of numbness or euphoria, or as previous chapters described, temporarily increase serotonin levels to mask emotional discomfort. In addition, the inability to change a behavior creates guilt and shame, which increase anxiety and stress, which in turn increase the need for the behavior. The cycle is difficult to break (6).

It is important to remember, when working with clients, that the key to success is understanding the driving force behind the behavior and helping the client develop coping skills that eliminate the need for the behavior she wishes to discontinue. In this context, there is no such thing as a good/bad, or desirable/undesirable, behavior. Rather, there is usually a reason why a behavior is employed. Once that reason is understood, action plans can be developed to allow the introduction of behaviors that are less destructive and shame-producing. Those reasons usually have their roots in childhood, when behavioral highways are first constructed.

Nutrition therapists should always work in close contact with clients' psychotherapists to be sure that food and exercise recommendations are achievable and take clients' current coping skills into consideration. When both therapists work together to develop a treatment plan, the client is more likely to be set up to succeed in treatment *(Box 5.1)*.

Box 5.1
CASE STUDY:
The Importance of a
Strong Treatment Team

> Barbara was a 25–year-old college student who sought help for her bulimia. In addition to purging, Barbara reported using 25 doses of laxatives a day and exercising 3 hours a day. Her diet history also revealed a significant caffeine addiction; most days she consumed 64 ounces of diet cola and coffee. In addition, she had many food rituals suggestive of a strong obsessive-compulsive component to her disorder. In the initial session, Barbara reported that she was experiencing more severe body discomfort than normal. She also reported that within the past week she had received a contraceptive injection from her primary physician, a member of her eating disorders treatment team.
>
> Rather than focus on food and food behaviors, the nutrition therapist focused her discussion on helping Barbara to understand the influence her hormone injection might have had on her weight and body feelings. From there, the discussion turned to how difficult it was for Barbara to tolerate even minimal fluctuations in fluid balance and weight, and how those intolerances triggered her need for laxatives, exercise, and diuretic beverages.
>
> From there, a treatment plan was developed that slowly introduced changes while minimizing bloating and constipation. Barbara chose to begin tapering her caffeine intake, as this was the easiest change for her to make. The changes in sleep habits, fluid retention, and bowel habits that this choice might produce were discussed so Barbara would tolerate them and not increase her use of laxatives or exercise.
>
> Barbara's physician was contacted and informed of her body discomfort. He responded to this information by scheduling a follow-up appointment with Barbara so alternative contraceptive interventions with less potential for side effects could be discussed. Barbara's psychotherapist was also contacted. She used her next session with Barbara to process the feelings that arose when Barbara felt bloated or constipated. Finally, Barbara's psychiatrist was also notified that a caffeine taper had been started. This information proved valuable in adjusting antidepressant medication doses as the taper progressed.
>
> Because Barbara had four health professionals supporting the caffeine taper, she also had a coping outlet that helped her tolerate the physiological and psychological changes this behavior change elicited. She commented in her next nutrition session that caffeine withdrawal was difficult, but because she was able to talk about its effects with a treatment team member on an almost daily basis, she was able to make the change.
>
> The side benefit from this coordinated intervention was that Barbara had ample opportunity to develop communication skills that helped her reduce her more ingrained behaviors: her laxative use and her compulsive exercise. The process was slow but generally consistent. There were setbacks, but Barbara was encouraged to learn that setbacks could be growth experiences.

Though a baby is initially completely dependent on her parents for survival, the ultimate goal or destination of a healthy parent-child relationship is for the parents to teach the child the skills she will need to function independently as an adult (7). In order for the transition from dependence to independence to take place, the parents must use a combination of unconditional love, limit setting, reasoning, and freedom.

CHOOSING THE DESTINATION

Unconditional love (or the lack of it) is one of the most important initial influences on a child. Infants initially experience unconditional love through the physical bonding created by being held and nursing. The importance of these initial influences has even been physically measured. One study found adrenocorticotropic hormone and cortisol levels increased in infants separated from their mothers for 24 hours and dropped when feeding was resumed, and digestive function improved when physical contact was restored (8).

Providing Unconditional Love

As the child develops, unconditional love is modeled in such family rituals as regular meal times, bedtime stories, holiday traditions, play times, and food customs (9). Rituals provide a sense of security and consistency, which in turn lay the foundation for self-esteem and confidence. The social skills that family rituals promote become the child's frame of reference for interacting with his peers, community, and culture.

Unconditional love is also the bond that provides a sense of acceptance through good and bad times. It creates a sense of self-worth based on who the child is (a son or daughter), rather than on external factors, such as appearance or achievements. Later in life, the confidence that develops out of growing up with unconditional love provides a foundation for addressing situations outside the nuclear family (10). Individuals who develop this foundation early in life tend to view unexpected events not as failures, but as opportunities to learn. Without this perspective, the child may never develop the confidence it takes to venture out and take the risks required to function independently.

Limit setting, or discipline, is important in the development of the concepts of safe/dangerous and right/wrong. Though some lessons must be learned the hard way, an inexperienced child facing a potentially physically or emotionally harmful situation needs parents to make decisions that keep her safe. For example, grabbing the child's hand and pulling her away from a busy street are important for her survival. Later the reasoning behind this limit can be discussed, but immediate limit setting is the most important parenting decision at the moment.

Limit Setting

It is natural for children to test limits. Even the best parents sometimes have difficulty maintaining the limits they have set, but it is important that this parenting function be maintained with consistency. One reason children test limits is to be reassured of their existence (7). If there are no limits or if there are no consequences for disregarding them, the child is left feeling unsafe. Most children complain outwardly when given limits, but rules create a sense of safety and ritual that help children feel cared about and safe. If a child is not given limits, he may misbehave or "act out," not to be disrespectful, but as a way of asking for a limit to be set.

Setting limits also conveys the concept that even though "no" may occasionally be the answer or there may be a negative consequence to not adhering to a limit, the relationship can still be constructive and based on unconditional love. Again, this concept is important to integrate into other relationships that develop outside the family unit as the child becomes more independent.

The nutrition therapist is often one of the first individuals in a client's life who sets firm limits. This sets the nutrition therapist up to be the "bad guy" and the target of client blame when things do not proceed as planned. Limit setting sends the message that old coping behaviors will no longer be useful, and creates the expectation that new behaviors need to be tried. The fear and grief involved in leaving the old and trying the new can be tremendous.

When limits are set in treatment, much bargaining is likely to occur. The nutrition therapist may be asked to lower calories goals, target weights, or weight gain expectations, or to delay his recommendation for inpatient treatment. It is precisely at this point that limits need to be held, regardless of the temptation to rescue the client from her discomfort. Though the outward behavior may be angry, accusatory, or unappreciative, the client is often inwardly relieved that someone has provided a safety net. Many nutrition therapists can tell of clients who returned months or even years later to say, "I hated you because you made me work hard . . . but I knew I could trust you to keep me safe."

Reasoning

A young child often has limits set without explanation. However, as a child grows, so do his cognitive abilities. It is important to provide reasoning for decisions so that when the child is functioning outside the family unit, he has the information he needs to make appropriate independent decisions (11).

Reasoning should be tailored to the child's cognitive level. For example, a 2-year-old might be told that she is not to go near the street, a 5-year-old child might be told that he must stop and look both ways before crossing the street, and a 10-year-old might be told that she can cross the streets in her immediate neighborhood but major intersections are off limits. Each of these instructions would be inappropriate for other cognitive levels, and the child would likely not be able to adhere to them.

Reasoning is also important, as it helps the child understand the rationale behind decisions that might otherwise seem harsh, unkind, or unloving. It is important for a parent to convey that even when unpleasant decisions, consequences, and emotions are encountered, unconditional love is still the foundation for the relationship. Limit setting without reasoning can leave a child feeling guilty, unloved, and even hated.

Because the nutrition therapist is often the team member who sets the numerical goals for treatment (eg, goal weight, calories, weight when inpatient treatment is necessary, weight when tube feeding is necessary, tube feeding rate), he can be perceived as the "bad guy" of the treatment team. It is important, when making any decisions requiring a change in protocol in such interventions, to take the time to explain to the client why the decision is being made as it is. Helping the client understand that the nutrition therapist's responsibility is to make decisions when the client is not able to make those decisions for herself, even to let the client know ahead of time what kind of decisions will be made if she cannot keep herself safe with her food behaviors, can help the client understand that these decisions are not made out of anger or frustration on the part of the nutrition therapist.

Allowing Freedom

Of the four components of parenting, allowing freedom is often the hardest for the parent to provide (7). Unconditional love, limit setting, and reasoning all place control of the relationship in the hands of the parent. Freedom, however, turns control over to the child, and with freedom comes the risk of a serious consequence for the child and even the parent. In addition, allowing freedom requires accepting the risk that the child may not continue to pursue a relationship with her parents. An insecure parent may fear that allowing freedom will end the relationship. However, without freedom, the child will never develop the ability to function independently.

In addition to the freedom to make decisions, a child needs the freedom to express his emotions. Whether it is anger, fear, joy, sadness, loneliness, shame, or guilt, an individual's emotions are a personal experience. A healthy parenting relationship recognizes this and teaches how to recognize and appropriately react to each of these emotions. When an angry child is told, "Don't feel sad" or "Go to your room and don't come out until you're not angry," he learns that his thoughts and feelings are not valid. He learns to ignore his emotions. The long-term consequence is that alternative responses to stressful situations develop. Ultimately, these responses can become dysfunctional communication or coping tools.

One of the most important skills a parent can teach a child is recognizing each of these basic emotions and developing ways to act on them once they are recognized. Anger is a natural response to certain situations; rather than ignoring or avoiding it, the child must learn to develop constructive outlets for anger when it arises. The same is true for other emotions. A parent's goal should be to foster her or his child's ability to recognize, appreciate, and appropriately communicate a range of emotions.

The relationship that develops when freedom is not given to a child is often dysfunctional and filled with hidden resentments and unspoken feelings that chip away at the parent/child bond. Though allowing freedom is a risk, it is also a chance to move the relationship to a deeper level, at which both parent and child participate willingly and respectfully. Much of the process of separation and individuation is trusting that the unconditional love, limit setting, and reasoning provided in the early years have created a bond that will continue once those controls have been lifted. The process of letting go can be frightening and even painful, but also rewarding to a parent who is confident enough to trust.

Psychological evaluations of eating disordered individuals provide insight into their family dynamics, and suggest that healthy parenting is one of the key factors necessary for the prevention of eating disordered behavior. *Table 5.1* illustrates some of the coping techniques commonly found in eating-disordered individuals.

Though each person seems to be born with her own physiological pattern of stress response, the basic blueprint can be greatly influenced by the surrounding environment (7,9,10,12). In other words, the child may be prone to anxiety and depression, but how she learns to cope with her anxiety and depression depends greatly on the parenting she receives and the behaviors she observes. In one study, binge eaters seemed to be more "positively emotional," while anorexic individuals were more "negatively emotional." The researchers suggested that the neural and behavioral systems of the anorexic individuals were not as activated as they were in binge eaters (12). This may have been a byproduct of malnutrition. However, a significant percentage of anorexic individuals were binge eaters before their anorexia developed. Could their behavior be a way for them to cope with emotions when no other tools were provided during development?

Much of psychological counseling involves modeling healthy parenting and communication skills to individuals who may not have experienced them in their immediate families *(Box 5.2)*. When clients do not act their chronological age (which frequently occurs), it is important to remember that healthy reparenting by the treatment team may be the most immediate therapeutic need. Maintaining this perspective can reduce the chance that transference and/or countertransference will sabotage treatment.

Sondra Kronberg in Chapter 16 discusses the importance of supervision for professionals in counseling. Supervision allows the professional to evaluate her interactions with clients and to determine whether or not she is functioning as a healthy "parent". The successful nutrition therapist must be able to unconditionally accept behaviors that on the surface may seem undesirable, to set limits when a client is being manipulative, to have the knowledge base necessary for providing reasoning for limits and interventions, to accept anger as a natural emo-

Table 5.1
Common Coping Styles

Style	Anorexia	Bulimia	Binge Eating
Low tolerance for emotional stress	xxxxx	xxxxx	
Poor social problem-solving skills	xxxxx	xxxxx	xxxxx
Social avoidance		xxxxx	
Feeling of lack of control	xxxxx	xxxxx	xxxxx
Reward dependence	xxxxx		
Novelty seeking		xxxxx	
Harm avoidance	xxxxx		
Avoidance of emotional intimacy	xxxxx		
Dependence on others	xxxxx	xxxxx	xxxxx

Sources: Birk (13), Bulik et al (14), Leal et al (15), Santoro (16), Williams et al (17).

Eating disorders can be viewed as an alternative language that develops when verbal skills do not provide an emotional outlet. When basic emotions such as anger and fear are not verbalized, they find other avenues of expression. This is a useful concept for many clients, as it removes the shame associated with their behavior and helps them logically organize their behavior. Clients often express frustration that family and friends did not recognize their dysfunctional behavior as their way of saying they were angry or hurt. This failure to be understood and validated tends to reinforce the uncommunicated emotion and exacerbate the behavior. Examples of dysfunctional communications include slamming a door instead of verbalizing anger and avoiding a friend's phone call rather than telling the friend she has done something hurtful. Common eating disordered behaviors include:

- Tearing food into small pieces to express anger
- Expressing fear of weight gain or fear of fat in place of a greater, less tangible fear
- Bingeing to avoid feeling lonely
- Avoiding finger foods to express shame (possibly over sexual abuse)
- Expressing guilt over food eaten, rather than over another behavior perceived as "bad"
- Restricting favorite foods to express sadness or lack of self-worth ("I don't deserve to eat that")

In many cases the nutrition therapist functions as an "interpreter" who recognizes what the individual is trying to say and can put words to behaviors that are often labeled as passive-aggressive. When dysfunctional behaviors are observed, some of the first questions asked should be: What is this individual trying to communicate? Is he angry? Lonely? Has something occurred at home that is causing distress? Is he in the middle of a difficult issue in psychotherapy? Is there an emotion about nutrition therapy that is not being communicated?

Viewing eating disordered behaviors as attempts to communicate rather than as mere actions that need changing has several functions. First, clients often feel they have found someone who understands them. This strengthens the bond with the nutrition therapist and encourages more honest disclosure. When clients are more honest about their behaviors, issues are more likely to be quickly identified. Finally, interventions can be designed that better address the root of the behavior.

Note that the examples above are only examples and are not hard-and-fast rules. Each eating disorder is unique, as are the situations and emotions that contribute to its development. The "linguistic" approach is most effective when the nutrition therapist focuses on asking questions and listening to the client, rather than diagnosing or categorizing. Techniques for achieving this rapport are provided in Section Three.

Box 5.2
The Language of Eating Disorders

tion, and to allow the client the freedom to make what may seem like undesirable choices. All of these skills will naturally challenge the clinician's own personal issues. Regular discussion with a skilled provider of supervision sessions can make this process a positive and exciting one, rather than a cause of professional burnout.

Normal Psychological Development

Erik Erikson (18) identified eight crucial stages of development that mark the gradual transition from childhood to adulthood (*Table 5.2*). At the beginning of each stage vulnerability is heightened, as changes are required in the individual's relationships with others. The first five stages occur between infancy and adolescence; at these points the four parenting basics described above are the skills that will successfully bring both parent and child through the change. If the relationship is healthy, these changes should progressively deepen the parent/child relationship.

Individuals who have had healthy foundations created in their families are likely to view these relationship changes as challenges. Individuals without these basic foundations are likely to view them as rejection and to enact behaviors that keep them in the stage where they feel comfortable. An unhealthy family relationship can leave a child "stalled" on her developmental highway, unable to progress through the remaining stages. As a result, she is more likely to be poorly equipped to handle emotional stressors appropriate to her chronological age, and may resort to adopting behaviors that mask, avoid, or numb the awareness of those stressors. These behaviors are often addictive and impulsive behaviors, such as eating disorders and substance abuse.

Table 5.2
Normal Stages of Psychological Development

Erikson Stage/Crisis	Typical Age	Characteristics/Goal	Consequences of Unsuccessful Transition
CHILDHOOD STAGES			
1. Trust vs Mistrust	0–1	Development of general sense of trust and hope	Inability to trust others
2. Autonomy vs Shame and Doubt	2	Development of motor, speech, sensory, and other skills that allow move toward autonomy	Overcompliance Compulsive defiance
3. Initiative vs Guilt	3–4	Development of understanding of roles within family; transfers into roles in other groups	Paralysis due to guilt
4. Industry vs Inferiority	5–12	Development of understanding of importance of work, capacity to cooperate in society	Persistent feelings of inferiority
5. Identity vs Role Confusion	13–18	Development of ability to be true to oneself and to others	Delinquency Inability to form identity
ADULT STAGES			
6. Intimacy vs Isolation	Early adulthood	Development of ability to form intimate relationships and sexual unions that call for self-sacrifice and compromise	Isolation
7. Generativity vs Stagnation	Middle adulthood	Focus shift toward procreativity and teaching next generation	Stagnation Boredom
8. Integrity vs Despair	Late adulthood	Attainment of wisdom	Depression Hypochondriasis Paranoia

Adapted from Satter (20)

Erikson and other psychologists theorize that much of the depression and dysfunction exhibited by some adults arise from inadequate progression through these developmental stages. Many adult clients may be very capable in the career or family roles they project to the outside world, but still be children emotionally. It is important to understand that such clients' emotional development may have been hindered and, when working with individuals who have dysfunctional families, to meet them where they are at emotionally. The goal of treatment can be to move them through stages that they have not been able to challenge on their own.

The concepts described above have pertinence in the development of healthy feeding behaviors as well. *Table 5.3* summarizes Erikson's developmental stages in terms of nutritional development, along with some consequences of not adequately progressing through these stages (19). Adequate transition through these stages requires application of the basic four parenting skills described above.

The self-assessment in *Box 5.3* is a good starting point for individuals who wish

Parenting to Develop Healthy Feeding Behaviors

Table 5-3
Normal Stages of Nutritional Development

Erikson Stage	Typical Age	Nutritional Characteristics	Consequences of Unsuccessful Transition
1. Trust vs Mistrust	0-1	General rooting/sucking/nursing Weaning Introduction to solids	Fussy eating habits Control battles Food neophobia
2. Autonomy vs Shame and Doubt	2	Learning to use eating utensils Trying new foods Eating with family, learning rules Overdeveloped sense of shame	Overcompliance Compulsive defiance Finickiness
3. Initiative vs Guilt	3-4	Learning food behaviors/preferences by observation Learning consequences of eating vs not eating (hunger vs satiety)	Aggression Lack of control Poor table manners Expression of guilt via eating/not eating
4. Industry vs Inferiority	5-12	Increased acceptance of different foods Sensitive to criticism for not meeting with approval More independent food choices away from home First experiments with dieting	Overcompliance/ overeating Learned helplessness
5. Identity vs Role Confusion	13-18	Eating for social acceptance to others (at-risk behaviors include dieting and vegetarian eating)	Rebellion Inability to form identity
6. Intimacy vs Isolation	Early adulthood	Development of the ability to form intimate relationships and sexual unions that call for self-sacrifice and compromise.	Isolation with bingeing or food restriction to avoid sexual development

Adapted from Satter (20)

to evaluate how their attitudes about food, appearance, and body weight may be influencing the food choices and behaviors of family members. As discussed in the physiological chapters, many food preferences are predetermined. The most a parent can and should do is provide adequate food and an environment that allows for individual preferences, instead of making these preferences a battleground for control (20). It is important to encourage exploration of a wide vari-

ED: by not breaking box, it moves the citation for the box to the next page, ok?

Box 5.3
Food Behavior
Self-Assessment

The things we say and do greatly impact the people around us. The following statements are designed to get you thinking about how your behaviors may be influencing someone else's ideas about food, weight, and appearance. These behaviors are not necessarily bad, but the more that apply to you and your family, the more likely it is that your behaviors are significantly influencing another's food behaviors.

1. I follow a low-fat diet and try to get the rest of the family to do the same.
2. I worry about what other family members eat.
3. I have been on many diets in the past.
4. I like to talk about recipes, cooking, and food.
5. I often comment about other individuals' weight.
6. I try to get other people to eat the way I do.
7. I eat differently when no one is around than when I eat with my family.
8. I monitor the weights of other family members.
9. I have suggested to other people that they should change their weight.
10. Food is used as a reward in our home.
11. Dinnertime is often in front of the television set.
12. I keep my own secret stash of _____. (You name the food.)
13. I have offered gifts to _____ as an incentive to lose/gain weight.
14. We have family nicknames like "Lardbottom" and "Thunder Thighs".
15. I identify people according to their physical characteristics (the thin one, the lady with the double chin, the pretty little girl).
16. I have been known to say, "You don't need that!" when a family member asks for seconds at the dinner table.
17. Family gatherings always revolve around some type of meal.
18. I bake/buy sweets for my family but I never eat them myself.
19. I bake/buy sweets for myself but I do not share them with my family.
20. We rarely sit down and eat together as a family.
21. I use food to comfort myself and/or others.
22. Desserts, chips, and food treats are often referred to as "bad", "sinful", "no-no's", or "fattening" in our home.
23. Food is withheld as a form of punishment in our home.
24. I have used food to quiet a crying child.
25. Dinner conversations revolve around how the meal was cooked.
26. I have been known to comment, "You're eating so much!" if someone at my table takes more food than I would have eaten.
27. I express opinions about what I think other family members should weigh.

ety of food types and to encourage the child to develop an internal sense of appetite, hunger, and satiety.

As children learn to choose foods and feed themselves, they may exhibit behaviors that challenge even the most patient and accepting parent. Though this phenomenon occurs in all types of behaviors, food behaviors often receive undue parental attention. Cultural norms often attach value judgments to food behaviors and choices (fast food is "bad", vegetarian is "good"), and a child who is experimenting with food choices may push food issue "buttons" in his parents. Fearful that these choices may reflect bad parenting or poor character, parents may be tempted to control these behaviors or to encourage food choices and behaviors more consistent with their own.

Progression through developmental stages can be disrupted in several ways. Prenatal nutrition may alter the development of the central nervous system *(Box 5.4)*. An overcontrolling parent can stifle growth. A disconnected parent or a chaotic family can be so preoccupied with issues beyond the child that adequate developmental stimuli are not provided. Or a trauma can focus attention on other immediate needs to the detriment of normal developmental behaviors. For example, a child who is hospitalized with a serious illness requiring tube feeding may not be exposed to normal foods on a regular basis that would foster the appetite and motor skills necessary for progression through succeeding developmental stages (21).

Missed developmental stages can manifest themselves as disordered eating

---

Box 5.4
Can Eating Disorders Be a Birth Defect?

Maternal nutrition experts have always promoted the importance of good nutrition in utero. Now evidence is surfacing that for good adult mental health, adequate nutrition is important throughout pregnancy and into childhood. Prenatal protein malnutrition has been observed to cause selective changes in the central serotonin mechanism (22). Inadequate glucose during pregnancy retards fetal brain development and the development of the fetal serotonergic system (23). As more information is gained about the function of serotonin and its relationship to mood and appetite, the long-term consequences of such altered brain development are becoming an important research issue.

Mothers of low birth weight and very low birth weight infants (who are more likely to have had inadequate nutrition during pregnancy) are more likely to have delayed breast stimulation and decreased pumping frequency after delivery (24). Since essential fatty acids and choline, found in breast milk, are crucial for nervous system development, they may also play a role in the development of intelligence (25). In fact, choline supplementation during pregnancy has been shown to increase spatial memory in the offspring of rats (26).

Are the children of women who are overly restrictive with their food intake during pregnancy predisposing their children to depression, eating disorders, and other addictions? This question is gradually being addressed in the literature (27–29). Before we promote particular dietary practices for women and children, it is important to consider the impact they can have on mental health.

behaviors later in life. To the astute nutrition therapist, food behaviors can provide diagnostic clues to important family events. While some food rituals are recent developments and part of the core eating disorder, others can be diagnostic indicators of when issues started to surface in childhood *(Box 5.5)*. An understanding of Erikson's basic developmental tasks can help the nutrition therapist develop a treatment plan that addresses the origins of these behaviors.

Box 5.5
CASE STUDY:
When Development Is
Delayed

Morgan was a 22-year-old who, in addition to her bulimia, presented with a list of food-hates that limited her food choices to cottage cheese and rice. She adamantly refused to eat any other foods she was offered. Morgan was in an inpatient treatment center that required that a regular, varied meal plan be offered regardless of individuals' food preferences. Having to sit in front of foods she did not eat only increased Morgan's defiance of the food plan.

During the initial psychosocial and nutrition assessments, it was learned that Morgan's parents had divorced when she was two. At that point her mother began to work out of the home. Mealtime was no longer a family event; Morgan's mother rarely cooked and was often too exhausted to argue when Morgan refused food. Mealtime was either a battleground or a silent, disconnected half hour at the table. As Morgan grew up, she gravitated toward eating alone, usually a microwaved meal in front of the television.

Morgan's nutrition therapist decided to spend a day's worth of mealtimes with Morgan to observe firsthand the difficult eating behaviors the nursing and dietary staff had reported. She witnessed several distinct behaviors:

- a tendency to eat foods only if they were separate from each other and not served as mixes or casseroles,
- a dislike for all vegetables,
- a tendency to play with food and eat with the hands despite being provided with silverware,
- increased anxiety if a new food was served, and
- childlike crying if a staff member attempted to change any of Morgan's food behaviors.

All of these were behaviors more appropriate to a 2- or 3-year-old. When the nutrition therapist discussed these findings with Morgan's psychotherapist, she learned that Morgan also displayed toddler-like social behaviors when participating in group activities. Morgan's psychotherapist was focusing mainly on her primary issue of abandonment, which had originated with her parents' divorce, and was providing assignments designed to guide her through the developmental stages she had missed while growing up.

Morgan's nutrition therapist developed a similar treatment plan for use at the table. She reviewed Erikson's developmental stages with the psychotherapist and Morgan, and they identified Morgan's developmental location. For each stage, Morgan and her nutrition therapist planned a series of challenges appropriate to her current developmental stage. These were coordinated with the psychological assignments her psychotherapist had created, and included:

continued

Stage 2 Autonomy vs Shame and Doubt

Intervention: Eat a variety of foods using a variety of eating techniques (eg, spaghetti, sandwiches, omelet) in the presence of nutrition therapist; nutrition therapist models appropriate behaviors to client.

Stage 3 Initiative vs Guilt

Intervention: Eat at the table with peers without disruption. Dislikes and other food problems addressed only if client follows community rules for such problem solving during mealtime.

Stage 4 Industry vs Inferiority

Intervention: Work in the kitchen, learn basic food preparation skills, help plan a meal.

Stage 5 Identity vs Role Confusion

Intervention: Try a variety of new foods. One-bite minimum trial for each food; "like and dislike" list created only with foods that are actually tried.

Box 5.5
(*continued*)

By moving back to the place where her development had strayed off course and bringing herself up to speed chronologically, Morgan was able to progress to a varied and age-appropriate meal plan without being challenged in a fashion that exceeded her developmental capabilities.

The four parenting skills described in this chapter were crucial to the success of this intervention. When Morgan sought treatment, she knew her behavior was inappropriate and she was ashamed of her inability to eat like the average 22-year-old. The unconditional acceptance of her treatment team and the individualization of her program helped to communicate that she was "ok" despite her behavior. Morgan was given the expectation that she would try new behaviors and that she would progress through treatment (setting limits), but the rationale behind her treatment plan was explained to improve the likelihood that she would trust and cooperate with interventions that were initially anxiety-producing (reasoning). Finally, she was asked to create her own challenges and interventions when appropriate to help develop confidence that she could continue these behaviors after discharge (freedom).

One year after treatment, Morgan contacted her treatment team to report that she had just eaten a "burrito with the works" at a local fast-food restaurant. She reported that she did have episodes when she reverted to her previous behaviors, but rather than feel guilty, she was learning to use these incidents as emotional barometers and to respond to them by exploring the possible triggers in her ongoing therapy.

Successfully implementing any new behavior, from eating to learning a new language, requires a period of acclimatization. The first few times a new behavior is employed, the effort seems deliberate and even stiff and uncomfortable. With time, as the new neural pathway is paved, the new behavior is implemented more readily and flows more smoothly. Eventually, the new behavior becomes the preferred behavior and occurs without a second thought. As long as environmental input is constant, the behavioral response is likely to be consistent. However,

MAINTAINING THE COURSE

when an environmental stressor changes the input to the brain, the elicited behavioral response may change. The brain may not have had a chance to develop a behavioral pathway to respond to a specific stressor, and the individual may revert to an old behavior.

For example, when one learns a foreign language, the process of memorization is tedious. Forming sentences requires much effort, and generating spontaneous conversation happens only with much concentration. Eventually, however, speaking the new language can become almost as natural a behavior as speaking one's native language, give or take a few accents or transposed words. However, in a stressful situation, such as an argument, individuals often revert to their native language or have more difficulty finding the words to express their feelings in the new language.

This phenomenon occurs with any learned behavior. Under stressful circumstances, the old behavior is much more likely to surface. This does not mean the new behavior has been "unlearned," but rather that on-ramps to the new behavior need to be constructed from previously unidentified stimuli. This takes time. When a particular situation triggers undesired behavior, this should be viewed not as a failure, but as a new situation for which new coping skills are needed. It is important to continue to identify and evaluate the on-ramps to the old behavior and, when possible, to redirect them to the new behavior.

An important part of the nutrition therapist's job is to help the client identify stresses that trigger the use of eating disordered behaviors. Often these behaviors are a source of shame to the client and she may not disclose them. It is important to maintain open lines of communication and to listen to behaviors described without judgment. They provide important clues to issues central to the eating disorder. Only when ongoing dialogue is possible can the appropriate evaluation and intervention be planned and executed (*Box 5.6*).

Box 5.6
CASE STUDY:
Identifying the
Core Issue

Katie was a 35–year-old binge eater who had been "in recovery" for 6 months. During that time, she successfully discontinued her nighttime binges and developed an eating pattern that included a variety of foods. She was excited about the weight loss that these changes had brought about. After 6 months, however, Katie's progress screeched to a halt. She began to experience food cravings and gradually returned to a nightly binge on Oreos and ice cream.

Ashamed about this regression, Katie did not initially report these changes to her nutrition therapist. Though she was working on her perfectionism with her psychotherapist, she still struggled with wanting to present as the model patient with her nutrition therapist, whose opinion she valued greatly.

Katie's nutrition therapist capitalized on this change of events. Instead of focusing on food behaviors, he evaluated Katie's weight history. He discovered that in the years Katie was dieting, she always seemed able to lose weight until she hit 135 pounds, at which point she resumed bingeing and weight gain. Together with Katie's psychotherapist, the nutrition therapist spent time reconstructing the events surrounding this particular weight, with special focus on Katie's earliest memory of being at this weight.

continued

Box 5.6
(*continued*)

After several sessions, Katie disclosed that as a college senior she had been date-raped. At that time she weighed 125 pounds. At a joint session with her psychotherapist and the nutrition therapist, this information was confirmed. Katie realized that as she approached the weight at which this trauma had occurred, she more closely resembled the person who had been traumatized. In addition, she gained more male attention with her weight loss, which she perceived as threatening rather than flattering. With the help of the nutrition therapist, Katie recalled that Oreos and ice cream were foods she was given by her mother to cheer her up. She had continued to use these foods for comfort as an adult.

Katie's nutrition therapist developed an eating plan that maintained Katie at a weight she perceived as "safe" (just above 140) while she processed her sexual trauma with her psychotherapist. Eventually she was able to resume an eating plan that moved her toward her target weight of 128 pounds. In the process, Katie was able to understand that her bingeing and food choices were not something to be ashamed of, but rather a valuable emotional barometer that helped her identify when her emotions and issues needed to be examined in therapy.

SUMMARY

- **Conditioning develops preferred behavioral pathways that have both physiological and psychological roots.**

- **A healthy (functional) family creates nurturing, productive behaviors by providing unconditional love, setting limits, reasoning, and allowing freedom.**

- **These four parenting skills are necessary for normal development into adulthood.**

- **Individuals who cannot change their behaviors may be struggling with alternative pathways resulting from parenting that did not employ these four skills.**

- **One of the most important functions of the treatment team is to model functional communication and counseling skills that the client did not receive in his own developmental history.**

- **Professional supervision helps the nutrition therapist evaluate her interactions with clients and maintain a healthy relationship with them.**

REFERENCES

1. Nichols M. *Family Therapy: Concepts and Methods.* Needham Heights, Mass: Allyn & Bacon; 1984.
2. Vogt BA, Finch DM, Olson CR. Functional heterogeneity in cingulate cortex: the anterior executive and posterior evaluative regions. *Cereb Cortex.* 1992;2(6):435–443.
3. Maekawa K, Sano M, Nakae Y. Developmental change of sucking response to taste in infants. *Biol Neonate.* 1991;60(Suppl 1):62–74.
4. Howard PJ. *The Owner's Manual for the Brain: Everyday Applications From Mind-brain Research.* Austin, Texas: Bard & Steven; 1994.
5. Fairburn CG. Cognitive-behavioral treatment for bulimia. In: Garner DM, Garfinkel

PE, eds. *Handbook of Psychotherapy for Anorexia Nervosa & Bulimia.* New York: The Guilford Press; 1985.

6. Garner DM, Rockert W, Olmsted MP, Johnson C, Coscina DV. Psychoeducational principles in the treatment of bulimia and anorexia nervosa. In: Garner DM, Garfinkel PE, eds. *Handbook of Psychotherapy for Anorexia Nervosa & Bulimia.* New York: The Guilford Press; 1985.

7. Rolfe R. *The 7 Secrets of Successful Parents.* Lincolnwood, Illinois: Contemporary Books; 1997.

8. Suchecki D, Rosenfeld P, Levine S. Maternal regulation of the hypothalamic-pituitary-adrenal axis in the infant rat: the roles of feeding and stroking. *Brain Res Dev Brain Res.* 1993;75(2):185–192.

9. Dorsa D. The importance of ritual to children. *Dissertation Abstracts Int.* 1994;55–12A: 3875.

10. Reuben SC. *Children of Character: A Parent's Guide.* Santa Monica, Calif: Canter Associates; 1997.

11. Rimm S. *Dr. Sylvia Rimm's Smart Parenting: How to Raise a Happy, Achieving Child.* New York: Crown Publishers, Inc; 1996.

12. Horner TN Jr, Utermohlen V. A multivariate analysis of psychological factors related to body mass index and eating preoccupation in female college students. *J Am Coll Nutr.* 1993;12(4):459–465.

13. Birk MW. Social problem-solving in bulimic and non-bulimic women. *Dissertation Abstracts Int.* 1994;56–02B:1100.

14. Bulik CM, Sullivan PF, Weltzin TE, Kaye WH. Temperament in eating disorders. *Int J Eat Disord.* 1995;17(3):251–261.

15. Leal L, Weise S, Dodd DK. The relationship between gender, symptoms of bulimia, and tolerance for stress. *Addict Behav.* 1995;29(1):105–109.

16. Santoro LE. A comparative analysis of intimate behavior among female bulimics in residential treatment, female bulimics in outpatient therapy, and non-eating disordered women. *Dissertation Abstracts Int.* 1994;53–07A:2303.

17. Williams GJ, Chamove AS, Millar HR. Eating disorders, perceived control, assertiveness and hostility. *Br J Clin Psychol.* 1990;29(Pt 3):327–335.

18. Erikson EH. *Childhood and Society.* New York: WW Norton; 1950.

19. Satter E. *How to Get Your Child to Eat . . . But Not Too Much.* Palo Alto, California: Bull Publishing Company; 1987.

20. Satter E. *Child of Mine: Feeding with Love and Good Sense.* Palo Alto, California: Bull Publishing Company; 1991.

21. Schauster H, Dwyer J. Transition from tube feedings to feedings by mouth in children: preventing eating dysfunction. *J Am Diet Assoc.* 1996;96(3):277–281.

22. Chen JC, Tonkiss J, Galler JR, Volicer L. Prenatal protein malnutrition in rats enhances serotonin release from hippocampus. *J Nutr.* 1992;122(11):2138–2143.

23. Koski KG, Lanoue L, Young SN. Maternal dietary carbohydrate restriction influences the developmental profile of postnatal rat brain indoleamine metabolism. *Biol Neonate.* 1995;67(2):122–131.

24. Hill PD, Brow LP, Harker TL. Initiation and frequency of breast expression in breastfeeding mothers of LBW and VLBW infants. *Nurs Res.* 1995;44(6):352–355.

25. de Andraca I, Uauy R. Breastfeeding for optimal mental development: the alpha and the omega in human milk. *World Rev Nutr Diet.* 1995;78:1–27.

26. Garner SC, Mar MH, Zeisel SH. Choline distribution and metabolism in pregnant

rats and fetuses are influenced by the choline content of the maternal diet. *J Nutr.* 1995;125(11):2851–2858.

27. Weekly SJ. Diets and eating disorders: implications for the breastfeeding mother. *NAACOGS Clin Issues Perinat Womens Health Nurs.* 1992;3(4):695–700.

28. Lifshitz F. Children on adult diets: is it harmful? Is it healthful? *J Am Coll Nutr.* 1992;11(Suppl):84S-90S.

29. Wachs TD. Relation of mild-to-moderate malnutrition to human development: correlational studies. *J Nutr.* 1995;125(8 suppl):2245S-2254S.

CHAPTER 6

Family Dynamics and Eating Disorders

MONIKA M. WOOLSEY, M.S., R.D.

To promote independence in their children, parents must be free of self-consuming agendas. A parent who is lonely, afraid, addicted, depressed, or otherwise distracted is likely to be over- or underinvolved in his or her child's life. Children in such families can develop an overdeveloped sense of dependence or obligation or disconnectedness. In each case, they are at high risk of developing an impaired ability to function independently and to form healthy relationships with others.

The behaviors seen in individuals with eating disorders often reflect dysfunctional relationship skills rooted in the client's family of origin. Such individuals are normally found in four types of dysfunctional families: enmeshed, disconnected, chaotic, or abusive. The first three types will be addressed in this chapter. Abuse, with a special emphasis on sexual abuse, is addressed by Karin Kratina in Chapter 7.

THE ENMESHED FAMILY In an enmeshed family, the parent-child relationship suffers from overinvolvement *(Box 6.1)*. One parent is usually emotionally detached and the other is left without a mature relationship connection (1). Rather than confront the problem with their spouse, such parents often seek an emotional release in another relationship.

Children in enmeshed families often serve as the spousal replacement for one or both parents (2). When such a bond is forged, the child often has difficulty later separating from the parent. If the child matured and developed as she should, the parent would be left without an emotional bond and would have to face the dys-

Box 6.1
CASE STUDY:
The Enmeshed Family

Margaret entered treatment after a semester at college. Since leaving home for school, she had lost 30 pounds; she presented at 5 feet 10 inches and 109 pounds. She did not notice her weight loss until a family friend visited and commented on the extreme change in her appearance.

Margaret's food journal described an austere diet, averaging about 800 calories a day. She had taken herself off the campus meal plan and was shopping for herself at local grocery stores. Her average food expenditure was $20 a week. When asked why she allotted so little money to food, Margaret said she had no idea what the appropriate amount of money was, as she had never been responsible for food shopping until she left home for school.

Margaret had additional problems in the grocery store. Many of the food items she was used to eating at home were not in the local grocery store, thus leaving her with the task of making decisions about replacement foods without any parental input. As she described it, choosing one salad dressing from the many available was so monumental a task that she bought none to avoid having to make the decision.

Margaret came to realize that she had rarely had to make such decisions while living at home. When she did have to choose a meal, outfit, or social engagement, her mother was often critical. As a result, Margaret came to live the life her mother dictated because it was easier than dealing with the conflict assertiveness would have brought on. Much of Margaret's mother's overinvolvement seemed the result of Margaret's parents' divorce, which had occurred when Margaret was 6 years old. Margaret's mother had never remarried and she did not have many friends, as she was too busy with Margaret to make other plans.

As Margaret's treatment advanced, her mother regularly called from home to check in with the treatment team. In addition, she called Margaret two or three times a week to check on her progress. This involvement frustrated Margaret, as she felt as though her treatment was being intruded on and as if she were a child rather than a young adult.

A large part of Margaret's treatment involved developing communication skills and assertiveness training that would enable her to individuate from her mother and appropriately handle the conflict that was likely to arise as a result of her new behaviors. Many of her nutrition assignments were exercises in making her own decisions, based on whether her choices provided nourishment and taste satisfaction. When a choice was determined to be less than optimal, problem solving was used to develop a strategy for the next shopping trip. Eventually Margaret was able to plan and carry out a meal plan that allowed her to maintain an ideal weight.

function in his or her marriage. The parent therefore (often subconsciously) acts to maintain the enmeshed relationship and to discourage independence.

Children who grow up in enmeshed families do not experience boundaries or privacy. It is often difficult to tell in these families where one person stops and the other starts. The parent becomes overly invested in the child's activities, leaving him with little time to individuate. If the child participates in sports, for example, the parent may spend as much time on the activity as the child. The child may participate in extracurricular activities the parent chooses, rather than those that fit her personality and interests.

One important consequence of enmeshment is that the child grows up without emotional freedom. The enmeshment parent dictates what emotions are acceptable, rather than teaching the child to recognize and freely express a wide range of feelings. The unspoken message in many of these families is that happiness is the only acceptable emotion, as this conceals family problems from the outside world. Problem solving and communication are sacrificed at all costs to project an outward image of happiness.

For example, if an issue between the parents is unexpressed anger, anger may be actively avoided to avoid bringing into focus the parental dysfunction. If a child in the family encounters a situation that arouses anger, the enmeshed parent is likely to act to suppress this emotion. She may change the subject, use food to soothe the child, or directly say, "Now, let's not get angry about this." Eventually the child learns that his emotions are not important and suppresses them. In addition, he becomes overly sensitive to the emotions of those around him and begins to act out their emotions. This allows the enmeshed parent to avoid her own emotions and issues, but also leaves little time and energy for individual expression on the part of the child.

Unfortunately, stifling one's emotions does not make them go away. Anger, sadness, guilt, shame, loneliness, and fear are emotions that naturally surface in the course of an average day. If a child has learned that verbalizing these emotions is not acceptable, the stress from these events will accumulate internally. The physiological consequence of accumulated stress that has no outlet, as previous chapters have detailed, is depression. However, in a family in which depression and its symptoms are inconsistent with the need to project a happy, conflict-free image, other behaviors develop so the individual can dissipate stress while meeting the family's behavioral expectations. These behaviors, as discussed in previous chapters, include compulsions, avoidance, and addictions such as eating disorders (3).

Individuals who grow up in enmeshed families have several fundamental psychological issues, including

- a sense of inadequacy and low self-esteem,
- an overdeveloped sense of responsibility for the feelings and behaviors of others, also known as *codependency,*
- strong feelings of guilt and shame, and
- a tendency toward perfectionism, which is a defense that hides feelings of guilt and shame from the outside world (3).

Enmeshment is a common finding in families in which there is an eating disorder. Parents of eating disordered individuals, particularly anorexics, tend to be more controlling than other parents; this tendency can be seen as early as the first year of life (4). Though this phenomenon is demonstrated in a variety of behaviors, it is a particular problem in the parental approach to food behaviors. Children in families that do not promote autonomy in food behaviors seem to be at risk for developing dysfunctional food behaviors as they progress through adolescence (4,5). For such children, food behaviors become an alternative language that communicates feelings not allowed to be verbally expressed.

A mother who is overly concerned about her daughter's weight and food intake and who controls food intake and food choices as a result may be teaching her daughter to chronically diet. A child in this situation may resort to out-of-control eating when she is in an unmonitored food environment (6). A mother who is overly concerned about a child's finickiness and who attempts to increase her child's food intake may actually increase finickiness and encourage the child to use the table as a place where he can control his emotional affairs (4,6). In both cases, the child is left without an emotional outlet or an opportunity to develop autonomy, and resorts to a tangible behavior that provides a means of emotional expression *(Box 6.2)*.

A child's weight can also become a focus in an enmeshed relationship (7–9). Preoccupation with the child's weight provides the enmeshed parent with a distraction from his own problems. However, overconcern with physical appearance

Box 6.2
Eating Disorders: An Inheritable Problem?

Mothers of individuals with eating disorders demonstrate a greater degree of eating disordered behaviors than mothers of non-disordered eaters (9). This observation has been noted numerous times in the literature; it has even been suggested that children of eating disordered mothers should be designated an at-risk group requiring special monitoring throughout their development (10,11). Though part of this correlation is likely due to an inherited biochemical predisposition to depression and related disorders, there is also a strong behavioral contribution. Mothers who experienced an eating disorder during the postnatal year

- were more intrusive with their infants during both mealtimes and play,
- expressed more negative emotion towards their infants during mealtimes but not during play,
- had infants with a more negative emotional tone, and
- had more conflictual mealtimes than controls.

Their infants were lighter and their weight was independently and inversely related to the amount of conflict observed during mealtime and the extent of the mother's concern about her own body shape (12). Over half of the mothers with a history of a diagnosable eating disorder were found to have an emotional disorder that impaired social functioning.

These observations suggest that the basic principles of parenting—unconditional love, limit setting, reasoning, and allowing freedom—are not consistently a component of the feeding relationship when the mother is struggling with emotional issues of her own. Diane Keddy (Chapter 15) has observed that a "second generation" of eating-disordered individuals is starting to emerge, and suggests that nutrition therapists who treat eating disordered women of childbearing age incorporate basic feeding concepts into nutrition education to minimize the impact of the eating disorder on the next generation.

teaches the child that love depends on appearance. A child in this situation often becomes a performer, excelling in school, sports, and/or social activities, as it provides an alternative source of love and attention. Individuals with anorexia are often high achievers, perfectionistic, and, outside of the eating disorder, appear to lead very successful lives. It is important to view this "perfection" as a mask that hides a deep well of low self-esteem.

THE DISCONNECTED FAMILY

At the other end of the spectrum is the disconnected family, in which bonding does not occur at all. This lack of emotional connection can occur for numerous reasons, including parental depression or mental illness or an environmental condition that consumes the family's energy, such as a serious illness, a situation that results in frequent or long separations (such as a job requiring travel), or parental abandonment or death (13–17). When the child's source of unconditional love is absent, he is deprived of the basic developmental experience that sets the stage for further emotional development. As a result, much of his life is spent searching for a replacement for this initial lost love. Common pursuits include perfectionism, materialism, unhealthy attachments to abusive or neglectful friends, and promiscuity (18).

In a disconnected environment, a crisis can serve to pull detached family members together for a short bout of problem solving (*Box 6.3*). If this is the only time the family bonds, the eating disordered individual quickly learns that her illness is the glue that holds together an otherwise broken family. If the family consistently resumes its disconnected ways once the crisis has passed, the eating disordered individual has no incentive to get better.

Our culture's focus on weight loss and thinness are particularly detrimental to the disconnected family member struggling for attention. Weight loss often brings positive and encouraging comments from relatives, peers, teachers, employers, and other acquaintances. If this is one of the individual's few achievements garner attention, weight loss, necessary or not, becomes an attention-getting behavior. However, once the comments stop, the individual finds she must continue to lose weight to continue receiving attention. The cycle becomes vicious, with a deadly outcome if not broken.

Exacerbations of the eating disorder can introduce the individual to a second source of love and bonding—the treatment team. It is not uncommon for an eating disordered individual to sabotage treatment in order to maintain his ties with the first healthy "family" he may have ever encountered. Though staying sick is not the most desirable physical state, it is desirable if it provides the security of family attention and caretaking by the treatment team. New behaviors that lack guaranteed outcomes are frightening and difficult to initiate.

Individuals who grew up in disconnected families often require therapeutic interventions that reconstruct the developmental stages that were missed during childhood. This type of therapy addresses the "inner child," the core personality

Box 6.3
CASE STUDY:
The Disconnected
Family

Kayla's entire family—mother, father, and older brother—came to her first session. Her brother was annoyed, as he was missing a baseball game. Kayla's father was ten minutes late, as he had just returned from a business trip and his arrival had been delayed. His wife politely requested that he turn off his pager and cellular phone so they would not interrupt the session. She was anxious about his late arrival, as she would have to leave the appointment promptly to preside at a local bar association meeting.

Kayla was sullen and quiet during this initial discussion, but brightened up when asked what she liked and disliked. She talked about her acting classes and upcoming auditions for the school play. Her father added that she was a good soccer player, and he enjoyed watching her games on the weekends. When Kayla gave her diet history, her mother said it was difficult to know exactly what Kayla ate because the family ate so few meals together, so no one could confirm whether what she said was true. When the family did eat together, Kayla seemed to have a good appetite.

Scheduling follow-up appointments was always difficult, as they always seemed to interfere with family members' work and social commitments. Assignments to participate in family outings were also met with resistance, as they required social sacrifices as well. With help, the family was able to work out a system of compromise that allowed each member to pursue individual interests and relationships but provided a consistent routine that helped Kayla feel she was connected to each family member. As these connections strengthened, Kayla no longer needed the eating disorder to bring the family together.

Kayla's food issues were not severe enough to be diagnosed as an eating disorder, but they were disordered and significant enough to have caused family concern. Fortunately, her family was committed to working to better their communication skills and followed through with the nutrition therapist's recommendations. This process took time, and did not progress perfectly.

This case, though not representing a bona fide eating disorder, illustrates the importance of assessing the psychosocial environment of an individual presenting with a food problem. Food behaviors often communicate what words cannot; encouraging the development of more appropriate relationship skills in such cases must be central to the treatment plan if disordered eating is to be prevented from developing into an eating disorder.

that acts out what it has learned it needs to do in order to receive love (16). This process is long and difficult, but functions to help improve the ability to develop trust, be emotionally intimate, and rely less on addictive and compulsive behaviors to relieve emotional distress.

THE CHAOTIC FAMILY

Another environment in which bonding does not occur is that of the chaotic family. In this situation, parental behavior is unpredictable and/or abusive, and is often due to an alcohol or drug addiction or other psychological problem in a parent (17,19). Because there is no consistent expression of either love or limits, the child has no frame of behavioral reference. Appropriate behavior that would be encouraged and rewarded in a functional family is often ignored or punished, but sometimes rewarded. Inappropriate behavior that would normally generate limit setting in the functional family also invokes inconsistent responses. The parental response is not dependent on the child's behavior, but on the parent's emotional state. The only real consistency in such environments is *inconsistency*.

Individuals who grow up in chaotic families often cope by becoming "people pleasers," constantly on the alert for environmental changes that signal an impending emotional outburst. They quickly learn to alter their behavior to accommodate the moods of others and to take blame for problems (even if they did not cause them) to reduce the chaos. They are conditioned to have very little tolerance for emotional distress and often act impulsively in an attempt to restore equilibrium *(Box 6.4)*.

Over time, the emotional energy it requires to constantly be on alert can drain the body physiologically. If this emotional drain continues without reprieve, behaviors develop that allow the individual to numb her awareness of her emotional

Box 6.4
CASE STUDY:
The Chaotic Family

Miranda always looked like a scared rabbit. Always at the edge of her seat with one leg shaking, this 16-year-old started when her nutrition therapist merely increased the volume of her voice. Miranda's father was an alcoholic, and her mother worked long hours at the office to avoid confrontations with her husband.

Miranda loved her dad. He was fun, like a big kid, and made her laugh with his funny jokes. But he had his bad days as well. Often the tension would break at the dinner table, one of the few places where Miranda's mother and father actually spent time together. If dinner was late, which it often was when Mom worked late, Dad had the opportunity to have a few pre-dinner drinks. By the time dinner was served, his temper was short and he had an issue to argue about with Mom. On those days, Miranda knew that if she did not finish dinner first and get started cleaning up the kitchen, she would also be on the receiving end of Dad's ill temper. She became skilled at anticipating mood changes and jumping into chores to avoid being punished for being lazy.

Miranda had had a bout with the flu a few years earlier. She never forgot the sense of physical euphoria and relief that vomiting brought her. From that point on, when the nausea and discomfort her family chaos brought on became too much to bear, she resorted to vomiting to make the feeling go away. Eventually her vomiting became spontaneous whenever she felt anxious.

Miranda's bulimia subsided only after her father entered treatment for alcohol abuse. Though the original family chaos subsided, Miranda needed therapy to learn to cope with the anxiety environmental changes brought on. She learned which environments made her feel unsafe, and how to relax to minimize their impact. With her nutrition therapist, she visited several of these environments (grocery stores and restaurants) to practice using relaxation skills to overcome the discomfort. She learned how to recognize her feelings and express them so they did not build up and explode.

Eventually Miranda was able to visit most restaurants and accept most social invitations. If she felt anxious about an upcoming event, she developed a routine of relaxation and writing in her journal that provided an outlet for her anxiety so she could participate in the events her peers invited her to join.

distress (eg, addiction to alcohol, drugs, sex, or gambling). Many of these behaviors also increase serotonin levels, which can temporarily relieve the depression that accompanies this scenario. In extreme cases, borderline personality disorders can develop (20)—the individual jumps from impulsive behavior to impulsive behavior, and life is consumed by the pursuit of relief from emotional distress and depression.

One of the most intense emotional distresses in these individuals is the fear of abandonment (21). Impulsive behaviors are often employed to keep others engaged in unhealthy relationships that might otherwise come to an end. These behaviors include seductive or controlling behavior, suicide attempts, and other dysfunctional activities that manipulate the actions of others to keep them engaged in the relationship.

Most individuals who act out dysfunctionally experience significant shame about what they are doing, which further intensifies the emotional distress. Despite this shame and a wish to break the cycle of impulsivity, the individual's need to dissipate her emotional and physiological distress is more pressing and overcomes genuine attempts to overcome behaviors she perceives as undesirable. The cycle becomes entrenched, and without help is difficult to break.

A consensus is gradually developing that there is a high incidence of physical, emotional, and sexual trauma in individuals with bulimia (22). Eating disordered symptoms are particularly prevalent in the children of alcohol abusers (23). In addition, there is a high rate of cross-addiction in bulimics (24). In other words, if an individual discontinues an undesirable behavior (eg, laxative abuse) without addressing the root cause of the behavior, another impulsive behavior (eg, alcohol abuse or shoplifting) is likely to surface as a means of coping with the resulting emotional distress. Children from chaotic families in which these incidents occur are thought to be more susceptible to eating disorders, particularly bulimia, because of the "numbing" quality these impulsive behaviors tend to have.

This finding does not suggest that all individuals who experience such traumas will develop an eating disorder. In fact, many individuals who have been abused do not. However, it does suggest that certain psychosocial backgrounds can place an individual at high risk for developing eating disorders and other maladaptive behaviors, and that it is important to evaluate the client's history to ascertain if such a profile is part of the big picture. If it is, the treatment plan should reflect this history and all treatment team members should work together to create an environment that models stability and unity. This may be the first time such a "functional family" is modeled to the client, and this example may help the client to visualize what is possible in his own life as he moves toward recovery.

Most dysfunctional families are combinations of the three types described above (25). If one parent is disconnected or struggling with an addiction, the other is likely to seek comfort with the child in an enmeshed fashion. The result might be a disconnected-enmeshed or chaotic-enmeshed combination. The relationship dynamics depend on whose needs in the system are dominant at any given time. For example, the chaotic model is most likely to dominate when an alcoholic parent is drunk and angry. When that parent is away at work, the enmeshed parent may seek out the child for an emotional release.

Enmeshed, disconnected, chaotic, and abusive families can be compared in terms of the ways boundaries and consistency characterize the relationships *(Figure 6.1)*. Inappropriate boundaries or consistency creates an environment in which dysfunctional communication is likely to occur.

Figure 6.1
Comparison of
Family Types

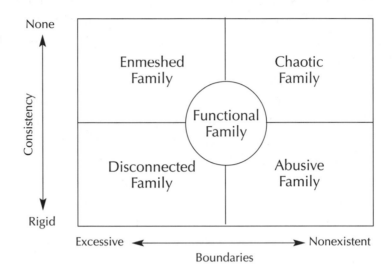

All parents make some decisions that negatively affect their children. The goal of parenting is not to be perfect, but to model as much as possible the four skills of granting unconditional love, setting limits, reasoning, and allowing freedom. In addition, fostering honest emotional communication when there is a problem can help all the individuals involved learn how similar situations can be more effectively handled. It is when dysfunctional patterns are more consistent than functional patterns that problems in development and predisposition to eating disorders and other addictions are likely to arise. The first step in change is understanding the system as it exists: its strengths, weaknesses, unchangeable aspects, and patterns that can respond to therapeutic intervention.

FAMILY MAPPING   Much of eating disorder therapy is actually family therapy, and revolves around teaching families how to incorporate these concepts into their parenting and relationship building. A common technique in family therapy for identifying relationships that need to be addressed is genogram construction (26). In this exercise, a family tree is drawn and personality characteristics are identified for the individual, his or her parents, their parents, and other relatives with a significant influence on family dynamics *(Figure 6.2)*. The purpose of this exercise is twofold. First, it provides a comprehensive understanding of the family system and demonstrates that an individual's behavior is never isolated, but the result of

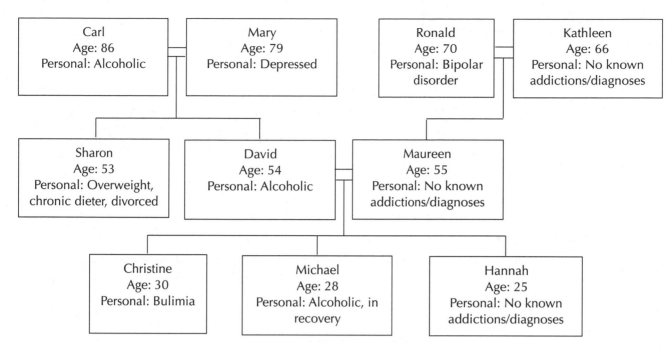

Figure 6.2
Sample Family Genogram

many family interactions. This moves the focus of change from the individual to the family, and illustrates what each individual in the system needs to do to support healthy communication and interaction. Second, it helps illustrate how dysfunctional behaviors are intergenerational. That is, a dysfunctional parent rarely spontaneously behaves dysfunctionally. He or she is more likely to be enacting behaviors that were learned in his or her family of origin, which were derived from parental families of origin, and so on. Achieving this comprehensive understanding of family dysfunction shifts the focus away from blaming one individual to understanding the complexity of dysfunction and discussing problem-solving behaviors the family can enact together to decrease the need for an addiction, such as an eating disorder, to do the communicating.

Family mapping is typically performed in psychotherapy, but a nutrition therapist can map out family food behaviors. Such an exercise can be a powerful way to gain insight into where dieting, cooking, exercise, and dysfunctional food behaviors were modeled and learned. Understanding how behaviors are learned and passed on can make it easier for the client to address behavior change (and why behaviors are difficult to change) more analytically and less emotionally.

An alternative to family mapping is family journaling *(Figure 6.3)*. A nutrition therapist can use this tool to explore family behaviors at the dinner table. Since food and food behaviors are the thought focus in the eating disordered individual, a journaling exercise using this focus can be a first step toward understanding family dynamics. What happens at meals is often a window to what happens in other situations, and can be a springboard into discussions that provide a more

1. *Mealtime as a Child*

    Do you remember mealtime as a child? _____ If you do, draw a picture that depicts your memory. In what room did you eat? Who cooked? Who served? Who cleaned? Who sat where? Was this a time you looked forward to and enjoyed? What topics of conversation were common? Who talked the most?

2. *Mealtime as an Adult*

    Draw a picture that depicts your current mealtime setting. In what room do you eat? Who cooks? Who serves? Who cleans? Who sits where? Is this a time you look forward to and enjoy? What topics of conversation are common? Who talks the most? How does your childhood mealtime influence your mealtime as an adult?

3. How many times a week do you sit at a table and eat dinner? _____

    Is dinner at a regularly scheduled time? _____

    Do different people in your family eat at different times? _____

    How many meals a week do you eat in front of the television? _____

    How many meals a week do you eat in your car? _____

    How many meals a week do you eat in a restaurant? _____

4. Describe a past pleasant family experience with food.

    _____

    _____

    _____

5. Describe a past unpleasant family experience with food.

    _____

    _____

    _____

6. Is there a food you currently regard as a problem food or binge food? _____ What is your childhood memory of this food? Is it related with something positive? Negative? A special event? A person?

Figure 6.3
My Family's Food Personality

complete picture of what happens in the family as a unit. From here, treatment plans can be developed that teach the client how to interact in ways that do not repeat dysfunctional family patterns.

Several concepts must be kept in mind when working with dysfunctional families. First, the initial step into treatment may be the family's first experience with sharing their problems with outsiders. There is likely to be much shame and defensiveness at first, as there may be family members who have been punished or shamed for the behaviors and problems for which they seek help. It is crucial to set judgment aside so that the client can honestly communicate and trust that his words will be heard and validated.

THE TREATMENT TEAM "FAMILY"

Second, one of the most important functions of the treatment team is to work together to model the type of behavior they would like to see adopted by the family that is seeking help. Since dysfunctional families lack an understanding of what functional behavior actually is, they are likely to enact the relationship dynamics that they have been conditioned to use for most of their lives. Enmeshed parents may attempt to find out what happened in therapy without their child's permission. Disconnected parents may be difficult to engage in therapy. Chaotic parents may be defensive and even explosive. Clients may "staff split," or pit staff members against each other, rather than acknowledge a dysfunctional behavior with which they have been confronted.

When dysfunctional individuals first encounter a treatment team that does not model or respond to old dysfunctional behaviors, they are likely to respond negatively to what they experience or to escalate their habitual dysfunctional behavior. Anger is a common response. It is important to understand that anger often masks emotional sensitivity and deflects confrontation in a dysfunctional system. Rather than avoiding or being immobilized by anger, the effective nutrition therapist recognizes that anger is communicating important thoughts and feelings that need further exploration. By acknowledging anger and validating in the angry individual that her feelings are important, the nutrition therapist builds trust and can begin true therapeutic work.

The nutrition therapist is a treatment team member who is especially susceptible to client anger. By virtue of her specialized area of knowledge, she is the most threatening member of the treatment team. To the client, her advice, calculations, and interventions stand to remove any and all coping behaviors and leave the client emotionally vulnerable. To the client who has been neglected, invalidated, or emotionally wounded in previous situations in which she was emotionally vulnerable, the nutrition therapist represents any number of individuals who have hurt him in the past. The nutrition therapist can come to represent a client's parent, grandparent, or any combination of individuals. This phenomenon is known as *transference* (27), as in the process feelings about and responses to a relationship from the past are transferred to a relationship in the present that in some way is similar.

Transference is crucial to identify *(Box 6.5)*. A client's response to healthy limits provides important information about the dynamics that shaped his behavior. Rather than rescue the client from his emotional discomfort, the nutrition therapist should acknowledge the discomfort and help him understand where it comes from. Once the origin of the behavior is identified, the client can learn new ways of coping that allow him to get his needs met without eliciting anger or dysfunctional behaviors.

Client behaviors may also trigger feelings and behaviors in members of the treatment team that represent issues from their past. This phenomenon is known as

**Box 6.5
Transference—
A Personal Note**

My tenure as director of dietary services for an inpatient program was at times stressful. It seemed as though every client who walked in the door came with the expectation that I would be waiting at the front door, basket of fat-free food in hand. They sometimes refused to be assessed by the rest of the treatment team if the nutrition assessment had not been completed. I diligently worked to put together a schedule that allowed all new clients to be seen within 24 hours of admission.

Despite my efforts, clients still complained. After my most detailed, empathic, creative sessions, other members of the treatment team told me that clients reported that I had been "cold," "short," "mean," and many other things that were always a surprise and at times hurtful when I had put forth my best, most compassionate effort.

It wasn't until I learned about the concept of transference that I began to relax about what was happening. I realized that from the client's perspective, I was the person most capable of doing harm. A simple dietary order could strip the client of the last shield of protection. A simple calorie recommendation could put control into my hands. All this was occurring at a point when the client had not yet developed trust.

I began to use transference as a therapeutic tool. Rather than escalate an argument over the amount of fat that was in a meal plan, I tried to be sensitive to any postures or facial expressions that communicated emotions words could not. If I sensed fear or anger, I asked about it in an empathetic fashion: "Wow! I can't imagine what it feels like to put your food choices into the hands of someone you don't even know!"

More often than not, I learned that I symbolized mothers, fathers, uncles, grandmothers, and other authority figures who had exercised their power in a dysfunctional, often abusive fashion. Clients occasionally related that it wasn't me they saw when they looked at me, but someone in their life who had caused them great emotional pain. Often they feared that if they were unable to live up to the (unrealistic) food standards they thought I would enforce, I would hurt them as others had in the past.

Taking the time to process this transference lengthened the initial assessment, but moved my client partnerships forward much more quickly than when I ignored transference and tried to stick to nutritional tasks. Allowing for these feelings to be expressed in a nutrition assessment was one of the most important skills I developed in my work with eating disorders.

countertransference (27). When working with eating disordered individuals, it is important for members of the treatment team to undergo thorough self-evaluations that identify emotions that might be easily triggered by a client's behavior *(Box 6.6)*. Otherwise it may be impossible to model healthy behavior to the family seeking help. Supervision, as discussed in Chapter 16, is the most effective means of receiving feedback and developing skills to ensure that countertransference does not interfere with treatment.

In an effective treatment team, members communicate frequently. This decreases the chances of splitting (clients' pitting treatment team members against each other). As different therapists tend to bring out different facets of a client's personality, communication can also help the team identify where transference and countertransference are occurring and develop interventions that eliminate the resulting behaviors or convert them into therapeutic incidents. Various forms of therapy can be used in the process of eating disorder treatment; these are detailed in Chapter 16. While the actual process of therapy may differ between clinicians, the goal should always be the same—to teach and model healthy family communication and parenting skills the client can take home and substitute for the dysfunctional behaviors that are causing distress.

I know I experience countertransference when:

- I get defensive with a client.
- I become judgmental with a client.
- I feel dread at merely seeing a client's name on my daily schedule.

With much practice and supervision, I have learned to identify these reactions as important signals that part of my personal past is facing me head on.

A countertransference reaction can cause me to predict failure or noncompliance in a client simply because he reminds me of someone who I knew could not adopt functional behaviors. It can cause me to cut a session short because the interaction is making me anxious. It can make me angry. It can leave me feeling exhausted after a session.

Anytime these phenomena appear, I take them to supervision for processing. Sometimes these reactions bring forth an important issue of my own that needs addressing. In the process, a former client almost always comes to mind. When I first began recognizing countertransference, I would think, "If I had just known this then . . . maybe I could have helped that person more effectively. . . ." With time, I have come to realize that no counseling session is ever flawless. The hope is that, at the end, both participants leave with a better understanding of themselves, their challenges, and ways they can become healthier and more functional.

Countertransference never disappears. But as I mature in my profession, what *has* disappeared is the angst over experiencing countertransference. What has appeared in its place is the ability to recognize it as a phenomenon that challenges me to continue to work through my own issues and not grow stagnant in my work. I have come to welcome this as one of the benefits of being a nutrition therapist.

**Box 6.6
Countertransference**

SUMMARY

- Children growing up in dysfunctional families do not develop adequate skills for expressing emotions or for interacting in relationships outside their families. They develop alternative means of communicating, which can often be eating disorders.

- Eating disordered individuals commonly come from four types of dysfunctional families: enmeshed, disconnected, chaotic, and abusive.

- An individual's experiences with food during her childhood (with her family of origin) can have a great impact on her behaviors with food as an adult.

- Clients seeking treatment for eating disorders may have little to no experience with a healthy support system. A healthy treatment team models the behavior of a functional family and is comfortable with emotions (including anger) that are likely to surface during the learning process of therapy.

REFERENCES

1. Minuchin S. *Families and Family Therapy*. Cambridge, Mass: Harvard University Press; 1974.

2. Hoffman L. *Foundations of Family Therapy: A Conceptual Framework for Systems Change*. New York: Basic Books; 1981.

3. Hartman A, Laird J. *Family-Centered Social Work Practice*. New York: The Free Press; 1983.

4. Paci A, Zappia V, Riciardi L, Bertini M, Zoppi C. Anorexia in the first year of life: case contribution. *Pediatr Med Chir*. 1988;10(1):63–72.

5. Birch LL, Fisher JA. Appetite and eating behavior in children. *Pediatr Clin North Am*. 1995;42(4):931–953.

6. Johnson SL, Birch LL. Parents' and children's adiposity and eating style. *Pediatrics*. 1994;94(5):653–661.

7. Leung AK, Robson WL. The toddler who does not eat. *Am Fam Physician*. 1994;49(8):1789–1792,1799–1800.

8. Jackson-Walker SM. The implications of separation-individuation difficulties and parent eating preoccupation for disordered eating in late adolescent women. *Dissertation Abstracts Int*. 1995;56–10B:182.

9. Pirke KM, Rodin J. Mothers, daughters, and disordered eating. *J Abnorm Psychol*. 1991;100(2):198–204.

10. Walther DL. The relationship between perceived family interactional patterns and symptoms of eating disorders, compared with symptoms of depression. *Dissertation Abstracts Int*. 1994;55–11B:5090.

11. Scourfield J. Anorexia by proxy: are the children of anorexic mothers an at-risk group? *Int J Eat Disord*. 1995;18(4):371–374.

12. Evans J, le Grange D. Body size and parenting in eating disorders: a comparative study of the attitudes of mothers towards their children. *Int J Eat Disord*. 1995;18(1):39–48.

13. Stein A, Woolley H, Cooper SD, Fairburn CG. An observational study of mothers with eating disorders and their infants. *J Child Psychol Psychiatry*. 1994;35(4): 733–748.

14. Burns K, Chethik L, Burns WJ, Clark R. Dyadic disturbances in cocaine-abusing mothers and their infants. *J Clin Psychol.* 1991;47(2):316–319.
15. Dahlman K. Affective capacity in mothers of eating disordered patients. *Dissertation Abstracts Int.* 1995;56–09B:5163.
16. Kneisl CR. Healing the wounded, neglected inner child of the past. *Nurs Clin North Am.* 1991;26(3):745–755.
17. O'Loughlin MA. The relationship of assertiveness and bulimia to psychological separation. *Dissertation Abstracts Int.* 1995;56–08B:4590.
18. Thienemann M, Steiner H. Family environment of eating disordered and depressed adolescents. *Int J Eat Disord.* 1993;4(1):43–48.
19. van der Kilk BA, Fisler RE. Childhood abuse and neglect and loss of self-regulation. *Bull Meninger Clin.* 1994;58(2):145–168.
20. Welch LA. Internalizing and externalizing psychopathology and personality in parents and their adolescent offspring. *Dissertation Abstracts Int.* 1995;56–10B:5818.
21. Kroll J. *PTSD/Borderlines in Therapy: Finding the Balance.* New York: WW Norton; 1993.
22. Bemporad JR, Beresin E, Ratey JJ, O'Driscoll G, Lindem K, Herzog DB. A psychoanalytic study of eating disorders. I. A developmental profile of 67 index cases. *J Am Acad Psychoanal.* 1992;20(4):509–531.
23. Chandy JM, Harris L, Blum RW, Resnick MD. Disordered eating among adolescents whose parents misuse alcohol: protective and risk factors. *Int J Addict.* 1994;29(4):505–516.
24. Chandy JM, Harris L, Blum RW, Resnick MD. Female adolescents of alcohol misusers: disordered eating features. *Int J Eat Disord.* 1995;17(3):283–289.
25. Yeomans FE, Selzer MA, Clarkin JF. *Treating the Borderline Patient: A Contract-Based Approach.* New York: Basic Books; 1992.
26. McGoldrick M, Gerson R. *Genograms in Family Assessment.* New York: WW Norton; 1985.
27. Kroll J. *The Challenge of the Borderline Patient.* New York: WW Norton; 1988.

CHAPTER 7

Sexual Abuse, Dissociative Disorders, and the Eating Disorders: Nutrition Therapy as a Healing Tool

KARIN M. KRATINA, M.A., R.D.

Nutrition therapists increasingly find themselves involved with clients who are concurrently being treated for sexual abuse issues. The Rader Center reports that approximately 85% of its inpatient clients report a history of some type of sexual assault (1); this figure has been confirmed by other inpatient treatment centers as well (2,3), and in the research literature (4–14). Unfortunately, most helping professionals, including nutrition therapists, receive little training in general or sexual abuse issues. These topics are rarely covered in school and require knowledge beyond that found in most professional training books.

The prevalence of sexual abuse history coexisting with eating problems mandates that part of the healing process involves understanding that these problems may be related to the abuse history. Nutrition therapists who can assist psychotherapists in moving abuse survivors through food- and weight-related issues need to be available to clients with sexual abuse histories that affect their relationship with food.

The purpose of this chapter is to provide information to nutrition therapists who are likely to encounter clients who have been sexually abused. While this chapter will shed light on food- and weight-related issues as they are experienced by the abuse survivor, as well as the treatment of those issues, it is important to note that there is disagreement in the field about the most effective methods of treatment for abuse victims. This chapter is designed to introduce nutrition therapists to an area of work that, while extremely difficult and demanding, is also highly rewarding.

Not everyone is suited for working with the sexually traumatized. A prerequisite for working with these clients is the ability to deal with one's own emotional reactions to the trauma of others. A level of comfort about sex in general is also necessary; uneasiness about human sexuality would exacerbate the professional's emotional reactions to the abuse. Nutrition therapists must avoid minimizing or discounting sexual abuse allegations or reacting with rage at the perpetrator. These responses can interfere with the clinician's ability to help clients.

While many clients choose not to discuss abuse with the nutrition therapist (and it would be inappropriate for the nutrition therapist to engage in extended conversations about the abuse), abuse issues often arise in the course of discussing food issues. The nutrition therapist must be able to recognize concerns, address the issues with the client, and discuss them with the psychotherapist and in supervision.

Sexual abuse has been documented in the literature since ancient times (16), but only recently has the public begun to recognize the prevalence of such abuse. The Child Abuse Prevention and Treatment Act, passed by Congress in 1973, provided for a National Center on Child Abuse and Neglect to promote research, conferences, and dissemination of information on the topic. The resulting accumulation of data has created an awareness of a phenomenon that was previously not openly discussed.

There are many reasons why sexual abuse was ignored or even condoned for so long. It is a situation most would rather not know about. In fact, sexual trauma has been called a syndrome of simultaneously "knowing and not knowing" (17). Sexual abuse, especially the abuse of children, is so terrible many do not want to discuss it (18). This creates a psychic pressure "not to know," which can lead to partial or complete repression by both victim and perpetrator. This resistance to knowing exists not only in those who have been abused, but also in professionals and in the public as a whole. Why is it that so many know yet also "don't know"? One suggestion is that recognition of the high incidence of sexual abuse challenges one's perceptions of the world (17,19). To maintain their perceptions, clinicians and researchers develop blind spots that occlude their ability to know. It is important to recognize that sexual abuse exists and to talk openly about the phenomenon. Breaking this cultural taboo is the first step toward transforming gender relations.

Recent allegations of false memory syndrome have further muddled the picture. The False Memory Syndrome Foundation (FMSF) of Philadelphia coined the term "false memory syndrome" (FMS). Overzealous therapists can cause their clients to access memories they may not have the coping skills to safely tolerate. Increased distortion of past events is also a risk, as is "remembering" trauma that never occurred. Memories are never completely factual; they are reassimilated over time and influenced by a child's perception (eg, "I caused it," "I thought I was being killed," or "I wanted to be special"). However, this does not necessarily mean that the person was not abused. On the contrary, the developmental distortions

RECOGNITION OF SEXUAL ABUSE

and the "concreteness of children's thinking" often make abuse more injurious because of the child's developmental limitations (19).

Even women who have not been sexually assaulted can suffer the signs and symptoms seen in abuse victims. In Western culture, learning to diet and living in fear of food can create a hatred of one's body and oneself, ie, can create a belief structure similar to that seen in a sexual abuse victim (1). This belief structure admonishes a woman

- not to like herself but, instead to see herself as inadequate and shameful;
- not to trust herself or her thoughts, memories, emotions, or symptoms;
- not to give a full, curious, and empathic hearing to her symptoms, but to eradicate them, sometimes by any means necessary; and
- not to dignify her pain by knowing her whole story.

THE NUTRITION THERAPIST'S ROLE

The nutrition therapist can play a pivotal role in the identification and treatment of sexual abuse victims since she is often sought out as the expert in food- and weight-related issues, areas in which abuse survivors typically feel a great deal of pain. Nutrition therapists who counsel chronic dieters, eating disordered individuals, and clients with mental health concerns need to realize they may be treating individuals who have been abused.

Dietetic training, traditionally based on the medical model (eg, externally regulated eating and weight loss) can effectively mask the symptoms and foster or reinforce dissociation from the body. In other words, traditional nutrition counseling can promote ignorance of the past. Addressing sexual abuse issues has traditionally been considered beyond the scope of our practice, and much of it is. However, it is important that nutrition therapists be well informed about their roles and responsibilities in responding to and treating survivors of abuse. If nutrition therapists are familiar with the appropriate and inappropriate responses before encountering victims of sexual abuse, they are more likely to respond in a therapeutic manner. Appropriate responses include

- creating a safe environment for the client to begin to understand his relationship with his body and food,
- reacting positively toward victims to prevent further trauma,
- reporting and processing any disclosures with the survivor's therapist if he is in therapy, and
- working collaboratively with other professionals to enhance treatment.

The nutrition therapist must make sure the client is in therapy with a qualified psychotherapist who is experienced in working with both sexual abuse and eating disorders. *If the client is not in therapy, the goal must be to direct her toward an appropriate therapist.* The nutrition therapist should know several local therapists who treat individuals with sexual abuse and dissociative disorders. To make an appropriate referral, the nutrition therapist should interview psychotherapists to determine their treatment philosophy, familiarity with eating disorders, the types of clients they prefer to work with, and their willingness to work collaboratively with a nutrition therapist. In addition, the nutrition therapist

- does not encourage the client to discuss past abuse in nutrition therapy sessions. If a client begins to discuss abuse, the nutrition therapist should listen empathically without judgment and be aware of her own reactions. When appropriate, the nutrition therapist may link abuse with the client's current relationship with food.

- does not mention under *any* circumstances to a client with no memories of abuse that difficulty with food may be due to past, as yet undetected trauma.

- provides food- and weight-related guidance *without structured guidelines* (20). While certain clients benefit from structure around food, many do not, and the problem can be exacerbated when structure is provided. When an individual requests rules for eating, the nutrition therapist needs to be aware that the request may actually have nothing to do with eating. The client may not feel safe addressing the issues at hand, and getting back to basics with structured eating guidelines may be easier. It may be a way of expressing disappointment in nutrition therapy, of saying that something is not working or he needs or wants something else from the nutrition therapist. The client may feel frightened; if the nutrition therapist's ideas about how to eat are not working, how good can the nutrition therapist be? The client may be angry or want to be rescued.

- explores symptoms in a respectful manner and gradually introduces healthier eating patterns while helping the client to compensate for the damage caused by the symptoms.

- understands that as the impulse to starve or binge is explored, painful memories may be exposed and symptoms may worsen. The psychotherapist may request that no changes be made in a client's food for a period of time since the eating disordered behavior may provide structure to a life that otherwise feels chaotic and out of control. The nutrition therapist must be able to work with the psychotherapist's requests and, if there is disagreement, discuss it with the psychotherapist . . . not the client.

THE IMPACT OF SEXUAL ABUSE

Much of the psychological trauma that arises from sexual abuse results from the betrayal of the child's trust by an adult, often a primary caregiver (4). This betrayal undermines the child's ability to trust not only the perpetrator, but other adults as well, and is compounded if other caregivers respond in an unsupportive manner. Typically children do not understand what is happening to them and cannot successfully fight back. Eventually they feel that they are inherently bad and deserve the abuse. Occasionally a child is able to figure out ways to not feel. *Dissociation*, one such "escape," is a highly creative and, paradoxically, adaptive way to both hide from and know the truth of one's experience. It allows a child who is being hurt to escape mentally. The body is hurt, but the child no longer feels it because her mind escapes to a safe place (1).

Dissociation allows escape by focusing intense attention elsewhere, away from the abuse, reducing awareness of the trauma. Commonly referred to as "zoning out" or "spacing out," it is an effective means of dealing with the hurt so the person can survive. Initially dissociation does numb the pain, but the pain is still present while the memory as well as the feelings and sensations associated with the abuse are locked away in the body, temporarily "forgotten," basically protected through dissociation. The result is what Costin (3) calls an "executive self" who functions as if no violation had occurred, keeps the family's secret, and acts as if all were well, and concurrently an "eating-disordered self" who stores the truth of the abuse and whose self-development is severely inhibited. It is typical for a survivor to present in therapy both as a capable, organized, highly functioning adult as well as a child stuck in time, disorganized, and incapable of running his life (21). According to Costin, food behaviors can also serve as a way to numb traumatic memories, to maintain physical symptoms to focus on, to reenact pain, and to self-soothe (3).

THE CONNECTION BETWEEN SEXUAL ABUSE AND EATING PROBLEMS

In their efforts to understand and cope with the abuse, many victims attribute the abuse to their physical appearance and feel ashamed of the role they believe it played in the abuse. There may be no conscious awareness of the connection between having been abused and experiencing the body as deficient. Our culture's messages that the body must be changed to be acceptable contribute to the body loathing experienced by the victims. Likewise, women who attribute sexual abuse to being too attractive may starve or overeat to change their body size as an unconscious strategy to defend against further victimization (22).

Those who have been abused may feel a loss of control over their bodies and their lives. This is significant because issues of control are known to contribute to the development of eating disorders. In an attempt to regain the lost sense of control, the eating disordered individual renounces needs, effectively isolating herself. Initially these efforts are effective, but over time they cease to work. The resultant hopelessness then may be displaced into food- and weight-related concerns. For example, the denial of the need to eat may be a metaphor for the denial of the need for any other person because the victim has learned through the abuse that others can be dangerous.

An eating disorder may serve to arrest psychosexual maturity, which, from the perspective of a victim of sexual abuse, can be a desirable outcome. Avoidance of normal weight, secondary sexual characteristics, and menstruation may be used by the survivor of abuse as a means of avoiding sexual contact and feelings, as well as other physiological reminders of abuse. Avoiding any sensory pleasure (food is a highly sensory experience) may enable the client to avoid uncomfortable feelings and memories.

Reestablishing safety and control becomes associated with consuming only "good foods" and avoiding "bad foods." Eventually foods may even be categorized as "safe" and "unsafe." An individual may categorize foods for a variety of reasons. The most obvious basis for categorization is the caloric or fat content of the food; the more calories or fat, the more "bad" or "unsafe" the food. If a client fears that a food has caused a binge or he feels out of control when consuming it, that food is regarded as bad or unsafe, as are the foods typically consumed in a binge.

Some experts have recommended that such terms as "good", "bad", "legal", and "illegal" be eliminated in relationship to food (23,24). Nutrition therapists can assist clients with this process, using terms such as "supportive" or "unsupportive" to categorize food.

FOOD AVERSIONS AND THEIR RELATIONSHIP TO SEXUAL TRAUMA

Individuals between 6 and 12 years of age are most susceptible to the development of food aversions, and girls are more prone than boys. Such aversions develop for a variety of reasons. Under normal circumstances, the most common reason is past gastrointestinal upset. Foods associated with this upset are correlated with physical discomfort and are often subsequently rejected (25). Food aversions can also develop when a person has been forced to eat certain foods. Finally, they can develop in those who have been sexually abused and often appear to be related to the abuse. Such an aversion can develop after even one pairing of the food with the aversive event. Physiological consequences of stress resulting from the abuse (eg, upset stomach) can become linked with other aspects of the abuse (eg, food that was used to lure the victim or keep him quiet). Possible interpretations of some common food aversions are provided in *Box 7.1*. These illustrate the important meanings food aversions can have. They should not be used to categorize or interpret such aversions.

Food aversions are difficult to extinguish. They cannot be reasoned away, possibly because their development is a survival mechanism in all animals, including humans. For instance, an animal might develop aversion if it experienced a negative reaction after consuming a poisonous food, resulting in its rejecting that food in the future. In the case of sexual abuse, the aversion is related to an indirect influence of the food on the event. While avoiding a food that is poisonous can be directly related to future survival, avoiding a food that is associated with sexual abuse does not address the true source of the trauma.

Food aversions can also develop when the abuse doesn't specifically coincide with the food or meals. After an aversion develops to a specific food, the aversion can be generalized to other foods with similar sensory properties. For example, the first client described in *Box 7.2*, who could not eat turkey, generalized this aversion to other white meats and eventually to all meats. Survivors can also generalize

**Box 7.1
Sample Interpretations
of Food Behaviors**

Self-Soothing/Anxiety Management

- Eating soothes sadness that otherwise would be too much for the client to bear.
- Having been told crying would bring punishment, the client needs eating to relieve sadness or pain.
- Having revealed a secret in the last session and fearing she will be punished as promised by her abuser, the client eats to allay anxiety.
- Eating soothes the client's overwhelming feeling of generalized shame.
- Starving provides a feeling of control over a fear of toxic self-nurturing.

Self-Abuse

- The client hates herself after eating, an emotion that can reenact the sadistic-masochistic relationship between her and her abuser.
- The client attempts to validate the belief that she caused all her pain by punishing herself with bingeing, purging, or starving.
- The client reenacts earlier deprivation of food intake related to the sexual assault as a form of retraumatization.
- The client squelches her desire for food or love to avoid disappointment. In addition, eating provides a reason for self-beratement.

Expression of an Aversion

- Eating chocolate can cover abusive associations with other tastes (eg, beer), although the client may see herself only as a chocoholic.
- Eating (or not eating) can transform the client's body size from that of the abused body to a size that does not remind her of the abuse.
- It is often easier for the client to talk about how she hates her body than it is to talk about how she hates her abuser.

---

aspects of abuse (eg, sexual organs) to foods with similar properties, such as phallic-shaped foods (bananas or hot dogs). One client was able to eat these foods when they were served cut up but not when they were served in whole. Foods that resemble sexual fluids (eg, cottage cheese and yogurt) can also be aversive.

Eating as It Parallels the Sexual Act

Few objects besides food and sex organs enter the human body. The loss of control over what happens outside the body as well as what enters the body is significant and seems to contribute to the pairing of food with sexual abuse. If abusers cannot be controlled, food can. Or at least our culture provides the illusion that food can be controlled. Refusing food becomes a powerful way to regain a sense of control over the body and the world that the abuser took away. For the survivor, the body both hides and expresses the secrets of what has happened to her.

How Abuse Influences Eating Behavior and Body Image

A child who dissociates and "forgets" an abusive event is often left with behavioral or somatic symptoms. Those who have been abused develop eating problems and body image distortions for many reasons, including family dynamics and intrapsychic adaptations (1).

Box 7.2
CASE STUDY:
Separating Food
from Feelings

Jeri sought treatment for anorexia. She reported having intense food aversions to "seafood, chicken, bananas, or anything whole." She liked these foods, but felt that eating them was "bad, wrong, and unthinkable." She explained that she had difficulty with the texture of most proteins, that they were chewy and "just not appealing." She described one incident when she attempted to eat a shrimp but ended up vomiting it, explaining she felt it "was dirty." Her difficulty with eating bananas had to do with her fear that they "are indigestible because they are too solid and bulky." Jeri's strongest food aversion was to protein, specifically chicken. She reported that she both disliked chicken and found it "okay."

The nutrition therapist noted that Jeri carefully avoided the words "I like chicken" and challenged her ambivalence by asking her to say, "I like chicken." The issue was referred to her psychotherapist. When Jeri finally said the words, she began to shudder and cry. Later, long-repressed memories of being sexually abused as a child began to surface. Her attitudes and feelings about certain foods as "dirty," "bad," "long," and "bulky" became more understandable when the foods were viewed as reminders of her abuse. In avoiding the foods to which she had aversions, Jeri was able to avoid the memories of being abused.

Victims of abuse frequently had poor experiences around feeding and did not learn how to respond appropriately to hunger and satiety signals. Often destructive family dynamics were played out at the dining room table. Women sometimes connect being starved or fed with abuse. Food is often used as a reward or punishment; in the abusive home it is often linked directly to the trauma *(Box 7.3)*.

Box 7.3
How Abuse Can Create
Food Aversions

Certain factors facilitate the pairing of food aversions and sexual abuse. Two common examples are the timing of the aversive event and the use of food as a reward.

Timing. If the timing of an aversive event coincides with meals or with eating, the likelihood of an aversion is increased. Often difficulty with food can be traced to abuse that occurred at or near dinnertime.

Maureen was sexually assaulted by her father during Thanksgiving dinner. As she sat staring at her helping of turkey, her father fondled her underneath the table. Meanwhile, he and her mother scolded her for refusing to eat her dinner. Memories of this event continue to make it difficult for her to eat, particularly turkey and other Thanksgiving foods.

Food as a Reward. Frequently children are given "treats" as inducements to engage in sexual activity or as bribes to keep them quiet.

Julie's uncle often took her to an out-of-the-way bench in the park. He placed her on his lap, and initially she enjoyed the attention. After a few visits he began to push her body back and forth on his lap. Although Julie did not understand what was happening, she was uncomfortable and tried unsuccessfully to get away. Her uncle held her while he masturbated, and told her that if she would quit crying, he would get her some ice cream. Eventually she sat in stony silence while he masturbated, but she continued to receive ice cream as a reward.

An abusive male relative may shame a growing girl's body. Unconsciously obsessed with the victim's sexually maturing body, the relative may project his own feelings of temptation and longing onto her. Victims are often told that they "asked for it." The victim can eventually internalize this "badness" and act accordingly. The result is a woman who actively devalues herself in a hostile manner. Her body image suffers in the process.

The sexually abused child sometimes unconsciously decides that her body and sex organs are "bad" to maintain the belief that her caregivers are "good". Her body becomes a source of shame, and she believes she deserves punishment. Altering eating patterns to influence body size can arrest sexual development, decrease the probability of sexual abuse, and minimize the need to deal with sexual urges or the inability to say "No." For another victim, making the body as attractive as possible might be the only way to escape being alone, since her body "is the only reason a man would be interested in her" (17).

BASIC PRINCIPLES IN NUTRITION THERAPY FOR THE TREATMENT OF SEXUAL ABUSE

It is important to understand that eating disorder symptoms fill a strong need for the client. The treatment team must communicate respect and empathy for that need, and model acceptance of the whole person, including the eating disorder. This creates an environment in which the client can identify and explore the confounding issues. The therapeutic process focuses on the meaning of the symptom while also addressing ways to contain the symptom and alternative coping strategies. The symptoms must then be linked to the client's history, including the abuse. The treatment team must generally hold a "position of belief" when working with survivors. However, since memories are not always accurate, it is the trauma in general that must be accepted. The team's stance becomes the opposite of the perpetrator's, conveying that "knowing the truth is both deeply courageous and the authentic way to secure safety" (1).

If a history of sexual abuse is disclosed, it is essential that the nutrition therapist work with a team of specialists. A client may have come to nutrition therapy hoping that focusing on her weight and eating would allow her to avoid painful memories. She may even have started psychotherapy and then quit when sessions moved closer to topics that were too threatening. Nutrition therapy is an essential component of eating disorder treatment, but it can never replace sexual abuse therapy. A nutrition therapist who works with sexually abused clients needs to maintain strong boundaries and keep clients focused on nutrition while redirecting them to other team members for discussions of the abuse (Box 7.4).

Several basic steps are important in the treatment of trauma victims: establishing safety, remembering and mourning the abuse, and reconnecting with real life (26). Because abuse is associated with disempowerment and disconnection from others, recovery must involve empowerment and development of new relationships.

The client must be treated with respect, and therapy boundaries must be honored. The client must not be emotionally overloaded with memory work (27). Until

> When a client discloses trauma, it is important to encourage her to take such disclosures to the team member most qualified to process them. Conversations regarding trauma should be empathically and carefully redirected to the client's relationship with food and body. Appropriate responses to redirect a client disclosing trauma include
>
> - "That must have been very hard for you."
> - "It's obvious to me that your relationship with food helped you to survive."
> - "Are you discussing this with your psychotherapist?"
> - "It seems that this abuse affects your current relationship with food in that . . . "
>
> It is important to ask your client if she has shared these topics with her psychotherapist. If she answers yes, inquire briefly into their work (although you should be aware of this through regular discussions with the psychotherapist) and then redirect to food- and weight-related issues. If she answers no, inquire as to why not. If she forgot to tell the psychotherapist or had just remembered the abuse, make sure she intends to process the information with the psychotherapist.
>
> If the client doesn't trust the psychotherapist or says, "You understand me better," *be very careful.* It may be that the psychotherapist truly does not understand the issues at hand, but more likely the client is *splitting*, or pitting treatment team members against each other to avoid confronting her issues. Redirect the client to the psychotherapist and *do not* let the client continue to split.
>
> Clients often say they prefer sessions with the nutrition therapist over the psychotherapist. It is critical that the nutrition therapist realize that the psychotherapist is typically discussing issues with the client that can make the client very uncomfortable. Unfortunately, nutrition therapists, in an attempt to be compassionate with and supportive of clients, often risk engaging in enabling behavior. This is fairly common when the nutrition therapist has had minimal supervision. The importance of maintaining strong boundaries and receiving supervision cannot be overemphasized.

Box 7.4
Redirecting the Client to the Psychotherapist

recently, the emphasis in trauma theory had been on the importance of a client's knowing the basic outlines of her story (1). However, overemphasis on remembering can cause unnecessary retraumatization. Clients differ markedly in how much memory is required for healing. It is possible to work through eating disordered symptoms and achieve a significant level of functioning with no memories of abuse.

The treatment team must guide the client to a sense of mastery in life and must not collude with the client's sense that she lacks control of her symptoms (such as by providing a meal plan or assisting in her weight loss.) It is important to help the client make the connection between her eating disordered symptoms and the feelings, thoughts, and memories related to abuse. Connection facilitates the process of client empowerment.

Dieting and the Trauma Survivor

The diet mentality—the belief that one ought to diet, ought to restrict, ought to be on a food plan, ought not to trust one's self as an eater, and instead ought to find a good diet program or plan and adhere to it—parallels the effects of trauma and/or abuse. Chronic dieting, bypassing hunger, creates an internal environment of deprivation and a lack of safety. It also creates the notion that fears, needs, and desires will not be accepted and that self-soothing cannot be achieved. Chronically bypassing hunger disorganizes and assaults body-self integration, and over time teaches and reinforces a pattern of body-self distortion.

Removing the food labels of "good" and "bad" taught by the world of dieting is indispensable to learning to eat with and respond to body hunger and satiation, as well as to letting go of compulsive emotional eating or starving. As long as some foods remain forbidden and "dangerous", those will be the same foods that are regarded as able to change painful internal self-states *(Box 7.5)*. Often those who move away from diets and adopt a nondiet lifestyle eventually choose to eat lower-fat diets. This is *very* different from eating low-fat because one was told to do so. One course is internally directed, the other externally directed.

Box 7.5
Decoding Food Behavior

As primitive defense structures, food preferences and aversions can contain a significant amount of information regarding abuse history. Their importance must be appreciated. For example, an anorexic with a very quiet, childlike voice might consume large amounts of strong condiments, such as mustard. Mustard is low in calories (small), but it has a very strong taste (voice). It could serve as a substitute for the difficulty the client has in raising her voice. Purging and restricting can be about ejecting abuse experiences and purifying the body. They can also be attempts to get rid of feelings such as anger.

Eating disordered behaviors can also be a traumatic reenactment of past abuse. Bingeing on dry crackers, which can scratch the throat, can be seen as self-abuse. Maria, a binge eater who ate fifteen to twenty apples each day and experienced gastrointestinal upset as a result, said she did so because they were low in calories and would help her maintain her weight. Eventually it was discovered that she really ate the apples to create gastric upset, and therefore to distract herself from feelings that caused her pain and discomfort.

Survivors of sexual abuse can unconsciously attribute to food and their bodies a variety of meanings. Food and the body can be "containers" for the projection of hating or dangerous thoughts and feelings.

The Nondiet
Approach

For the survivor of sexual abuse, learning to trust food desires has special meaning. However, becoming attuned to the body and its nutritional needs is not easy. The victim of abuse has learned to ignore, repress, and dissociate from her bodily desires *(Box 7.6)*. Therefore, it may be difficult for her to decide exactly what foods will satisfy her hunger. One of the biggest challenges in this work is helping clients learn to know and experience their bodies and nutritional needs as real without reinforcing a diet mentality. Psychotherapists and nutrition therapists need to use nutritional information in a nurturing way. This takes time, effort, and creativity, and is a very individualized process.

In work with survivors, nutritional knowledge frequently becomes irrelevant. The nondiet approach is particularly useful with this population. It encourages

Box 7.6
CASE STUDY:
What Is the Client
Really Saying?

Cheryl sought inpatient treatment for bulimia. She had been sexually abused as a child and raped as a young adult. She joined an eating disorder group, and had intense emotional reactions to issues discussed in the group, making such demeaning remarks as, "This is stupid. I hate talking about food and what people eat." When her reactions were analyzed, Cheryl admitted that talking about food stirred up feelings of anxiety, as well as urges to vomit and purge. She indicated that she often became dissociative whenever she discussed eating issues.

During one session, Cheryl reported having trouble breathing and heightened anxiety. She was reluctant to discuss this, but appeared agitated and angry. Soon her anger and anxiety gave way to expressions of sadness and pain. Cheryl began to connect her difficulty with discussing foods and eating to sexual abuse. Eating certain foods, as well as talking about eating, stirred up memories of forced fellatio. She felt that the abuse was contained in her body, and identified her accompanying urge to vomit with an attempt to get rid of the abuse. She realized she avoided discussing eating because she feared recalling the abuse. She also avoided foods to avoid the pain associated with the abuse.

- total health enhancement and well-being, rather than weight loss or achievement of a specific "ideal weight,"
- self-acceptance and respect for the diversity of healthy, beautiful bodies, rather than the pursuit of an idealized weight at all cost,
- the pleasure of eating well, based on internal cues of hunger and satiety, rather than on external food plans or diets, and
- the joy of movement, encouraging all physical activities, rather than prescribing a specific routine of regimented exercise (28).

This approach moves the focus of control from the cognitive (a diet or a meal pattern) to the body's internal messages. Clients learn to

- determine when to eat by listening to internal signals of hunger,
- determine how much food is needed by listening to the body's signals of satiety and fullness,
- discern when a food is wanted for reasons other than physical hunger and determine the desired course of action, and
- temper the above with a relaxed interpretation of what science tells us is best for our health.

The reader is referred to the reading list at the end of this book for sources on this approach.

When people eat according to their hunger and satiation, they eventually reach a size that is within their natural weight range. This may or may not conform to the size they consider their ideal. However, the process of eating in response to hunger is often so gratifying that most people find greatly increased physical and psychological comfort in their body, whatever its size. The ability to accept oneself at any size means that a profound shift has occurred. The body has become a safe place.

The Importance of Detailed Inquiry

Since compulsive eating, food restriction, and a distorted body image are among the most important avenues of expression for survivors of abuse, the nutrition therapist must carefully examine eating and body image distortion incidents and know what issues should be referred to a psychotherapist specializing in eating disorders.

Each time the psychotherapist and nutrition therapist ask the client about his eating disordered behavior, there is a new opportunity to find out what happened in terms of the trauma and its effects. Eating and body image are avenues of non-verbal expression that arise when verbal disclosure is prohibited. A trauma survivor must not ignore his attempts to express himself in relation to food or body image. The nutrition therapist must be willing to discuss the food- and weight-related behavior and not avoid it so as to enable the client to see what happened to him and what his responses have been. This must happen over and over again until the client has integrated this new way of thinking about and responding to past and present events.

DISSOCIATION AND DISSOCIATIVE IDENTITY DISORDER

Nutrition therapists may encounter clients who dissociate and who have diagnosable dissociative disorders. This is especially likely if they work with eating disordered clients, particularly those who have been sexually abused. In fact, eating disorders may be among the presenting symptoms of dissociation (29). Dissociation is common in these clients.

Dissociation occurs along a range, from mild to extreme. It can involve such ordinary activities as daydreaming or getting lost in an absorbing book, exciting movie, or good music. Daily activities that involve automatic functioning, such as taking a long drive in a car or working on the computer, can become dissociative. Most people have experienced taking a long trip and suddenly realizing they cannot remember the last several miles. Some individuals have a greater capacity to dissociate and may present as "absent-minded professor" types who get lost in the creative process. More pronounced but still within the normal range are certain reactions to traumatic situations, such as forgetting details of a car accident. Dissociation can be used to escape reality; for instance, a child might get lost in video games to escape the chaos of a dysfunctional family (30).

More acute dissociative disorders include somnambulism (sleepwalking), hysterical blindness or paralysis, derealization (not feeling or experiencing one's body), and amnesia. Eating disorders are found at this end of the range. Dissociative identity disorder (DID), previously termed multiple personality disorder (MPD), and similar dissociative disorders are the extreme result of chronic dissociation.

Frequent dissociation causes great panic, sadness, suffering, and even danger. Clients with this disorder interpret current events as if they were as threatening as the original abuse that might have been the impetus for the condition. Individuals who dissociate can function surprisingly well, often holding complex jobs quite successfully. Unfortunately, there are also significant periods of decompensation (loss of ability to appropriately perform basic activities of daily living), which require intensive care (31).

Individuals who dissociate are often secretive. Nutrition therapists should report symptoms of dissociation to the psychotherapist or refer the client to a psychotherapist experienced in evaluating and treating this condition.

Nutrition Therapy and Dissociation

While the specific treatments of DID are debated, there is agreement that treatment must be individualized. Kluft (26) has assembled general principles for the successful treatment of dissociative clients. Several of the principles that are pertinent to nutrition therapy are outlined below.

Maintain Firm Boundaries

Dissociation is a condition that originates in broken boundaries. Had the client not been overwhelmed during childhood, a dissociative defense would not have developed. Therefore, successful treatment requires a secure treatment frame and firm, consistent boundaries. It is quite common for the therapist to become fascinated by the dissociative client, as well as overwhelmed by her pain and apparent neediness. This can result in boundary violations that will ultimately complicate and prolong treatment. The client needs the nutrition therapist to be a consistent, compassionate, and considerate person who safeguards the treatment settings and remains in the role of the therapist. To break the ground rules of therapy is to recapitulate the boundary violations of the client's childhood and to demonstrate that the nutrition therapist is corruptible rather than reliable. Insufficient limit setting often occurs at the beginning of treatment because these clients are so interested in eating. It is easy to spot this in hindsight, but not so easy when the client is hurting badly and in crisis. While it may be difficult to look at and accept criticism of insufficient limit setting, it is important to know that the client, on some level, will feel stifled by the nutrition therapist's overinvolvement and will be relieved when healthy limits are set and maintained.

Focus on Mastery and the Client's Active Participation.

Dissociative clients often feel out of control as a result of the unavoidable, unwanted experiences they endured. This is one reason providing a client with a diet can be counterproductive. The nutrition therapist's goal is to move a client to internally regulated eating. As an adult, the dissociative client often feels helpless in the face of his symptoms. He comes to feel that his locus of control is external. Therapy must include the development of active problem-solving skills and the recognition of the difference between physical hunger and emotions. In addition, developing a battery of appropriate communication, conflict resolution, and coping skills to address the variety of situations that arise in the course of the day allows the client to develop a sense of power and effectiveness that reduces the need for food behaviors to be used as an expressional outlet. Any time the client is not taking an increasingly active role in the therapeutic process, the situation should be closely scrutinized.

Establish and Maintain a Strong, Therapeutic Alliance

Without a strong therapeutic alliance in which the dissociative client is actively involved, the nutrition therapist will find it difficult to confront the client who is resistant or noncompliant. Nutrition therapists and psychotherapists typically ask how their clients feel about pursuing a specific subject. Often it is useful to ask the client's permission to approach a particular task.

A client who is in a good therapeutic alliance but not prospering in treatment may be working to please or appease the nutrition therapist. She may be experiencing the therapeutic work as something to be endured to obtain the nutrition therapist's care, rather than seeing that it has value in and of itself. Such clients need help understanding the true nature of the therapy.

A Note of Caution

The dissociative client will test and retest the nutrition therapist. Though this can happen with all members of the multidisciplinary team, this interaction can be especially intense when it occurs between the client and the nutrition therapist. The nutrition therapist is the individual who specializes in food and weight issues, and therefore can become an easy scapegoat when the client is working through emotionally charged issues. Food is more tangible and concrete than those issues. The client may prefer to escape to the office of the nutrition therapist and focus on food when topics such as sexual abuse, which the psychotherapist is addressing, come to feel frightening and unsafe (*Box 7.7*). Because food is linked with a multitude of meanings (eg, nurturing, punishment, reward, and shame), the

**Box 7.7
Important Concepts in the Treatment of Dissociative Disorders**

- Don't work harder than the client.
- Don't make exceptions for the dissociative client that you wouldn't make for other clients.
- Maintain flexible but firm boundaries.
- Don't expect—or ask—the client to trust you completely. You will have to earn his trust, just as he will have to earn yours.
- While it is important to recognize and acknowledge different parts of the client, always maintain a conceptualization of the client as a whole.
- Hold the client responsible for her behavior. The client as a whole is responsible for the behavior of any of the parts represented by her personalities.
- Encourage and model acceptance of all the client's personalities. At the same time, make clear that some *behaviors*, such as violent or self-injurious behaviors, are not acceptable in therapy. The client will probably need help understanding that someone can accept and respect a person while maintaining limits regarding his behavior.

nutrition therapist can become a tangible representation of these feelings and is subject to being the target of blame for any anger, frustration, or other emotion the client may be feeling.

SUMMARY

- The nutrition therapist must remain alert to the possibility that abnormal eating behaviors represent defenses against disowned feelings or parts of dissociated memories.

- All dietitians should be aware that eating disorder and weight management clients could be abuse survivors and that weight loss programs and structured eating plans may be counterproductive with such clients.

- All nutrition therapists working with these clients should familiarize themselves with sexual abuse and the treatment of abuse survivors. Eating disorder specialists need to be skilled in working with trauma and the range of dissociative disorders.

- Regular professional supervision and consultation with referring therapists is important for developing competency in working with individuals with a history of sexual abuse.

- Both the nutrition therapist and the psychotherapist need to understand the nature of the unique relationship between the client and the nutrition therapist.

- It is impossible to treat severely dysfunctional clients without getting angry at them and dreading to come to work at times. Regular supervision can help to create awareness of these interactions and develop the skills to use them in a positive fashion.

REFERENCES

1. Gutwill S, Gitter A. Eating problems and sexual abuse: theoretical considerations. In: Bloom C, Gitter A, Gutwill S, Kogel L, Zaphiropoulos L, eds. *Eating Problems: A Feminist Psychoanalytic Treatment Model.* New York: Basic Books; 1994.
2.. Bloom C, Gitter A, Gutwill S, Kogel L, Zaphiropoulos L. *Eating Problems: A Feminist Psychoanalytic Treatment Model.* New York: Basic Books, 1994.
3. Costin C. Body image disturbance and eating disorders in sexual abuse. In: Schwartz MF, Cohn L. *Sexual Abuse and Eating Disorders.* New York: Brunner/Mazel, Inc; 1996.
4. Everill JT, Waller G. Reported sexual abuse and eating psychopathology: a review of the evidence for a causal link. *Int J Eating Disord.* 1995;18(1):1–11.
5. Goodwin JM, Attias R. Eating disorders and survivors of multimodal childhood abuse. In: Kluft RP, Fine CG, eds. *Clinical Perspectives on Multiple Personality Disorder.* Washington, DC: American Psychiatric Press; 1993.
6. Hall RCW, Tice L, Beresford TP, Wooley B, Hall AK. Sexual abuse in patients with anorexia nervosa and bulimia. *Psychosomatics.* 1989;30:79–88.
7. Herzog DB, Staley JE, Carmody S, Robbins WM, van der Kolk BA. Childhood sexual abuse in anorexia nervosa and bulimia nervosa: a pilot study. *J Am Acad Child Adolescent Psychiatry.* 1993;32(5):962–966.
8. Kearney-Cooke A. Group treatment of sexual abuse among women with eating disorders. *Women Ther.* 1988;7:5–22.

9. Mallinckrodt B, McCreary BA, Robertson AK. Co-occurrence of eating disorders and incest: the role of attachment, family environment and social competencies. *J Counseling Psychiatry.* 1995;42(2):178–187.

10. Morrison J. Childhood sexual histories of women with somatization disorder. *Am J Psychiatry.* 1989;146:239–241.

11. Root MP, Fallon P. The incident of victimization experiences in a bulimic sample. *J Interpersonal Violence.* 1988;3:161–173.

12. Smolak L, Levine MP, Sullins B. Are childhood sexual experiences related to eating disordered attitudes and behaviors in a college sample? *Int J Eating Disord.* 1990;9:167–178.

13. Vanderlinden J, Vandereycken W. Dissociative experiences and trauma in eating disorders. *Int J Eating Disord.* 1993;13:187–194.

14. Waller G. Sexual abuse is a factor in eating disorders. *Br J Psychiatry.* 1991;159:664–671.

15. Waller G, Halek C, Crisp AH. Sexual abuse as a factor in anorexia nervosa: evidence from two separate case series. *J Psychosomatic Res.* 1993;37(8):873–879.

16. Schultz LG. Child sexual abuse in historical perspective. *J Social Work Hum Sexuality.* 1982;1:21–35.

17. Schwartz MF, Cohn L, eds. *Sexual Abuse and Eating Disorders.* New York: Brunner/Mazel, Inc; 1996.

18. Gentry CE. Incestuous abuse of children: need for an objective view. *Child Welfare.* 1978;62:355–364.

19. Janorr-Bulman R. The aftermath of victimization: rebuilding shattered assumptions. In: Figley C, ed. *Trauma and Its Wake.* Vol 1. New York: Brunner/Mazel; 1985.

20. Kratina KM, Albers M, Meyer R. Eating disorders. In: Guyer L, ed. *Handbook of Medical Nutrition Therapy: The Florida Diet Manual.* Tallahassee: The Florida Dietetic Association; 1995.

21. Faller KC. *Child Sexual Abuse: An Interdisciplinary Manual for Diagnosis, Case Management and Treatment.* New York: Columbia University Press; 1988.

22. Kearney-Cook A, Striegel-Moore RH. Anorexia nervosa and bulimia nervosa: a feminist psychodynamic approach. *Int J Eating Disord.* 1994;15(4):305–319.

23. Keddy D. The "fat-free backlash"—who's to blame? *SCAN's Pulse.* 1995;14:11.

24. Kratina KM, King NL. In the trenches: dealing with the "fat-free backlash." *SCAN's Pulse.* 1995;14:8–10.

25. Ackerman D. *A Natural History of the Senses.* New York: Vintage Books; 1990.

26. Kluft RP. Basic principles in conducting the psychotherapy of multiple personality disorder. In: Kluft RP, Fine CD, eds. *Clinical Perspectives on Multiple Personality Disorder.* Washington, DC: American Psychiatric Press; 1993.

27. Fine CG. Treatment stabilization and crisis prevention: pacing the therapy of the multiple personality disorder patient. *Psychiatr Clin North Am.* 1991;14(3):661–767.

28. Kratina KM, King NC, Hayes D. *Moving Away from Diets: Healing Eating Problems and Exercise Resistance.* Lake Dallas, Texas: Helm Publishing, Inc; 1996.

29. Ross CA. *Multiple Personality Disorder: Diagnosis, Clinical Features and Treatment.* New York: John Wiley and Sons; 1989.

30. Torem MS. Dissociative states presenting as an eating disorder. *Am J Clin Hypn.* 1986;39:137–142.

31. Putnam FW, Guroff JJ, Silberman EK, Barban L, Post RM. The clinical phenomenology of multiple personality disorder: review of a hundred recent cases. *J Clin Psychiatry.* 1986;41:285–293.

CHAPTER 8

Sociocultural Influences on Eating Disorders

MONIKA M. WOOLSEY, M.S., R.D.

Despite the growth of the nutrition profession since its founding in 1917, the many advances in understanding of nutrition, and numerous public education efforts, eating disorders are epidemic today. One percent of American women are estimated to be anorexic, 5 percent bulimic, and as many as 20 percent of college women fall into one category or the other (1). In addition, the number of Americans who meet the current criteria for obesity has increased; 33 percent are currently obese, up from 26 percent 20 years ago (2).

Is the nutrition profession part of the solution or part of the problem? Or are there other factors that more strongly influence eating habits than nutrition knowledge and that need to be examined and accommodated in nutrition counseling work?

CONTRIBUTING FACTORS

Following are some important cultural trends that merit consideration as possible factors in the increased incidence of eating disorders.

Longer Workdays

Electricity and mass production have stretched the workday at both ends. Over 22 million Americans work in jobs outside the traditional 9-to-5 schedule (3). In response to that development, more retail operations have turned to 24-hour schedules. Twenty-four-hour gas stations and grocery stores, a relatively new development, are now common.

Rather than follow nature's cues for day's beginning and end, Americans have externalized their sleeping and waking schedules to accommodate these new trends. This is a change that disrupts normal circadian cycles and also increases

147

time pressure. It is also likely to be a major influence on many of the dietary trends repeatedly documented in the *Journal of The American Dietetic Association* over the years. Americans eat fewer breakfasts, more fast foods, more fat, more sugar, and less varied nutrients than they did in years past. More calories come from carbonated beverages and fewer from milk (4). Fewer meals are eaten at home and more are consumed in automobiles or in front of the television (5). These observations cannot be blamed on ignorance, as Americans are well informed about nutrition. If it is sleep deprivation and not lack of knowledge that prevents one from eating breakfast, then it must be stress and sleep management skills, not nutrition education, that is the answer to effectively changing the problem behavior. Nutrition professionals must adapt their approach to these new realities.

New Forms of Telecommunication

The workday has been lengthened even more by downsizing and rapid changes in telecommunication technology, which make possible additional work at home. Home offices, e-mail, and voicemail, all designed as tools to increase work flexibility and efficiency and make life easier, have instead tended to detract from family time and mealtime. Two decades ago the phone, daily mail, and interoffice memos were the main business communication tools. All could be left behind for shorter or longer breaks. Now cellular phones, pagers, e-mail and voicemail, laptop and hand-held computers, and Internet kiosks and coffeehouses make it possible to receive communications 24 hours a day, and the expectation often is that the receiver will respond immediately.

Where families once spent time engaging each other in conversation, they now often spend it in contact with electronic devices. When these devices replace personal, face-to-face communication, they erode a basic human need for bonding. When the human connection is lost, self-esteem and self-efficacy can suffer. The resulting stress demands an outlet, and all too often the outlet is food. Or dieting may have appeal, not because it results in weight loss, but because it creates at least superficial order in a life that otherwise feels chaotic.

Longer Commutes

Americans spend more time in their cars than ever before. The movement of families to increasingly distant suburbs has been a major influence. In California, affordable housing is often a 2-hour drive from work. In Colorado, a rustic dream home in the mountains can be a 2-hour drive from the office. When both parents work outside the home, the commute to and from day care and afterwork sports activities further increases time behind the wheel. This increased time spent commuting has two significant consequences. First, it is time that cannot be invested in relationship development and relaxing activities. Second, commuting, and driving in particular, is inherently stressful, eliciting reactions ranging from anxiety to road rage (6).

Working Mothers

Though most would agree that women have benefited from increased career choices, the increase in mothers working outside the home has created dilemmas that cannot be overlooked. Though women are approaching equal treatment in their jobs, such equality has yet to be seen in most households. A working woman is likely to be responsible for 75 percent of household chores (7). For many, the end of the work shift signifies the beginning of the "home shift." There is little time for anything but household responsibilities in the hours between job and sleep.

Images of families gathered together at the dinner table are heartwarming but outdated. Many meals are eaten at work or in restaurants or cars. One study found that 75 percent of all adults eat at least one meal away from home each week (8). At the same time there has been a decrease in the variety of foods consumed. The most popular items ordered in restaurants today are generally low in nutrient density and high in calories. "Supersizing," a recent trend in fast food restaurants, is another source of additional calories. Once a meal is purchased, it is likely to be completely consumed, especially when it is eaten behind the wheel, where sensations signaling fullness may be overlooked if safe driving is the main focus.

In households in which meals are purchased and consumed outside the home more often than they are prepared and consumed together at home, basic tasks of menu planning, shopping, and food preparation are not modeled. Children who grow up without participating in food preparation activities that were once taken for granted leave home without having learned skills basic for survival. If their frame of reference for food choices is advertisements, the majority of which are for foods of marginal nutritional value, young adults are likely to make choices that compromise their medical and emotional health and promote the development of dysfunctional eating.

Single Parents

Thirty percent of all families are headed by single parents (9), whose efforts to juggle household responsibilities plus parenting *completely* fill their day. If that parent is a woman, her standard of living is likely to be significantly lower than that of her male counterparts (10). An individual working full time and raising a family alone has little time for anything other than her basic domestic responsibilities, and even finding time for these is a challenge. Food becomes an afterthought or outlet for stress. When a diet of fast food and "stress" food results in weight gain, the parent's response is often to swing to the other extreme with a restrictive diet. There is little room for any middle eating ground.

Single-parent households also have a significant impact on children. Children in single-parent families have been found to have significantly more emotional and behavioral problems than those in two-parent families (11). When single-parent households are the result of death or divorce, the children have experienced a significant life change. In addition, they have likely lost a significant role model and support person, which may decrease their ability to communicate feelings directly as they arise and increase their need for an alternative form of communication, such as disordered eating.

Multitasking

Juggling career and family responsibilities is a challenge in any household. Americans have had to become proficient at "multitasking", performing several tasks simultaneously, such as eating, reading, and listening to phone messages. Multitasking reduces the attention focused on any one activity and leaves little time or energy for listening to internal signals. The central nervous system transmits messages about changes in energy levels. These can be ignored for a short time, but they become louder the longer they are ignored. As long as a structured day and external commitments dominate an individual's consciousness, he can effectively ignore any messages his body might be communicating. However, when the schedule slows down and thoughts, feelings, and sensations that have amassed over the day begin to surface (for example, at night, when binge eating is most common), they surface with a vengeance!

An individual who increases her stress level by packing more commitments and more stressful activities into her day without regularly refueling with the chemicals she needs to meet these demands will eventually lose the ability to cope. The result is a sense of being overwhelmed, of feeling helpless, hopeless, and ineffective. These are cardinal symptoms of depression, the diagnosis that most commonly coexists with an eating disorder.

Children's Issues   As noted above, it is not just the adult world that is stressful. Where children once spontaneously played unsupervised with their friends, today they are often sent to day care or limited to a few scheduled play times a week. Children who do have parents at home may have difficulty finding playmates who are not in day care. Or it may not be safe to play unsupervised.

Organized sports model teamwork and provide regular physical activity, but they sometimes leave the child with a schedule as hectic as his parents'. Children who do not participate in sports or clubs may find themselves home alone, with little available entertainment. These children are likely to engage in more passive activities such as watching television, playing computer games, and "surfing" the Internet. The average child watches approximately 21 to 23 hours of television a week, the equivalent of a part-time job (12)!

Children who have grown up in environments in which daily routine, life skills, and relationship maintenance are not priorities have difficulty creating personal structures in a world that is increasingly hurried and chaotic. If they are not raised to believe they are worthy just as they are, black or white, science buff or artist, high weight or low weight, they enter the adult world looking for a place that offers acceptance. Unfortunately, if they have bonded more with sports and television personalities than with their family, they may be highly susceptible to messages they receive from institutions that place their own monetary gain ahead of the individual's personal growth and development. Those messages may suggest that material possessions, sexual activity, expressions of anger, and addictions to certain chemicals and foods offer a sense of belonging or identity that has not been obtained from the family.

Homogenized Standards of Acceptance   American culture rests on the premises that everyone is equal and that diversity is important. However, these premises do not always translate into practice. Americans of Hispanic, Asian, African, and East Indian descent all have established presences in this country, but the standard of beauty often doesn't reflect our national differences.

Resistance to diversity can also be seen in the grocery store. Consumers ask for—and get—a variety of food choices, but they also demand simple diets or food plans that will eliminate the need to make those choices. Advertisers capitalize on the latter trend by suggesting their products will eliminate the need to weigh choices, offer peace of mind, perhaps even enhance self-esteem. The anxious, busy consumer is likely to conclude that any stress she experiences comes from not meeting some external standard.

Looking for self-worth in material things rarely works. New clothes, a trimmer body, or a dream vacation may bring temporary relief, but they do not address the root cause of the low self-esteem. When the quick fix fades and the insecurity and depression return, it can be tempting to search out another quick fix, such as a new diet. Some of the more common quick-fix solutions that relate to food behaviors are summarized below.

QUICK-FIX SOLUTIONS TO COMPLICATED PROBLEMS

The models and actresses who play out media messages are selected by a few producers, editors, and other media executives. Unfortunately, these individuals tend to favor a single look: young, slender, often blond. Even Hispanic media tend to use lighter-skinned, Anglo-looking reporters and actors. The weight standard has drifted downward over the years to the point where the average beauty pageant contestant today has a weight-for-height ratio that borders on anorexia (13).

Thinness Is Beauty, Thinness Is Health

Standards of health have been influenced by this size prejudice. "Healthy" and "low-fat" have become interchangeable. While a low-fat diet is beneficial to cardiovascular health, 40 grams of fat a day, the traditional low-fat prescription, is only 20 percent of the calories in an 1800-calorie diet. Many people today aim for 10, 5, or even 1 gram of fat. In their passion to prevent heart disease, dietitians and other health professionals have neglected to define a lower limit of desirable fat intake, which may be promoting depression and disordered eating. Though public health education and marketing theory suggest that messages must be simplified to reach larger audiences, dietitians must take care that they don't oversimplify to the point of creating new problems.

Health professionals should work to eliminate perpetuate size discrimination and overemphasis on fat. Most nutrition studies measure success by weight change. In fact, there are few outcome studies of changes in self-esteem, self-efficacy, and body image that do not also evaluate changes in weight. To maintain credibility, health professionals should reevaluate whether the message that weight loss translates into improved health is appropriate. They also need to consider the psychological factors that may play a part in a client's obesity, and refrain from automatically recommending weight loss if her health is good.

The growing body of psychological and behavioral research strongly suggests that eating well is more than achieving a target weight. The most logical professional for teaching this skill is the nutrition professional. Moving away from the emphasis on weight allows dietitians to help their clients relearn to recognize and respond to internal cues, to prioritize their commitments, take care of themselves, and put enjoyment back in their lives.

Stimulants Can Make You Feel Better

Caffeine, nicotine, alcohol, and other stimulants are common means of coping with environmental overstimulation. Many of these compounds are also appetite suppressants. They help the user avoid eating, the activity that most effectively maintains nervous system function. Today food is less often part of a social ritual and more often an afterthought when a growling stomach or headache sends a reminder that the last meal was eaten several hours earlier. By the time the day finally slows down and hunger signals can finally be acknowledged, they are amplified by circadian rhythms. When physical and emotional signals that have been suppressed all day are finally acknowledged, intense food cravings can be a problem.

Evening is also frequently the time for relaxing in front of the television. The messages television transmits may only intensify food cravings and hunger: advertisements project images of people who seem to have it all, and programs show still more people who can solve even serious problems within an hour. These images create false expectations that solutions to stress and low self-esteem are available in a "quick fix" format. When these expectations are not met in real life, it is easy to dull the awareness of failure by altering one's consciousness with stimulants or addictions. Most people know that these are not real solutions, but because of exhaustion, poor self-image, or learned helplessness, in susceptible individuals these behaviors repeatedly win out over positive, self-nurturing behavioral choices.

You Can Have It All!

The purpose of marketing is to create a perceived need for a product. Stylish clothes, convenience foods, and makeup are not essential for beauty, acceptance, and self-esteem, but advertisers must create a need for their products to increase sales. Much advertising is designed to increase sales by making consumers dissatisfied with themselves:

Are you really ok?
Have you looked in the mirror lately?
A gray hair?
An extra pound?
The wrong car?

The subtle, unspoken message that is communicated is:

You need our product to hide your unacceptability.

To continue to make a profit, manufacturers must continually create new standards. Once a product has gained acceptance, consumers have purchased it, and sales have tapered off, a new product must be created, along with a new ad campaign to promote it. In an instant, millions of people thousands of miles apart can simultaneously learn what new dress, compact disc, or hairstyle is not to be lived without. As attention spans have decreased, so have product lifespans. Products enter and leave the market at an increasingly rapid pace.

One of the most traumatic environments for a person with an eating disorder to enter is the grocery store. Not because there is food, not necessarily because there is fat, but because there are so many choices. In 1998 alone, 11,037 new food products reached American grocery stores (14). Shopping is no longer a matter of getting some bread, some cereal, and some pasta. Obtaining these three simple items requires myriad decisions:

> *Should I get corn flakes or rice flakes?*
> *Should I get the regular corn flakes, the fat-free corn flakes . . . or what about the generic corn flakes?*
> *Should I get the house pasta or the fresh pasta?*
> *Should I get the garlic-basil flavor or the lemon-pepper?*
> *Fettucini or rotini?*

And so on. For an individual who may already be overwhelmed by personal problems, grocery shopping is an exhausting proposition, not a simple task. Self-styled nutrition experts can exacerbate the problem with too much focus on charts and graphs, calories and fat grams, and not enough on the central task, to procure the ingredients for a healthy meal. In the process, learned helplessness and an unwillingness to try even small changes can develop. An alternative approach, encouraging any change, no matter how small, is a step in the right direction.

Sex, Drugs, and Rock 'n Roll Are Where It Is

Some researchers propose that sexual abuse is at the root of a high percentage of eating disorders, but others question this theory. (See Chapter 7.) What the debate overlooks is that a much more pervasive influence may be "unwanted sexual exposure." Sexuality is a constant in our culture. Advertisements for mundane objects such as tires use it. Beauty pageants promote it. Television standards have loosened so that what was once a "late" topic now appears routinely at any time of day. It is estimated that children watching television are exposed to over 14,000 sexual situations and innuendoes a year (12). In addition, the Internet has become a haven for sexual material.

Children and teens who spend more time in front of the television and the computer than ever before are exposed to ideas and attitudes that may not be appropriate for early developmental stages. As portrayed in the media today, sexuality promises acceptance and physical and emotional pleasure. It can also serve as a stress release, a means of numbing oneself, and an addictive behavior.

For some children, sex becomes a means of bonding when more appropriate means are not available. For other children, the prospect of reaching adulthood and dealing with sexuality as it is presented by the media scares them into starving to prolong childhood or eating to dull the painful awareness adolescence brings. If a child struggling with weight gain is also struggling with her sexuality, she may not be communicating fear of fat as much as fear of adulthood. Nutrition professionals need to be aware of the possibility of such an underlying issue, and if it is identified, to help to decrease susceptibility to these messages. Learning self-acceptance and self-esteem at any size helps children and teens reject inappropriate messages and invitations and develop interest in activities that do not diminish their self-image.

Spirituality Is the Answer

Over the last decade there has been a growing realization that dependence on the media for entertainment is not always positive. A resurgent interest in spirituality suggests that Americans have grown weary of materialism and are looking elsewhere for affirmation and purpose. From fundamentalist Christianity to New Age metaphysics, individuals are searching for guidance through the maze of decisions and pitfalls life presents. Spirituality can play a very important role in the development of self-esteem. Most religions stress that all people, no matter how physically or emotionally unacceptable they perceive themselves, are valuable and worthwhile. In a supportive context, this message can transform lives and create hope. However, religion can also set standards so high that its members cannot possibly meet them, creating the potential for guilt and shame.

Spirituality is an important part of a person's identity that can promote a client's recovery if it fosters self-acceptance and encourages living with balance, but not if it becomes an addiction. The nutrition therapist must appreciate and affirm the client's belief structure if the shame and guilt that often accompany disordered eating patterns are to be lifted and appropriately addressed (*Box 8.1*).

**Box 8.1
Food Behaviors That May Suggest Religion Is Being Used to Express Guilt**

Adopting a religion (eg, Hinduism) that may encourage the restriction of food.

Adopting the food rules of a religion but not being able to describe its basic tenets and philosophy.

Rigidly adhering to religious food rules but lacking similar rigidity in other areas of life.

Avoiding foods because they create a sense of being "dirty".

Engaging in compensatory or self-mutilating behaviors as punishment for food behaviors (eg, running extra miles, purging, restricting for being "bad").

Being unable to express guilt or shame except for food behaviors (eg, "I feel guilty for eating that." "I'm a bad person because I can't control my food intake.").

Exhibiting excessive ritualism or praying in combination with eating.

Working for the social good has allowed many to create families beyond their biological ones. Having a cause to work for can provide a sense of purpose and belonging, but some of the methods can stem from or lead to eating disorders. Attaching a "politically correct" purpose to one's food behaviors delays the need to look at those behaviors as reflections of more personal issues, and can even gain affirmation from peers. Eating disordered individuals often become involved in animal rights issues, for example.

It is important to understand that while vegetarianism and other food-related social causes can be productive and health-promoting activities, if adopted for the wrong reasons, these behaviors can mask important psychological and psychiatric issues and even be life threatening. Nutrition therapists can help clients decide whether these activities are appropriate, given their personal physiological and psychological history.

Social Causes Can Ease Your Pain

For some, the need to belong supersedes any other need they might have. These individuals may not have had the opportunity to experience healthy bonding within their families. Such individuals are susceptible to the preachings of organizations motivated to control. "False families," such as cults, gangs, and paramilitary organizations, give members a sense of belonging and fill basic needs for many fragile individuals. The rigidity of their rules and thinking provide structure, guidance, and answers. Anyone who has felt rejected by society is susceptible to the lure of an organization that seems to offer unconditional acceptance. This can include anyone who is poor, who is a member of a minority group, who is too large, who does not eat "right", who has not finished school, *who is different.*

Nutrition therapists can make a difference. They can model unconditional acceptance, provide encouragement rather than judgment, and foster a sense of purpose and belonging in the client, rather than stressing compliance with an imposed diet. As the nutrition therapist's office is often the first place those with eating disorders turn when they feel out of control, the nutrition therapist can be crucial in helping those individuals to consider positive, self-affirming behavior changes.

It's Easier Not to Care

As marketed, diets promise beauty, acceptance, and a life free of problems. To the obese or eating disordered individual, they promise control in an out-of-control world. Though they promise to do this only with food, they are often viewed as the key to control over other problems as well. They make decisions for someone who is overwhelmed by decisions. They provide the illusion that there are concrete, simple answers for abstract and complicated problems. The language of dieting, full of words like "good," "bad", "cheat", and "guilt", reinforces the narrow thinking the individual may already have developed. Diets can be an easy focus for feelings of guilt and shame that belong to other issues and emotions, thereby providing a means of avoiding the issues behind the eating problem.

Diets have an extremely low success rate, yet advertisements for diets promise

Diets Can Make You Beautiful and Acceptable

that this time . . . *this* time . . . they will work. When they don't, the consumer is blamed for lack of willpower. Moreover, diets can actually exacerbate depression and low self-esteem. For someone who is already feeling ineffective and powerless, a diet reinforces those feelings.

Nutrition therapy can help the individual who may have come seeking a diet to enhance her self-esteem to explore other avenues for achieving this in a fashion that actually works. Weight may normalize indirectly as food is no longer used or abused as a means of expressing a negative self-image. When nutrition therapy addresses the root of the problem, the same food plan that was impossible to achieve can eventually become the client's natural eating style.

THE EMPOWERMENT MODEL: A NEW DIRECTION FOR NUTRITION PROFESSIONALS

The medical model of nutrition counseling has been the focus of nutrition training and counseling. It has also served as the financial basis for much of nutrition therapy, as weight loss counseling is the focus of many nutrition professionals' practices. Outcome studies use weight loss as a gauge of success. Nutrition professionals have convinced the public to incorporate "low-fat" and "low-cholesterol" into their everyday vocabularies. They have even engaged the media in educating Americans about the importance of balanced nutrition, but still Americans have become excessively heavy . . . or lean . . . or continued to yo-yo between the two extremes. Such trends in the face of widespread nutrition education programs suggest that the message or its method of delivery needs reexamination.

It is important to understand not just what foods are important for physical and mental health, but how the environment affects food-related behavior. An individual's environment, perceptions of daily events, interpersonal relationships, and self-image all affect weight and health. The eating disordered often disconnect from feelings and sensations in order to cope. The medical model may exacerbate their inability to cope by providing them with external cues to eat and not helping them understand the internal cues that contradict the dietary instructions. Imposing standards of behavior that fit the clinician's ideas of what is the right way to eat does not allow clients to respond to their internal cues. Nutrition professionals need to help clients understand that reliance on external stimuli may be the cause of the distress that brought them into counseling.

There is a changing paradigm in the nutrition field. Called the "empowerment model," it is a style of counseling that returns control to the individual in crisis. It recognizes that individuals need some structure to feel in control, but also that external structures, such as diets, are not as effective as internal. It encourages self-acceptance, self-expression, and emotional awareness. When clients acknowledge their emotions, employ appropriate communication and conflict resolution skills, and replace self-loathing with self-nurturing, food regains its place as a source of nourishment and enjoyment, not a tool of punishment or an item to fear.

Nutrition therapy for disordered eating is different from nutrition education. It adds psychological counseling to the medical model and focuses on connecting mind and body. The goal of nutrition therapy is achieving psychological, physical, and emotional balance. When that balance is achieved, extreme under- or overconsumption are no longer necessary and eating becomes a nurturing activity. Nutrition counseling often mandates standards of behavior and outcomes inconsistent with those desirable for eating disordered clients by reinforcing their deficits. Nutrition therapy, in contrast, identifies goals and plans a path that will identify deficits and meet challenges. Where traditional nutrition counseling takes an authoritarian tone, nutrition therapy makes the client the center of the team.

This new paradigm has several advantages for nutrition therapists:

- It includes the mechanisms of hunger, appetite, satiety, and aversion, which helps restore normal responses to stress and eating.
- It can help clients understand the interaction between physiological influences and psychological behavior,
- It positions dietitians as the professionals who can liberate the public from rigid food rules and promote food as a source of nourishment and enjoyment.

The nutrition therapist has the combination of medical and psychological training to facilitate the new paradigm.

Of course, working with this new model requires new thinking, approaches, and communication styles, as well as self-examination. The following steps can help nutrition therapists prepare for this shift in thinking.

Strengthen Counseling Skills

If eating right were simply about knowing what to do, there would be no need for nutrition therapy. In addition to educating clients, nutrition therapists need to help them understand why they make the choices they do, and why they sometimes can't seem to make the choices they want to. An understanding of basic psychological concepts and counseling techniques is the foundation for building this kind of expertise. The self-assessment in *Box 8.2* is a good starting place for nutrition therapists who want to evaluate their existing skills.

Promote Self-Acceptance

Promoting self-acceptance in others first requires self-acceptance on the part of the nutrition therapist. A therapist who models self-acceptance can

- talk positively about her own body. Remarks about one's "pear shape" or "slow metabolism" should be avoided. Turning down a piece of office coffeecake with the explanation that losing a few extra pounds is a goal should not be an ongoing or predominant behavior.
- like what she sees in the mirror and model that self-acceptance in the presence of colleagues and clients.
- mark a successful outcome for a client by the development of insights rather than by weight change.
- avoid immediately seeking to raise or lower calories if a client does not lose

Box 8.2
Basic Counseling Skills:
A Self-Assessment Quiz

Ask yourself the following questions to evaluate your counseling style and determine the kind of counseling environment you create for clients.

Ambience
Is there privacy?
Is the setting conducive to communication?

Expectations
Do my client and I have similar expectations? Are they reasonable?

Building Rapport
Am I friendly and personable?
Do I welcome clients and help them feel comfortable?
Am I nurturing and supportive? Am I patient?

Establishing a Dialogue
Do I ask open-ended questions?
Can I pose questions that elicit useful information from my client?

Listening and Reflection
Do I listen without interrupting?
Can I "read between the lines"?
Do I restate to my client what he or she has said to obtain clarification?

Frame of Reference
Can I put my personality aside and listen without judgment?
Am I able to empathize? Can I see through my client's eyes?

Respect
Do I extend the same professional courtesies to all my clients?
Do I always respect confidentiality?

Silence
Can I sit comfortably with a few moments of silence rather than trying to "find the right words" to answer every concern?

Sharing and Feedback
Do I share personal experiences in a way that enhances the session?
Do I give and accept feedback impartially?

Ethics and Teamwork
Do I know when to refer a client to another health professional?

Self-Examination
Have I cleared up my own food issues?
Am I defensive? Do I set boundaries?
Am I able to allow clients to express a full range of emotions?
Can I successfully confront an uncooperative client?
Can I terminate a counseling relationship with grace and respect?

From L Licavoli, Dietetics goes into therapy, *J Am Diet Assoc*, 1995;95:751–752. Reprinted with permission of the American Dietetic Association.

or gain weight. Such occurrences should be used instead as opportunities to discuss what positive changes besides weight are occurring.

- allow clients ride through "plateau" times with the goal of gaining increased insight, rather than assuming that not meeting weight goals implies non-compliance.

The nutrition therapist's attitudes about clients are portrayed at least as much by body language actions as by the spoken word. Self-acceptance allows the nutrition therapist to view the process of therapy as an introspective journey, rather than a number-oriented goal. The progress is less easily measured, but the results are usually more rewarding and long-lasting for both the client and the nutrition therapist.

Self-acceptance makes possible client acceptance, at 100 pounds or 300 pounds. For the client, self-acceptance is the first step in stress management. When an individual comes to believe he is a worthy and valuable member of society regardless of his weight, the stress of shame and rejection that may be the root cause of his problem begins to decrease. Communicating unconditional support of this process has special meaning, as the nutrition therapist is the member of the treatment team whose opinion about weight and acceptance is most valid in the client's eyes.

For therapists working with clients who need to gain weight, it is important to be comfortable with weight recommendations that may exceed one's own weight. It is also important to feel comfortable with recommending dietary practices that are in the client's best interest but not necessarily consistent with one's personal choices. This includes, when appropriate, recommending increased fat intake, encouraging meat intake, and helping a client with her fear of fast food restaurants, even if these choices are not one's own. In other words, it is important to differentiate personal values from professional recommendations.

Understand Nonverbal and Subtle Communication

The nutrition therapist needs to become acquainted with the person who has sought his help. Is she really saying she wants to lose weight? Or is she saying things feel out of control and she doesn't know where to start to piece them back together? Is it better to give her a 1,200-calorie diet or to help her understand the relationship between stress and eating behaviors? Is it better to help her to diminish her hunger or to recognize and respond appropriately to hunger? Is it better to help her understand the process of psychotherapy and to seek it out if necessary? Moving past the "whats" of client behaviors and into the "whys" is an important component of the empowerment model. It means providing just enough structure to help the client get back on track without imposing so much that the client does not learn to respond to personal physical and emotional cues.

Promote Size Acceptance

Recommending a target weight for a client that is above the recommendation on the height/weight chart if it seems appropriate for her body type and there are no apparent medical complications may cause the client discomfort. So can telling a client she is healthy where she is even if she desires weight loss. But helping her to understand that a slight weight gain with age is natural and even appropriate and to consider whether a diet is really the answer and weight is really the problem is an important component of the empowerment model.

Even scientific researchers have a tendency to reflect the culture's weight bias. Dean Ornish's program, for example, includes a low-fat diet (15,16), but critiques of the "Ornish approach" rarely mention that it also includes meditation, social connection, and personal reflection. Do clients lose weight on Dean Ornish's program because they have followed his diet, or because they have adopted behaviors other than eating to manage stress? These are issues the next generation of nutrition researchers would benefit from investigating.

The nutrition therapist's office communicates much about her attitude toward size acceptance. The waiting area should have magazines that do not portray thinness as a beauty standard and advertise diets. It should offer a variety of reading material that focuses on other topics or that promotes size acceptance. If a scale is in the office where counseling takes place, it should be positioned so that it is not the first thing the client sees when she comes into the office. Finally, office furniture should be selected that is comfortable for bodies of all sizes.

Develop Relationships with Mental Health Professionals Who Allow for Treatment of the Whole Person

The nutrition therapist should create alliances with mental health professionals in the community who promote self-acceptance and size acceptance. He should create an alliance and publicize his approach. He should become familiar with self-efficacy inventories that can document the effectiveness of his approach. Finally, he should be assertive about sharing the results of his nondiet focus with the other professionals he works with *(Box 8.3)*.

Create Tolerance for a Variety of Ideas

Issues of size acceptance are not as measurable as issues of weight and body composition. Though the client and the nutrition therapist may subscribe to vastly differing personal value systems, the therapist must understand and honor the client's cultural and religious beliefs. Again, self-acceptance is the goal. The client will trust the nutrition therapist more when the therapist communicates tolerance for the client's personal style and choices. If this trust is developed early in treatment, personal choices that seem to be contributing to a client's problems will be more effectively addressed without the nutrition therapist's being perceived as judgmental *(Box 8.4)*.

Vegetarianism, for example, is a personal choice that clients often attach to a religion, such as Buddhism or Hinduism, or to the animal rights movement in order to elevate its validity. Vegetarianism, Buddhism, and animal rights are neither right nor wrong choices, but if any of them are hindering a client's ability to nourish herself, they need to be addressed. An ability to work with less tangible aspects of the eating problem will help the nutrition therapist to explore these behaviors.

Avoid Black-and-White Thinking and Judgmental Language

The nutrition therapist should consider word choice. Do such words as "good", "bad", "avoid", "cheating", "off-the-wagon", "healthy", "artery-clogging", frequently pepper conversations? The nutrition therapist should work to adopt language that validates the client's personal choices, whatever they may be.

For Parents, Educators, Coaches, Athletes, Dance and Gymnastic Instructors

1. Examine, explore, and, if necessary, modify fantasies about your unborn child (eg, "Will she be pretty . . . , Will she be rich . . . , Will she be . . . ").

2. Examine your own attitudes, beliefs, prejudices, and behaviors about food, weight, body image, physical appearance, health, and exercise.

3. Replace unhealthy attitudes with healthy ones.

4. Replace excessive eating and exercise habits with more moderate ones.

5. Do not talk about or behave as if you are constantly dieting.

6. Do not "model" or otherwise communicate the message that you cannot dance, swim, wear a bathing suit, or enjoy a picnic because you do not look a certain way or weigh a certain amount.

7. Encourage healthy eating in moderation.

8. Allow all foods in your home.

9. Encourage eating in response to body hunger.

10. Notice often and in a positive way how varied people are—how they come in all colors, shapes, and sizes. (Show appreciation for diversity in race, gender, ethnicity, intelligence, etc.)

11. Become critical consumers—pay attention to and openly challenge media messages. Talk with your children about the pressures they feel to diet and "look good." Talk about advertisements and magazine covers and the way they convey a narrow image of attractiveness. Explain to your children that even models' pictures are altered to create a "perfect" look.

12. Convey to children that weight and appearance are not the most critical aspects of their identity and self-worth.

13. Build self-esteem. (The most important gift adults can give to children is self-esteem. When adults show children that they value and love them unconditionally, children can withstand the perils of childhood and adolescence with fewer scars and traumas. Children who feel good about themselves are less likely to reject their bodies, stop eating, or eat too much. They survive disappointments without blaming themselves. Self-esteem is a universal vaccine that can immunize youngsters from eating problems, body image distortion, exercise abuse, and many other problems. Providing it is the responsibility of both parents. Girls especially need support and validation from their fathers. The male opinion becomes increasingly important to them as they proceed through adolescence, but too often men do not recognize their importance to their children's self-esteem.)

14. Encourage open communication. Convey over and over again the most important aspects of identity and self-worth—*Don't Weigh Your Self-Esteem, It's What's Inside That Counts.* (Teach children how to communicate. Encourage children to talk openly and honestly and really listen to them; let them know that they are cared for and valued. Being encouraged to assert themselves allows them to say no to pressures to conform. Feeling loved and confident allows them to accept that they are unique, and when upset, they know they have the skills and the support to risk talking about their feelings.)

Box 8.3

Prevention Guidelines and Strategies: 52 Ways to Lose the "3D's" (*Dieting, Drive for Thinness, and Body Dissatisfaction*)

continued

Box 8.3
(*continued*)

15. Encourage critical thinking. (The only sure antidote to the tendency to conform to the powerful seduction of the media is the ability to think critically. Parents have to begin encouraging critical thinking early, and educators have to continue the mission. We need to teach kids *how* to think, not *what* to think, and need to encourage them to disagree, challenge, come up with alternatives, and so forth. Girls especially need to learn that men are not the ultimate authorities and that they have something important to contribute . . . that they don't have to "stop knowing." The more certain girls feel of their place in the world, the less likely they will be seduced to conform to the three D's—Dieting, Body Dissatisfaction, and the Drive for Thinness.)

16. Develop a value system based on internal values. (How is it that "the most important book you will read this summer" according to the *New York Times*, is one entitled *Teaching Your Children Values*, by Linda and Richart Byre? How is it that we need a "month-by-month program" to help our children develop honesty, courage, self-reliance, loyalty, justice, respect, and other critical human qualities? What happened to the days when these were precisely the values that most families struggled to impart without a "how-to-manual"? We must teach our children to equate certain values with personal worth, including care and concern for others, wisdom, loyalty, fairness, self-care and self-respect, personal fulfillment, curiosity, self-awareness, the capacity for relationships, connectedness and intimacy, individuality, confidence, assertiveness, a sense of humor, ambition, and motivation.)

17. Help children accept and enjoy their bodies and encourage physical activities.

18. Discourage the idea that a particular diet or body size will automatically lead to happiness and fulfillment.

19. Don't use food as a reward or punishment. That sets food up as a potential weapon for control.

20. Don't constantly criticize your own shape. ("I'm so fat, I've got to lose weight.") Self-deprecation implies that appearance is more important than character.

21. Don't equate food with positive or negative behavior. (The dieting parent who says she was "good" today because she didn't "eat much" implies that avoiding food is good behavior. Similarly, "don't eat that; it will make you fat" implies that being fat makes one unlikable.)

22. Be aware of warning signs of eating disorders before puberty. Watch for

    • refusing typical family meals,
    • skipping lunch at school,
    • negative comments about self and others like "I'm too fat; she's too fat,"
    • clothes shopping that becomes stressful,
    • withdrawal from friends,
    • irritability and depression,
    • any signs of extreme dieting, bingeing, or purging.

23. Love, accept, acknowledge, appreciate, and value your children, out loud, no matter what they weigh.

continued

24. Trust your children's appetite. Never try to limit their caloric intake unless requested to do so by a physician for a medical problem.

25. Learn about and discuss with your sons and daughters the dangers of trying to alter body shape through dieting.

26. Don't support beauty pageants, pornography, or other "institutions" that depict women as objects for the pleasure of men, objects without personal integrity.

27. Give boys and girls the same opportunities and encouragement and be careful not to suggest that females are less important than males. Take females more seriously for what they say, feel, and do, and less seriously for what they look like.

28. Teach children about good relationships and ways to deal with difficulties when they arise. (Males and females alike use food to express themselves in dealing with difficult feelings in relationships. They eat too much or too little, instead of confronting problems head-on. Because of the messages that suggest that the perfect body will dissolve all relationship problems, young people often put energy into changing their bodies instead of their feelings and/or their relationships. Interpersonal satisfaction that comes from well-negotiated and fulfilling relationships is much more enduring than the temporary relief that food bingeing, purging, or quick weight loss have to offer.)

29. Teach children about spirituality.

For Men
(Specific recommendations for primary prevention of eating disorders that men can do as citizens, husbands, and fathers, developed by Michael Levine, PhD, Kenyon College Gambier, Ohio)

30. Develop a historical perspective on the politics of the control of women's bodies.

31. Work toward and speak out for women's rights to fair pay, to safety, to respect, and to control of their bodies.

32. Demonstrate respect for women as they age in order to work against the cultural glorification of youth and a tightly controlled, single body type. (Why is it that men become distinguished as they age, while women become wrinkled and need facelifts?)

33. Learn to nourish women's spirits so they won't feel an empty hunger for beauty and for unhealthy amounts of food.

34. Educate your children about the existence, the experience, and the ugliness of prejudice and oppression, whether it is directed against people of color or people who are overweight.

35. Raise non-sex-stereotyped children by modeling and living gender equality at home.

36. Demonstrate respect for all women, especially your wives, the mothers of your children.

37. Remain close to and supportive of your daughters as they experiment and struggle with body image, grooming and cosmetic issues, flirtatiousness and sexuality, etc.

Box 8.3
(continued)

continued

Box 8.3
(*continued*)

38. Talk to your sons about the way body shape and sexuality (for both boys and girls) are manipulated by the media and the struggle their girlfriends have in trying to conform or not to conform.

39. Model patience, compassion, tenderness, fallibility, and, most important, the capacity and desire to listen.

For Mental Health Professionals

40. Educate yourself about the warning signs of eating disorders. (See guidelines for parents, above).

41. In your work with children, emphasize self-esteem, critical thinking, self-assertion, and communication skills. Remember that these strengths will inoculate children against pressure they experience to change and harm their bodies in the pursuit of "perfection, goodness, and happiness."

42. Become political and sociocultural advocates; invite children you work with to challenge the ways in which our culture glorifies thinness.

43. Encourage the young men you work with to examine their "weightist" attitudes and behavior toward women.

44. Become knowledgeable about and able to discuss the scientific evidence concerning a variety of complex topics, including

   - the physical development of boys and girls during puberty,
   - "set point" regulation and defense of body weight,
   - the futility and dangers of dieting,
   - ways in which our culture has exaggerated the "risks" of being overweight.

45. Develop systems whereby you can connect to teachers and coaches, who can in turn reach out to help children who are expressing problems with their eating and body image. (Build referrals to competent treatment sources into the system.)

46. Strengthen and support families so they are able to more effectively provide the security, acceptance, support, and direction that children need to "childproof" themselves from negative media influence. (As the family becomes stronger, the influence of the Three D's will become weaker.)

47. Help parents reclaim their rights as experts. (In this world of advanced technology, we have experts for everything including child rearing. Empower parents to listen to their children and find solutions that will be best for them.)

48. Recognize how our changing world alters what children need from parents today. (Sociocultural pressures surrounding drugs, sexuality, weight, body image, and perfectionism require great character strength, self-assurance, and decision-making in young children. Support parents to give more attention to children in these areas.)

49. Appreciate with families how we *all* use food for the wrong reasons. (Help families understand the power and role of food in their own lives as it soothes, rewards, or punishes. Both parents should be actively involved in meal planning and preparations so that food and nurturing do not appear to

continued

be exclusive tasks for women. Encourage families to return to the traditional evening family meal in any way they can. Many families have dropped the tradition, and the children have suffered and experienced loss.)

50. Educate your community about the risks of the three D's and the dangers of eating disorders while at the same time being careful not to promote or teach young people how to become eating disordered. (In some ways, children are actually the highest risk audience).

51. Better audiences are school personnel, parent groups, athletic directors, and day care personnel. Have a system in place if a child does have a problem and be supportive of the child's family and friends. You may work with the family while someone else is working with the patient. Give information and support; reduce shame and guilt. Blaming parents guarantees treatment failure. Work with families to create and restore healthy eating and interaction patterns.

52. Be optimistic; an ounce of prevention is worth a pound of cure!

Copyright, Paula Levine, PhD. Adapted with permission from Eating Disorders Awareness and Prevention, Inc.

Box 8.3
(continued)

Christopher was distressed. He had been regularly attending nutrition sessions for six months, yet his weight continued to rise. He began to notice back pains and knee pains that told him he had exceeded his healthy weight range. Christopher diligently recorded in his journal when his cravings for ice cream surfaced. He easily made the connection between certain emotions and eating, but his weight continued to rise.

Finally, one day Christopher came to counseling with the announcement that he had "bottomed out," that the costs of his behaviors far outweighed the benefits and he knew it was time to address his food habits. When asked what this would entail, he said that he had decided it was time to tell his father he was homosexual. Through nutrition therapy and psychotherapy, he became aware that his weight had begun to increase when he told his mother about his sexual orientation but had not had the courage to tell his father.

When he finished sharing his revelation, Christopher commented that having a heterosexual psychotherapist and nutrition therapist who consistently communicated support and understanding through the "noncompliant" times, despite the differences in sexual orientation, had given him the confidence he needed to confront this highly emotional issue. He also said the unconditional acceptance he received helped him to feel that, no matter what the outcome of the upcoming conversation with his father, he had qualities that were of value to his world, and that there was a positive future for him.

Christopher still struggles with emotional eating, but he has learned to use it as his barometer for issues he needs to confront, rather than a demonstration of failure.

Box 8.4
CASE STUDY:
Unconditional
Acceptance
Facilitates
Communication

Promote Empowerment

A client comes to a nutrition therapist to learn how to make her own decisions. The empowerment approach focuses on developing the client's confidence in making her own choices, rather than making choices for the client. Every choice should be embraced as a learning experience *(Box 8.5)*. In nutrition therapy, allowing for the bizarre and validating whatever choice is made models unconditional acceptance and removes the temptation to rebel. It also provides an environment in which the client may, possibly for the first time, consider what he does and doesn't like. From this point, most individuals drift toward a diet that is reasonably healthy by traditional nutritional standards. Only this time, perhaps for the first time, they are willfully choosing it and not eating it because someone else said they should or shouldn't.

Avoid Valuing Weight Change Above Everything Else

Even when dealing with anorexics, focusing on weight gain values the superficial above the internal, where change is most important. The nutrition therapist should develop the ability to provide her service without always weighing the client. She should have the client develop a list of ten markers of progress that are not related to changes in weight, such as increased desire to socialize, decreased mood lability, and increased spontaneity. Assessment tools should be included in the initial evaluation that do not address weight or body composition. The more that cognitive and emotional change is emphasized, the more likely it is that the client will be able to make the behavioral changes that had not occurred by overtly working for them.

Consider the Issues Behind the Choice to Be a Nutrition Therapist

Nutrition therapists should ponder why they became nutrition professionals. Those who entered the profession to resolve their own weight issues under supervision should work to resolve them. Otherwise, there is a possibility of communicating (even subconsciously) size discrimination. Entering the profession to help a family member with a weight problem may result in countertransference reactions to clients that impair the ability to free the clients from food issues.

The goal of nutrition therapy is to empower clients to make their own choices and feel good about them. As a profession, nutrition therapists should reflect the

Box 8.5
CASE STUDY:
Empowering Choices

Linda's four-year-old daughter was developing a reputation as the family's picky eater. Rather than force young Sierra to eat what she didn't want to eat, Linda asked Sierra if she would like to be in charge of the menu one night each week. Sierra was thrilled. Her first attempt, M & Ms with macaroni and cheese (because it looked pretty), was not palatable, even to Sierra. Even so, it was consumed by the family and respected as Sierra's choice, and she continued to take charge of dinner one night each week. Sierra learned, through the process of elimination, what she did and did not like. Gradually she drifted toward menu choices that were balanced and consistent with what her mother was making the rest of the week. Because she was allowed to move to this place on her own, Sierra did not rebel and accepted the choices on her own.

general population, with a variety of physical characteristics, including size. Tolerance for size differences within the profession is an important step toward tolerance for these differences in the rest of the population *(Box 8.6)*.

Box 8.6
The Voice of Experience:
One Dietitian's Story

The roots of my eating disorder trace back to my early teens. Although never overweight, I was fearful of falling into the diet traps and weight patterns of my three older sisters and mother. They were forever dieting, yet unsuccessful in losing weight. Because of this, I knew at an early age I wanted to become a dietitian. There had to be an easier, healthier, and more successful way to diet, and I wanted to help.

I was raised in a large family, and food was always plentiful. My mother was extremely busy raising nine children and food was often used as a way to nurture us. Mom was forever cooking and baking. Family affairs centered around food, and food was frequently the topic of conversation. I found myself at the age of thirteen journaling about food, calories, and diets. Unlike my sisters and friends, I was a late bloomer and became very conscientious of not only my weight, but also my body image.

Because my father was a "functional" alcoholic and a workaholic, I learned at an early age to value hard work. Growing up, I discovered that the more I could "do", the more recognition and attention I received from my parents. Although I shared many of my siblings' characteristics, I was also different from them. I was the only one to graduate from college and leave my home state. I am one of only two not to marry at an early age. I became the family hero and received a lot of reinforcement for my achievements. My family believed in me more than I did, and was always encouraging me to do things despite my doubts, anxieties, and fears. I was frequently told, "Don't worry, you can do it." Although I didn't know it at the time, I learned to disengage from my inner feelings and to rely on the feelings of others.

During college, I learned about what did and did not represent a healthy diet and lifestyle. The more I learned, the healthier I began to eat, but my obsession over calorie counting and weight continued. Upon graduation, I moved away from home to do an internship. That year I also began experimenting with bulimia. I was lonely and anxious and periodically found comfort in food. After few years, this experimenting turned into a full-time compulsion.

The bulimia peaked during the summer of 1989, when my personal and professional life were completely out of control. I was offered a major job promotion that was too good to refuse. I immediately became enmeshed with my job, and my personal life suffered. Instead of allowing myself to feel what was going on inside, I worried and ate my feelings away. That summer brought several personal tragedies (the murder of a special friend, the death of a grandmother, stalking by an acquaintance) that I was unprepared for. I was filled with myriad feelings and didn't know how or what to do with them. Food became my best friend and my enemy. It was always there for me, whether I was feeling high or low. It sometimes relaxed me with its anesthetic side effects, and at other times make me feel like a crazed, out-of-control monster.

continued

My life became a paradox. I was now a dietitian who looked and played the part. I learned everything I could about dieting, and with this newly acquired knowledge was able to help everyone but myself. I wanted so badly to be a role model for the profession. I had always been discouraged by the number of dietitians who were overweight and didn't practice what they preached. I felt like a hypocrite and a fake. For years I used my profession as a mask. Who would ever suspect a young, aspiring dietitian was battling an eating disorder? It was a battle that for the first few years I thought I could win on my own. After all, I knew what I was doing and what I needed to overcome it all. I was invincible!

It wasn't until I realized things were getting worse that I confided in some coworkers and family members and sought professional treatment. It took me awhile to find a psychotherapist I felt comfortable with and, most important, trusted. Unfortunately, that meant commuting 300 miles round trip and I wasn't able to see her as frequently as necessary. Although every visit was valuable and I learned a great deal about myself, the disease was progressing (despite many periods of temporary "freedom" from it). My therapist was a strong Christian and taught me a great deal about the role of spirituality in the recovery process. I learned about unconditional acceptance and how to deal with my feelings of guilt and shame. After a year of yo-yo recovery, my therapist encouraged me to consider an inpatient therapy program. She felt I needed a safe place where I could focus all my attention and energy on the bulimia. The program's philosophy was holistic and comprehensive in nature, and involved several treatment modalities.

Admitting myself into the program was a humbling experience. Fellow patients quickly learned of my profession, and again I felt like a hypocrite. All my life I'd wanted to be successful and to prove to others that they could be, as well, if they took a few risks and worked hard. Needless to say, I felt like a failure and a disgrace to my profession.

Knowing I'd be meeting with a dietitian didn't make it any easier, but she made me realize from the beginning that I wasn't immune to an eating disorder. Difficult though it was, I placed my trust in the dietitian and found her to be an extremely important person in my recovery. She taught me the importance of not only having the intellectual knowledge, but also being able to translate that knowledge into personal and professional behaviors and actions. Incorporating the principles of good nutrition made a major difference in my nutritional status and was a cornerstone in my recovery process.

I remain in recovery today, and am much stronger and healthier than I was when the bulimia first surfaced. The disease is multifaceted, and so is my recovery plan. Although recovery isn't always easy, committing to living a more healthy, balanced lifestyle has helped me tremendously.

Avoid Blaming the Victim

Nutrition therapists should recognize the cultural issues that affect clients. They should not complain or blame, but look for positive actions that can promote cultural change, as detailed in Box 8.3. Eating disordered and disordered eating clients have been victimized enough; it is important to model positive conflict resolution and problem solving in client-counselor interactions with them.

SUMMARY

- Disordered eating results from a combination of physiological, psychological, and cultural influences. Traditional medical models of nutrition therapy tend to address mainly the physiological component of the problem. When psychological and cultural issues are not considered, nutrition intervention can have a negative influence on an individual's recovery.

- Many behaviors that accompany a disordered eating profile result from additive environmental stress that overloads physiological coping mechanisms and challenges those whose psychological coping skills are compromised.

- Nutrition therapy needs to include life skills training that reduces an individual's perceived stress and improves perceived self-effectiveness.

- The purpose of nutrition counseling under the new empowerment paradigm is to enable a client to make internalized food choices free of guilt and shame.

- An individual's reasons for entering the nutrition profession may interfere with his or her ability to effectively use the empowerment model. Awareness of one's psychosocial profile can decrease the chance that such interference or transference will hinder effective work in the profession.

REFERENCES

1. Brownell KD, Fairburn CG, eds. *Eating Disorders: A Comprehensive Handbook.* New York: Guilford Press; 1995.

2.. Kuczmarski RJ, Flegal KM, Campbell SM, Johnson CL. Increasing prevalence of overweight among US adults: the National Health and Nutrition Examination Surveys, 1960 to 1991. *JAMA.* 1994;272(3):238–239.

3. Sleep strategies for shift workers. http://www.sleepfoundation.org/publications/shiftworker.html. Accessed Nov 9, 2000.

4. Kant AK, Schatzkin A. Consumption of energy-dense, nutrient-poor foods by the US population: effect on nutrient profiles. *J Am Coll Nutr.* 1994;13(3):285–291.

5. Haines PS, Hungerford DW, Popkin BM, Guildey DK. Eating patterns and energy and nutrient intakes of US women. *J Am Diet Assoc.* 1992; 92(6):698–704,707.

6. The Subcommittee on Surface Transportation Hearing, July 27, 1997, Road Rage: Causes and Dangers of Aggressive Driving. http://www.house.gov/transportation/surface/sthearin/ist717/ist717.htm. Accessed Nov 9, 2000.

7. Kushnir T, Kasan R. Major sources of stress among women managers, clerical workers, and working single mothers: demands vs. resources. *Public Health Rev.* 1992–93;20(3–4):215–229.

8. 1999 Lunch Study: Restaurateurs Put Food Back into Lunch Hour. http://www.restaurant.org/rusa/1999/october/9910p22.htm. Accessed Nov 9, 2000.

9. The evolving American family. *Stat Bull Metrop Insur Co.* 1993;74(2):2–8.

10. Teachman JD, Paasch KM. Financial impact of divorce on children and their families. *Future Child.* 1994;4(1):63–83.

11. Clark JJ, Sawyer MG, Nguyen AM, Baghurst PA. Emotional and behavioral problems experienced by children living in single-parent families: a pilot study. *J Paediatr Child Health.* 1993;29(5):338–343.

12. Derksen DJ, Strasburger VC. Children and the influence of the media. *Prim Care.* 1994;21(4):747–758.

13. Wolf N. *The Beauty Myth: How Images of Beauty are Used Against Women.* New York: Anchor Books; 1992.

14. *Trends in the United States: Consumer Attitudes and the Supermarket, 1999.* Washington, DC: Food Marketing Institute; 1999.

15. Ornish D. Can lifestyle changes reverse coronary heart disease? *World Rev Nutr Diet.* 1993;72:38–48.

16. Gould KL, Ornish D, Kirkeeide R, Brown S, Stuart Y, Buchi M, Billings J, Armstrong W, Ports T, Scherwitz L. Improved stenosis geometry by quantitative coronary arteriography after vigorous risk factor modification. *Am J Cardiol.* 1992; 69(9):845–853.

CHAPTER 9

Introduction to Diagnosis and Classification of Mental Disorders

MONIKA M. WOOLSEY, M.S., R.D.

The American Psychiatric Association (APA) recommends that clinicians use a multiaxial system to assess mental disorders (1). Also referred to as the DSM-IV system, this method of classification includes five separate axes *(Box 9.1)*. In comparison with the traditional medical diagnostic model, this system provides means for constructing a comprehensive profile of the client. Medical diagnoses are part of the APA system; however, psychiatric, psychological, and sociocultural profiles are also included. This format allows the clinician to

- gain insight into how the client perceives and responds to her environment,
- design treatment plans with interventions that are consistent with the client's learning style,
- appreciate the psychological barriers that affect the client's ability to adhere to the treatment plan, and
- draw from a wide range of possible outcomes (behavioral, educational, and medical) that can be measured to evaluate success with treatment.

The following chapters in this section will discuss in detail the first three axes of the APA System of Diagnosis and Classification. The final two axes, while not as complex diagnostically, contain important information that the clinician can use to personalize and individualize treatment. Axis IV describes any environmental or personal issues that can affect the client's response to intervention. Categories listed under Axis IV include occupational problems, educational problems, housing problems, and problems related to the social environment. Examples are provided in the three diagnostic presentations included in this chapter.

**Box 9.1
Axes Included in
Multiaxial Assessment
of Mental Disorders
(DSM-IV)**

Axis I	Clinical Disorder
	Other Conditions That May Be a Focus of Treatment
Axis II	Personality Disorders
	Mental Retardation
Axis III	General Medical Conditions
Axis IV	Psychosocial and Environmental Problems
Axis V	Global Assessment of Functioning

Axis V is expressed as a numerical score on the Global Assessment of Functioning Scale *(Box 9.2)*(1). It provides an overall evaluation of how the client is able to function in her everyday world, given the diagnoses and situations she is currently experiencing. This score is fluid, and represents the client's state at the time of testing. While scoring is the responsibility of the client's mental health professional, understanding the meaning of the score and the limitations of the client is important if the nutrition therapist is to design interventions that capitalize on her current capabilities without expecting a response that is beyond her current state of functioning.

Traditional dietetics training tends to focus on medical diagnoses and outcomes. Though the medical axis is the "best fit" for the focus of a nutritional treatment plan, the diagnoses and information provided in the other axes can significantly enhance the nutrition therapist's ability to demonstrate a positive outcome. A diabetic's most important medical goal, for example, might be to reduce blood glucose and glycosylated hemoglobin measurements. However, if she is also depressed and binge eating in response to this depression, this may be the core issue to address in order to effect the desired biochemical changes. A client who is being treated for depression may be at risk for lowered zinc intake because of loss of appetite, which may further reduce his sense of taste and desire to eat. A treatment team that uses a comprehensive diagnosis system is more likely to intervene in a fashion that accelerates progress. Without this system, interventions are likely to conflict and delay the client's ability to move out of her eating disorder. Examples of classifications for each of the axes are provided in *Boxes 9.3–9.5*.

In most traditional nutrition counseling settings, a client is likely to present with only his Axis III, or medical, diagnoses. The traditional model for nutrition counseling places the nutrition therapist at the end point of treatment, where the problem requiring treatment has been identified and the nutrition therapist is mainly responsible for implementing a diet prescription decided upon by the referring professional. This model of identification, referral, and treatment may be inadequate for a combination of reasons:

- Managed care has shortened the length of physician visits, which limits the ability to ask the number of questions often necessary to connect psychosocial stressors to health problems and eating habits. A physician may identify

Box 9.2
Global Assessment of
Functioning (GAF) Scale

Consider psychological, social, and occupational functioning on a hypothetical continuum of mental health————illness. Do not include impairment in functioning due to physical (or environmental) limitations.

CODE

100–91 Superior functioning in a wide range of activities. Life's problems never seem to get out of hand, is sought out by others because of his or her many positive qualities. No symptoms.

90–81 Absent or minimal symptoms (eg, mild anxiety before an exam), good functioning in all areas, interested and involved in a wide range of activities, socially effective, generally satisfied with life, no more than everyday problems or concerns (eg, an occasional argument with family members).

80–71 If symptoms are present, they are transient and expectable reactions to psychosocial stressors (eg, difficulty concentrating after family argument); no more than slight impairment in social, occupational, or school functioning (eg, temporarily falling behind in schoolwork).

70–61 Some mild symptoms (eg, depressed mood and mild insomnia **or** some difficulty in social, occupational, or school functioning (eg, occasional truancy, or theft within the household), but generally functioning pretty well, has some meaningful interpersonal relationships.

60–51 Moderate symptoms (eg, flat affect and circumstantial speech, occasional panic attacks) **or** moderated difficulty in social, occupational, or school functioning (eg, few friends, conflicts with peers or coworkers).

50–41 Serious symptoms (eg, suicidal ideation, severe obsessional rituals, frequent shoplifting) **or** any serious impairment in social, occupational, or school functioning (eg, no friends, unable to keep a job).

40–31 Some impairment in reality testing or communication (eg, speech is at times illogical, obscure, or irrelevant) **or** major impairment in several areas, such as work or school, family relations, judgment, thinking, or mood (eg, depressed man avoids friends, neglects family, and is unable to work; child frequently beats up younger children, is defiant at home, and is failing at school.

30–21 Behavior is considerably influenced by delusions or hallucinations **or** serious impairment in communication or judgment (eg, sometimes incoherent, acts grossly inappropriately, suicidal preoccupation) **or** inability to function in all areas (eg, stays in bed all day; no job, home, or friends).

20–11 Some danger of hurting self or others (eg, suicide attempts without clear expectation of death; frequently violent; manic excitement) **or** occasionally fails to maintain minimal personal hygiene (eg, smears feces) **or** gross impairment in communication (eg, largely incoherent or mute).

10-1 Persistent danger of severely hurting self or others (eg, recurrent violence) **or** persistent inability to maintain minimal personal hygiene **or** serious suicidal act with clear expectation of death.

Note: Use intermediate codes when appropriate, eg, 45, 68, 72.
American Psychiatric Association (1). Used with permission.

a problem that has manifested and recognize that intervention would be beneficial, but may not have the time to pursue the problem past that point. A nutrition assessment is typically at least an hour in duration, which provides more opportunity to develop rapport and ask questions than a shorter appointment time.

- The client's medical problem may be the first measurable manifestation of a deeper problem. A psychosocial stressor may have been in existence for quite a long time, but until its consequences can be measured with a blood test, urine test, or blood pressure reading, the client may not have viewed the stressor as a problem requiring intervention.

- The client may have experienced distress as a result of the psychosocial stressor but may not feel comfortable talking about it. The medical issue may be "safer", and thus easier to focus on.

- The client may be aware that he has emotional and physical problems in need of intervention, but may not have realized that the problems were related to each other.

- The client may recognize that she has emotional and physical problems and hope that the concrete nature of nutrition information (eg, grams to count, portions to calculate, weight change to measure) will provide answers and eliminate the need to discuss painful emotions. She may have even been told by other practitioners that her problems have a mind-body connection, and hope the nutrition therapist will contradict that conclusion.

- If the client has an eating disorder, the very nature of that disorder causes him to connect events and problems to food eaten and body weight measured, rather than to psychosocial stressors.

**Box 9.3
Diagnosis and
Classification of
Individuals with
Binge Eating Disorder
(DSM-IV)**

Axis I	Eating Disorder Not Otherwise Specified: Binge Eating Disorder
	Major Depressive Disorder, Recurrent, Moderate, Seasonal Pattern
Axis II	Histrionic Personality Disorder
Axis III	Hypercholesterolemia
	Hypertension
Axis IV	Occupational Problems:
	Unhappy in career as a nurse
	Problems Related to Social Environment:
	Social life has decreased because friends and relatives work a different shift than she does
	Other Psychosocial and Environmental Problems:
	Difficulty adjusting to her workshift
Axis V	Current GAF = 56
	Highest GAF in Past Year = 60

American Psychiatric Association (1). Used with permission.

Axis I	Bulimia Nervosa
	Post-Traumatic Stress Disorder
Axis II	Borderline Personality Disorder
Axis III	Severe Constipation
	Esophagitis
Axis IV	Problems with Primary Support Group:
	Separation from husband
Axis V	Current GAF = 41
	Highest GAF in Past Year = 55

American Psychiatric Association (1). Used with permission.

Box 9.4
Diagnosis and Classification of Individuals with Bulimia Nervosa (DSM-IV)

Axis I	Anorexia Nervosa
	Major Depressive Disorder, Recurrent, Severe
Axis II	Obsessive-Compulsive Personality Disorder
Axis III	Malnutrition
	Amenorrhea
	Iron Deficiency Anemia
Axis IV	Environmental Problems and Problems Related to the Social Environment:
	Adjusting to college and being away from family
Axis V	Current GAF = 37
	Highest GAF in Past Year = 55

American Psychiatric Association (1). Used with permission.

Box 9.5
Diagnosis and Classification of Individuals with Anorexia Nervosa (DSM-IV)

For all these reasons, it is important that the nutrition therapist do a nutrition assessment that evaluates aspects of the client's life that extend beyond his eating habits. It is also important to consider that an eating disorder may exist even if one has not been identified or the identified issue is medical in nature (eg, diabetes, hypertension, or hyperlipidemia). Eating disorders almost never exist independently of other problems, but rather as a component of problems that manifest emotionally as well as physically. The nutrition therapist needs to feel comfortable functioning as a point of identification, screening, and referral, as well as in the traditional role of education.

Clients often hope that a diet or nutrition consultation will provide a simple, concrete answer to a complicated, threatening problem. If it appears that nutrition may be only a part of the problem, it is important to ascertain the client's comfort level with the non-nutrition-related issues. One way to move toward integrating emotional and physical issues is to use an outcome study that measures changes and progress that may be related to weight but that cannot be measured in the traditional fashion. The Diet Mentality Quiz *(Figure 9.1)* shows outcomes

Tell how often you feel like the descriptions in each statement, using the following numbers:
1–always; 2–very often; 3–often; 4–sometimes; 5–rarely; 6–never

1. _____ I am unhappy with myself the way I am.

2. _____ I am constantly thinking about changing the way I look (thinner, more muscular, smaller nose, etc).

3. _____ I weigh myself several times a week.

4. _____ The number on the scale influences whether I feel good about myself or not. (If the number is where I want it to be, I feel good about life and myself. If the number is higher or lower than I want it to be I feel lousy about myself.)

5. _____ I think about burning calories when I exercise.

6. _____ I eat for reasons other than being physically hungry (tired, bored, lonely, upset, because food is there).

7. _____ I can't tell when I am hungry or full.

8. _____ I eat too quickly, not taking time to pay attention to my meal and taste, savor, and enjoy my food.

9. _____ I don't take time to do activities that I really enjoy that are just for me.

10. _____ I swing between times when I enjoy healthy eating and times when I eat out of control.

11. _____ I spend a lot of time worrying about how I look.

12. _____ I go through periods ranging from not eating anything to "pigging out" on food.

13. _____ I think all-or-nothing; if I can't do it all, or can't do it well, I don't even try.

14. _____ I try to do everything my friends ask of me.

15. _____ I try to do things perfectly, and if I don't succeed, I get really down on myself.

16. _____ I criticize myself when I don't achieve exactly what I set out to do (or don't reach my goals).

_____ Total + 4 = _____ Your Score

Source: Omichinski L (2). Used with permission.

Figure 9.1
Diet Mentality Quiz

other than weight change that can be used to measure progress. A client can answer a questionnaire such as the Diet Mentality Quiz during the initial appointment and again later in treatment. For individuals who focus on weight change as the only measure of progress and who feel frustrated by a lack of "progress", a review of other positive changes that have been made can keep them motivated. For individuals who have made important changes and who still do not feel better, the Diet Mentality Quiz can help identify which feelings are sensitive to dietary change and which may respond better to psychological counseling *(Box 9.6)*. In addition, the pre-diet and post-diet scores can provide helpful insights to a psychotherapist who is eventually brought onto the team to address issues that have not responded to nutrition therapy.

It is important to remember that, despite the nutrition therapist's best efforts, some clients will not respond to nutrition therapy. This is not an indication that nutrition therapy has failed or that the client has failed, but that the core problem was not the result of a nutrition-related problem. For some individuals, the problem may be a neuroendocrine (Axis I) imbalance, such as depression, anxiety, or obsessive-compulsive disorder, that will need medication to improve. For others, a personality issue may require psychotherapy to learn communication and coping behaviors that will make it easier to implement recommended nutrition therapies. It is important to recognize when Axis I and Axis II diagnoses exist so the appropriate team members can be involved in creating an effective treatment plan. *Box 9.7* lists some common characteristics of clients that may indicate

Question	Score/Initial Appointment	Score/8 Weeks Later
1	4	5
2	1	4
3	6	6
4	4	6
5	2	6
6	4	4
7	4	5
8	3	4
9	3	6
10	4	5
11	4	4
12	3	5
13	5	6
14	1	3
15	4	6
16	4	6

Box 9.6
Sample Pre- and Post-Diet Mentality Scores for Client Who Was Referred for Psychotherapy After Eight Weeks of Nutrition Therapy

Note: This client initially presented for help with bulimia. While he improved in every area measured, the ending scores on items 2, 6, 11, and 14 suggested that other issues were influencing his food behavior. Two months after completing the post-diet test, he was diagnosed with bipolar disorder. With the help of medication and group psychotherapy, he is stabilized and functional in his home and school environment and rarely uses food to cope with stress.

Box 9.7
Indications That an Axis I and/or Axis II Diagnosis Might Coexist with a Medical Diagnosis

- The client cannot understand basic information, continuously needs things repeated.
- Conversations appear to go in circles.
- The client's emotional state seem to derail productive problem solving.
- The client appears to sabotage assignments/self, either intentionally or unintentionally.
- The practitioner feels anxious on seeing the client's name on the schedule.
- The client brings out anger in the practitioner.
- The practitioner goes out of his way to accommodate the client, then feels taken advantage of.
- The client leaves the practitioner feeling exhausted after a session or phone conversation.

that an Axis I or Axis II diagnosis is part of the overall problem. Note that Axis I and Axis II diagnoses have a strong potential to bring out negative feelings and anxiety in the practitioner. For this reason, it is especially important to enlist the help of mental health professionals so that these tendencies do not interfere with the client's getting the help he needs.

In some settings, a client's medical and mental health documentation may not be on the same chart. This separation may be designed to protect the client's confidentiality. In a purely medical setting, documentation may pass through the hands of clinicians, office assistants, and medical records personnel. Mental health documentation is handled in a much more protective manner, and rightly so; information regarding an individual's mental status can affect employment, court decisions, and other significant aspects of an individual's life. Such information should be handled with care and provided to only those clinicians who need it in their work with the client *(Box 9.8)*.

The confidentiality issue also affects communications between clinicians. Legally, any professional who has received information in confidence is not allowed to share that information with any other person without the express written permission of the client. The nutrition therapist must respect this confidentiality and ask the client to sign a release for so the nutrition therapist can obtain the information needed for treatment planning. Similarly, out of respect for the client, the nutrition therapist must maintain confidentiality and release information only to those professionals, family members, or others who are designated in the release form *(Figure 9.2)*.

When documenting nutrition therapy sessions, the nutrition therapist must consider who will be reading the notes in the future. In a private practice setting, when documents are solely for the use of the individual practitioner, more detailed notes may be used. In a clinic setting where many practitioners chart jointly in one document and nonprofessionals have access to this documentation, detailed personal notes may still be taken, but sensitive personal and psychosocial information is best noted in generic terms.

Subjective:	Client says the past week was difficult for her. Was not able to meet her goal of including a fat exchange at each meal and had a tendency to fall back into "safe foods," rather than using the expanded meal plan she had been working on the past few weeks. Noticed that food rituals began to reappear. Also reported running an hour each day to manage anxiety.
Objective:	Weight was not recorded. Food/mood journal was reviewed, and connections between caloric intake, food choices, and emotions were discussed.
Assessment:	Client appears to have several psychosocial stressors that affect her ability to enact nondisordered food and exercise behaviors.
Plan:	(1) Continue to help client make connection between stress, emotions, and behavioral choices.
	(2) Continue to keep food/mood journal.
	(3) Develop "safe day" menu for client to use when anxiety affects coping skills.
	(4) Encourage client to share the week's events with support group.

Note: In this session the client revealed that her psychotherapist was beginning to work with her on issues relating to her marriage, which suffered from domestic abuse. The anxiety of considering separation was the core issue, but these specifics were excluded to protect the client's confidentiality.

**Box 9.8
Sample Documentation
of Eating Disorder
Therapy Session**

Because nutrition therapists are relatively new members of the mental health team, their interest in their clients' mental health issues may not be understood by the team psychotherapists. Psychotherapists may be reluctant to share information because they have a legal and ethical obligation the protest their clients' privacy.

Nutrition therapists can promote strong collaborative relationships with their mental health colleagues by

- framing questions in a way that explains the relevance of mental health information to the nutrition treatment plan;
- demonstrating healthy boundaries and not interacting with clients outside of their scope of practice (addressing psychological issues only as they relate to food behaviors);
- educating team members about the many connections between nutritional status, nutrient balance, and behavior.

A nutrition therapist who is willing to invest time in relationship building is likely to create value for his services as he develops a reputation for facilitating recovery in clients in a more comprehensive fashion than was possible without nutrition therapy *(Box 9.9)*. The mental health team is more likely to be open to working with a nutrition therapist who is perceived as an asset to their work, rather than someone who may be interfering with clients' progress.

AUTHORIZATION TO OBTAIN/RELEASE CONFIDENTIAL INFORMATION

I, _____, hereby authorize _____

to release my treatment records and to discuss my case with the following professionals:

Name: _____

Address: _____

_____

Phone: _____

Name: _____

Address: _____

_____

Phone: _____

I understand that my records and treatment are confidential and cannot be released without my express written consent, unless legally obliged. I am also aware of my right to revoke, in writing, this consent at any time, excepting any disclosure that has already occurred.

Date: _____

Client: _____
(signature)

Address: _____

_____

Parent/Guardian: _____

_____
(signature required if client is a minor)

Figure 9.2
Sample Release Form

Soon after I began working at a local outpatient eating disorder clinic, I received a phone call from one of the psychotherapists. She wanted to know why I asked questions that were not directly related to nutrition, why I made referrals to mental health professionals, and why I was interested in a client's Axis II diagnoses. I explained that there were several reasons these pieces of information were important.

First, in my years as a nutrition therapist, I had seen thousands of clients. My experience with those who presented over their ideal weight (which was confirmed in the literature) was that most did not eat breakfast and struggled with appetite and hunger all day as a result. I also knew from experience that merely handing these clients a diet that included a breakfast would not effect the desired behavior change. I learned as I worked more closely with mental health professionals that the behavior itself was often not as important as why that behavior was chosen in the first place. In the case of skipped breakfasts, I learned that if I asked why a client didn't eat breakfast and pursued my assessment past the typical "I don't have time" answer, these clients often reported insomnia, disrupted sleep patterns, and even nightmares that kept them up much of the night, leaving them exhausted the next morning. As a result, they got up too late with little to no time to think about eating. Such sleep disruptions were classic signs and symptoms of depression. If they were not normalized, there was not much I could do to normalize eating. In other words, I could be effective in my nutrition work only with the help of a psychiatrist and psychologist.

Second, if I did not know at least basic information about a client's mental health profile, I might very likely be drawn into a dysfunctional communication pattern that would sabotage what the psychotherapist was attempting to achieve. "Splitting" is extremely common in working with mental health clients. If I knew a client's Axis I and Axis II diagnoses, I also knew to some degree what types of medications and interventions this client was being exposed to, and I could tailor my assignments and expectations accordingly. A client might complain of feeling worse since initiating treatment and indicate a desire to discontinue working with a therapist. If I could help the client understand that what he was feeling might not be "worse" but "awareness of a range of emotions," and framed my conversations based on the learning/perception/response styles his Axis I/Axis II profile described, I might help encourage the client to stay in treatment and to understand what the psychotherapist was working to accomplish. Not understanding the goals and expected outcomes of my team members could negate weeks of invested treatment time.

Finally, I explained that many clients coming to my office for the first time would more appropriately seek psychotherapy. However, the stigma often attached to mental health care prevented them from seeking the appropriate professional. In this early stage of awareness, the client might know that something "isn't right" or "feels out of control" but hope that a solution might be found in a diet. In other words, in the eyes of the client, I might be the least threatening health professional she could turn to for help. In such cases, my ultimate job might be not to provide nutritional advice, but to begin assessment and perform triage. If I could ask basic questions and recognize early in the counseling relationship that this client had a problem that would eventually require interventions beyond my expertise, I could help this client get the help she needed. My best service might be to develop trust

Box 9.9
Making the Mental Health Connection Work

continued

Box 9.9
(*continued*)

with the client and enable her to move into the mental health system that she previously had not considered as a treatment option.

With time, this psychotherapist and I developed a healthy working relationship. We came too understand and respect each other's specialties and scopes of practice, and trust that we support each other in our work. The trust took some time to develop, but was worth the effort. Not only did we increase referrals to each other, but we were able to see changes in our clients that occurred much more quickly than when we were tentative with our own relationship.

SUMMARY

- **The American Psychiatric System of Diagnosis and Classification provides means for constructing the client's physical and mental profile.**

- **Though each of the axes in the PA system may reflect the diagnostic skills and treatment responsibilities of specific members of the treatment team, it is important for each member of the team to understand the impact of each axis on his or her own treatment planning and intervention.**

- **The flow of a patient through a typical health care setting may result in an individual presenting for nutrition therapy before any existing Axis I or Axis II diagnoses have been formally identified. It is important to recognize the basic symptoms of these diagnoses and to include the appropriate caregivers in the client's treatment plan, as not addressing them may set the client up to fail with recommendations provided in nutrition therapy.**

- **Confidentiality regarding mental health and psychosocial information is crucial in order to protect the rights of the client; documentation should be protected and released only to those individuals designated by the client.**

REFERENCES

1. *Diagnostic and Statistical Manual of Mental Disorders.* 4th ed. Washington, DC: American Psychiatric Association; 1994.
2. Omichinski L. *You Count, Calories Don't.* 3rd ed. Winnipeg, Canada: Tomos Books; 1993.

CHAPTER 10

Axis I: Diagnoses and Psychiatric Interventions

MONIKA M. WOOLSEY, M.S., R.D.

An Axis I diagnosis pertains to the psychiatric component of the eating disorder, and is therefore managed primarily by the team psychiatrist and psychologist. In the treatment of eating disorders, these professionals have three important areas of responsibility: diagnosis, medication, and psychological therapy. Each area can significantly affect the client's nutritional progress; likewise, nutritional status can affect the client's response to psychiatric and psychological treatment. Frequent communication between the team psychiatrist, psychologist, and nutritionist is essential so that their combined interventions can result in successful treatment. Psychological therapy is discussed in more detail in the following chapter; this chapter will focus on nutritional implications as well as diagnosis, medication, and treatment planning for Axis I diagnoses.

DIAGNOSIS

The eating disorder itself—anorexia nervosa, bulimia nervosa, or eating disorder not otherwise specified—is a psychiatric diagnosis that is listed under Axis I. Binge eating disorder is currently categorized as a "research category." Its use is being tested in the current version of the *Diagnostic and Statistical Manual of Mental Disorders-IV* (1), and is being considered for inclusion as a separate diagnosis in future versions of the manual.

Eating disorders are often not separate, but reflect an individual's relationship with food at the time of the interview. Over time, an eating disorder can begin as binge eating, progress to anorexia nervosa, and shift to bulimia. With some individuals, the type of eating disorder diagnosed communicates the prevailing issues at the time of treatment. For example, if control issues are dominant, anorexia might manifest. If therapy for control issues has progressed and the client and family have successfully addressed problem areas, other issues that were buried beneath the control issue might surface. Memories of a physical or sexual trauma might surface. Anger about a parent's divorce might come to light. For these reasons, it is important for the psychiatrist or psychologist to take a thorough chronological history before assigning a diagnosis to the client's condition. The nutrition therapist's interview might bring to light important food-emotional connections; however, definitive mental health assessment and diagnosis are the responsibility of the team psychologist or psychiatrist.

A diagnosis of bulimia indicates that a compensatory mechanism is part of the client's presentation. Compensatory mechanisms include self-induced vomiting, caloric restriction, compulsive exercise, diet pill use, and diuretic/laxative abuse. A nutrition assessment should not only cover caloric intake and output, but characterize the individual bulimic behaviors. *Table 10.1* summarizes the most common types of bulimia engaged in. This list is not all-inclusive, but illustrates the types of questions that need to be asked in order to understand the nature and purpose of the symptoms for which the individual is seeking help.

If some combination of anorexia, bulimia, and binge eating is identified, a careful history should be conducted to assess the presence of other psychiatric conditions. The "mixed disorder" has a more serious comorbid psychopathology than the "pure disorder"; treatment plans will likely need adjustment to accommodate these coexisting conditions. Mixed-disorder individuals tend to have significantly lower body weights than pure-disorder individuals, and to be more likely to use laxatives and less likely to engage in self-induced vomiting (2). This subgroup also tends to be less verbal and therefore tends to exhibit more behaviors that act out their communication to others (2).

Table 10.1 Common Behavior Patterns Found in Bulimia Nervosa Clients	Pattern	Incidence
	Finger-induced purging with occasional use of diet pills, diuretics, and/or laxatives	62%
	Finger-induced purging and regular use of <50 laxatives a day	25%
	Binge eating without finger-induced purging but with regular use of ≥50 laxatives a day	3%
	Binge eating without finger-induced purging but with regular use of Ipecac	1.6%
	Bulimia Subtypes	
	Overt bulimia	2%
	Sexually evocative bulimia	2.9%
	Obsessive-ritualistic bulimia	2%
	Masochistic bulimia	4.9%

44% of persons with bulimia overeat, 19% undereat. In those who overeat, 37% of their meals contain more than 1000 calories. These large meals are consumed predominantly in the afternoon and evening and consist mainly of dessert and snack foods.

Source: Hall et al (2).

Because guilt and shame over behaviors is common, clients are often defensive in their initial interviews. They may not disclose important psychiatric information to the psychiatrist but freely discuss their insomnia with the nutrition therapist. Likewise, the psychiatrist may get more detailed information about food behaviors than the nutrition therapist. This behavior can be frustrating, but performs an important function for the client, many of whom have dysfunctional backgrounds and histories of abuse and neglect. Guilt and shame are often prevailing emotions at the initiation of treatment. The fear that being truthful about behaviors will bring judgment and rejection makes honesty difficult for many clients. Finally, as undesirable as some of the presenting behaviors might be, they have been (from the client's perception) a means of coping; the fear of having these behaviors taken away with no concept of what replacement behaviors will be is overwhelming. Clients are also frequently accustomed to triangulation because it is the predominant communication style in their family of origin. As a result, they may attempt to use triangulation when communicating with treatment team members (ie, speaking about nutrition needs with the psychiatrist with the expectation that this information will be passed on to the nutrition therapist).

Though psychiatry, psychology, and nutrition are completely different specialties, it is important for each team member to understand the work of the others so that important information is provided to the professional most able to provide help with that issue, regardless of how the client chooses to disclose it. Client interviews are best structured so that some questions are asked by multiple team members and answers can be compared for discrepancies. After all intake interviews have been completed, answers can be compared and a "big picture" assessment can be made. This comprehensive approach then becomes the blueprint for treatment planning from which all team members work.

Eating disorders commonly coexist with other medical and psychiatric conditions, and it is important to evaluate a client for the possible existence of comorbid conditions. The psychiatrist or psychologist is the treatment team member most qualified to make a formal diagnosis and to identify these additional diagnoses *(Box 10.1);* any information gained in the nutrition assessment that may be

COMORBID CONDITIONS

Unipolar depression
Bipolar depression
Obsessive-compulsive disorder (OCD)
Seasonal affective disorder (SAD)
Post-traumatic stress disorder (PTSD)
Attention deficit-attention deficit/hyperactive disorder (ADD/ADHD)
Paranoid schizophrenia
Substance abuse

Box 10.1 Comorbid Axis I Conditions Commonly Seen with Eating Disorders

of value to these professionals should be shared so that diagnosis and treatment planning are expedient and accurate. This chapter will describe important aspects of each of these diagnoses and provide considerations to be made in the nutritional treatment plan that account for the additional complications these diagnoses place on an individual's ability to participate in day-to-day life and food consumption.

MEDICATION ADMINISTRATION

Psychiatric medications are an important part of treatment. They are often used to "jump-start" a client out of circular or addictive behavior patterns that behavioral therapy alone has not been able to correct. Or, if a diagnosis can be attributed to an inherent chemical imbalance, medications may be prescribed as a permanent intervention. As these medications can alter behavior and thought processes, they can also alter a client's response to nutrition interventions. It is important to understand the functions of these medications and to tailor nutrition therapy to the client's capabilities within her medication regimen. A list of common psychiatric medications is provided in *Table 10.2.*

The nutrition therapist is often the first treatment team member the client sees. This is to be expected because, from the client's perspective, the eating disorder is an eating problem. However, if an eating disorder is suspected or if reported behaviors suggest that the client's diagnosis is more complicated, a psychiatric and/or psychological consultation should be recommended. In many clients, behaviors will not change without such an intervention. The client's inability to follow through with assignments and assigned interventions will only compound the guilt and shame that likely drive the eating disorder in the first place. To increase the probability of successful treatment, the nutrition therapist should proactively engage other members of the treatment team who can implement interventions that support the desired changes.

Antidepressants

Because depression is such a frequent comorbid condition in eating disordered individuals, antidepressants are commonly prescribed. Three categories of antidepressants are currently approved by the Food and Drug Administration: monoamine oxidase inhibitors, tricyclics, and selective serotonin reuptake inhibitors. Each type functions to correct a biochemical imbalance in the brain that has fostered the development of depression. Table 10.2 lists the major antidepressant medications by category, generic name, and trade name.

Monoamine oxidase inhibitors (MAOIs) were the first class of antidepressants to be developed. They slow down the biochemical degradation of the neurotransmitter norepinephrine (3). Though most eating disordered individuals use other antidepressant regimens, some are still prescribed MAOIs. Their nutritional implications are important to understand.

Because MAOIs block the monoamine oxidase pathway, they also impair the body's ability to metabolize some dietary components. When these components

Trade Name	Generic Name	Manufacturing Company	
Adderall	mixed amphetamines	Shire Richwood Pharmaceutical Company Florence, Kentucky	**Table 10.2** **Common** **Psychiatric** **Medications**
Anafranil	clomipramine	Novartis Pharmaceuticals East Hanover, New Jersey	
Asendin	amoxapine	Lederle Laboratories Pearl River, New York	
Ativan	lorazepam	Wyeth/Ayerst Laboratories Philadelphia, Pennsylvania	
Aventyl	nortryptiline	Eli Lilly and Company Indianapolis, Indiana	
BuSpar	buspirone	Bristol-Myers Squibb Princeton, New Jersey	
Celexa	citalopram	Forest Pharmaceuticals St Louis, Missouri	
Centrax	prazepam	Parke-Davis Pharmaceuticals Morris Plains, New Jersey	
Cylert	pemoline	Abbott Laboratories North Chicago, Illinois	
Depakote	divalproex sodium	Abbott Laboratories North Chicago, Illinois	
Dexedrine	dextroamphetamine	Smith Kline Beecham Philadelphia, Pennsylvania	
Effexor	venlafaxine	Wyeth-Ayerst Laboratories Philadelphia, Pennsylvania	
Elavil	amitryptiline	AstraZeneca Pharmaceuticals Wilmington, Delaware	
Eskalith	lithium carbonate	Smith Kline Beecham Philadelphia, Pennsylvania	
Haldol	haloperidol	Ortho McNeil Pharmaceutical Corporation Raritan, New Jersey	
Klonopin	clonazepam	Roche Laboratories Nutley, New Jersey	
Lamictal	lamotrigine	Glaxo-Wellcome Research Triangle Park, North Carolina	
Librax	chlordiazepoxide	Roche Laboratories Nutley, New Jersey	
Libritabs	chlordiazepoxide	Roche Laboratories Nutley, New Jersey	
Librium	chlordiazepoxide	ICN Costa Mesa, California	
Lithobid	lithium carbonate	Solvay Pharmaceuticals Marietta, Georgia	
Ludiomil	maprotiline	Novartis Pharmaceuticals East Hanover, New Jersey	
Luvox	fluvoxamine maleate	Solvay Pharmaceuticals Marietta, Georgia	
Marplan	isocarboxazid	Roche Laboratories Nutley, New Jersey	
Mellaril	thioradazine	Novartis Pharmaceuticals East Hanover, New Jersey	
Nardil	phenelzine sulfate	Parke-Davis Pharmaceuticals Morris Plains, New Jersey	
Navane	thiothixine	Pfizer Pharmaceuticals New York, New York	
Neurontin	gabapentin	Parke-Davis Pharmaceuticals Morris Plains, New Jersey	

	Trade Name	Generic Name	Manufacturing Company
Table 10.2 (*continued*)	Norpramin	desipramine	Hoechst Marion Roussel Kansas City, Missouri
	Pamelor	nortryptiline	Novartis Pharmaceuticals East Hanover, New Jersey
	Parnate	tranylcypromine sulfate	Smith Kline Beecham Philadelphia, Pennsylvania
	Paxil	paroxetine hydrochloride	Smith Kline Beecham Philadelphia, Pennsylvania
	Paxipam	halazepam	Schering-Plough Kenilworth, New Jersey
	Prolixin	fluphenazine	Bristol Myers Squibb Princeton, New Jersey
	Prozac	fluoxetine hydrochloride	Eli Lilly and Company Indianapolis, Indiana
	Remeron	mirtazapine	Organon, Inc West Orange, New Jersey
	Risperdal	risperidone	Janssen Pharmaceuticals, Inc Titusville, New Jersey
	Ritalin	methylphenidate hydrochloride	Novartis East Hanover, New Jersey
	Serax	oxazepam	Wyeth-Ayerst Laboratories Philadelphia, Pennsylvania
	Seroquel	quetiapine fumarate	AstraZeneca International Wilmington, Delaware
	Serzone	nefazodone hydrochloride	Bristol-Myers Squibb Princeton, New Jersey
	Sinequan	doxepin	Pfizer Pharmaceuticals New York, New York
	Thorazine	chlorpromazine	Smith Kline Beecham Philadelphia. Pennsylania
	Tofranil	imipramine	Novartis Pharmaceuticals East Hanover, New Jersey
	Tranxene	clorazepate	Abbott Laboratories North Chicago, Illinois
	Valium	diazepam	Roche Pharmaceuticals Nutley, New Jersey
	Vivactil	protryptiline	Merck & Company West Point, Pennsylvania
	Wellbutrin	bupropion	Glaxo-Wellcome Research Triangle Park, North Carolina
	Xanax	alprazolam	Pharmacia & Upjohn Peapack, New Jersey
	Zoloft	sertraline hydrochloride	Pfizer Pharmaceuticals New York, New York
	Zyprexa	olanzapine	Eli Lilly and Company Indianapolis, Indiana

accumulate, they may place the client at risk for hypertensive crisis. The MAOI diet is well known to most nutrition therapists; however, there are important considerations in the eating disordered client prescribed MAOIs. Many of the foods to be avoided on the MAOI diet are "fear foods" (foods commonly avoided by those with eating disorders, such as cheese and sausage). The person with anorexia may use this as an excuse to avoid these foods. Other antidepressants that do not require food restriction, if indicated, may be more appropriate. For the person with bulimia or binge eating disorder, the foods to be avoided may be binge foods. Reducing their intake at the initiation of treatment may not be realistic, and the risk of hypertensive crisis may be increased. Again, another medication may be more appropriate.

The medication decision is always the responsibility of the psychiatrist. However, the nutrition therapist may collect information in his assessment regarding the client's ability to follow a dietary regimen mandated by her medications. This information is important to share with the psychiatrist so that she can make the most appropriate decision regarding which medication to prescribe. Constructive communication is important.

Tricyclic antidepressants reduce the reuptake of serotonin and norepinephrine from a synapse after a nerve impulse has been transmitted. Increased synaptic levels of serotonin increase neuron stimulation and overall CNS responsiveness. Though successful in the treatment of eating disorders, their side effects can be particularly distressing to the client struggling with appetite dysfunction and body image: cotton mouth, increased appetite, and weight gain. It is important to help clients understand these in the context of their treatment if they are determined to be the most appropriate medication.

Selective serotonin reuptake inhibitors (SSRIs) are also reuptake inhibitors, but act specifically on serotonin concentrations. This category of antidepressant is the newest and most widely used in the treatment of eating disorders. Prozac was the first of the SSRIs to become available in the United States. Since then Paxil, Zoloft, Luvox, and Celexa have also been brought to market. Each of these medications alters serotonin metabolism using a slightly different mechanism, and there are individual responses to each. The end result of each is a relief of depressive symptoms, usually within 6 to 8 weeks of initiation of treatment (4).

Alterations in serotonin metabolism have been correlated with obsessive-compulsive disorder (OCD) and seasonal affective disorder (SAD), as well as with unipolar depression (5,6). SSRI medications may be indicated if these conditions exist, even if depression is not diagnosed (5). It is important to determine the condition for which the medication was described, as each of these diagnoses requires a slightly different approach in nutrition therapy sessions.

The impulsivity and compulsivity of clients prescribed SSRIs can affect the medication's effectiveness in several ways. First, because the medication takes several weeks to take effect, clients often give up and cease taking it before they achieve benefit. Second, if a client is actively purging, he is likely not receiving therapeutic levels of the drug. Third, SSRIs can alter sleep patterns, which directly affect meal patterns. Evaluating these possible scenarios, providing information that promotes compliance, and referring the client to the psychiatrist when a problem is noted are all important components of the nutrition session. Again, these issues may not arise in the psychiatrist's appointment, but are valuable pieces of information that should be accounted for in his medication decisions.

In general, antidepressants alter the biochemistry of the CNS so that it can respond to external stimuli in an appropriate fashion. As the neurochemistry of the brain is better understood, medications with more specific mechanisms of action (and fewer side effects) are being developed. The biochemical imbalance being corrected may be due to an ongoing external stress, or it may be a physiologically inherent condition that would exist in the absence of stress. Regardless of the cause of the imbalance, antidepressants are an important part of the treatment of eating disorders.

Appetite Suppressants

The knowledge of neuroendocrine physiology that created the SSRI class of antidepressants was recently taken one step further. As neuron anatomy was elucidated, it became clear that not only are there receptors for neurotransmitters, but these receptors are quite specialized in their function and physiological responsibilities. Thus far, at least 14 different subreceptors with different physiological functions have been identified (6); while one of these serotonin subreceptors is responsible for sleep-related stimuli, another primarily controls appetite, and so on.

Fenfluramine and dexfenfluramine operate on the same principle as SSRI medications. The main difference is that their impact is seen in a very specific serotonin receptor (5-HT3), the one responsible for appetite regulation and suppression (7). The concept is similar to that of a Patriot missile, in that these compounds attack very specific problem areas, rather than hitting a general area of operation in the hope that the specific problem area will be included in the target range. Phentermine, the medication that was often administered in combination with fenfluramine, is a norepinephrine stimulant (7). Used in combination, these medications were popularly referred to as "phen-fen".

At the time of this printing, fenfluramine was no longer available for prescription. Despite the fact that this appetite suppressant was not the answer to obesity that it was hoped to be, and was seemingly abused by many, there were many things to be learned from our short experience with these medications. In addition to appetite suppression, these medications had numerous endocrine effects, as summarized in *Box 10.2.* As explained in Chapter 2, the disruption in eating patterns found in individuals with eating disorders can often be traced back to an acute or chronic stress that taxed the neuroendocrine system past its ability to respond. The appetite suppressants appear to "jump-start" the individual out of a dysfunctional stress response that was not able to shut off on its own.

Appetite suppressants also affect many metabolic functions *(Box 10.3),* which reinforces the theory that there is an interaction between stress and many common obesity-related problems. Perhaps these findings help explain why participants in programs such as that promoted by Dean Ornish can reduce their cholesterol levels (8). In addition to making dietary changes, these individuals are taught to participate regularly in some type of stress reduction exercise, such as meditation or yoga, and to process daily stressors in a support group format.

These medications also have many behavioral impacts, which are likely a

**Box 10.2
Endocrine Impact
of Fenfluramine
and Fluoxetine**

Endocrine Impact of Fenfluramine (9-11)

Decreased cortisol-releasing hormone (CRH) and cortisol concentrations

Improved ACTH response to CRH

Decreased norepinephrine secretion

Decreased nighttime secretion of growth hormone

More distinct circadian rhythms in ACTH secretion

Decreased cortisol response to restraint stress

Improved receptor responsiveness

Endocrine Impact of Fluoxetine (12,13)

Normalization of prolactin levels

Decreased thyroid-stimulating hormone response to thyroid-releasing
   hormone

Reduced urinary NE/T3 ratio

reflection of the neurochemical changes they promote *(Box 10.4)*. It was the fact that phen-fen appeared to eliminate food-related behaviors that diets had not been able to over the long term that made phen-fen such a phenomenon.

It is important to note that fluoxetine (Prozac) has been found to have endocrine and metabolic effects similar to those of fenfluramine and dexfenfluramine. What this may suggest is that many individuals who responded well to appetite suppressants were individuals whose disrupted eating patterns were a symptom of a much more comprehensive problem, such as anxiety, depression, or obsessive-compulsive disorder. In focusing on the most obvious symptom, these individuals may have been overlooking the cause of the problem. Perhaps this is why appetite suppressants did not "fix" disordered eating and were effective only as long as they were taken. An individual who does not learn how to manage stress

**Box 10-3
Metabolic Impact
of Fenfluramine
and Fluoxetine**

Metabolic Impact of Fenfluramine (14-16)

Reduced diastolic blood pressure

Reduced serum cholesterol level

Improved insulin sensitivity

Decreased adipose and hepatic free fatty acid release

Decreased serum triglycerides

Decreased blood glucose response to restraint stress

Metabolic Impact of Fluoxetine (17,18)

Increased metabolic rate and body temperature

Reduced glycosylated hemoglobin

Reduction in dietary fat intake

Reduction in feeding-reward behavior that high-fat diet tends to reinforce

Hypophagia

Suppressed intake of high-carbohydrate, low-protein diet

Reduction in nocturnal eating

Change in sleep patterns

Increased taste aversion

Prolonged active circadian cycle

Reversed learned helplessness

and to cope with life in an assertive and constructive fashion will continue to absorb environmental stressors that disrupt his physiological function to the point where it alters eating behaviors. Again, this supports the need for medical/psychiatric intervention to be teamed with cognitive behavioral therapy in working with disordered eating.

Though the medical complications fenfluramine created (pulmonary hypertension and cardiac valve failure) led to its being banned by the Food and Drug Administration, the data collected may have helped the medical and nutritional communities view feeding behaviors from a slightly different perspective. Several conclusions can be drawn from the phen-fen experience:

- Feeding behavior has a strong physiological component that may not always respond to traditional "behavior modification" models of nutrition therapy,
- Environmental events perceived as stressful can have physiological consequences that alter feeding behavior,
- Medical problems such as hypertension and hypercholesterolemia, often associated with overweight, may be more closely associated with a predisposing "stressed" physiological state than with the weight itself, and
- The psychological treatment plan is just as important as the medical in working with eating disordered clients.

From a nutritional standpoint, one of the most important concepts that should be drawn from this issue is that basic evaluations for life stress and depression should be included in the assessment of a client presenting with altered eating patterns. If this evaluation proves to be positive, referral to a psychiatrist and/or psychologist should eventually be made.

Clients with eating disorders often have obsessional thinking patterns that are difficult to break without intervention by these specialists. Though fenfluramine is no longer available, many of these clients might benefit from a similarly acting drug, such as an SSRI antidepressant, from cognitive behavioral therapy, or from a combination of medication and behavioral intervention. These decisions need to be made by mental health professionals, but since these clients often first present in the nutrition therapist's office, recognizing the need for a team approach and initiating the appropriate referrals can be one of the most important services in the course of treatment that the nutrition therapist can provide.

The nutrition therapist will be most effective if she understands how Axis I diagnoses affect an individual's ability to perceive and respond to the world around her. Often these comorbid conditions render the client vulnerable to labels such as "noncompliant," "difficult," and "unmotivated". This is often far from the case! If these clients were not motivated, they would not have gone to the trouble to seek out advice from the medical community.

AXIS I DIAGNOSES

It is important to remember that an Axis I diagnosis denotes a variation in the cognitive process. It is not a deficit or a flaw, but a biological variation in cognition. Understanding how each of these diagnoses affects an individual's ability to follow recommendations can improve the nutrition therapist's ability to design interventions that are consistent with the client's current cognitive state and that serve to enhance a sense of self-esteem and self-effectiveness.

The remainder of this chapter describes the diagnoses and provides a summary of the nutritional implications each diagnosis is likely to have for the eating disordered client.

MAJOR DEPRESSIVE EPISODE: DIAGNOSIS

A. Five (or more) of the following symptoms have been present during the same 2-week period and represent a change from previous functioning; at least one of the symptoms is either depressed mood or loss of interest or pleasure. Do not include symptoms that are clearly due to a general medical condition or mood-incongruent delusions or hallucinations.

1. Depressed mood most of the day, nearly every day, as indicated by either subjective report (eg, feels sad or empty) or observation made by others (eg, appears tearful). Note: In children and adolescents, can be irritable mood.

2. Markedly diminished interest or pleasure in all, or almost all, activities most of the day, nearly every day (as indicated by either subjective account or observation made by others).

3. Significant weight loss when not dieting or weight gain (eg, a change of more than 5% of body weight in a month), or decrease or increase in appetite nearly every day. Note: In children, consider failure to make expected weight gains.

4. Insomnia or hypersomnia nearly every day.

5. Psychomotor agitation or retardation nearly every day (observable by others, not merely subjective feelings of restlessness or being slowed down).

6. Fatigue or loss of energy nearly every day.

7. Feelings of worthlessness or excessive or inappropriate guilt (which may be delusional) nearly every day (not merely self-reproach or guilt about being sick).

8. Diminished ability to think or concentrate, or indecisiveness, nearly every day (either by subjective account or as observed by others).

9. Recurrent thoughts of death (not just fear of dying), recurrent suicidal ideation without a specific plan, or a suicide attempt or a specific plan for committing suicide.

B. The symptoms do not meet criteria for a Mixed Episode.

C. The symptoms cause clinically significant distress or impairment in social, occupational, or other important areas of functioning.

D. The symptoms are not due to the direct physiological effects of a substance (eg, a drug of abuse, a medication) or a general medical condition (eg, hypothyroidism).

E. The symptoms are not better accounted for by bereavement; ie, after the loss of a loved one, the symptoms persist for longer than 2 months or are characterized by marked functional impairment, morbid preoccupation with worthlessness, suicidal ideation, psychotic symptoms, or psychomotor retardation.

American Psychiatric Association (1). Used with permission.

SEASONAL PATTERN FOR MOOD DISORDER: DIAGNOSIS

nset of Major
r Depressive
ular appear-

mania) also
ears in the

urred that
ia A and B,
uring that

tially out-
occurred

Major Depressive Episode and Seasonal Pattern: Nutritional Implications

ing dis-

ervosa,

once or depres-

Common Medications

Anafranil, Asendin, Aventyl, Celexa, Effexor, Elavil, Ludiomil, Luvox, Marplan, Nardil, Norpramin, Pamelor, Parnate, Paxil, Prozac, Remeron, Serzone, Sinequan, Tofranil, Vivactil, Wellbutrin, and Zoloft

Goals of Treatment

- Restore neurochemical imbalances.
- Restore normal appetite and food behaviors.
- Restore normal sleep patterns.
- Restore normal daily function.
- Develop emotionally appropriate stress response.

Nutritional Concerns

- Neurochemical imbalances may alter macronutrient appetite. There may be a craving for carbohydrates and a decreased taste for protein and/or fat.
- Binges may have become a habit as an attempt to self-medicate.

- Altered sleep patterns may have created a pattern where breakfast is skipped and night eating is where most calories are consumed.
- Depression and stress can either increase or decrease bowel function. Constipation and diarrhea are common; managing stress and depression should be the primary goal, with adequate hydration and fiber being secondary and tertiary goals. Dietary interventions can play into the individual's tendency to medicate discomforts inappropriately with food.

Nutritional Interventions (achieve gradually as treatment progresses)

- Meal plans should specify a lower acceptable limit of protein and fat intake, preferably no less than 25 percent of calories as fat (by the end of treatment) and no less than 7 ounces of protein or equivalent per day.
- Carbohydrates should be included at each meal, with an emphasis on complex carbohydrates. However, simple carbohydrates are acceptable and should not be considered "off limits" or bad. They are best consumed as a mealtime supplement rather than as a snack or as the focus of a meal (eg, muffin for breakfast).
- Food journals should be encouraged as a way to look at stress patterns and to determine how environmental stress promotes carbohydrate cravings and urges to binge/restrict.
- Carbonated drinks can create a feeling of bloating and increase body image focus. Limit to one a day.
- Caffeine has laxative and antidepressant qualities. Excessive caffeine can mask depression and make it difficult for the psychiatrist to properly dose antidepressant medications. Limit to two 8-ounce servings a day.
- Aspartame may be a trigger for some depressed individuals. Consider limiting intake to one product a day (see Chapter 15).
- Alcohol and stimulant use may be cross-addictions. Monitor for use and possible abuse.
- Difficulty adhering to the first seven recommendations should be an emotional barometer of environmental triggers exceeding the individual's capacity to cope. Psychiatrist and therapist should be kept abreast of client's progress in these areas.

A. A distinct period of abnormally and persistently elevated, expansive, or irritable mood lasting at least 1 week (or any duration if hospitalization is necessary).

B. During the period of mood disturbance, three (or more) of the following symptoms have persisted (four if the mood is only irritable) and have been present to a significant degree:

    1. inflated self-esteem or grandiosity

    2. decreased need for sleep (eg, feels rested after only 3 hours of sleep)

    3. more talkative than usual or pressure to keep talking

    4. flight of ideas or subjective experience that thoughts are racing

    5. distractibility (ie, attention too easily drawn to unimportant or irrelevant external stimuli)

    6. increase in goal-directed activity (either socially, at work or school, or sexually) or psychomotor agitation

    7. excessive involvement in pleasurable activities that have a high potential for painful consequences (eg, engaging in unrestrained buying sprees, sexual indiscretions, or foolish business investments)

C. The symptoms do not meet criteria for a Mixed Episode.

D. The mood disturbance is sufficiently severe to cause marked impairment in occupational functioning or in usual social activities or relationships with others, or to necessitate hospitalization to prevent harm to self or others, or there are psychotic features.

E. The symptoms are not due to the direct physiological effects of a substance (eg, a drug of abuse, a medication, or other treatment) or a general medical condition (eg, hyperthyroidism).

MANIC EPISODE: DIAGNOSIS

American Psychiatric Association (1). Used with permission.

A. A distinct period of persistently elevated, expansive, or irritable mood, lasting throughout at least 4 days, that is clearly different from the usual nondepressed mood.

B. During the period of mood disturbance, three (or more) of the following symptoms have persisted (four if the mood is only irritable) and have been present to a significant degree:

    1. inflated self-esteem or grandiosity

    2. decreased need for sleep (eg, feels rested after only 3 hours of sleep)

    3. more talkative than usual or pressure to keep talking

    4. flight of ideas or subjective experience that thoughts are racing

    5. distractibility (ie, attention too easily drawn to unimportant or irrelevant external stimuli)

HYPOMANIC EPISODE: DIAGNOSIS

6. increase in goal-directed activity (either socially, at work or school, or sexually) or psychomotor agitation

7. excessive involvement in pleasurable activities that have a high potential for painful consequences (eg, engaging in unrestrained buying sprees, sexual indiscretions, or foolish business investments)

C. The episode is associated with an unequivocal change in functioning that is uncharacteristic of the person when not symptomatic.

D. The disturbance in mood and the change in functioning are observable by others.

E. The episode is not severe enough to cause marked impairment in social or occupational functioning, and there are no psychotic features.

F. The symptoms are not due to the direct physiological effects of a substance (eg, a drug of abuse, a medication, or other treatment) or a general medical condition (eg, hyperthyroidism).

American Psychiatric Association (1). Used with permission.

Manic and Hypomanic Episodes: Nutritional Implications

Primary Characteristics

- Hypomania is a common finding in binge eating disorder (25).
- In bulimia, a concomitant diagnosis of bipolar depression tends to indicate a more severe and chronic symptomatology than if bulimia exists without a comorbid diagnosis (25)
- Seasonal affective disorder commonly coexists with bipolar depression (25).

Common Medications

Depakote, Eskalith, Klonopin, Lamictal, Lithobid, and Neurontin.

Goals of Treatment

- Minimize mood vacillations.
- Restore normal sleep patterns.
- Restore normal daily function.

Nutritional Concerns

- Lithium carbonate is a salt and may increase thirst.
- Weight gain may result from increased salt and fluid intake, which may trigger body image issues and urges to restrict or purge.
- Serum lithium levels must be kept stable in order for medication to function as it should. Any purging activity will affect lithium levels and decrease the medication's effectiveness.
- Manic swings drastically influence food behaviors. In a mood depression, food may not be consumed at all. In a mood elevation, food may be consumed in

excess. These drastic changes in food behavior may leave the client feeling out of control and exacerbate eating disordered thinking, guilt, and shame.

- Shifts between hypermania and hypomania can significantly affect a client's sleep patterns and therefore food intake. Any drastic shifts in food consumption should be brought to the attention of the psychiatrist.

- Clients with bipolar disorder often recognize that there is something wrong. Their first point of entry into treatment may be the nutrition therapist's office, as they may think their energy swings are due to dietary deficiencies or imbalances. Diagnoses of chronic fatigue, hypoglycemia, or other energy-related syndromes that have not responded to appropriate treatment merit the involvement of other mental health professionals. A technique that often engages these individuals is to work with them for a specified period of time on dietary interventions; if after strict adherence to protocol symptoms do not subside, then further workup (ie, a psychiatric visit) is recommended.

- Often addictive behaviors such as alcohol use, laxative use, or stimulant use are a bipolar individual's attempt to self-medicate his emotional symptoms. These behaviors, especially alcohol use, frequently surface first in nutrition therapy sessions. When cross-addiction is identified, this information should be shared with the rest of the treatment team.

POST-TRAUMATIC STRESS DISORDER: DIAGNOSIS

A. Has experienced or witnessed or was confronted with an unusually traumatic event that has BOTH of these elements:

    1. The event involved actual or threatened death or serious physical injury to the patient or to others, and

    2. The individual felt intense fear, horror, or helplessness.

B. The person repeatedly lives the event in at least one of these ways:

    1. Intrusive, distressing recollections, thoughts, and/or images.

    2. Repeated, distressing dreams.

    3. Through flashbacks, hallucinations, or illusions, feeling or acting as if the event were recurring (includes experiences that occur when intoxicated or awakening).

    4. Marked mental distress in reaction to internal or external cues that symbolize or resemble some part of the event.

C. The person repeatedly avoids the trauma-related stimuli and has numbing of general responsiveness (absent before the traumatic event), as shown by three or more of these:

    1. Tries to avoid feelings, thoughts, or conversations concerned with the event.

    2. Tries to avoid activities, people, or places that recall the event.

    3. Cannot recall an important feature of the event.

    4. Experiences marked loss of interest of participation in activities that were formerly important.

    5. Feels detached or isolated from other people.

    6. Experiences restriction in ability to love or feel other strong emotions.

    7. Feels life will be brief or unfulfilled (lack of marriage, job, children).

D. The patient has at least two of the following symptoms of hyperarousal that were not present before the traumatic event:

    1. Insomnia

    2. Angry outbursts or irritability

    3. Excessive vigilance

    4. Increased startle response

E. The symptoms have lasted longer than one month.

F. The symptoms cause clinically important distress or impair work, social, or personal functioning.

American Psychiatric Association (1). Used with permission.

Primary Characteristics

- Inpatient treatment centers report that as many as 85% of their eating disorder clients report a history of sexual assault(26).

Common Medications

Refer to sections on unipolar depression and anxiety disorder.

Goals of Treatment

- Normalize sleep patterns, circadian rhythms, and appetite patterns.
- Manage impulsivity and improve ability to institute long-term changes.
- Increase tolerance for physical, emotional, sensory, and environmental change.
- Develop a battery of emotional and expressive skills that can replace impulsive behaviors as a form of coping.

    Refer to Chapter 7 for a detailed discussion of post-traumatic stress disorder and eating disorders.

Nutritional Concerns

- Clients will have a tendency to be impulsive. This will be seen in session attendance, inability to follow through with assignments, and difficulty with long-term follow-through on behavioral changes. Part of this is due to physiological alterations in cognition, and part of it will eventually require behavioral intervention. It is important to set achievable goals, concrete and reliable limits, and a minimum standard of behavior. In order to set limits that are reasonable, frequent contact with the clients' psychiatrist and psychologist are necessary. Expectations should be standard across the treatment team.
- Clients need to understand and adhere to rules for attendance and payment. Making allowances reduces the client's trust and may only encourage more manipulation by the client to determine if limits really exist.
- As the client approaches traumatic memories and thoughts, he may avoid the psychotherapist and psychiatrist and seek to focus on nutrition counseling. He may justify this behavior with complaints about the other team members, or stop working with other team members. Regardless of the reason, the client needs to understand that the team works together as a unit and any changes in the treatment plan need to be agreed upon by the entire team. It may be necessary to discontinue seeing the client until he has resumed interactions with the team members he has been avoiding.
- Food intolerances and fears related to the trauma are common. All five senses can be involved in retraumatization. At certain times in treatment it may be appropriate to limit exposure to certain trigger foods. However, the ultimate goal is to break associations between the foods and the trauma. If

Post-Traumatic Stress Disorder: Nutritional Implications

the client makes associations, he should be advised to discuss them with his psychotherapist.

- Challenges need to be introduced in small steps. Trust building may take weeks of work before any real food issues can be addressed.

- Food journals are an excellent tool for keeping the client in the present and discouraging dissociative eating. If a client is too fragile to complete a food journal, it is important to acknowledge this and not assume she is being rebellious or noncompliant.

- Lifeskills experiences are important, as the client may have a heightened startle response in environments that involve food and are chaotic (eg, restaurants and grocery stores). The first restaurant visit may be most successful if it occurs in a small cafe with only a few items on the menu, during off-hours, with a trusted peer. Combining a food challenge with an environmental challenge may introduce too much environmental stimulus.

A.   Either obsessions or compulsions

Obsessions as defined by

1. recurrent and persistent thoughts, impulses, or images that are experienced at some time during the disturbance as intrusive and inappropriate and that cause marked anxiety or distress,

2. the thoughts, impulses, or images are not simply excessive worries about real-life problems,

3. the person attempts to ignore or suppress such thoughts, impulses, or images, or to neutralize them with some other thought or action,

4. the person recognizes that the obsessional thoughts, impulses, or images are a product of his own mind (not imposed from without, as in thought insertion).

Compulsions as defined by

1. repetitive behaviors (eg, hand washing, ordering, checking) or mental acts (eg, praying, counting, repeating words silently) that the person feels driven to perform in response to an obsession or according to rules that must be applied rigidly.

2. the behaviors or mental acts are aimed at preventing or reducing distress or preventing some dreaded event or situation; however, these behaviors or mental acts either are not connected in a realistic way with what they are designed to neutralize or prevent or are clearly excessive.

B.   At some point during the course of the disorder, the person has recognized that the obsessions or compulsions are excessive or unreasonable.

C.   The obsessions or compulsions cause marked distress, are time consuming (take more than 1 hour a day), or significantly interfere with the person's normal routine, occupational (or academic) functioning, or usual social activities or relationships.

D.   If another Axis I disorder is present, the content of the obsessions or compulsion is not restricted to it (eg, preoccupation with food in the presence of an eating disorder; hair pulling in the presence of trichotillomania; concern with appearance in the presence of body dysmorphic disorder; preoccupation with drugs in the presence of a substance use disorder, preoccupation with having a serious illness in the presence of hypochondriasis; preoccupation with sexual urges or fantasies in the presence of a paraphilia; or guilty ruminations in the presence of major depressive disorder).

E.   The disturbance is not due to the direct physiological effects of a substance (eg, a drug of abuse, a medication) or a general medical condition.

American Psychiatric Association (1). Used with permission.

Obsessive-Compulsive Disorder: Nutritional Implications

Primary Characteristics

- Females with OCD are more likely to have a past history of eating disorder and/or unipolar depression (27,28).
- 11%-13% of females with OCD have a history of anorexia nervosa (28).
- An additional 23% of females with OCD also have "subclinical" eating disorders, or behaviors that meet some but not all ED diagnostic criteria (29).
- 2/3 of individuals with OCD also have a history of unipolar depression (29).
- Other diagnoses commonly coexisting with OCD include panic disorder, social phobia, Tourette's syndrome, hypochondriasis, trichotillomania, and delusional disorders (30,31).
- Neurochemical and behavioral expression of both ED and OCD occur on a continuum; at one end, eating disorders and OCD are expressed through constrained behaviors of an avoidant quality. At the other end, both disorders are characterized by disinhibited approach behavior (32).

Common Medications

Anafranil, Asendin, Aventyl, Celexa, Effexor, Elavil, Ludiomil, Luvox, Marplan, Nardil, Norpramin, Pamelor, Parnate, Paxil, Prozac, Remeron, Serzone, Sinequan, Tofranil, Vivactil, and Zoloft

Goals of Treatment

- Remove ritualistic behaviors that interfere with activities of daily living.
- Improve the ability to make decisions from a variety of choices.
- Decrease perfectionism and fear of failure/rejection.

Nutritional Concerns

- Ritualistic behaviors keep the client in behavioral ruts that often reduce food choices to a minimum. Moving out of these ruts is difficult and increases the probability that adequate nutrition is being consumed.
- Ritualistic behaviors keep the client regimented in routines that, if disrupted, also disrupt food intake. For example, if dinner must occur at 6 PM and traffic delayed arriving home until 6:45 PM, dinner may not be eaten.
- Ritualistic behaviors decrease spontaneity. Social invitations may be declined because they do not coincide with the individual's set of rules. The more rigid the rituals, the more likely it is that the client is isolating from society, which increases susceptibility to depression.
- Severely ritualistic individuals may tolerate only weight or caloric goals that fit into their ritual system. For example, an individual who is fixated on the number 3 may eat only 3 foods at a meal, chew food in numbers divisible by 3, and accept only goal weights or calorie levels that are divisible by 3.
- There is a tendency to categorize foods as good and bad, and to eliminate entire food groups.

- Vegetarian ED individuals should be evaluated to rule out the possibility that this food practice is a manifestation of OCD.
- Decision making is an agonizing process. When presented with choices, the individual may avoid having to make an imperfect decision by making no decision at all. Food refusal in anorexia can often reflect the individual's inability to make the decision to eat, rather than a need for control.

Nutrition Interventions

- Limit the client's choices (ie, keep meal plans and assignments simple, avoid complicated food charts/tables) until she has developed confidence in her decision making skills.
- Encourage a minimal fat intake to increase response to medications. Severely underweight individuals may be so fat-deprived that their nervous system is unresponsive to antidepressant medications.
- Provide exposure therapy challenges. Introduce the client to small doses of situations and foods he fears the most. Break challenges into small but manageable steps. (Look at a picture of a cookie, buy a package of cookies, touch a cookie, take a bite of cookie, etc.)
- Provide assignments with no right or wrong way to complete them. Meal plans and fat gram counting play into perfectionism.
- When a client has difficulty following through with an assignment, consider that the assignment may have threatened to disrupt daily rituals past the point of emotional tolerance.

ATTENTION DEFICIT/ HYPERACTIVITY DISORDER: DIAGNOSIS

A. Either (1) or (2)

1. Six (or more) of the following symptoms of inattention have persisted for at least 6 months to a degree that is maladaptive and inconsistent with developmental level:

Inattention

(a) often fails to give close attention to details or makes careless mistakes in schoolwork, work, or other activities,

(b) often has difficulty sustaining attention in tasks or play activities,

(c) often does not seem to listen when spoken to directly,

(d) often does not follow through on instructions and fails to finish schoolwork, chores, or duties in the workplace (not due to oppositional behavior or failure to understand instructions),

(e) often has difficulty organizing tasks and activities,

(f) often avoids, dislikes, or is reluctant to engage in tasks that require sustained mental effort (such as schoolwork or homework),

(g) often loses things necessary for tasks or activities (eg, toys, school assignments, pencils, books, or tools),

(h) is often easily distracted by extraneous stimuli,

(i) is often forgetful in daily activities.

2. Six (or more) of the following symptoms of hyperactivity-impulsivity have persisted for at least 6 months to a degree that is maladaptive and inconsistent with developmental level:

Hyperactivity

(a) often fidgets with hands or feet or squirms in seat,

(b) often leaves seat in classroom or in other situations in which remaining seated is expected,

(c) often runs about or climbs excessively in situations in which it is inappropriate (in adolescents or adults, may be limited to subjective feelings or restlessness),

(d) often has difficulty playing or engaging in leisure activities quietly,

(e) is often "on the go" or often acts as if "driven by a motor,"

(f) often talks excessively.

Impulsivity

(g) often blurts out answers before questions have been completed,

(h) often has difficulty awaiting turn,

(i) often interrupts or intrudes on other (eg, butts into conversations or games).

B. Some hyperactive-impulsive or inattentive symptoms that caused impairment were present before age 7 years.

C. Some impairment from the symptoms is present in two or more settings (eg, at school [or work] and at home).

D. here must be clear evidence of clinically significant impairment in social, academic, or occupational functioning.

E. The symptoms do not occur exclusively during the course of a Pervasive Developmental Disorder, Schizophrenia, or other Psychotic Disorder and are not better accounted for by another mental disorder (eg, Mood Disorder, Anxiety Disorder, Dissociative Disorder, or a Personality Disorder).

American Psychiatric Association (1). Used with permission.

Attention Deficit/ Hyperactivity Disorder: Nutritional Implications

Primary Characteristics

- Appetite fluctuates with medication dosage.
- Has difficulty in chaotic food environments.
- May abuse caffeine and other stimulants.

Common Medications

Adderall, Cylert, Dexedrine, and Ritalin

Goals of Treatment

- Improve ability to concentrate on activities of daily living.
- Improve ability to focus and make critical decisions.
- Improve ability to communicate effectively.

Nutritional Concerns

- Substances that function as stimulants in most people may function as calming agents in these individuals. Excessive intake of caffeine and other stimulants may be explained by the client as "something I do to help me focus."
- Clients may follow diet regimens that restrict artificial flavors and colors as well as sugar. It is important to determine whether these dietary interventions are genuinely therapeutic or whether they are being used as an excuse to restrict food intake.
- In uncontrolled ADD/ADHD, caloric needs may exceed predicted calculations, even if the hyperactivity is not physically observable. When medication is initiated, meal plans may need to be adjusted to accommodate the new metabolic rate.
- Ability to understand instructions and process information may completely change once medication is implemented. Information provided early in treatment may need to be repeated once medication has begun and a behavioral response is observed.

- Environments that increase sensory stimulation tend to increase agitation and decrease concentration. Sensory overstimulation of this kind is likely to occur at restaurants, grocery stores, buffets, parties, receptions, etc. It is important to interview the client to discern whether any of these environments cause difficulty, and to include experiences in the treatment plan that help the client learn to focus and successfully participate in visits to these environments. For example, designing a shopping list in conjunction with a grocery store map allows one to shop with only one trip down each aisle, decreasing exposure to stimuli and therefore decreasing anxiety. Restaurants with less complicated menus are better choices for "first dates" and other special occasions that are already stressful; they are also best visited early or late to avoid the chaos of the rush.

- Ability to understand instructions and process information may completely change once medication is implemented. Information provided early in treatment may need to be repeated once medication has begun and a behavioral response is observed.

- Ritalin is a stimulant, and therefore has the ability to suppress appetite. Clients who use this medication to manage ADD/ADHD may not feel hungry during the day when the medication is typically active. Reduced food intake in this scenario may not be intentional restriction, but a natural response to altered physiological signals. As the medication wears off in the evening, appetite may be increased if the client has not eaten enough during the day. Clients need to be educated about the impact of this medication on their appetite signals. Cylert is a longer-acting medication and in many cases allows clients to experience normal appetite patterns that do not trigger eating disordered sensations or responses.

A. Excessive anxiety and worry (apprehensive expectation), occurring more days than not for at least 6 months, about a number of events or activities (such as work or school performance).

B. The person finds it difficult to control the worry.

C. The anxiety and worry are associated with three (or more) of the following six symptoms (with at least some symptoms present for more days than not for the past 6 months). Note: Only one item is required in children.

   1. restlessness or feeling keyed up or on edge
   2. being easily fatigued
   3. difficulty concentrating or mind going blank
   4. irritability
   5. muscle tension
   6. sleep disturbance (difficulty falling or staying asleep, or restless unsatisfying sleep).

D. The focus of the anxiety and worry is not confined to features of an Axis I disorder, eg, the anxiety or worry is not about having a Panic Attack (as in Panic Disorder), being embarrassed in public (as in Social Phobia), being contaminated (as in Obsessive-Compulsive Disorder), being away from home or close relatives (as in Separation Anxiety Disorder), gaining weight (as in Anorexia Nervosa), having multiple physical complaints (as in Somatization Disorder), or having a serious illness (as in Hypochondriasis), and the anxiety and worry do not occur exclusively during Posttraumatic Stress Disorder.

E. The anxiety, worry, or physical symptoms cause clinically significant distress or impairment in social, occupational, or other important areas of functioning.

F. The disturbance is not due to the direct physiological effects of a substance (eg, a drug of abuse, a medication) or a general medical condition (eg, hyperthyroidism) and does not occur exclusively during a Mood Disorder, a Psychotic Disorder, or a Pervasive Developmental Disorder.

American Psychiatric Association (1). Used with permission.

GENERALIZED ANXIETY DISORDER: DIAGNOSIS

Primary Characteristics

- There are increased rates of depression and anxiety in anorexia nervosa, bulimia nervosa, and binge eating disorder (24).
- In bulimia, the incidence of anxiety is equal to the incidence of depression (24).
- In whites, disordered eating attitudes have been significantly positively correlated with feelings of anxiety and depression; this is not true with other ethnic groups (33).

Generalized Anxiety Disorder: Nutritional Implications

Common Medications

Ativan, BuSpar, Centrax, Klonopin, Librax, Libritabs, Librium, Luvox, Paxil, Paxipam, Prozac, Serax, Tranxene, Valium, Xanax, and Zoloft

Goals of Treatment

- Improve cognitive processes so that anxiety does not impair or paralyze functioning in activities of daily living.
- Widen the window of tolerance for fluctuations in environmental and emotional change, improve "distress tolerance."
- Develop a battery of coping skills that can replace dysfunctional skills such as restricting, purging, and compulsive exercise.

Nutritional Concerns

- A person who is anxious on the inside may not present as anxious on the outside. Often a person with anxiety disorder will manifest this anxiety in the form of increased metabolism. A client who has difficult maintaining weight may not be restricting, but may be struggling with a level of anxiety that is difficult to "keep up with" in the form of adequate caloric intake.
- Plateaus in weight gain or weight loss may be the first signs that an important emotional issue is surfacing or insomnia is worsening. Pharmacological, therapeutic, and stress management intervention can at times be more successful at restoring weight progress than a focus on increased calories or decreased physical activity.
- The excessive physical activity (ie, pacing, standing, leg shaking) that is often observed with an eating disorder may be more reflective of internal anxiety in need of an outlet than an intentional desire to burn calories to lose weight. It is important to discern the source of this hyperkinetic behavior, as telling a client that her presentation is intentional when it is not may only escalate the anxiety and behavior.
- There can be a tendency to want to limit physical activity because of the calories it burns. Again, if the anxiety is not being managed from a psychiatric, therapeutic, and stress management perspective and physical activity limitation is the only intervention, anxiety may only increase. A more practical approach is to teach the client how to use exercise appropriately, without compulsion. For example, short (eg, 15-minute) bouts of exercise after a long day can help the transition from a stressful workday to the home environment. Also, discourage exercises that are repetitive (eg, running, exercise machines) and encourage exercises that are more creative/expressive (eg, jazz dance, ballet). These exercises also provide a secondary outlet (communication) for the anxiety that has accumulated.
- Environments that increase sensory stimulation tend to increase agitation and decrease concentration. Sensory overstimulation of this kind is likely to

occur at restaurants, grocery stores, buffets, parties, receptions, etc. It is important to interview the client to discern whether any of these environments cause difficulty, and to include experiences in the treatment plan that help the client learn to focus and successfully participate in visits to these environments. (Refer to ADD/ADHD for examples.)

SCHIZOPHRENIA: DIAGNOSIS

A. *Characteristic Symptoms:* Two (or more) of the following, each present for a significant portion of time during a 1-month period (or less if successfully treated):

1. delusions
2. hallucinations
3. disorganized speech (eg, frequent derailment or incoherence)
4. grossly disorganized or catatonic behavior
5. negative symptoms (ie, affective flattening, alogia, or avolition)

B. *Social/Occupational Dysfunction:* For a significant portion of the time since the onset of the disturbance, one or more major areas of functioning such as work, interpersonal relations, or self-care are markedly below the level achieved prior to the onset (or when the onset is in childhood or adolescence, failure to achieve expected level of interpersonal, academic, or occupational achievement).

C. *Duration:* Continuous signs of the disturbance persist for at least 6 months. This 6-month period must include at least 1 month of symptoms (or less if successfully treated) that meet Criterion A (ie, active-phase symptoms). During these prodromal or residual periods, the signs of the disturbance may be manifested by only negative symptoms or two or more symptoms listed in Criterion A present in an attenuated form (eg, odd beliefs, unusual perceptual experiences).

D. *Schizoaffective and Mood Disorder Exclusion:* Schizoaffective Disorder and Mood Disorder with Psychotic Features have been ruled out because either (1) no Major Depressive, Manic, or Mixed Episodes have occurred concurrently with the active-phase symptoms; or (2) if mood episodes have occurred during active-phase symptoms, their total duration has been brief relative to the duration of the active and residual periods.

E. *Substance/General Medical Condition Exclusion:* The disturbance is not due to the direct physiological effects of a substance (eg, a drug of abuse, a medication) or a general medical condition.

F. *Relationship to a Pervasive Developmental Disorder:* If there is a history of Autistic Disorder or another Pervasive Developmental Disorder, the additional diagnosis of Schizophrenia is made only if prominent delusions or hallucinations are also present for at least a month (or less if successfully treated).

American Psychiatric Association (1). Used with permission.

Schizophrenia: Nutritional Implications

Primary Characteristics

- Psychotic depressive subjects were more likely to demonstrate psychomotor disturbance, to report morbid conditions (ie, feeling sinful and guilty, feeling deserving of punishment), to report constipation, terminal insomnia, appetite/weight loss, and loss of interest and pleasure (34).

- In one study, all ED individuals with schizophrenia had also been diagnosed with depression (35).
- There may be an affinity between the diagnoses of anorexia nervosa and schizophrenia (35).
- Significant social difficulties persist in this population even after treatment (35).

Common Medications

Haldol, Mellaril, Navane, Prolixin, Risperdal, Seroquel, Thorazine, and Zyprexa

Goals of Treatment

- Minimize distraction from delusions and conflicting cognitive information.
- Improve tolerance for new environments and activities.

Nutritional Concerns

- Somatic delusions, a hallmark behavior in this subpopulation, can exacerbate/complicate body image distortions already present within the eating disorder diagnosis. It is important to distinguish whether distorted body perceptions are related to the eating disorder or to the schizophrenia, as the former will be responsive to cognitive behavioral body image therapy but the latter may not be.
- "Hearing voices" is a commonly reported schizophrenic phenomenon. These voices can communicate a variety of messages relating to the eating disorder, including, "You're fat," "You don't deserve to eat," and "Stop eating right now."
- Though all eating disordered individuals have similar thoughts in their belief system, in schizophrenia these "voices" are much more concrete and persistent. It is important to determine whether the individual is experiencing thought distortion or hearing "voices", as the first perception is more responsive to behavioral therapy, the second one to psychotropic medications.
- Regardless of how irrational the client's thoughts may appear, it is important to accept them as her reality. If the irrational thoughts about body, food, or food reactions stem from the schizophrenia, cognitive behavioral therapy may not successfully change the thought process. It is best to validate the client's perception to develop trust and to develop a treatment plan that emphasizes the client's strengths. Arguing or working to convince the client that she should think otherwise may only increase her paranoia and distrust.
- Small doses of Risperdal are often prescribed to potentiate the activity of other psychotropic medications. Risperdal in an individual's medication regime is not always indicative of a diagnosis of schizophrenia.

SUMMARY

- Axis I diagnoses are medical diagnoses that describe problems of the central nervous system. Diagnosis of Axis I disorders is normally made by the team psychiatrist or psychologist.

- Clients with Axis I disorders may disclose information in nutrition therapy that is important for medical diagnosis, medication management, and treatment planning. Communication among team members is crucial for effective treatment.

- Axis I diagnoses are likely to coexist with eating disorders. It is important to understand the perception and response styles of clients with these disorders in order to design effective treatment plans.

- Axis I disorders often require medication in addition to behavior intervention. A client who is not responding to behavioral therapy should undergo a psychiatric assessment. If medication is recommended, nutrition therapy should include education regarding the importance of complying with the psychiatrist's recommendations.

- Appetite suppressants often have mechanisms of action similar to those of psychoactive medications. Understanding these mechanisms can suggest other interventions that may elicit similar effects on appetite.

REFERENCES

1. *Diagnostic and Statistical Manual of Mental Disorders.* 4th ed. Washington, DC: American Psychiatric Association; 1994.

2. Hall RC, Blakey RE, Hall AK. Bulimia nervosa: four uncommon subtypes. *Psychosomatics.* 1992;33(4):428–436.

3. Comer RJ. *Abnormal Psychology.* 2nd ed. New York: WH Freeman and Company; 1995.

4. Dubovsky SL. Beyond the serotonin reuptake ihibitors: rationales for the development of new serotonergic agents. *J Clin Psychiatry.* 1994;55(Suppl):34–44.

5. Wurtman JJ. Carbohydrate craving: relationship between carbohydrate intake and disorders of mood. *Drugs.* 1990;39(Suppl 3):49–52.

6. Leonard BE. Serotonin receptors—where are they going? *Int Clin Psychopharmacol.* 1994;Suppl 1:7–17.

7. Samanin R, Garattini S. Neurochemical mechanism of action of anorectic drugs. *Pharmacol Toxicol.* 1993;73(2):63–68.

8. Gray DS, Fujioka K, Devine W, Bray GA. A randomized double-blind clinical trial of fluoxetine in obese diabetics. *Int J Obes Relat Metab Disord.* 1992;16(Suppl 4):S67–S72.

9. Appel NM, Owens MJ, Culp S, Zaczek R, Contrera JF, Bissette G. Role for brain corticotropin-releasing factor in the weight-reducing effects of chronic fenfluramine treatment in rats. *Endocrinology.* 1991;128(6):3237–3246.

10. Bernini GP, Argenio GF, Del Corso C, Vivaldi MS, Birindelli R, Franchi F. Serotoninergic receptor activation by dextrofenfluramine enhances the blunted pituitary-adrenal responsiveness to corticotropin-releasing hormone in obese subjects. *Metabolism.* 1992;41(1):17–21.

11. Ditscunheit HH, Flechtner-Mors M, Dolderer M, Fulda U, Ditscunheit H.

Endocrine and metabolic effects of dexfenfluramine in patients with android obesity. *Horm Metab Res.* 1993;25(11):573–578.

12. Pijl H, Koppeschaar HP, Willekens FL, Frohlich M, Meinders AE. The influence of serotonergic neurotransmission on pituitary hormone release in obese and non-obese females. *Acta Endocrinol Copenh.* 1993;128(4):319–324.

13. Bross R, Hoffer LJ. Fluoxetine increases resting energy expenditure and basal body temperature in humans. *Am J Clin Nutr.* 1995;61(5):102–1025.

14. Ornish D. *Dr. Dean Ornish's Program for Reversing Heart Disease.* New York: Ivy Books; 1996.

15. Holdaway IM, Wallace E, Westbrook L, Gamble G. Effect of dexfenfluramine on body weight, blood pressure, insulin resistance and serum cholesterol in obese individuals. *Int J Obes Relat Metab Disord.* 1995;19(10): 749–751.

16. Richter WO, Donne MG, Schwandt P. Dexfenfluramine inhibits catecholamine stimulated in vitro lipolysis in human fat cells. *Int J Obes Relat Metab Disord.* 1995;19(7): 503–505.

17. Rowland NE, Dunn AJ. Effect of dexfenfluramine on metabolic and neurochemical measures in restraint-stressed ob/ob mice. *Physiol Behav.* 1995; 58(4):749–754.

18. Gray DS, Fujioka K, Devine W, Bray GA. Fluoxetine treatment of the obese diabetic. *Int J Obes.* 1992;16(9):717.

19. Blundell JE, Lawton CL. Serotonin and dietary fat intake: effects of dexfenfluramine. *Metabolism.* 1995;44(2, Suppl 2):33–37.

20. Fisler JS, Underberger SJ, York DA, Bray GA. d-fenfluramine in a rat model of dietary fat-induced obesity. *Pharacol Biochem Behav.* 1993;45(2):487–493.

21. Mancini MC, Aloe F. Nocturnal eating syndrome: a case report with therapeutic response to dexfenfluramine. *Rev Paul Med.* 1994;112(2):569–571.

22. McCann UD, Yuan J, Ricaurte GA. Fenfluramine's appetite suppression and serotonin neurotoxicity are separable. *Eur J Pharmacol.* 1995;183(1–3):R5-R7.

23. Hill-Melton CA. An examination of depression in a subclinical eating disorder female population. *Dissertation Abstracts Int.* 1995;55-O2B:577.

24. Kaplan ME. The presence of current and lifetime depressive and anxiety disorders in eating disordered individuals. *Dissertation Abstracts Int.* 1994; 54–05B:2755.

25. Mury M, Verdoux H, Bourgeois M. Comorbidity of bipolar and eating disorders: epidemiologic ad therapeutic aspects. *Encephale.* 1995;21(5):545–553.

26. Tobin DL, Molteni AL, Elin MR. Early trauma, dissociation, and late onset in the eating disorders. *Int J Eating Disord.* 1995;17(3):305–308.

27. Castle DJ, Deale A, Marks IM. Gender differences in obsessive compulsive disorder. *Aust NZ J Pyschiatry.* 1995;29(1);114–117.

28. Fahy TA, Osacar A, Marks I. History of eating disorders in female patients with obsessive-compulsive disorder. *Int J Eating Disord.* 1993;14(4):439–443.

29. Rubenstein CS, Pigott TA, L'Heureux F, Hill JL, Murphy DL. A preliminary investigation of the lifetime prevalence of anorexia and bulimia nervosa in patients with obsessive compulsive disorder. *J Clin Psychiatry.* 1992;53(9):309–314.

30. Rasmussen SA, Eisen JL. The epidemiology and differential diagnosis of obsessive compulsive disorder. *J Clin Psychiatry.* 1994;55(Suppl):5-10; discussion 11–14.

31. McElroy SL, Phillips KA, Keck PE Jr. Obsessive compulsive spectrum disorder. *J Clin Psychiatry.* 1994;55(Suppl):33–51; discussion 52–53.

32. Jarry JL, Vaccarino FJ. Eating disorder and obsessive-compulsive disorder: neurochemical and phenomenological commonalities. *J Psychiatry Neurosci.* 1996;21(1): 36–48.

33. Dolan B, Lacey JH, Evans C. Eating behavior and attitudes to weight and shape in British women from three ethnic groups. *Br J Psychiatry*. 1990;157:523–528.

34. Parker G, Hadzi-Pavlovic D, Brodaty H, Austin MP, Mitchell P, Wilhelm K, Hickie I. Sub-typing depression. II. Clinical distinction of psychotic depression and non-psychotic melancholia. *Psychol Med*. 1995;25(4):825–832.

35. Shiraishi H, Koizumi J, Suzuki T, Yamaguchi N, Mizukami K, Hori M, Tanaka Y. Eating disorder and schizophrenia. *Jpn J Psychiatry Neurol*. 1992;46(4):859–867.

CHAPTER 11

Screening and Assessment Tools for Axis I Eating and Weight Disorders

MICHAEL BRAUN, M.S.

According to Jacobson (1), a comprehensive pretreatment evaluation approach includes four components: detection, assessment, diagnosis, and population screening. *Detection,* or identification, is the first-level screening procedure that determines the presence or absence of disease. It can also identify clients who would benefit from referral to a specialist for further examination. *Assessment* procedures typically rank clients along a continuum (a concept that is gaining increased application with better understandings of binge eating and chronic dieting). A true *diagnosis* might be made after establishing the cause and nature of the disorder and evaluating its history, present signs and symptoms, and laboratory data/special tests. This information leads to a better understanding of the etiology, development, and expression of the disorder, and is used to formulate appropriate treatment plans and establish prognosis and possible outcomes of treatment. *Population screening* should lead to early diagnosis and thereby improved treatment. However, in many cases, screening also serves to identify advanced cases that have not come to the attention of clinicians.

DETECTION

The above terminology was initially devised in reference to alcohol abuse. However, given the abundance of literature documenting the similarities between eating disorders and alcohol abuse (ranging from etiologies and shared risk factors through their consequences for physical and mental health), these evaluation-related terms will suffice as guideposts for this chapter. Leon et al identified similarities between alcohol abusers and disordered eaters as early as 1979 (2). They found that individuals with several addictive-type behaviors (eg, binge eating, anorexia nervosa, and smoking) scored similarly on the MacAndrew Addiction (MAC) Scale of the Minnesota Multiphasic Personality Inventory (MMPI), which was originally developed to measure proneness to alcoholism. They noted that their findings (and similar findings from other studies) suggested that an elevated score on the MAC could indicate addiction proneness in the disordered eating clientele they assessed. This conclusion is important, as it connects a nutritional behavior to a psychological/psychiatric condition.

Brownell and Fairburn (3) also connected previously distinct findings from researchers in psychiatry, psychology, nutrition, physiology, metabolism, pharmacology, and surgery. One important paradigm their work advanced was the connection between the diagnosis of an eating disorder and the diagnosis of obesity. Until recently the obesity field had focused on medical perspectives, such as physiology and health risks, while eating disorder research has had stronger roots in psychiatry. Brownell and Fairburn discussed commonalities between the two that support the implementation of standardized detection, assessment, diagnosis, and screening procedures across the entire spectrum of disordered eating:

- a similar basic physiology of hunger and satiety,
- distorted body image, researched considerably with eating disorders but relatively ignored in relationship to obesity,
- the phenomenon of binge eating, now recognized to be a problem in up to 25 percent of obese clientele seeking treatment, and
- similar etiologies.

Interestingly, attitudes toward dieting tend to separate the two fields. Despite the fact that eating disorders and obesity have more similarities than differences, dieting is considered a pathological behavior in the former condition and a solution to the latter.

Williamson's textbook, *Assessment of Eating Disorders: Obesity, Anorexia and Bulimia Nervosa* (4), was one of the first to include obesity and compulsive overeating (now referred to as binge eating disorder) as eating disorders, along with the two more traditionally known eating disorders, anorexia nervosa and bulimia nervosa. This researcher has advanced key rationale for classifying obesity similarly to the eating disorders:

- 20 to 40 percent of obese patients have significant problems with compulsive binge eating,
- compulsive bingeing is much more prevalent in obese populations than in individuals of normal weight,
- though the obese typically do not engage in extreme weight control behaviors such as starving or purging, compulsive bingeing is often a presenting behavior,

- binge eating individuals (bulimic as well as nonbulimic) typically recognize that their bingeing is abnormal and experience negative emotions after bingeing, which often precipitates more bingeing,

- bingers are typically dissatisfied with their body size but do not have a distorted sense of body size or desire an unrealistically thin body (the latter characteristics of bulimia nervosa clearly distinguish it from binge eating disorder).

In addition, individuals with binge eating disorder, anorexia nervosa, and bulimia nervosa share certain secondary psychopathologies, including depression, anxiety, obsessive/compulsive habits, interpersonal sensitivity, interpersonal and family problems, personality disorders, substance abuse, and stress.

ASSESSMENT AND DIAGNOSIS

The psychopathology and general clinical characteristics usually seen in clients with bulimia nervosa and anorexia are widely accepted and well documented. Less is known about the psychopathology of binge eating disorder and other eating disorders that fall outside of bulimia nervosa and anorexia. Although tremendous advances have been made in the technology of assessment, there is no universally accepted protocol for assessing eating disorders. However, a consensus does exist on the value of a multitrait and multimethod approach to assessment.

Several approaches have been developed for gathering information from eating disorder clientele, including clinical interviews, symptom checklists, self-report measures, clinical rating scales, self-monitoring, standardized test meals, and direct behavioral observation. The most commonly used are semistructured clinical interviews, self-report measures, and self-monitoring (5).

Clinical Interviews

Standardized, semistructured clinical interviews represent the primary method for collecting information on eating disorders. The Eating Disorder Examination (EDE) is the most well-validated clinical interview, has generated perhaps the most research, and is the current interview method of choice (6). Client responses are categorized on four subscales: restraint, eating concerns, shape concerns, and weight concerns.

The EDE is popular because it

- can be used to arrive at a diagnosis,
- is sensitive to treatment effects,
- defines different forms of overeating based on the amount of food eaten and the presence or absence of loss of control,
- assesses specific eating disorder symptoms,
- allows for a detailed appraisal of the specific eating disorder psychopathology,
- permits the investigator to clarify meanings behind a client's responses to questions, and

- is more accurate than self-monitoring measures in identifying ambiguous symptoms, such as those associated with binge eating.

The EDE can be used in a variety of detection, assessment, and diagnosis situations. However, it can take an hour or more to administer, and requires a trained interviewer. This may decrease its value in certain assessment environments, especially when group administration or anonymity is required.

Much of the literature on the assessment of binge eating is based on the study of clients with bulimia (7). However, with the recent increased interest in binge eating in obese clients, a much wider range of clients are being assessed for binge eating. The EDE appears to be the best choice for assessing binge eating, largely because of measurement problems that can occur. Wilson observes that, when eating is especially chaotic, it can be extremely difficult for the assessor or the client to determine when one binge episode stops and another starts (7).

The EDE has several additional advantages over alternative methods of assessment for binge eating disorder:

- it is the only instrument that directly assesses the diagnostic criteria of all eating disorders,
- it is the only instrument that directly assesses the different forms of overeating,
- the clear definitions for large eating episodes and loss of control provide diagnostic significance for these distinctions,
- it is unmatched in its depth and breadth of assessment, and
- it provides the most detailed and direct assessment of dietary restriction of any assessment instrument.

Self-Report Measures The three most widely used self-report measures, the Eating Attitudes Test (EAT), the Eating Disorder Inventory (EDI), and the BULIT-R, are summarized in *Table 11.1*. A continuum of assessments has clear advantages over the dichotomous (ie, yes/no) *DSM-IV* diagnosis for bulimia nervosa. In addition to diagnosing the client's current condition, these measures provide information about the condition's etiology and duration, which is important in community-based studies. They may also better reveal the severity of weight control efforts and the persistence of symptoms of eating disorders at different times.

A study by Drewnowski and coworkers (8) confirmed that bulimia nervosa represents a pathological extreme of a broader continuum of behavior aimed at weight control and that many women exhibit bulimic behavior without meeting the diagnostic criteria for bulimia nervosa. Greater eating pathology was associated with increased desire for thinness. While nondieters wished to lose an average of 1.6 pounds, those with bulimia wished to lose an average of 12.4 pounds. In addition, greater eating pathology was linked to higher reported frequency of dieting and a greater number of dieting strategies used during the previous month, as well as with higher ratings of self-reported depression and stress.

Assessment Tool	Characteristics	Table 11.1
Bulimia Test(BULIT-R)	• A 28-item, multiple-choice, self-report measure based on the DSM-IV criteria for bulimia nervosa (6). A reliable psychometric measure of the severity of bulimia nervosa.	**Self-Report Measures Common in Eating Disorders Assessment**
Cognitive Behavioral Dieting Scale (CBDS)	• A 14-item scale that measures current dieting behavior and related thought in the 2 weeks prior to testing. • Measures thoughts and behaviors related to current dieting intended for weight loss. • Predicts calorie intake and negative caloric balance. • Provides a method for operationalizing dieting. • Provides a construct that is different from restraint. • Assesses dieting behavior on a continuum.	
Eating Attitudes Test (EAT)	• 26-item measure of global eating disorder symptoms.	
Eating Disorder Inventory (EDI)	• Provides a psychological profile with the use of three subscales: (1) drive for thinness, (2) bulimia, and (3) body dissatisfaction. • Contains five subscales that assess more general psychological traits: ineffectiveness, perfection, interpersonal distrust, interoceptive awareness, and maturity fears.	
Eating Pathology Scale	• Classifies bulimic behavior into five subgroups: probable bulimia, dieters at risk for bulimia, intensive dieters, casual dieters, and nondieters.	
Emotional Eating Scale (EES)	• A 25-item scale. • Assesses coping with negative affect/emotion by eating. • Contains three subscales, Anger/Frustration, Anxiety, and Depression, that correlate highly with measures of binge eating.	
Matching Familiar Figures Test (MFFT)	• Can be used in assessments geared toward cognition in disordered eating clientele. • Clients may be subdivided according to eating behavior and psychopathological characteristics. • Distinguishes cognitively reflective from cognitively impulsive clients.	
Revised Eating Disorder Inventory (EDI-2)	• Adds three new subscales to the original EDI assessment: asceticism, impulse regulation, and social insecurity.	

Sources: Garner and Garfinkel (5), Drewnowski et al, (8) Koslowsky et al (9), Cooper et al (10), Martz et al (11), Arnow et al (12).

The five-category Eating Pathology Scale (EPS), described in the Drewnowski study, provides a new way of classifying a nonclinical population according to the frequency and severity of bulimic symptoms. Three percent of the respondents were classified as having bulimia, but 10% or more regularly engaged in bulimic behavior and were at risk for developing bulimia. Dieting to lose weight was found to be the *normative* behavior (31% intensive dieters, 42% casual dieters), and relatively few respondents were classified as nondieters (4–18%).

At least two important considerations from this study underscore the need for related intervention/prevention efforts (8):

- new cases of bulimia nervosa (at follow-up) were drawn exclusively from the intensive dieters and the at-risk group (at baseline), which suggests that prevention strategies should be targeted at younger individuals, and
- further investigations are needed of psychological and social factors that hinder or promote the development of eating disorders in women.

The EPS classifications were also used to demonstrate the clear association between clinical eating disorder behaviors and substance abuse in women (11). Drewnowski and coworkers found that such increases in dieting severity are positively associated with increasing prevalence of alcohol use, as well as increasing frequency of heavy drinking and drinking enough to alter mental state. In fact, these researchers found that the differences among dieting severity groups in the qualitative use of alcohol as a mood-altering substance were even larger than indicated by the simple frequency of alcohol use. They concluded that chronic dieting may serve as an important factor in the development of substance abuse in young women.

With regard to the Matching Familiar Figures Test (MFFT), researchers found that clients with bulimia responded more quickly than did those with anorexia, suggesting that not only are clients with bulimia more behaviorally impulsive than those with anorexia, but they are also more cognitively impulsive (13). Clients with anorexia in this study seemed to exhibit a "reflective" cognitive style compared with those with bulimia. The authors conclude that extreme cognitive styles may contribute to resistance in treatment and/or relapse in clients with anorexia or bulimia.

Self-report measures are relatively economical, quickly and easily administered, easy to score, and free of bias from interviewer-subject interactions. However, the risk of anonymous reporting is a decreased accuracy of reporting, especially regarding ambiguous behaviors such as binge eating. This type of assessment should be supplemented by symptom frequency data derived from an interview or a symptom checklist (6).

Self-Monitoring   Self-monitoring requires that clients record the following information in diaries: food intake, extreme weight control behaviors, general thoughts or feelings. Self-monitoring is considered a valuable assessment tool, and it probably yields more accurate information regarding eating behaviors and eating disorder symptoms than methods that require retrospective reports or generalizations about behavior. However, it may be unacceptable to certain clients, as it raises awareness of behaviors that arouse guilt and shame, and it may influence the frequency of the behaviors being monitored.

Beglin and Fairburn (14) conducted a detailed comparison of the first two methods for assessing the features of eating disorders, and found several discrepancies. Both methods produced similar results related to the less ambiguous behavioral features (eg, self-induced vomiting and dieting), but self-report questionnaires generated higher scores than interviews in assessing more complex features (eg, binge eating and concerns about shape). Interestingly, both methods underestimated body weight. These researchers also report that self-report questionnaires may be used in the place of investigator-based interviews when features that do not pose problems of definition are being assessed.

Some researchers have argued that, in assessing eating disorders, interviews are to be preferred to self-report questionnaires because many of the core features are particularly complex (14). A trained interviewer can increase the reliability of assessment scores because he is able to use standardized definitions for terms such as "binge" and "loss of control." The meaning of these terms can vary widely in the population that is being evaluated.

Clinical Interviews vs Self-Report Measures

Both self-report questionnaires and investigator-based interviews have been used to identify binge eaters. The Binge Eating Scale (BES) is a questionnaire that was developed to assess the severity of binge eating in obese individuals and has been widely used in the identification of research subjects. However, the EDE, the current "gold standard" of clinical eating disorder diagnosis, has the advantage of providing detailed descriptions of binge episodes, and thus more accurate evaluation of the amounts of food eaten, feelings of loss of control, and frequency of episodes.

A simple, accurate way to identify obese binge eaters is needed. Greeno et al (15) compared the EDE with the BES in search of a simple and accurate way to identify obese binge eaters, since binge eating is a common problem among the obese. In their study of 126 women seeking treatment for obesity, they found the BES accurately identified 92.9% of non-binge eaters (confirmed by the EDE) but only 51.8% of binge eaters. They concluded that there are limitations to self-report questionnaire measures of binge eating. However, they added that there is still a role for self-report questionnaires such as the BES as screening tools because the BES

POPULATION SCREENING IN ADULTS

- is extremely accurate in identifying non-binge eaters,
- can be used to identify subjects who have problems with their eating, even when they do not meet the criteria for binge eating disorder, and
- is useful for "first-pass screening" to identify individuals with severe binge eating problems.

They added that "the fact that 50% of high BES scorers are found to meet criteria for binge eating disorder is far higher than the base rate of 8% found in the community . . . and argues for the utility of this instrument for initial screening" (p 159). Perhaps more important, identification of related characteristics can play a large role in improved prevention of and early intervention in the development of more problematic eating behaviors/disorders.

Several other clinical interviews are currently used to assess the specific psychopathology of eating disorders, and binge eating in particular, including the Clinical Eating Disorder Rating Instrument (CEDRI), Structured Interview for Anorexia & Bulimia Nervosa (SIAB), Interview for the Diagnosis of Eating Disorders (IDED), and Binge Eating Disorder Interview (BEDI). Wilson (7) describes how the relative merits of each method depend on the purpose of the screening tool. Self-report questionnaires are useful as measures of overall severity but have major limitations related to diagnosis and clinically relevant descriptions of binge eating. Self-monitoring has broader clinical applicability and provides the most direct evaluation of the frequency and temporal pattern of eating behavior. Perhaps its major limitations are that the recording is often made retrospectively and that clients have to decide whether a perceived overeating episode constitutes a binge. This latter is difficult for clients to do reliably, and ideally self-monitoring should be used in conjunction with a detailed clinical interview such as the EDE.

As with anorexia nervosa and bulimia, the BULIT-R has been used to assess binge eating. However, instead of the EDI and EAT, commonly used in the assessment of anorexia nervosa and bulimia, several other tests have been used in binge eating disorder. These include the Binge Scale (BS), the Binge Eating Scale (BES), the Bulimic Investigatory Test (BITE), and the EDE-Q.

The BS, a 9-item scale designed to measure behavior and attitudes associated with binge eating, was the first questionnaire with this objective. It has good internal consistency and test-retest reliability. The BES is a 16-item tool devised to assess binge eating in obese clientele. It measures both the behavioral features of binge eating and associated feelings and cognitions, and has good test-retest reliability. The BITE is also a 36-item test with adequate psychometric properties, which assess the psychopathology of eating disorders. Wilson points out that neither the BULIT-R nor the BITE has been used much in research on binge eating. The EDE-Q is a 38-item questionnaire of the specific psychopathology of eating disorders, which is derived from the previously discussed EDE and has good potential in assessing binge eating by self-report questionnaire.

Internalized Eating Disorder Shame Scale

Shame is a significant problem in eating disorder clients, especially those with bulimia (16,17). Eating disorder inpatients exhibit the highest score in the Internalized Eating Disorder Shame Scale (ISS) of any clinical group studied, including substance abusers, clients with affective disorders and other psychiatric disorders, and post-traumatic stress disorder. Both anorexia and bulimia clients who were administered the ISS and EDI exhibited a significant relationship between the severity of their eating disorder and the degree of internalized shame (16).

The psychologically paralyzing human experience of shame was virtually neglected as a factor in mental health until the early 1980s, but shame plays a powerful role in eating disorder, compulsive overeating, addiction and recovery, dysfunctional family systems, childhood sexual abuse, aging, and disability (18). Nathanson (19) has done perhaps the most extensive work on shame, compassion, and psychopathology, and discusses related influences on instability of mood, interpersonal relationships, self-image, and other factors that are intimately related to disordered eating behaviors. In addition to the psychometric data, case study interviews were analyzed for thematic content and were found to confirm many theoretical postulates in the literature that pertain to eating disorder clientele, including

- feelings of inadequacy,
- hypercriticism of self,
- wishes to avoid others,
- defenses against shame (eg, perfectionism, envy, and struggles for power and control),
- intense fears of abandonment,
- wishes to be someone else, and
- feelings of contamination/self-disgust.

The ISS has excellent potential in the screening and assessment in disordered eating clientele.

Tools for Nutrition Assessments

Reiff and Reiff (20) have developed a package of instruments, each of which can be administered by nutrition therapists:

- *Precounseling Intake Form*—is used to collect basic personal information (eg, marital history, mental health history, family mental health history, therapy history, diet history).
- *Eating Disorder Intake Form*—is designed for nutrition therapists to use in collecting factual information (eg, medication history, exercise history, current somatic symptoms, obsessions about food, weight, hunger, and body image, expectations of nutrition therapy).
- *"Dying to Be Thin" Questionnaire*—indicates tendencies toward anorexia nervosa, bulimia nervosa, or other eating disorders. This tool is not designed to be a diagnostic instrument, but rather to serve as a way to identify thought patterns/beliefs commonly found among eating disorder clients. The questions are written in a nonthreatening way; the form works especially well for clients who are in denial. It is also effective as a means of determining recovery after treatment.
- *Longitudinal Weight and Life Event History*—examines the relationship between the food- and weight-related behaviors history and major life events and mood changes (eg, periods of depression, grief, contentment,

elation). This form may also be used to determine history, type(s), and severity of behavior patterns.

POPULATION SCREENING IN CHILDREN AND ADOLESCENTS

There is a need for a sensitive measure of eating disorder psychopathology that is appropriate for use with children. Although attempts have been made to describe the clinical features of eating disorders of childhood onset (ie, age 14 years or less), none has provided a systematic replicable assessment of psychopathology.

Screening in Children

The EDE was designed for use with adults, and extra care needs to be taken with some EDE items with younger girls, a clear advantage of investigator-based interviews over self-report measures. An investigator-based interview allows for questions to be explained clearly and adapted for better understanding by the child. More specifically, Bryant-Waugh and coworkers (21) incorporated the following modifications in the EDE in order to assess children:

- assessment of the critical overvalued ideas about weight and shape,
- reformulation of some of the questions to assess intent rather than actual behaviors, and
- rephrasing of certain questions to be more suitable for children.

This slightly modified version of the EDE is appropriate for use with children between the ages of 8 and 14 years, with some minor difficulties in administration and coding. The authors' pilot study shows that some children obtain global and subscale scores consistent with adult norms for females with eating disorders. They also suggest that further studies of this kind are needed to clarify the significance of apparent anomalies found in their study.

Another promising instrument for measuring disturbed eating attitudes and behaviors in middle-school girls is the Children's Eating Attitudes Test (chEAT), a 26-item self-report questionnaire (22). This instrument has adequate internal reliability. A 23-item version has even better reliability. Concurrent validity has also been demonstrated for the 26-item version, (again, slightly better for the 23-item version), in that correlations between the chEAT and independent measures of weight management and body dissatisfaction were significant. The chEAT was also found to have an additional factor, in comparison to the EAT-26, that tapped restricting and purging behaviors.

The Diagnostic Interview Schedule for Children, 2nd edition (DISC-2.1) can also be used to obtain assessment data from this age group. Fisher et al (23) examined the sensitivity of this instrument for certain "rare" disorders, including eating disorders, major depressive episode, obsessive-compulsive disorder (OCD), psychotic disorders, and substance abuse disorders. The strategy used in their study was found to be useful for assessing the DISC's sensitivity for these disorders, but they noted that additional work examining the specificity of the DISC remains to be done. The instrument should prove to be a useful adjunct in clinical settings, given the ease and relatively low cost of its administration.

Van Furth et al (24) examined whether parental expressed emotion (EE) ratings, based on the Camberwell Family Interview (CFI), were predictive of the course of illness in a sample of families with an eating disordered adolescent. Results generated by these researchers underscore the importance of involving the family in the treatment of adolescent eating disorders, a factor that makes related assessment in this age group a unique challenge. Specifically, the researchers found that it is important to pay close attention to the mother's thoughts, feelings, and behavior concerning her ill daughter, and that "helping mother and daughter to differentiate and separate through a constructive noncritical approach to the presenting problems may be a crucial factor in breaking through the perpetuating cycle of criticism and illness" (p 30).

In the 1960s the first reliable measures of family interaction were developed, leading to intensified research interest in the link between eating disorders and family interactions. The Expressed Emotion Index (EEI), developed in 1972, is one of the most well-established measures of family affective attitudes. According to van Furth and colleagues, the EEI is traditionally rated from an audiotaped, semistructured interview (the CFI). Examples of factors assessed in the CFI/EEI include criticism, hostility, warmth, emotional overinvolvement, and positive remarks.

Research into the influence of family interaction (as measured in expressed emotion variables) and the evaluation of family therapies in eating disorders has revealed a relationship between parental expressed emotion and dropout from eating disorder treatment. However, no study to date has documented a relationship between expressed emotion (rated from a family interview) and therapy outcome, or investigated the relationship between expressed emotion and the course of illness in eating disorders.

The CFI and EEI elucidated several distinctive patterns in eating disorder families:

- A higher degree of negative parental affect and a lower degree of positive parental affect correlated with a longer duration of treatment.
- Clients with a critical or less supportive parent were more difficult to treat.
- Mothers who were critical were also more overinvolved, whereas fathers were either critical or overinvolved.
- A more critical maternal attitude was predictive of a poorer outcome following treatment and at follow-up.
- Maternal criticism was a better predictor of outcome than other variables, such as diagnosis, duration of illness, body weight, body mass index, premorbid weight, age at onset, present age, and gender.
- Maternal criticism could predict changes in psychiatric states over a treatment period (24).

The precise nature of the relationship between expressed variables and the perpetuation and course of adolescent eating disorders needs further examination.

Screening in Adolescents

PSYCHOLOGICAL SCREENING IN COMMERCIAL WEIGHT LOSS PROGRAMS

Obese clientele drawn from treatment settings are likely to exhibit psychiatric symptoms (eg, high rates of depression, anxiety, poor body image, and maladaptive eating behavior), and may be at greater risk for having comorbid psychiatric diagnoses (25). Historically, however, there were no notable assessments of psychiatric symptoms in clients seeking treatment at commercial weight reduction programs, which historically have not supported psychiatric assessment, intervention, or research. Most of the current treatment of obesity in the US is carried out in these programs (which constitute a $33 billion annual industry with a 95% failure rate [26,27]).

Goldstein and coworkers (25) used the following self-report measures to study the prevalence and severity of psychiatric/psychopathologic symptoms in a group of commercial weight reduction clients, as compared with a group of patients seeking outpatient medical treatment for obesity:

- Depression (Beck Depression Inventory, BDI)—The BDI has been the most widely used assessment tool in clinical and nonclinical research. This 21-item scale assesses the presence and severity of affective, cognitive, motivational, vegetative, and psychomotor components of depression. Each item relates to a particular symptom of depression, and respondents indicate on a scale of 0 to 3 the severity of the current state of each symptom. Although the BDI was developed for use with adults, it has also been used successfully with children. A 13-item version of the BDI is also available.

- Anxiety (Spielberger State & Trait Anxiety Inventories, SSTAI)—The SSTAI has two similar 20-item questionnaires, designed to assess immediate and ongoing symptoms of anxiety and their severity.

- Body Shape Questionnaire (BSQ)—This 34-item questionnaire assesses subjective body dissatisfaction and preoccupation with body size and shape.

- Sheehan Disability Scale (SDS)—This 3-item questionnaire measures the impact of symptoms (not specifically defined as psychiatric or medical) on three areas of functioning—vocational, social, and familial.

The researchers reported that

- severe depressive symptoms were found in 15.0% of the commercial weight reduction clients, as compared with only 2.3% of the medical treatment group (despite the fact that the latter patients were in worse physical health),

- clients presenting for weight reduction were more preoccupied and dissatisfied with body shape in a manner that was unrelated to actual body size,

- commercial weight reduction program clients exhibited moderate anxiety levels similar to those of the medical patients, but had slightly greater social, family, and occupational impairment.

The authors generated a number of hypotheses to explain the high rates of depressive symptomatology found in this newly investigated sample. Clients with comorbid depressive symptoms may present for weight reduction treatment preferentially, as they may attribute their dysphoria to their weight, a misguided notion corroborated by advertisements for commercial weight reduction programs touting a relationship between weight loss, happiness, and success. Not surprisingly, commercial weight reduction clients had higher rates of body dissatisfaction than those seeking medical treatment, reflecting a possibility that these clients suffer from body image distortion. They may need to be evaluated more closely for the presence of undiagnosed or subclinical eating disorders.

The preliminary findings presented here are meaningful and suggest that commercial weight reduction programs are attracting people with high rates of depressive symptoms. Given the lack of onsite medical supervision at most commercial weight reduction programs, these symptoms may not be thoroughly evaluated. Several strategies may be appropriate to implement in these settings:

- more vigorous screening of commercial weight reduction program clients for psychiatric symptoms,
- differential treatment strategies for clients presenting with depressive symptoms, as depression per se may lead to weight gain or to decreased compliance with treatment,
- evaluation of clients of average weight attracted to commercial weight reduction programs and their motivation for engaging in such treatment. Treatment strategies designed to correct distortions of body image rather than to promote weight loss may be more appropriate.

COMMUNITY SCREENING

Selzer et al (28) provide a fine example of how, over the last two decades, the development of clinically validated instruments for the evaluation of eating disorder symptomatology has allowed for an expansion of epidemiological research into community settings. However, they explain that efficient detection has continued to be a challenge to psychiatric epidemiologists for several reasons:

- The relatively low prevalence of eating disorders in community samples greatly reduces the diagnostic/screening efficacy of instruments effective in clinical populations.
- The presentation of eating disorders in the community differs from that in clinical samples, where instruments are usually validated.
- Subclinical disorders are more common in the community than in clinical populations, so application of a clinically validated instrument to general population surveys is uncertain.

- Fixed-format questionnaires (eg, the EAT-26) are the usual instruments of choice for case detection in surveys, but their efficiency is limited. Structured interviews compare favorably with questionnaires in efficiency of case detection, but have disadvantages related to cost and training.

Selzer and colleagues developed a branched format, computerized questionnaire (BET). This approach may overcome the disadvantages of interviews, in which individuals may be less likely to divulge emotionally laden symptoms connected to shame and embarrassment. The mean time for subjects to complete the BET was only 15.3 minutes. Though modification and further evaluation of this instrument is needed, it holds promise as a practical tool for use with large populations.

SUMMARY

- **A comprehensive approach for evaluating and treating clients with eating disorders includes detection, assessment, diagnosis, and population screening.**
- **There is no universally accepted protocol for assessing eating disorders. Assessment commonly takes the form of a clinical interview, self-report, or self-monitoring.**
- **Assessment of children and adolescents should accommodate their emotional and chronological ages. It should also evaluate family dynamics that may affect the clinical presentation.**
- **Research suggests that commercial weight loss programs tend to attract clientele with significant depressive symptoms. These programs might improve their effectiveness if they screened clients for depression and included interventions (in addition to weight loss counseling) that can help resolve depressive symptoms.**
- **Population screening for eating disorders using the available assessment tools is quite costly. However, instruments are being developed that may encourage the use of population screening.**

REFERENCES

1. Jacobson GR. A comprehensive approach to pretreatment evaluation: I. Detection, assessment, & diagnosis of alcoholism. In: Hester RK, Miller WR, eds. *Handbook of Alcoholism Treatment Approaches.* New York: Pergamon Press; 1989.
2. Leon GR, Kolotkin R, Korgeski G. MacAndrew Addiction Scale and MMPI characteristics associated with obesity, anorexia and smoking behavior. *Addictive Behaviors.* 1979;4:401–407.
3. Brownell KD, Fairburn CG. *Eating Disorders and Obesity: A Comprehensive Handbook.* New York: Guilford Press; 1995.
4. Williamson DA. *Assessment of Eating Disorders:Obesity, Anorexia, and Bulimia Nervosa.* New York: Pergamon Press; 1990.
5. Garner DM, Garfinkel PE. *Diagnostic Issues in Anorexia Nervosa and Bulimia Nervosa.* New York: Brunner/Mazel; 1998.
6. Fairburn CG, Cooper Z. The eating disorder examination In: Fairburn DC, Wilson GT, eds. *Binge Eating: Nature, Assessment and Treatment.* 12th ed. New York: Guilford Press; 1993.

7. Wilson GT. Assessment of binge eating. In: Fairburn DC, Wilson GT, eds. *Binge Eating: Nature, Assessment and Treatment.* 12th ed. New York: Guilford Press; 1993.

8. Drewnowski A, Yee DR, Kurth CL, Krahn DD. Eating pathology and DSM-II-R bulimia nervosa: a continuum of behavior. *Am J Psychiatry.* 1994;151:8–11.

9. Koslowsky M, Scheinberg Z, Bleich A, Mark M, Apter A, Danon Y, Solomon Z. The factor structure and criterion validity of the short form of the Eating Attitudes Test. *J Pers Assess.* 1992;58(1):27–35.

10. Cooper Z, Cooper PJ, Fairburn CG. The specificity of the Eating Disorder Inventory. *Br J Clin Psychol.* 1985;24(Pt 2):129–130.

11. Martz DM, Sturgis ET, Gustafson SB. Development and preliminary validation of the cognitive behavioral dieting scale. *Int J Eating Disord.* 1996;19(3):297–309.

12. Arnow B, Kenardy J, Agras WS. The Emotional Eating Scale: the development of a measure to assess coping with negative affect by eating. *Int J Eating Disord.* 1995;18(1):79-90.

13. Kaye WH, Bastiani AM, Moss H. Cognitive style of patients with anorexia nervosa and bulimia nervosa. *Int J Eating Disord.* 1995;18(3):287–290.

14. Beglin SJ, Fairburn CG. Assessment of eating disorders: interview or self-report questionnaire? *Int J Eating Disord.* 1994;16(4): 363-370.

15. Greeno CG, Marcus MD, Wing RR. Diagnosis of binge eating disorder: discrepancies between a questionnaire and clinical interview. *Int J Eating Disord.* 1995;17(2): 153–160.

16. Andrews B. Bodily shame in relation to abuse in childhood and bulimia. *Br J Clin Psychol.* 1997;36(Pt 1):41–49.

17. Cook DR. *Internalized Shame Scale: Professional Manual.* Menomonie, Wis: Channel Press; 1994.

18. Kaufman G. *Shame: The Power of Caring.* Cambridge, Mass: Schenkman; 1994.

19. Nathanson DL. Shame, compassion, and the "borderline" personality. *Psychiatr Clin North Am.* 1994;17(4):785-810.

20. Reiff D, Reiff KL. *Eating Disorders: Nutrition Therapy in the Recovery Process.* Gaithersburg, Md: Aspen Publications; 1992.

21. Bryant-Waugh RJ, Cooper PJ, Taylor CL, Lask BD. The use of the eating disorder examination with children: a pilot study. *Int J Eating Disord.* 1996;19(4):391–397.

22. Maloney MJ, McGuire J, Daniels R, Specker B. Dieting behavior and eating attitudes in children. *Pediatrics.* 1989;84(3):482–489.

23. Fisher PW, Shaffer D, Piacentini JC, Lapkin J, Kafantaris V, Leonard H, Herzog DB. Sensitivity of the Diagnostic Interview Schedule for Children, 2nd edition (DISC-2.1) for specific diagnoses of children and adolescents. *J Am Acad Child Adolesc Psychiatry.* 1993;32(3):666–673.

24. van Furth EF, van Strien DC, Martina LM, van Son MJ, Hendriskx JJ, van Engeland H. Expressed emotion and the prediction of outcome in adolescent eating disorders. *Int J Eating Disord.* 1996;20(1):19-31.

25. Goldstein LT, Goldsmith SJ, Anger K, Leon AC. Psychiatric symptoms in clients presenting for commercial weight reduction treatment. *Int J Eating Disord.* 1995;17(2): 153–160.

26. Begley CE. Government should strengthen regulation in the weight loss industry. *J Am Diet Assoc.* 1991;91(10):1255–1257.

27. Goodrick GK, Foreyt JP. Why treatments for obesity don't last. *J Am Diet Assoc.* 1991;91(10):1243–1247.

28. Selzer R, Hamill C, Bowes G, Patton G. The Branched Eating Disorders test: validity in a population. *Int J Eating Disord.* 1996;20(1):19–31.

CHAPTER 12

Axis II: Personality Disorders

LISA M. VARNER, Ph.D., R.D.

Personality disorders frequently occur with eating disorders such as bulimia nervosa and anorexia nervosa (1). The purpose of this chapter is to review the essential features of the personality disorders and to provide nutrition professionals with recommendations for approaches to treating clients with Axis II disorders.

FUNCTION OF AXIS II

It is usually Axis I symptoms that bring clients in for treatment. Personality disorders are included on a separate axis, Axis II, to ensure they are considered in treatment planning. Otherwise, personality disorders could be disregarded when attention is directed to the usually very prominent Axis I disorders (1).

Up to 80% of patients seen in mental health clinics present with a personality disorder (2), and it is not unusual for patients to have more than one personality disorder (1). Personality disorder diagnoses are important to note and consider, as they can interfere with the treatment of eating disorders or other Axis I disorders. Treatment team members must recognize the presence of personality disorders and their possible influence on eating- and weight-related problems (3–5).

DEFINITIONS

The general diagnostic criteria for personality disorders are indicated in APA's *Diagnostic and Statistical Manual-IV* (DSM-IV) and listed in *Box 12.1*. Personality disorders are basically disorders of traits or character. They are often referred to as characterological disorders. Personality disorders reflect an indi-

A. An enduring pattern of inner experience and behavior that deviates markedly from the expectations of the individual's culture. This pattern is manifested in two (or more) of the following areas:
   1. cognition (ie, ways of perceiving and interpreting self, other people, and events)
   2. affectivity (ie, the range, intensity, lability, and appropriateness of emotional response)
   3. interpersonal functioning
   4. impulse control

B. The enduring pattern is inflexible and pervasive across a broad range of personal and social situations.

C. The enduring pattern leads to clinically significant distress or impairment in social, occupational, or other important areas of functioning.

D. The pattern is stable and of long duration and its onset can be traced back at least to adolescence or early adulthood.

E. The enduring pattern is not better accounted for as a manifestation of consequence of another mental disorder.

F. The enduring pattern is not due to the direct physiological effects of a substance (eg, a drug of abuse, a medication) or a general medical condition (eg, head trauma).

American Psychiatric Association (1). Used with permission.

Box 12.1
General Diagnostic Criteria for a Personality Disorder

vidual's long-standing (since at least adolescence or early adulthood) tendency to perceive and respond to the environment in broad and maladaptive ways that extend across time and situations (3).

Only when personality traits are inflexible and maladaptive and result in significant impairment in social, occupational, or other important areas of functioning or in subjective distress do they meet the criteria for a personality disorder diagnosis. To be considered a personality disorder, this enduring pattern of inner experience and behavior cannot be better accounted for as a manifestation of an Axis I disorder (1). For example, the social withdrawal that often is part of major depressive disorder should not be mistaken for the social isolation that is a major feature of several personality disorders.

Personality disorders are difficult to treat for a variety of reasons. First, they are typically long-standing, having often developed in childhood. In addition, by definition personality disorders consist of maladaptive personality traits that have become ingrained over time and thus are resistant to change. In addition, many persons with personality disorders refuse to acknowledge that their difficulties in life may have anything to do with their own thoughts and behaviors, and thus see no reason to change (1,2). Also, since personality disordered individuals also tend to have Axis I disorders, which led to their seeking treatment, the focus of treatment is often directed more toward the Axis I problem(s) (eg, anorexia nervosa, bulimia nervosa, or major depressive disorder) than the Axis II disorder(s).

PERSONALITY DISORDER CLUSTERS

The DSM-IV organizes personality disorders into three clusters. Cluster A includes the paranoid, schizoid, and schizotypal personality disorders. These are often referred to as the "odd cluster," as persons with these disorders often appear to be eccentric or remarkably unusual. Cluster B includes antisocial, borderline, histrionic, and narcissistic personality disorders; individuals with these disorders exhibit relatively dramatic and egocentric behaviors and characteristics. Individuals with Cluster C personality disorders (avoidant, dependent, and obsessive-compulsive) share anxious and fearful attributes (1,2).

Numerous studies have reported the existence of personality disorders in eating disorder clients, most commonly in those with bulimic symptoms (4,5,6). Bulimic individuals are most likely to receive borderline (40%) or histrionic (13%) personality disorder diagnoses, while anorexics are most often diagnosed as avoidant (33%) or dependent (10%) (7). Thus, anorexic and bulimic patients are most often diagnosed with Cluster B and C personality disorders. Little research exists on personality disorders in individuals with eating disorder not otherwise specified. However, evidence to date indicates significantly lower Axis I and Axis II symptomatology in nonpurging binge eaters (which could include individuals with binge eating disorder) than in purging binge eaters (8).

Several studies indicate that personality disorders are associated with both disordered eating and reported sexual abuse (9-11). It appears that behaviors characteristic of borderline personality disorder (eg, impulsivity, poor anger control, self-harm, unstable relationships, and mood affective disturbance) are particularly relevant to the development and maintenance of eating disorders in sexual abuse victims (11,12). A proposed model suggests that sexual abuse can cause specific borderline symptoms to develop, and the borderline personality style in turn negatively affects eating- and weight-related behavior (13).

ASSESSMENT OF PERSONALITY DISORDERS

Relatively few measures are currently available to directly assess the presence of personality disorders. The Millon Clinical Multiaxial Inventory-III (MCMI-III) is one instrument psychiatry and psychology professionals can use to screen for personality disorders. This self-report measure contains eleven subscales that correspond to personality problems and nine clinical subscales that tap various Axis I problems, such as depression and anxiety.

An earlier version of the MCMI-III, called the MCMI, was used by Williamson (5) to determine base rate personality problem subscale scores in a sample of compulsive eaters, bulimics, and anorexics. In general, the results indicated higher scores and more problematic personality symptoms in anorexics and bulimics than in compulsive overeaters (5).

Psychiatry and psychology professionals may also use the Personality Disorder Scales of the Minnesota Multiphasic Personality Inventory-II (MMPI-II) to evaluate for the presence of personality disorders. Scales have been developed for each of the personality disorders, as defined by the DSM-III (14,15).

In addition to using one or both of these instruments, psychiatry and psychology professionals must assess for personality disorders by conducting clinical interviews. The clinician should, in the course of this interview, evaluate long-term patterns of functioning, with particular emphasis on the stability of traits over time and across different situations. Supplementary information from other informants (eg, parents or spouses) also can be helpful in making diagnostic decisions about the presence or absence of Axis II disorders (1).

TYPES OF PERSONALITY DISORDERS

The *DSM-IV* lists nine categories of personality disorders. Each can exist with eating disorders and other Axis I diagnoses. The rest of this chapter describes these disorders. Case studies illustrate how the disorders might present in a nutrition therapy setting and how they might affect food behaviors. These case studies illustrate how complex clinical presentations can be. A person with hyperlipidemia might also be depressed; his lipid profile might indicate as much about his mood and stress levels as his dietary habits.

Disordered eating characteristics, as well as Axis I and Axis II characteristics, have many variations in intensity of presentation. It is important not to assume that, because Axis I or II diagnoses have not been assigned, they do not exist. An individual with an eating disorder will tend to relate food and eating to problems that are not food related. The nutrition therapist is often such an individual's point of entry into the health care system. A competent nutrition therapist will evaluate all clients for possible psychosocial complications and coordinate a team approach that addresses nutritional as well as medical and emotional needs.

Paranoid Personality Disorder

Box 12.2 indicates the diagnostic criteria for paranoid personality disorder. The essential feature of this disorder is a pattern of pervasive distrust and suspiciousness of others, which leads to the assumption (without supporting evidence) that others are out to exploit, harm, or deceive. Individuals with paranoid personality disorder are reluctant to confide in or become close to others, as they believe that information they provide could be used against them. They also may refuse to answer personal questions and may misperceive offers of help as criticisms (1).

Reports in the literature indicate paranoid personality disorder accounts for 1.7% to 2.6% of all psychiatric cases and 4.0% to 5.2% of all personality disorders. However, experts believe that these rates may be low, in part because those with paranoid personality disorder rarely seek treatment and thus are disproportionately

**Box 12.2
Diagnostic Criteria for
Paranoid Personality
Disorder**

A. A pervasive distrust and suspiciousness of others such that their motives are interpreted as malevolent, beginning by early adulthood and present in a variety of contexts as indicated by four (or more) of the following:

1. suspects, without sufficient basis, that others are exploiting, harming, or deceiving him or her,

2. is preoccupied with unjustified doubts about the loyalty or trustworthiness of friends or associates,

3. is reluctant to confide in others because of unwarranted fear that the information will be used maliciously against him or her,

4. reads hidden demeaning or threatening meanings into benign remarks or events,

5. persistently bears grudges (ie, is unforgiving of insults, injuries, or slights),

6. perceives attacks on his or her character or reputation that are not apparent to others and is quick to react angrily or to counterattack,

7. has recurrent suspicions, without justification, regarding fidelity of spouse or sexual partner.

B. Does not occur exclusively during the course of schizophrenia, a mood disorder with psychotic features, or another psychotic disorder and is not due to the direct physiological effects of a general medical condition.

American Psychiatric Association (1). Used with permission.

omitted from clinical samples (16). Paranoid personality disorder is not particularly common in eating disorder patients.

It has been proposed that paranoid personality disorder results from sadistic treatment in childhood or a failure to be protected from excessive tension and anxiety during childhood. In both instances, the child comes to view the world as an unfriendly, unstable place in which others will harm him or her (17).

Given these characteristics, it is not surprising that individuals with paranoid personality disorder often prove a challenge for health care professionals, including nutrition therapists. In fact, it often is a challenge to convince these individuals to come in for treatment because of their underlying distrust and suspicion of others. When they do present for treatment, it may be difficult to obtain accurate personal information from them. In addition, the rigidity often observed in paranoid individuals makes them less likely than others to embrace or successfully implement change. Millon (18) warned therapists that therapeutic work with paranoid personalities is very difficult because they believe that therapy signifies weakness and dependency, which are aversive to them. Furthermore, these clients often intimidate health care professionals with their arrogance and anger.

Experts on personality disorders have recommended that health care professionals who work with paranoid personalities attempt to build trust slowly, maintaining a "quiet, formal, genuine respect for the patient" (18,19). The nutrition therapist working with a paranoid client may want to implement behavioral interventions involving food shopping, preparation, and dietary intake toward the beginning of therapy, since these interventions would be relatively unthreatening *(Box 12.3)*. As trust builds over time, treatment may progress to include such goals as increasing self-efficacy about food-related behavior, realistically appraising problems, and improving coping skills related to food and weight.

**Box 12.3
CASE STUDY**
Paranoid Personality Disorder

M.L. was a 30-year-old married, white woman who presented for treatment at an inpatient eating disorders treatment facility following a 20-pound weight loss over the past four months. She reported that she had begun restricting her food intake and losing weight after she spotted her husband's ex-girlfriend at a local sporting event.

The client noted that she had always been "suspicious" of this woman's intentions, even though she had never talked with her, and said she was convinced that the ex-girlfriend was having an affair with her husband. M.L.'s husband insisted that he had not been unfaithful and had not, in fact, talked with his ex-girlfriend since he had begun dating M.L. However, he noted that his wife had felt threatened by his ex-girlfriend throughout their five-year relationship, for what he called "no reason." M.L. indicated that she was motivated to lose weight in order to "compete" with this ex-girlfriend's "stick-thin body," and she described using food restriction, self-induced vomiting, laxatives, and diet pills in the past four months in her efforts to lose weight.

The nutrition therapist working with M.L. spent a great deal of time establishing rapport with her so that she could develop trust in their relationship and in the nutrition therapist's expertise. The nutrition therapist first implemented dietary interventions with a high likelihood of success to increase M.L.'s confidence in the nutrition therapist and the overall treatment. The nutrition therapist elected not to have M.L. participate in the eating disorders group because of her difficulty in trusting others. This lack of trust would likely have limited her ability to share her problems with other group members. In addition, the nutrition therapist feared that M.L.'s arrogance and anger would intimidate other group members.

Schizoid Personality Disorder

Box 12.4 indicates the essential features of schizoid personality disorder. Individuals with this disorder typically exhibit a basic indifference to social relationships. They have a restricted range of emotional experience and expression, and seem content to live their lives as loners. These individuals often demonstrate social skills deficits (eg, poor eye contact, difficulty in initiating and maintaining conversations) (2).

Some researchers have suggested a relationship between schizoid personality disorder and the Axis I disorder called schizophrenia, but at present the evidence for this relationship is not substantial. One researcher found that only 9% of children with strong schizoid features went on to develop schizophrenia in adulthood. Individuals with schizoid personality disorder sometimes develop major

**Box 12.4
Diagnostic Criteria for
Schizoid Personality
Disorder**

A. A pervasive pattern of detachment from social relationships and a restricted range of expression of emotions in interpersonal settings, beginning by early adulthood and present in a variety of contexts, as indicated by four (or more) of the following:

   1. neither desires nor enjoys close relationships, including being part of a family,
   2. almost always chooses solitary activities,
   3. has little, if any, interest in having sexual experiences with another person,
   4. takes pleasure in few, if any, activities,
   5. lacks close friends or confidants other than first-degree relatives,
   6. appears indifferent to the praise or criticism of others,
   7. shows emotional coldness, detachment, or flattened affectivity.

B. Does not occur exclusively during the course of schizophrenia, a mood disorder with psychotic features, another psychotic disorder, or a pervasive developmental disorder and is not due to the direct physiological effects of a general medical condition.

American Psychiatric Association (1). Used with permission.

depressive disorder, which often occurs with schizotypal, paranoid, and avoidant personality disorders (1). Due to limited research on schizoid personality disorder, the prevalence and etiology of this Axis II disorder remain unclear (16). However, this disorder is not particularly common in eating disorder patients.

Nutrition therapists who work with persons with schizoid personality disorder will readily note the clients' social skills deficits. Their relative disinterest in social relationships may also make it difficult to establish and maintain a good therapeutic relationship. Nutrition therapists should not expect these individuals to be talkative or enthusiastic, but should understand that relationships with the treatment team member may be among their most in-depth social connections (*Box 12.5*). However, these clients will probably not value these connections much and can tax health care professionals' empathy and warmth. Nutrition therapists should meet with these clients in individual sessions before placing them in a nutrition therapy or education group to evaluate their appropriateness for the group. These clients should only be placed in groups that are supportive and not too demanding initially (20).

Schizotypal Personality Disorder

The predominant features of schizotypal personality disorder are presented in *Box 12.6*.

Like persons with schizoid personality disorder, individuals with schizotypal personality disorder demonstrate social skills deficits, have few interpersonal relationships, and typically strike others as "odd" or "strange." However, they also exhibit peculiar thoughts or beliefs, which are not usually present in schizoid

S.L., a 52-year-old single, white woman, presented to a county public health department for treatment of uncontrolled type 2 diabetes. During her nutrition assessment, a pattern of binge eating was identified. The client reported having been employed "off and on" as a dishwasher, though she currently was unemployed. She said she had no close relationships, and this did not seem to cause her concern. She reported spending most her time by herself at her apartment, caring for her seven cats. She said she had never learned how to drive a car, nor had she ever been involved in a dating relationship.

The nutrition therapist who worked with S.L. did not expect easy rapport with this client, nor did she blame herself for the relative lack of rapport established. The nutrition therapist determined that S.L. would not be appropriate for a diabetes education group because her lack of social skills and her relative disinterest in forming or maintaining relationships. Instead, the nutrition therapist provided nutrition education in individual sessions with as much emphasis as possible on visual aids and materials S.L. could take home and read on her own. Because S.L. seemed unlikely to call health care professionals or other for support, the nutrition therapist asked her to return for periodic follow-up sessions in order to be a support and resource as needed.

Box 12.5
CASE STUDY
Schizoid Personality Disorder

A. A pervasive pattern of social and interpersonal deficits marked by acute discomfort with, and reduced capacity for, close relationships, as well as by cognitive or perceptual distortions and eccentricities of behavior, beginning by early adulthood and present in a variety of contexts as indicated by five (or more) of the following:

1. ideas of reference (excluding delusions of reference),
2. odd beliefs or magical thinking that influences behavior and is inconsistent with subcultural norms (eg, superstitiousness, belief in clairvoyance, telepathy, or "sixth sense" in children and adolescents, bizarre fantasies or preoccupations),
3. unusual perceptual experiences, including bodily illusions,
4. odd thinking and speech (eg, vague, circumstantial, metaphorical, overelaborate, or stereotyped),
5. suspiciousness or paranoid ideation,
6. inappropriate or constricted affect,
7. behavior or appearance that is odd, eccentric, or peculiar,
8. lack of close friends or confidants other than first-degree relatives,
9. excessive social anxiety that does not diminish with familiarity and tends to be associated with paranoid fears rather than negative judgments about self.

B. Does not occur exclusively during the course of schizophrenia, a mood disorder with psychotic features, another psychotic disorder, or a pervasive developmental disorder.

American Psychiatric Association (1). Used with permission.

Box 12.6
Diagnostic Criteria for Schizotypal Personality Disorder

patients. These peculiar beliefs and thoughts are not consistent with cultural norms, and tend to influence the individual's behavior. Examples may include the schizotypal person's claims that he can "feel" or "sense" things that others cannot. The speech and conversation of schizotypal individuals may be peculiarly vague or abstract, and they may be seen talking to themselves. In addition, their appearance may be disheveled and unkempt (2,16). Schizotypal personality disorder is present in about 3% of the general population (2).

There are several theories about the etiology of schizotypal personality disorder. Some researchers believe that this disorder is a precursor to or less severe form of schizophrenia (1), while others have speculated that the peculiar thoughts and beliefs may develop early on as a form of autostimulation in response to inadequate cognitive and emotional input during childhood (16).

Individuals with this personality disorder typically seek treatment for depression or anxiety, rather than for the personality disorder features per se. From 30% to 50% of those with this personality disorder have a concurrent diagnosis of major depressive disorder when admitted to a clinic setting. A considerable percentage also have other personality disorders, including paranoid and borderline (1) (Box 12.7).

As with the other Cluster C personality disorders, nutrition therapists may find it extremely challenging to even establish rapport, much less a therapeutic relationship, with individuals with schizotypal personality disorder. Nutrition therapists may find assessment and counseling of these individuals difficult because of

Box 12.7
CASE STUDY
Schizotypal Personality Disorder

H.I. was a 25-year-old single, obese, Asian man referred to a psychiatrist by his mother, who was concerned about his long-standing disinterest in making friends and his inability to hold a job. She was also disturbed about his recent insistence that he "felt an evil presence" in certain rooms of the house in which they lived (ie, his bedroom and the family room). H.I. had avoided these rooms for the past two months and had been sleeping on the dining room floor to avoid "the evil presence."

The psychiatrist referred H.I. to a nutrition therapist to help him with weight management. The nutrition therapist realized prior to the nutrition assessment session that H.I. would likely be hard to interview because of his social skills deficits. She asked that his mother accompany him to nutrition assessment and counseling sessions to provide information that H.I. could or would not provide. The nutrition therapist was thus better able to determine his dietary history, family food preparation, and eating patterns. She determined that H.I. would not benefit from participation in a weight management group because of his lack of interest in establishing relationships and in obtaining support from others. In addition, she speculated that other group members might be disturbed by his unusual beliefs and unkempt appearance. The nutrition therapist reminded herself throughout treatment that H.I.'s relative lack of warmth and participation in sessions were not due to her professional and personal deficits, but were to be expected given the client's personality disorder.

their social skills deficits and dysfunctional belief and thought patterns. Individuals with schizotypal personality disorder generally are not appropriate for group treatment interventions because of their social skills deficits, their anxiety in social situations, and the discomfort other group members may well experience in their presence.

Antisocial Personality Disorder

Box 12.8 presents the DSM-IV diagnostic criteria for antisocial personality disorder. Individuals with this disorder have repeatedly exhibited (without remorse) irresponsible, impulsive, and aggressive behaviors since childhood. Typically antisocial individuals engage in actions such as violating the law, becoming involved in physical fights, lying, and being reckless about their own and others' personal safety (2,20). They exhibit poor judgment and fail to learn from past problems and mistakes (1).

The lifetime prevalence of antisocial personality disorder is 2.5% to 5.0% in the general population, with men more likely to carry this diagnosis. Many individuals with antisocial personality disorder have other personality disorders, particularly borderline and narcissistic. In addition, substance abuse disorders are quite common in antisocial individuals (1,20).

Box 12.8
Diagnostic Criteria for Antisocial Personality Disorder

A. There is a pervasive pattern of disregard for and violation of the rights of others occurring since age 15 years, as indicated by three (or more) of the following:

1. failure to conform to social norms with respect to lawful behaviors as indicated by repeatedly performing acts that are grounds for arrest,
2. deceitfulness, as indicated by repeated lying, use of aliases, or conning others for personal profit or pleasure,
3. impulsivity or failure to plan ahead,
4. irritability and aggressiveness, as indicated by repeated physical fights assaults,
5. reckless disregard for safety of self or others,
6. consistent irresponsibility, as indicated by repeated failure to sustain work behavior or honor financial obligations,
7. lack of remorse, as indicated by being indifferent to or rationalizing having hurt, mistreated, or stolen from another.

B. The individual is at least 18 years old.

C. There is evidence of conduct disorder with onset before age 15 years.

D. The occurrence of antisocial behavior is not exclusively during the course of schizophrenia or a manic episode.

American Psychiatric Association (1). Used with permission.

Antisocial personality disorder appears to evolve from a combination of biological, psychological, and social factors. There is strong evidence for a genetic component, and frontal lobe brain dysfunction may also be involved. In addition, dysfunctional family characteristics (eg, parental conflict and abuse) and poor parenting techniques (especially harsh and erratic punishment) are predictive of antisocial personality disorder, as are being from a poor, urban environment and a large family. It has been speculated that persons with antisocial personality disorder also have learning deficits that prevent them from learning cultural norms (20).

Nutrition therapists who work with antisocial clients should be aware that they may be resistant to entering and staying in treatment. When considering treatment planning, keep in mind that antisocial patients become bored easily and are highly stimulation-seeking. Expect antisocial clients to possibly be deceptive about their history and present treatment adherence status. If possible, seek to corroborate important information by contacting other health care professionals or the clients' significant others. Note that antisocial clients often seem charming and agreeable during treatment sessions, when in actuality they are "conning" the health care professional to shorten the treatment process (*Box 12.9*). Thus,

Box 12.9
CASE STUDY
Antisocial Personality
Disorder

P.R., a 35-year-old divorced, white man, was voluntarily admitted to an inpatient substance abuse treatment center. Further questioning revealed that he had a long history of driving while intoxicated, drug dealing, and theft, and it appeared he was entering the hospital to avoid an upcoming court date. P.R. reported a history of almost daily alcohol and marijuana use dating from age 13 and a history of weekend cocaine use since age 18. Both of his parents were alcoholics. His wife divorced him 5 years ago because of his substance abuse. He had been unemployed for the past year after being fired for being intoxicated on the job. He had two children whom he had not seen since his divorce, and he failed to pay child support.

P.R. was referred to a nutrition therapist after laboratory tests indicated hyper-triglyceridemia. The nutrition therapist learned he ate primarily one large meal in the evening, consisting of fast food and sugary sweets. She noted numerous disordered eating behaviors as she conducted her assessment. She found the client very attentive, almost flirtatious, at the beginning of the nutrition assessment session. However, he soon began to lose interest in the session and occasionally interrupted the nutrition therapist with irrelevant questions when she tried to obtain a diet history. He also laughed after answering some of her questions, which made her suspicious of the accuracy of his responses. The nutrition therapist found that she had to work very hard to keep this client on task.

She discovered that the best strategy for working with him was to meet with him on several occasions for only brief periods each time, so that his attention was better maintained. She also decided not to include P.R. in a group nutrition education class because of his tendency toward disruptive behavior and decreased attention over time. She found he responded well to activities in which he was involved. Thus, she had him use food models and actual food samples to practice meal planning, and she also took him through the cafeteria line and helped him make appropriate meal choices as part of a nutrition education session.

nutrition therapists who work with antisocial clients should be "on their toes," as the potential is there for these clients to be manipulative and untruthful. Nutrition therapists should also be aware of the strong potential for substance abuse in these clients and the related nutritional implications.

Borderline Personality Disorder

The diagnostic criteria for borderline personality disorder are shown in *Box 12.10*. Clients with this disorder exhibit a long history of instability in mood, interpersonal relationships, and self-image. They may also present with recurring suicidal threats and gestures, self-mutilating behavior, rapid mood shifts, impulsivity, and intense interpersonal relationships (1,2). Borderline personality disorder is relatively common in eating disorder clients, particularly those who binge and purge (1,4,5). Persons with borderline personality disorder have intense fears of abandonment. They may initially idealize lovers and potential caregivers, including the health care professionals working with them. However, borderline clients may switch quickly from idealizing individuals to devaluing them if they perceive that these individuals are not caring or giving enough (1).

Individuals with borderline personality disorder often present with one or more Axis I disorder(s), most commonly mood, panic, substance use, eating, gender identity, attention-deficit, and post-traumatic stress disorders. There are many theories about the etiology of borderline personality disorder. Numerous studies suggest that some form of childhood trauma or family conflict may be

---

Box 12.10 Diagnostic Criteria for Borderline Personality Disorder

A. A pervasive pattern of unstable interpersonal relationships, self-image, and affects, and marked impulsivity beginning by early adulthood and present in a variety of contexts, as indicated by five (or more) of the following:

1. frantic efforts to avoid real or imagined abandonment,
2. a pattern of unstable and intense interpersonal relationships characterized by alternating between extremes of idealization and devaluation,
3. identity disturbance: markedly and persistently unstable self-image or image of oneself,
4. impulsivity in at least two areas that are potentially self-damaging (eg, spending, sex, substance abuse, reckless driving, binge eating),
5. recurrent suicidal behavior, gestures, or threats, or self-mutilating behavior,
6. affective instability due to a marked reactivity of mood,
7. chronic feelings of emptiness,
8. inappropriate, intense anger or difficulty controlling anger,
9. transient, stress-related paranoid ideation or severe dissociative symptoms.

American Psychiatric Association (1). Used with permission.

involved. It also has been suggested that individuals with borderline personality disorder have a biologically based deficit in mood regulation (21).

The prevalence of borderline personality disorder is estimated to be about 2% in the general population, approximately 10% in individuals seen in outpatient mental health clinics, and about 20% in psychiatric inpatients. In clinical populations with personality disorder diagnoses, 30% to 60% carry the borderline personality disorder diagnosis (1). About three fourths of those diagnosed with borderline personality disorder are female (1).

Nutrition therapists who work with bulimic clients or in an inpatient psychiatric hospital will undoubtedly at some time have clients with this personality disorder. It is important for nutrition therapists to provide a stable and predictable environment for borderline clients. It is not uncommon for borderline individuals to be intense and emotionally labile during sessions, which may prove to be draining for the professional. Eating disorders patients with borderline personality disorder are especially likely to exhibit dichotomous thinking (also known as all-or-nothing thinking) about many aspects of their lives, including not only relationships but also food intake, purging, and weight. For example, they may consider their food intake to be "good" or "bad" (rather than some more realistic point in between), or they may think of themselves as either "skinny" or "fat" (when in reality they may be of relatively average weight). Borderline clients may initially present as very motivated and interested individuals who quickly establish a bond with the nutrition therapist. However, nutrition therapists should be cautious, because it is not unusual for these clients to later become demanding or to accuse the nutrition therapist of not meeting their needs (Box 12.11). It is also not uncommon for borderline clients to generate "crises" (eg, suicidal gestures or attempts, relationship breakups) during the course of treatment, which could negatively affect progress. Nutrition therapists who work with borderline clients should carefully assess for and (if present) monitor substance use and binge eating and purging behaviors.

Narcissistic Personality Disorder

Individuals with this disorder display a pervasive grandiose sense of self-importance, lack of empathy, and a hypersensitivity to the evaluation of others. These individuals commonly exploit others and are preoccupied with their own success, beauty, brilliance, or power. They may inflate their accomplishments, devalue the accomplishments of others, ruminate about "long overdue" admiration and privilege, and compare themselves favorably with privileged or famous persons. Despite their proclamations of superiority, persons with this disorder have fragile self-esteem and are very sensitive to criticism and defeat. They may react to blows to self-esteem with rage or social withdrawal (1,2).

Persons with narcissistic personality disorder are particularly vulnerable to comorbid depression because of their fragile self-esteem (22), and depression is often the reason they seek treatment (1). The prevalence of narcissistic personality disorder is estimated to be 2% to 16% in psychiatric populations and less

Box 12.11
CASE STUDY
Borderline Personality
Disorder

B.T., a 23-year-old single, white woman, presented to an inpatient psychiatric hospital after she cut her wrists with a razor blade during a suicide attempt. A psychiatric evaluation indicated a 5-year history of depression, anxiety, and binge eating and purging behavior, with occasional self-mutilating behavior (eg, cutting her skin with a knife). During the past year, the patient had engaged in weekend binge drinking. She reported being sexually abused as a child by her stepfather and date-raped at age 20. She reported a history of "stormy" family, peer, and romantic relationships and in fact made this suicide attempt after her boyfriend of 3 months informed her that he wanted to end their relationship.

The nutrition therapist who worked with B.T. easily established rapport with her. In the first session B.T. was very open about how disturbed she was by her binge eating and purging and how desperately she wanted to normalize her eating behavior. In the second session, the nutrition therapist found B.T. to be moody and uncooperative, indicating that she felt "too upset" by a previous psychotherapy session to continue the nutrition counseling session. After she was discharged from the hospital, she saw the nutrition therapist on a weekly basis for outpatient nutritional counseling. However, progress was impeded by her desire to discuss her most recent troubling events, rather than nutritional concerns. B.T. stopped coming to nutrition counseling sessions 1 month after discharge but reappeared 3 months later, stating that she had just begun a new relationship and wanted to get herself "back on track."

The nutrition therapist found that she made the most progress with this client when she helped her see the relationship between her moods and binge eating and purging, and this message was reinforced by B.T.'s psychotherapist as well. This client had to frequently be reminded of the negative effects of her all-or-nothing thinking, which was evident in her description of food intake as "bad" or "good" and her insistence that she was either "fat or thin; there is no in-between." B.T. was able to make progress when she sensed that the nutrition therapist was a steady and stable supporter of her recovery.

than 1% in the general population (1). The essential features of narcissistic personality disorder are shown in *Box 12.12.*

Most theories about the etiology of narcissistic personality disorder suggest that an unempathic, neglectful, or devaluing parent sets the stage for its development. A very different theory is that this disorder results from overly indulgent parents who instill in their children the belief that every wish is their command, that they can receive without giving in return, and that they deserve prominence without even minimal effort (22).

Nutrition therapists working with narcissistic individuals may find that they frequently question their credentials, training, and other qualifications, as well as the treatment protocol. Nutrition therapists should expect the narcissist's attitude and inquiries, as well as the defensiveness that they feel as a result. It is important to keep in mind that the anger and defensiveness these clients may produce in health care professionals is normal and is likely no different from what others experience when in their presence.

Nutrition therapists should maintain a confident stance with narcissistic clients

**Box 12.12
Diagnostic Criteria
for Narcissistic
Personality Disorder**

A pervasive pattern of grandiosity (in fantasy or behavior), need for admiration, and lack of empathy, beginning by early adulthood and present in a variety of contexts, as indicated by five (or more) of the following:

1. has a grandiose sense of self-importance (eg, exaggerates achievements and talents, expects to be recognized as superior without commensurate achievements),

2. is preoccupied with fantasies of unlimited success, power, brilliance, beauty, or ideal love,

3. believes that he or she is "special" and unique and can only be understood by, or should associate with, other special or high-status people (or institutions),

4. requires excessive admiration,

5. has a sense of entitlement (ie, unreasonable expectations of especially favorable treatment or automatic compliance with his or her expectations),

6. is interpersonally exploitative (ie, takes advantage of others to achieve his or her own ends)

7. lacks empathy; is unwilling to recognize or identify with the feelings and needs of others

8. is often envious of others or believes that others are envious of him or her,

9. shows arrogant, haughty behaviors or attitudes.

American Psychiatric Association (1). Used with permission.

and set clear limits on the therapeutic relationship. They should also expect narcissistic clients to attempt to test these limits in order to obtain "special" status. For example, narcissistic clients may attempt to have health care professionals see them during unusual hours to prove their status as "special clients." They may quit attending treatment sessions, or may come to sessions having collected information that opposes the proposed treatment plan, expecting the health care professionals to defend their treatment protocol. Narcissistic clients often try to present themselves in the "best light" and thus may hide or obscure important information (eg, lack of adherence to the recommended meal plan) (22) *(Box 12.13)*.

**Histrionic
Personality
Disorder**

The diagnostic criteria for the histrionic personality disorder are indicated in *Box 12.14.* Histrionic personality disorder is characterized by excessive emotionality and attention seeking. Histrionic individuals often seek reassurance, approval, and praise; are inappropriately seductive; are self-centered; and demonstrate exaggerated emotional expression. They are uncomfortable or feel unappreciated when they are not the center of attention, in which case they may do something dramatic to draw attention to themselves (1,2). The prevalence of histrionic per-

K.I., a 43-year-old white man, presented to a hospital emergency room office with complaints of severe headaches following a recent job loss and divorce. He made a point of denying to the emergency room staff any wrongdoing in his employment and marital problems, but he was unable to explain why these problems had occurred. K.I. indicated that he had grown up in a wealthy family and reported having graduated "at the top" of his class in college. He repeatedly mentioned to the hospital staff his superior skills as an accountant, but an occupational history indicated numerous job changes and he supplied vague reasons for these changes. K.I. reported distant family relationships and no close friends, stating that others seem to feel "threatened" by his intelligence.

K.I. was referred to a nutrition therapist after laboratory tests revealed hypercholesterolemia. The nutrition therapist working with K.I. found him to be arrogant in the first session. He refused to consider that his lipid profile might reflect emotional stress and stress eating. He questioned her credentials and training and asked her to "back up with evidence" her dietary recommendations. In follow-up appointments, he presented her with information he had found on the Internet that deviated from her recommendations, and he asked her to justify her position.

The nutrition therapist found that it was important to use a very confident manner with K.I. and to treat him with respect, despite the anger she sometimes felt in his presence. She also noted that K.I. preferred a very formal relationship with health care professionals. She elected not to have K.I. participate in a nutrition education group because of his arrogant manner and his tendency to make others feel defensive.

Box 12.13
CASE STUDY
Narcissistic Personality Disorder

A pervasive pattern of excessive emotionality and attention seeking, beginning by early adulthood and present in a variety of contexts, as indicated by five (or more) of the following:

1. is uncomfortable in situations in which he or she is not the center of attention,

2. has interactions with others that are often characterized by inappropriate, sexually seductive, or provocative behavior,

3. displays rapidly shifting and shallow expression of emotions,

4. consistently uses physical appearance to draw attention to self,

5. has a style of speech that is excessively impressionistic and lacking in detail,

6. show self-dramatization, theatricality, and exaggerated expression of emotion,

7. is suggestible (ie, easily influenced by others or circumstances),

8. considers relationships to be more intimate than they actually are.

American Psychiatric Association (1). Used with permission.

Box 12.14
Diagnostic Criteria for Histrionic Personality Disorder

sonality disorder is estimated to be 2%–3% in the general population and 10%-15% in inpatient and outpatient mental health settings (1). This personality disorder is much more common in women than in men (23). Individuals with histrionic personality disorder often present with other Axis I and II disorders, especially anxiety disorders (1).

Many theories of the etiology of histrionic personality disorder are psychoanalytic in origin, suggesting arrested ego development at the early genital stage. The result of this arrested development is egocentricity, exhibitionism, emotionality, suggestibility, and sexual provocativeness (23).

Nutrition therapists may find sessions with histrionic clients to be emotionally charged. Histrionic individuals may attempt to gain the nutrition therapist's attention through dramatic means, such as suicidal threats or crying. They may initially seem extremely enthusiastic about treatment, but their enthusiasm is often short-lived. These individuals are difficult to have in group sessions or educational programs because of their inordinate need for attention, which may prove disruptive and irritating for other group members. Nutrition therapists should avoid treating these clients in ways that may convey that they are "special" (eg, seeing them for longer periods or at hours not normally observed for client care), as these clients regularly overstep boundaries in their effort to obtain attention (20) (Box 12.15).

Avoidant Personality Disorder

The DSM-IV criteria for avoidant personality disorder are shown in Box 12.16. Individuals with this disorder are easily hurt by disapproval, avoid developing social relationships unless guaranteed acceptance, and fear being embarrassed. They exhibit a pervasive pattern of interpersonal avoidance, as well as extreme sensitivity to criticism or disapproval. Avoidant personality disorder involves more than just shyness. It is an active avoidance of interpersonal contact (2,16).

There are several theories about the development of avoidant personality disorder. Researchers have suggested that biological, genetic, and social factors contribute to producing an infant who is very irritable and withdrawn, leading to parental rejection. This parental rejection, in turn, results in a depletion of the child's natural energy and optimism, making self-deprecation and social alienation more likely. The resulting lowered self-esteem contributes to the child's difficulty in making friends, which serves to validate the family's negative evaluation of the child. Social interaction is avoided because of the anxiety it produces, and the avoidant style is perpetuated (16).

The prevalence of this disorder in the general population is 0.5%-1.0%. In outpatient mental health clinics, about 10% of patients are reported to have avoidant personality disorder. The disorder is equally common in men and women (1). Mood and anxiety disorders and anorexia nervosa are fairly common in individuals with avoidant personality disorder (1,4,5). Interestingly, it has also been suggested that there are a significant number of avoidant individuals in the alcoholic population (16).

Nutrition therapists who work with clients with avoidant personality disorder

Box 12.15
CASE STUDY
Histrionic Personality
Disorder

M.T. was a 37-year-old, married white woman who presented to a psychologist in private practice with complaints of panic attacks and binge eating behavior. She was dressed for her first therapy session in a sheer black dress with a low neckline and sobbed throughout the session. M.T. reported that her panic attacks began after her husband started a new job, which required him to often travel out of town on business. She stated that the panic attacks had become increasingly frequent and severe, to the point that she felt she had to give up her self-described "glamorous job" in the "entertainment industry." When questioned further, M.T. admitted that she had worked as a receptionist at a local radio station. She reported a long history of "up-and-down" relationships with friends and family members, due to what she reported as their "lack of appreciation" of her kindness and support.

The psychologist referred M.T. to a nutrition therapist to help her gain control over her binge eating behavior. The nutrition therapist conducted a diet and weight history. During the initial session, M.T. cried frequently and related a lifelong history of "emotional eating" with accompanying weight gain, which she subsequently tried to lose by restricting food intake. M.T.'s eating and weight gain had reportedly gotten "out of control" after she left her job. Self-monitoring with food diaries indicated that during the day she often ate out of boredom, feeling sad about having to leave work, and anxiety about her husband's absences from the home.

Early in treatment, the nutrition therapist made great efforts to kindly define for M.T. the limits on their relationship. She chose not to invite this client to participate in an eating disorders group because she believed M.T. would try to monopolize the conversation and use other attention-seeking strategies. The nutrition therapist found that M.T. responded best when she was asked to make incremental lifestyle changes for which she was strongly reinforced. She noted that she had to make a special effort to keep M.T. on task during sessions, as she often seemed to prefer to discuss her latest problems and emotional concerns.

Box 12.16
Diagnostic Criteria for
Avoidant Personality
Disorder

A pervasive pattern of social inhibition, feelings of inadequacy, and hypersensitivity to negative evaluation, beginning by early adulthood and present in a variety of contexts, as indicate by four (or more) of the following:

1. avoids occupational activities that involve significant interpersonal contact because of criticism, disapproval, or rejection,
2. is unwilling to get involved with people unless certain of being liked,
3. shows restraint within intimate relationships because of the fear of being shamed or ridiculed,
4. is preoccupied with being criticized or rejected in social situations,
5. is inhibited in new interpersonal situations because of feelings of inadequacy,
6. views self as socially inept, personally unappealing, or inferior to others,
7. is unusually reluctant to take personal risks or to engage in any new activities because they may prove embarrassing.

American Psychiatric Association (1). Used with permission.

should make a special effort to establish rapport with them and to make them feel comfortable and accepted. They should minimize negative comments and offer frequent reassurances. Any criticism should be carefully worded and expressed in a manner that conveys continued acceptance and a desire to continue to work with the client to achieve goals. These clients respond very well to positive reinforcement, such as compliments, so nutrition therapists should provide plenty of compliments when appropriate *(Box 12.17)*. Avoidant clients may have difficulty, especially initially, in group settings. When they are involved in group therapy or educational classes, the nutrition therapist should try to ensure that they feel included and obtain positive feedback from the nutrition therapist and other group members.

Box 12.17
CASE STUDY
Avoidant Personality
Disorder

R.M. was a 23-year-old, single white woman who presented to a psychotherapist at a private mental health clinic with symptoms of depression and anorexia nervosa. She told the psychotherapist that as a child she had been shy, eager to please, and easily hurt by criticism from family and peers. R.M. indicated that after being rejected by a peer in sixth grade, she "retreated into a world of studying," and as a result became a "straight A" student. She lived at home with her parents while attending college and stated that she was "very close" to her family. After college, R.M. took a job about 300 miles from her family home. She reported feeling extremely lonely and socially withdrawn during the past year, during which time she also began restricting her food intake to lose weight. She denied any purging behavior. R.M. reported losing 25 pounds in the past year (from 115 to 90 pounds at 5 feet, 4 inches tall). She indicated that she had made no new friends since her move, mostly because she feared rejection.

The nutrition therapist working with R.M. made special efforts to establish rapport with her in the first session, and she praised R.M. for initiating treatment at this time. The client seemed somewhat shy at first, but over the course of several nutrition counseling sessions (during which time the nutrition therapist provided plenty of support and positive reinforcement) she responded well. The nutrition therapist was careful to tell R.M. in the first session that she would continue to support her even if R.M. was not able to complete all of her goals each week, and she encouraged R.M. to continue to come to their sessions even if the previous week had produced little progress.

R.M. was invited to begin attending an eating disorders group, and this seemed to cause her some anxiety. The nutrition therapist took time to explain how the group operated, and she introduced R.M. to the group co-leader prior to her first group session. R.M. and the nutrition therapist spent time in the session discussing the pros and cons of attending a group, and the client was able to come to her own conclusion that her attendance might be helpful. At the first group session, the group co-leaders made efforts to make certain that R.M. felt involved, and on occasion they posed nonthreatening questions to her in the group to help her to become a more active participant. Over time, R.M. grew more confident in her relationships with group members and health care professionals and was then willing on her own to take a more active role in the group and in sessions.

Box 12.18 presents the essential features of dependent personality disorder. This personality disorder is characterized by a pervasive pattern of dependent and submissive behavior (eg, having difficulty making everyday decisions without excessive reassurance from others; permitting others to make important decisions; agreeing with people even when one believes they are wrong; having difficulty initiating projects; and being easily hurt by disapproval) (1,2).

A psychoanalytic theory is one of the more common theories used to explain the origins of this personality disorder. It has been suggested that individuals with dependent personality disorder experienced arrest at the oral stage of ego development, with resulting pessimism, passivity, and dependence (23). It also has been speculated that these individuals grew up in environments in which "abuse plus dominance equaled love" (20).

Dependent personality disorder is among the most frequently encountered personality disorders in mental health treatment setting, with a mean prevalence rate of 27% in clinical populations and 1.8% in nonclinical populations. It is much more common among women than men (1,23).

Clients with dependent personality disorder also frequently carry a diagnosis

Dependent Personality Disorder

A pervasive and excessive need to be taken care of that leads to submissive and clinging behavior and fears of separation, beginning by early adulthood and present in a variety of contexts, as indicated by five (or more) of the following:

1. has difficulty making everyday decisions without an excessive amount of advice and reassurance from others,
2. needs others to assume responsibility for most major areas of his or her life,
3. has difficulty expressing disagreement with others because of fear of loss of support or approval,
4. has difficulty initiating projects or doing things on his or her own (because of a lack of self-confidence in judgment or abilities, rather than a lack of motivation or energy),
5. goes to excessive lengths to obtain nurturance and support from others, to the point of volunteering to do things that are unpleasant,
6. feels uncomfortable or helpless when alone because of exaggerated fears of being unable to care for himself or herself,
7. urgently seeks another relationship as a source of care and support when a close relationship ends,
8. is unrealistically preoccupied with fears of being left to take care of himself or herself.

American Psychiatric Association (1). Used with permission.

**Box 12.18
Diagnostic Criteria for Dependent Personality Disorder**

of avoidant or borderline personality disorder. In addition, dependent personality disorder is common in clients who present with Axis I disorders, particularly depression, nicotine dependence, alcohol abuse, and agoraphobia with panic (23).

Nutrition therapists should make special efforts to establish boundaries and limits in the therapeutic relationship with dependent clients. Nutrition therapists and other health care professionals should avoid taking on an "authoritarian" role with or becoming "rescuers" of these clients. Rather, nutrition therapists should work with the clients toward the goal of increased independence in life skills and activities, including meal planning and food procurement and preparation (*Box 12.19*). Dependent clients often appear very "needy," and this can bring out care-taking instincts in many members of the treatment team. However, to reiterate, nutrition therapists should avoid allowing dependent clients to become overly reliant on their relationship. When overreliance does occur, terminating services,

Box 12.19
CASE STUDY
Dependent Personality
Disorder

L.M. was a 26-year-old, single, obese, African-American woman. She presented to an outpatient mental health center following the break-up of a 9-month romantic relationship. L.M. stated that she had "always had a boyfriend," and she reported feeling anxious and depressed at the thought of being alone. Her boyfriend reportedly had ended their relationship because of what he described as her "clinginess" and her frequently voiced concerns that he would "find somebody else." L.M. said that since her boyfriend had left her the previous week, she had been unable to eat, sleep, or go to work. During that time she also had engaged in binge eating behavior, with a resulting 5-pound weight gain.

The nutrition therapist who worked with L.M. clearly defined in their first session the time and content structure of the proposed nutrition assessment and counseling sessions, as well as her payment and telephone consultation policies. She said she would serve as a source of information and support for L.M., but she also said L.M. should learn to independently make and implement more positive food- and weight-related decisions and behaviors.

The client reported a 10-year history of binge eating without purging as a way of coping with stress and emotional problems. The nutrition therapist and psychotherapist helped L.M. identify other means of coping, as well as behavior modification strategies that could reduce the likelihood of her binge eating. The client was especially encouraged to learn ways of coping beyond social support so as to increase her self-reliance and independence.

At first L.M. attempted to overstep the stated boundaries by making frequent between-session telephone calls to the nutrition therapist. However, the nutrition therapist handled this situation by emphatically restating and maintaining her telephone policy and suggesting that L.M. record all her questions between sessions and bring them to the next session to discuss.

The client was invited to participate in a binge eaters group, and she did well in this group. The group coleaders asked other group members to provide her with supportive feedback about her relationships with men and her negative coping strategies, and she was attentive to what they had to say. The coleaders (including the nutrition therapist) also had the group members offer ideas to L.M. about ways to be more independent.

even at a very appropriate juncture in treatment, can prove exceedingly difficult and the client may create a "crisis" or devise a reason why continued services are necessary. When in a group setting, these clients often respond well to feedback from other group members.

The DSM-IV criteria for obsessive-compulsive personality disorder are shown in *Box 12.20*. This disorder is often confused with the Axis I diagnosis of obsessive-compulsive disorder. Obsessive-compulsive personality disorder is characterized by personality traits of perfectionism, inflexibility, preoccupation with details and rules, unreasonable insistence that others follow one's methods or standards for doing things, overconscientiousness, and restricted affect. Obsessive-compulsive disorder is characterized by repetitive thoughts and behaviors that the individual perceives as beyond his or her control (1). Interestingly, most persons with obsessive-compulsive personality disorder do not meet the criteria for obsessive-compulsive disorder (1).

Research indicates genetics, psychodynamics, and social learning history are

Obsessive-Compulsive Personality Disorder

A pervasive pattern of preoccupation with orderliness, perfectionism, and mental and interpersonal control, at the expense of flexibility, openness, and efficiency, beginning in early adulthood and present in a variety of contexts, as indicated by four (or more) of the following:

1. is preoccupied with details, rules, lists, order, organization, or schedules to the extent that the major point of the activity is lost,

2. shows perfectionism that interferes with task completion (eg, is unable to complete a project because his or her own overly strict standards are not met),

3. is excessively devoted to work and productivity to the exclusion of leisure activities and friendships (not accounted for by obvious economic necessity),

4. is overly conscientious, scrupulous, and inflexible about matters of morality, ethics, or values (not accounted for by cultural or religious identification),

5. is unable to discard worn-out or worthless objects even when they have no sentimental value,

6. is reluctant to delegate tasks or to work with others unless they submit to exactly his or her way of doing things,

7. adopts a miserly spending style toward both self and others; money is viewed as something to be hoarded for future catastrophes,

8. shows rigidity and stubbornness.

American Psychiatric Association (1). Used with permission.

Box 12.20 Diagnostic Criteria for Obsessive-Compulsive Personality Disorder

involved in the etiology of obsessive-compulsive personality disorder (1,2). Obsessive-compulsive personality disorder does seem to run in families, and there is evidence that overcontrolling, rigid, rule-bound, and exacting parenting (which disallows spontaneity and flexibility in moral development and socialization) plays a role (24).

Many of the features of obsessive-compulsive personality disorder are associated with what is typically considered "Type A" personality characteristics (eg, hostility, competitiveness, and time urgency), and these clients may thus be at risk for cardiovascular disease. Obsessive-compulsive personality disorder appears in about 1% of the general population and 3%-10% of individuals treated at mental health clinics (1).

Nutrition therapists working with individuals with this personality disorder may find that they prefer a relatively more formal therapeutic relationship than do some other clients *(Box 12.21)*. They tend to prefer very structured sessions and homework assignments. They are typically highly controlled, both emotionally and behaviorally. In addition, they usually exhibit little or no sense of humor.

Box 12.21
CASE STUDY
Obsessive-Compulsive
Personality Disorder

S.Y., a 40-year-old Asian woman, presented to a family medicine physician with complaints of gastrointestinal distress. A clinical interview revealed a woman with a very serious demeanor and significant perfectionism and overcontrolling tendencies. S.Y. reported that she took great pride in being extremely efficient and organized. For example, she stated that if she spotted a folder in her office that was out of place, she felt "very bothered" and had to stop whatever she was doing to "immediately take care of it." She also reported that she had been taught as a child to control her emotions.

S.Y.'s gastrointestinal distress began following her husband's diagnosis with cancer, which she said made her feel "very out of control." She was attempting to manage her distress by restricting foods that she connected to the problem. By the time she had her first appointment with the nutrition therapist, the list of foods she allowed herself to eat had been reduced to eight. Repeated blood pressure readings indicated hypertension, and she was referred to a nutrition therapist for nutrition assessment and counseling.

S.Y. presented at her nutrition assessment session with notebook, pen, and all of her blood pressure readings in hand. The nutrition therapist found that S.Y. provided excessively detailed responses to all her questions. She also attempted to write down all of the nutrition therapist's suggestions and comments.

The nutrition therapist began the next session by requesting that S.Y. listen carefully to what she said, rather than trying to write everything down. She assured S.Y. that the major points she was making were recorded in the handouts, and that S.Y. could later ask her about anything that was not clear. She was also careful not to give S.Y. too many handouts, as she suspected that S.Y.'s perfectionistic tendencies might cause her to try to digest too much information too soon. The nutrition therapist made certain that S.Y. obtained a sense of control and success by having her define and attempt specific and manageable dietary goals each week. She chose not to have S.Y. participate in a nutrition education group because of her overcontrolling nature and tendency to be very demanding of others.

These clients may be resistant to making lifestyle changes because of their rigidity. However, they also are more willing than clients with other personality disorders to follow directions provided by those they perceive as authority figures (which could include nutrition therapists and other health care professionals).

The personality disorder not otherwise specified category is applied in two situations: (1) if an individual's personality pattern meets the general criteria for a personality disorder and traits of several personality disorders are present but the full criteria are not met; or (2) if an individual's personality pattern meets the general criteria for a personality disorder but he or she is considered to have a personality disorder that is not included in the DSM-IV Classification System (eg, passive-aggressive personality disorder).

Personality Disorder Not Otherwise Specified

Passive-aggressive personality disorder was included in all previous DSMs but not in the DSM-IV. The disorder may still, however, be noted and the classification may prove useful in treatment considerations. The essential behavior pattern in passive-aggressive personality disorder is indirectly expressed resistance to social and occupational expectations, which results in chronic ineffectiveness. The resistance results from hostility, although the client will typically deny this hostility if questioned. The actual behavior that is expressed may be passive or aggressive, but physical aggression is rare. Examples of passive-aggressive behavior include being chronically late to appointments, meetings, and other events (as a means of "getting back" at someone in charge of the session) and indirectly expressing anger at group members by "becoming sick" at a crucial time so as to ensure the group project cannot be completed by the specified deadline. Nutrition therapists who work with passive-aggressive clients should be aware that they may sabotage their own treatment by missing or being late to appointments or by "losing" important assignments *(Box 12.22)*.

Passive-Aggressive Personality Disorder

M.K. was a 30-year-old, married white woman with a 5-year history of binge eating and purging, which began shortly after her marriage. She presented to an inpatient eating disorders facility after her husband told her that he would divorce her if she did not get help for her bulimia.

In her first session with M.K., the nutrition therapist noted the client's resistance to establishing rapport. M.K. appeared unwilling even to make eye contact. She told the nutrition therapist that she was in treatment at her husband's insistence.

An eating disorders assessment revealed that this client typically binged and purged after she argued with her husband. She made little effort to hide these behaviors from him; in fact, she often made certain that he was aware of her actions.

M.K. failed to follow through with most recommendations made by the nutrition therapist. Once discharged, she did not show up for three scheduled outpatient nutrition counseling sessions. The nutrition therapist was careful to attribute M.K.'s lack of success to her personality and her relationship with her husband, rather than her nutrition therapist's lack of effectiveness as a health care professional.

**Box 12.22
CASE STUDY**
Passive-Aggressive
Personality Disorder

SUMMARY

- An estimated 20%-30% of psychiatric patients seen in clinics present with an Axis II personality disorder. Their personality disorders represent the largest class of psychiatric disorders.

- The DSM-IV organizes the personality disorders into three clusters: Cluster A consists of paranoid, schizoid, and schizotypal; Cluster B includes the "dramatic" personality disorders: antisocial, borderline, narcissistic, and histrionic; and Cluster C includes avoidant, dependent, obsessive-compulsive, and personality disorder not otherwise specified.

- Eating disorders patients often present with Cluster B and C personality disorders, particularly borderline, histrionic, dependent, and avoidant. Personality disorder diagnoses are especially common in clients who exhibit binge eating and purging behaviors.

- Personality disorder diagnoses are important for nutrition therapists to note and consider because of their potential impact on treatment. An essential feature of personality disorders is their negative impact on interpersonal relationships, including the client's relationships with treatment team members. By being aware of Axis II features, nutrition therapists can develop treatment approaches to improve the likelihood of successful outcomes.

REFERENCES

1. *Diagnostic and Statistical Manual of Mental Disorders.* 4th ed. Washington, DC: American Psychiatric Association; 1994.

2. Turkat ID. Behavioral intervention with personality disorders. In: Turner SM, Calhoun KS, Adams HE, eds. *Handbook of Clinical Behavior Therapy.* 2nd ed. New York: John Wiley & Sons, Inc; 1992.

3. Rosehan DL, Seligman ME. *Abnormal Psychology.* 3rd ed. New York: WW Norton Company; 1995.

4. Williamson DA, Barker SE, Norris LE. Eating disorders. In: Sutker PB, Adams HE, eds. *Comprehensive Handbook of Psychopathology.* 2nd ed. New York: Plenum Press; 1993.

5. Williamson DA. *Assessment of Eating Disorders:Obesity, Anorexia, and Bulimia Nervosa.* New York: Pergamon Press; 1990.

6. Connors ME. Developmental vulnerabilities for eating disorders. In: Smolak L, Levine MP, Striegal-Moore R, eds. *The Developmental Psychopathology of Eating Disorders: Implications for Research, Prevention and Treatment.* Mahwah, MJ: Lawrence Erlbaum Associates; 1996.

7. Piran N, Lerner P, Garfinkel PE, Kennedy SH, Brouillete C. Personality disorders in anorexic patients. *Int J Eat Disord.* 1988;7:589-599.

8. McCann UD, Rossiter EM, King RI, Agras WS. Nonpurging bulimia: a distinct type of bulimia nervosa. *Int J Eat Disord.* 1991:10;679-687.

9. Waller G. Sexual abuse and eating disorders: borderline personality disorder as a mediating factor? *Br J Psychiatry.* 1993;162:771-775.

10. Waller G. Childhood sexual abuse and borderline personality disorder in the eating disorders. *Child Abuse Neglect.* 1994;18:97-101.

11. Shearer SL, Peters CP, Wuaytman MS, Ogden RL. Frequency and correlates of childhood sexual and physical abuse histories in adult female borderline inpatients. *Am J Psychiatry.* 1990;147:214-216.

12. Wonderlich S, Swift WJ. Borderline versus other personality disorders in the eating disorders: clinical description. *Int J Eat Disord.* 1990;9:629–638.

13. Waller G, Everill J, Calam R. Sexual abuse and the eating disorders. In: Alexander-Mott L, Lumdsen DB, eds. *Understanding Eating Disorders.* Washington, DC: Taylor & Francis; 1994:77–97.

14. Greene RL. *The MMPI-2/MMPI: An Interpretative Manual.* Needham Heights, Mass: Simon & Schuster; 1991.

15. Morey LC, Smith MR. Personality disorders. In: Greene RL, ed. *The MMPI: Use With Specific Populations.* Philadelphia: Grune & Stratton; 1988.

16. Thompson-Pope SK, Turkat ID. Schizotypal, schizoid, paranoid, and avoidant personality disorders. In: Sutker PB, Adame HE, eds. *Comprehensive Handbook of Psychopathology.* 2nd ed. New York: Plenum Press; 1993.

17. Cameron N. *Personality Development and Psychopathology: A Dynamic Approach.* Boston: Houghton-Mifflin; 1963.

18. Millon T. *Disorders of Personality:DSM-III. Axis II.* Minneapolis: National Computer Systems; 1981.

19. Beck AT, Freeman A. *Cognitive Therapy of Personality Disorders.* New York: Guilford; 1990.

20. Meyer RG, Deitsch SE. *The Clinician's Handbook: Integrated Diagnosis, Assessment, and Intervention in Adult and Adolescent Psychopathology.* 4th ed. Boston: Allyn & Bacon; 1996.

21. Sutker PB, Buff F, West JA. Antisocial personality disorder. In: Sutker PB, Adams HE, eds. *Comprehensive Handbook of Psychopathology.* 2nd ed. New York: Plenum Press; 1993.

22. Widiger TA, Trull TJ. Borderline and narcissistic personality disorders. In: Sutker PB, Adams HE, eds. *Comprehensive Handbook of Psychopathology.* 2nd ed. New York: Plenum Press; 1993.

23. Blashfield RK, Davis RT. Dependent and histrionic personality disorders. In: Sutker PB, Adams HE, eds. *Comprehensive Handbook of Psychopathology.* 2nd ed. Plenum Press; 1993; 396–409.

24. Johnson SM. *Character Styles.* New York: WW Norton & Co; 1994.

CHAPTER 13

Axis III: Medical Complications of Eating Disorders

TRUDY ALEXANDER, R.D.

The physiological effects of malnutrition are well documented through historical experiences with involuntary starvation, such as result from expeditions, acts of nature, and war (1). This information has laid the foundation for the identification and treatment of the voluntary starvation practiced by individuals with eating disorders.

Malnutrition and starvation place undue stress on the body. Months and years of nutritional deprivation from either external forces or self-induced behaviors create quite a grim presentation. Medical complications are similar, although additional complications may be found in bulimia. One major difference between involuntary and self-imposed starvation is that, when offered food, the victim of involuntary starvation accepts it, while the eating disordered individual continues the destructive behaviors. Educating eating disordered clients on their current health status and potential for future complications if they continue their behavior is an important part of nutrition therapy.

Eating disorders and their resulting malnutrition create both nutritional deficiencies and medical complications. Both will be reviewed in this chapter, as an understanding of both is necessary when performing a detailed nutrition assessment that accurately depicts the client's health status. *Tables 13.1* and *13.2* and *Box 13.1* detail the most common signs and symptoms found in eating disorders.

RECOGNIZING EATING DISORDERS

Because the identification of an eating disorder can be complicated by the possibility of other diseases that mimic or mask the client's symptoms, the nutrition therapist may be called upon to assist in the identification process. Crohn's dis-

Deficiency	Syndromes
Calcium	Osteoporosis—diminished bone mass Osteomalacia—normal bone mass, compromised composition Rickets, seen in children
Chromium	Reduced glucose tolerance Increased incidence of diabetes Depleted glycogen reserves Retarded growth Aortic lesions associated with elevated cholesterol
Copper	Depressed iron absorption Decreased white blood cell count Bone demineralization Defective red blood cell formation
Iodine	Goiter Physical and mental retardation in young Miscarriage/failure of fetal development
Iron	Anemia Poor wound healing Weakness Lassitude Joint aches Reduced immune response Elevated plasma cholesterol Demyelination and degeneration of nervous system Reproductive failure Pronounced cardiovascular lesions Defects in pigmentation and structure of hair Pale mucous membranes of underside of eye or in mouth Malaise Headaches Peripheral edema Labored breathing Cardiac arrhythmia Spoon- or ridge-shaped nails
Magnesium	Neuromuscular symptoms such as muscle spasm, twitching, tremors (tetany), which can affect cardiovascular and renal systems; in severe cases may include convulsions and lapse into coma Elevated serum cholesterol
Phosphorous	Fatigue Loss of appetite Bone demineralization
Potassium	Pervasive muscle weakness Poor intestinal tonus resulting in abdominal bloating Heart rhythm abnormalities Weakened respiratory muscles
Sodium	Muscle cramps Reduced plasma volume Weakness Headache Vascular collapse Loss of appetite Nausea Diarrhea Loss of body weight due to dehydration

Table 13.1

Most Common Mineral Deficiencies Found in Eating Disorders

continued

Table 13.1

Deficiency	Syndromes
Sodium	Excess hydration to maintain body weight
Zinc	Delayed growth and sexual maturation
	Loss of taste and smell acuity and appetite
Impaired liver function	
	Esophageal lesions
	Hair loss
	Dry, pink, scaly skin
	Increased irritability

Sources: Guthrie (2), Burton and Willis (3), Berdanier (4-6), Kanarek and Mark-Kaufman (7).

Table 13.2
Most Common Vitamin Deficiencies Found in Eating Disorders

Deficiency	Syndromes
Ascorbic acid	Listlessness
	Fatigue
	Weakness
	Impaired physical performance, particularly in legs
	Muscle cramps
	Vertigo
	Aching bones and joints
	Dry, rough skin
	Numerous bruises
	Bleeding gums
	Inappropriate temperature sensation
	Decreased glucose tolerance
	Depressed serum cholesterol
Biotin	Dermatitis
	Skin rash
	Conjunctivitis
	Hair loss
	Muscular atrophy
	Developmental delay
	Seizures
	Visual and auditory losses
Vitamin B-12°	(See Iron in Table 13.1.)
Folic acid	Neural tube defects in fetal development
Niacin	Blackened, rough skin lesions
	Insomnia
	Loss of appetitei
	Weight loss
	Soreness of mouth and tongue
	Indigestion
	Diarrhea
	Abdominal pain
	Vertigo
	Headache
	Numbness
	Nervousness
	Apprehension
	Mental confusion
	Forgetfulness
Riboflavin	Poor growth
	Loss of appetite
	Cracks at the corners of the mouth

continued

Deficiency	Syndromes	Table 13.2
		(continued)
Thiamin	Loss of appetite Impaired digestion Colitis, constipation, or diarrhea Loss of reflexive responses in feet and/or hands Paralysis of eye muscles(ophthalmoplegia) Disorientation Dementia	
Vitamin A	Retarded growth Reduced reproductive capacity Disturbed gastrointestinal tract Changes in epithelial tissues producing greater incidences of respiratory infections and diarrhea Loss of taste and smell sensations resulting in loss of appetite Dry, rough skin Eye conditions xerophthalmia, keratomalacia, and night blindness	
Vitamin D	Bone deformities (See Calcium in Table 13.1.)	
Vitamin E	Infertility Loss of antioxidant activity	
Vitamin K	Anemia Hemorrhage Prolonged blood coagulation	

°Even though body stores are small, it can take up to 6 years for symptoms to appear.
Sources: Guthrie (2), Burton and Willis (3), Berdanier (4-6), Kanarek and Mark-Kaufman (7).

ease, malabsorption syndrome, diabetes mellitus, thyrotoxicosis, chronic diarrhea and vomiting, brain tumors, and cancer are often considered first as medical reasons for a client's condition (8–10). The nutrition therapist can substantiate the existence of the eating disorder by doing a nutritional assessment that includes the client's disordered eating habits, including extreme food behaviors, caloric intake, and activity levels, distorted body image, and fear of gaining weight, none of which is likely to be present in the above diseases.

		Box 13-1
Loss of appetite	Amenorrhea	**Signs and Symptoms**
Poor hair and nail texture and strength	Reduced digestive motility	**of Protein Calorie**
Hepatomegaly	Increase in sleep	**Malnutrition**
Growth failure in children	Bradycardia	
Peripheral edema	Weakened immune system	
Apathy	Slowed metabolism	
Skin lesions	Decreased hormone production and receptor sites	
Diarrhea		
Anemia		
Tissue wastage	Sources: Guthrie (2), Burton and Willis (3),	
Hypothermia	Berdanier (4–6).	
Hypotension		

Two other barriers, denial and secrecy, create problems in identifying the eating disordered individual. Health issues can be underreported, minimized, or denied to the primary care physician. These individuals often prefer to be seen in emergency rooms or outpatient clinics when medical intervention is needed. When primary care physicians (gynecologists, pediatricians, or internists) suspect an eating disorder, they may send their patients to a nutrition therapist for assessment and confirmation of an eating disorder. It is often the nutrition therapist who discovers the full range of secretive eating behaviors and who understands the depth of malnutrition that exists. Based on his assessment and observations, the nutrition therapist may also be in the position of recommending that a client seeks psychological and/or medical intervention and/or requesting that the physician order medical tests. In short, the nutrition therapist is an integral part of the multidisciplinary team treating eating disorders.

It is important to recognize advanced clinical complications caused by malnutrition and to be able to discuss these complications with the client, the client's family (when appropriate), and the team physician. Even if the client's current medical condition produces normal laboratory tests, it is important to educate the client and team regarding the potential seriousness of continuing the behavior. This is particularly true when a client is in denial about the existence of an eating disorder.

DIAGNOSTIC CONSIDERATIONS

In treatment, concern for the eating disordered client's quality of life (and life itself) takes precedence over the client's denial and control issues. Almost anything can go wrong with the body in an eating disorder. The more common complications are the focus of this chapter. It is important to remember that every client is different and the symptoms manifested depend on a number of factors, including age, nutritional status prior to the onset of the eating disorder, length of time the eating disorder has existed, severity of eating disordered behaviors, and number and combination of behaviors practiced. Clients with mixed anorexia and bulimia are at risk for developing the most serious complications and may take longer to stabilize (*Table 13.3*).

The category of eating disorders known as binge eating disorder (BED) is not included as an official diagnosis in the DSM-IV. This disorder is unlike anorexia and bulimia in that people who have BED are usually overweight, are usually not protein/calorie deprived, and do not purge, abuse laxatives or diuretics, or engage in strenuous exercise. While they may experience many of the same psychological characteristics as those with anorexia and bulimia, their physical status and possible medical complications are significantly different. Health problems seen with BED are primarily related to obesity: vitamin/mineral deficiencies, heart disease, type 2 diabetes, poor exercise habits, high blood pressure, high serum cholesterol levels, gallbladder disease, amenorrhea, and some forms of cancer.

System	Complication
Cardiovascular	Bradycardia
	Arrhythmias
	Hypotension
	Electrocardiogram abnormalities
	Congestive cardiac failure
Gastrointestinal	Decreased gastric motility and emptying
	Epigastric pain (bloating, distention, constipation)
	Gastric dilation and perforation
	Complicated by a history of vomiting:
	Esophagitis
	Esophageal perforations
	Oral—gum disease, enamel erosion, tooth decay
	Benign enlargement of parotid salivary glands
	Complicated by a history of laxative abuse:
	Impaired colon function
	Tearing, fissuring, and scarring of the anus
Renal	Decreased glomerular filtration rate
	Decreased urine concentrating capacity
	Pyuria
	Proteinuria
	Hematuria
	Electrolytic abnormalities:
	Hypokalemia
	Hyponatremia
	Hypochloremia
	Hyperphosphatemia in vomiting cases
	Hypophosphatemia in refeeding process
	Hypokalemic nephropathy
	Peripheral edema (may also occur in refeeding process)
	Dehydration or excessive hydration
Endocrine	Delayed onset or interruption of pubertal development
	Amenorrhea and infertility
	Impotence
	Low basal levels of plasma luteinizing hormones (LH) and follicle stimulating hormones (FSH)
	Increased secretion of growth hormone
	Abnormal thyroid function resulting in hypothermia, cold intolerance, and decreased metabolic rate
	Altered pituitary function resulting in elevated plasma cortisol
	Altered fat, carbohydrate, and protein metabolism)
Neurological	Pseudoatrophy of brain
	Enlarged inner and outer cerebrospinal fluid space
	Sleep disturbances
	Alterations in functioning of sympathetic nervous system
Other	Osteoporosis
	Anemia
	Leukopenia
	Herpes simplex

Table 13.3

Common Complications of Eating Disorders

Sources: Kanarek and Mark-Kaufman (7), Comerci (11), Giannini, Newman, and Gold (12), Sharp and Freeman (13), Hall and Thomas (14), Carney and Andersen (15), Rock and Curran-Celentano (16).

It is important to recognize the differences between BED and obesity without associated eating disorder. Binge eating disorder involves eating large quantities of food in a limited amount of time (as in bulimia), often alone and in sufficient amounts to feel full, followed by feelings of guilt. There is a tendency with BED to alternate between episodes of binge eating and episodes of restriction. While weight loss is frequently the outcome of BED treatment, low-calorie diets are not recommended. In fact, a history of attempting and failing to follow low-calorie diets and lose weight may have increased stress sufficiently to produce the pattern of binge eating in the first place. Healthy, balanced meal patterns that teach moderation and portion control, along with cognitive-behavioral therapy, is usually the best approach with these clients. While some clients may complain, most will agree that keeping food journals is an effective way to stay focused.

TREATING NUTRITIONAL DEFICIENCIES

The medical examination, nutritional assessment, and appropriate laboratory tests provide the treatment team with a clear picture of the client's status. With this information, the medical nutrition therapist can begin the process of altering the client's eating/behavior patterns. Of primary concern are dehydration and protein and calorie deprivation. Correcting these conditions play an important role in stabilizing the client for psychotherapy. Without proper nourishment, the client may respond poorly to psychotherapy.

The list of common complications of eating disorders clearly illustrates the magnitude of the impact of this disorder on the body. Triaging the treatment of each of these associated medical problems is important in order to increase the client's chance of survival; of all the mental disorders, eating disorders have some of the highest mortality rates.

Cardiovascular complications are the most urgent to address (17–19). While refeeding is a priority, slow, cautious renourishment is necessary in order to avoid overloading a cardiovascular system weakened by malnutrition.

Both anorexia and bulimia can produce dehydration. Usually offering sufficient liquids corrects this. In the initial stages of stabilization, where possible, it is recommended that fluid input/output be recorded. Establishing a specific amount of liquid to be consumed may be required for those clients in whom the status of the renal system must be further assessed. Setting fluid requirements client also helps to correct the common problem of constipation, and prevents clients from overhydrating to temporarily influence weight and dull appetite.

Tube Feeding

There are times when the client's physical condition and inability to adapt to a more nutritional food intake (from active resistance or disturbed cognition) may necessitate tube feeding (20). If the client's cardiac status and central nervous system function are impaired, response to psychotherapy is likely to not be effective (21). In such cases, the decision to use tube feeding should be presented as an alternative, not as a "punishment" for noncompliance. It is important to determine when such an intervention should be implemented immediately, in preference to giving the client time to "prove" she can adopt healthier eating patterns voluntarily. The reality in most cases is that if the client were able to do so, she would not be seeking hospitalization for help. Her bid to delay the tube feeding may be part of her disease. The treatment team should be comfortable with the use of tube feeding in severely malnourished clients who appear unable to make the decision to eat independently of intervention.

The most common method of tube feeding used is the nasogastric tube. However, to avoid problems with gastric reflux and possible purging, it is recommended that the tube ending be placed in the duodenum. Clients who fear the weight gain that a tube feeding stands to produce may attempt to sabotage the procedure (*Box 13.2*). A nutrition therapist who is managing the refeeding of eating disorder clients must provide a well-monitored environment that minimizes the possibility of tube feeding manipulation.

Lowering the delivery rate on the feeding pump.
Using sharp objects (jewelry, pins, etc) to poke holes in the feeding tube.
Filing the tube to reduce thickness, then bending the tube at that point to spill the feeding.
Removing the feeding bag from its hanging pole and swinging it, thus creating air pockets that clog the tube.
Purging through the surgical opening (with a percutaneous endoscopic gastrostomy feeding).
Biting a hole in the tube.
Placing the nasogastric tube in another place (in a plant, out the window, in the mattress).
Diluting the feeding formula.

**Box 13.2
Sample Behaviors
Used to Manipulate
Tube Feedings**

Renourishment considerations are the same with tube feedings as they are with food. Caloric levels are usually started not much higher than the client's estimated intake at the time of assessment and should be slowly increased (approximately 100 calories a day). Cardiac monitoring is advised for the severely emaciated and dehydrated client. If refeeding appears to be taxing the heart, the rate should be slowed until the client's status has stabilized. Dietary sodium, potassium, and phosphate levels may need to be increased or decreased, depending on what laboratory tests indicate (22). Edema (pedal and sacral) is common; tube-feeding protocols should include provisions to monitor for these physical indications of fluid retention.

Gastrointestinal Complaints

Unless proven otherwise, the client's gastrointestinal complaints should be considered real. Recording all complaints that might require further medical intervention is advisable. Most clients who have relied heavily on diuretics, laxatives, or enemas will need some weaning. The rate and procedure should reflect the quantity, method, and length of time laxatives were used. Severe, chronic users of these compounds often require more diligent medical monitoring and a slower weaning process.

High-fiber diets are appropriate for individuals with anorexia and bulimia. However, the amount of fiber and the consistency of the diet should factor in the client's ability to tolerate them. In the severely malnourished client, too much fiber may constipate. The resulting gastrointestinal stasis may exacerbate symptoms by creating gas, bloating, and body image preoccupation. During this time, the client needs constant reassurance that normal gastric motility and gastric emptying will be restored slowly during the first week. Total recovery of these processes may take longer for those with very restricted food intakes or a protracted history of purging and laxative abuse. Normal bowel function also takes time to return, and may be complicated by rectal tearing. Adjustment in the diet should take into consideration all of these conditions and complaints.

The nutrition therapist can take advantage of the early refeeding process, using it to help the client understand how his body works and what happens when malnutrition and self-abusive behaviors impair normal functioning. In addition, as the body changes, the gastrointestinal tract fills with food, and rehydration occurs, the associated feelings are important to process. While rapid change in weight and hydration is often a life-saving intervention, to the client who typically fears and fights change, these new sensations can be threatening and terrifying.

Other Complications   Those who have been purging may experience dental hypersensitivity to temperature and taste due to loss of enamel, dental caries, and gum disease (23–25). They may also experience painful throat, esophagus, and parotid glands (9). Using fingers and objects to stimulate gagging may have caused perforations that will take time to heal. The parotid glands may be swollen from contact with gastric acids. Dietary alterations to accommodate these complications can encourage the client to choose a less restrictive intake.

Medical complications involving the neuroendocrine system require the establishment of a balanced, good nutrition program that provides for a healthy body weight before normal operations return. The impact of stress on the neuroendocrine system cannot be underestimated. Stress and the client's response to it were most likely present before the eating disorder began, and may have even facilitated the eating disorder's onset. Stress (physiological, emotional, and environmental) is likely to persist after treatment. One of the major goals of psychotherapy is to teach new mechanisms for coping with this stress. Maintaining a nutritionally sound mind and body provides the environment in which healthy coping is most likely to occur.

Less common complications may also arise, but are not discussed here. Also not addressed here are complications that are easily reversed (eg, infertility), at least in the short term, or complications that arise over the long term (eg, osteoporosis). The individual and societal cost of these and other health issues are just beginning to be documented.

THE ROLE OF THE NUTRITION THERAPIST

The nutrition therapist working with eating disorders plays a different role from those he or she usually plays. Listening to clients is often more important than educating them. It is important to help the malnourished client understand the positive effects of refeeding while minimizing the physical discomfort the intervention is likely to create. Nutritional stabilization is critical for preparing the client to begin her psychological healing and recovery. Facilitating this process and watching the client regain both physical and emotional health is one the most exciting and rewarding parts of being the medical nutrition therapist on an eating disorder treatment team.

SUMMARY

- Malnutrition creates physiological stresses and conditions that are important to identify in medical and nutrition assessments.

- It is important to identify and document signs and symptoms of nutritional deficiency, which is commonly found in eating disorders.

- Self-abusive behaviors (ie, diuretic, laxative, and enema use) may have created systemic fragilities that need to be accommodated with dietary modifications.

- Cardiac stabilization is the priority of medical nutritional intervention and dictates all other refeeding interventions.

- It is important for the treatment team to assume responsibility for refeeding (ie, initiate tube feeding) if the client does not demonstrate the ability to adequately refeed and maintain medical/nutritional stability.

REFERENCES

1. Young H, Jaspars S. Nutrition, disease and death in times of famine. *Disasters.* 1995;19(2): 94–109.
2. Guthrie HA. *Introductory Nutrition.* 5th ed. St Louis: CV Mosby Co; 1988.
3. Burton BR, Willis R. *Human Nutrition.* New York: McGraw-Hill Book Co; 1988.
4. Berdanier CD. *Advanced Nutrition: Micronutrients.* Boca Raton, Fla: CRC Press; 1998.
5. Berdanier CD. *Advanced Nutrition: Macronutrients.* BocaRaton, Fla: CRC Press; 1995.
6. Berdanier CD. *CRD Desk Reference for Nutrition.* Boca Raton, Fla: CRC Press; 1998.
7. Kanarek R, Mark-Kaufman R. *Nutrition and Behavior: New Perspectives.* New York: Van Nostrand Reinhold; 1991.
8. Stark ME. Challenging problems presenting as constipation. *Am J Gastroenterol.* 1999;94(3): 567–574.

9. McClain CJ, Humphries LL, Hill KK, Nickl NJ. Gastrointestinal and nutritional aspects of eating disorders. *J Am Coll Nutr.* 1993;2(4):466–74.

10. Nussbaum MP, Shenker IR, Shaw H, Frank S. Differential diagnosis and pathogenesis of anorexia nervosa. *Pediatrician.* 1983-1985;12(2-3):110–117.

11. Comerci GD. Medical complications of anorexia nervosa and bulimia nervosa. *Med Clin North Am.* 1990;74(5):1293–1310.

12. Giannini AJ, Newman M, Gold M. Anorexia and bulimia. *Am Fam Phys.* 1990;41(4):1169–1176.

13. Sharp CW, Freeman CP. The medical complications of anorexia nervosa. *Br J Psychiatry.* 1993;162:452–462.

14. Hall RC, Thomas PB. Medical complications of anorexia and bulimia. *Psychiatr Med.* 1989;7(4):165–192.

15. Carney CP, Andersen AE. Eating disorders: a guide to medical evaluation and complications. *Psychiatr Clin North Am.* 1996;19(4):657–679.

16. Rock CL, Curran-Celentano J. Nutritional management of eating disorders. *Psychiatr Clin North Am.* 1996;19(4):701–713.

17. Kohn MR, Goldern NHY, Shenker IR. Cardiac arrest and delirium: presentations of the refeeding syndrome in severely malnourished adolescents with anorexia nervosa. *J Adolesc Health.* 1998;22(3):239–243.

18. Cooke RA, Chambers JB, Singh R, Todd GJ, Smeeton NC, Treasure J, Treasure T. QT interval in anorexia nervosa. *Br Heart J.* 1994;72(10):69–73.

19. Schocken DD, Holloway JD, Powers PS. Weight loss and the heart: effects of anorexia nervosa and starvation. *Arch Intern Med.* 1989;149(4):877–881.

20. Arii I, Yamashita T, Kinoshita M, Shimizu H, Nakamura M, Nakajima T. Treatment for inpatients with anorexia nervosa: comparison of liquid formula with regular meals. *Psychiatr Clin Neurosci.* 1996;50(2):55-59.

21. Szmukler GE, Andrewes D, Kingston K, Chen L, Stargatt R, Stanley R. Neuropsychological impairment in anorexia nervosa: before and after refeeding. *J Clin Exp Neuropsychol.* 1992;14(2):347–352.

22. Sheridan PH, Collins M. Potentially life threatening hypophosphatemia in anorexia nervosa. *J Adolesc Health Care.* 1983;4(1):44–46.

23. Rytomaa I, Jarvinen V, Kanerva R, Heinonen OP. Bulimia and tooth erosion. *Acta Odontol Scand.* 1998;56(1):36–40.

24. Hazelton LE, Faine MP. Diagnosis and dental management of eating disorder patients. *Int J Prosthodont.* 1996;9(1):65–73.

25. Zachariasan RD. Oral manifestations of bulimia nervosa. *Women's Health.* 1995;22(4):67–76

CHAPTER 14

Nutrition and Nervous System Function

MONIKA M. WOOLSEY, M.S., R.D.

As with other organ systems, diet profoundly affects neurotransmitter function. However, while other organs select dietary metabolites from the circulation, the central nervous system (CNS) lies behind an additional protective wall, the blood-brain barrier, that filters out unnecessary and toxic metabolites and allows needed compounds to pass through into the cerebrospinal fluid *(Figure 14.1)*. Dietary amino acids, glucose, vitamins, and minerals diffuse through the blood-brain barrier in proportion to their relative concentrations in the blood. Thus, dietary habits can affect cerebrospinal fluid by altering the total amount of metabolites available for absorption and by altering blood metabolite proportions and absorption across the blood-brain barrier.

MACRONUTRIENTS

The neurotransmitters serotonin, norepinephrine, dopamine, and acetylcholine originate in the cerebrospinal fluid. Each neurotransmitter has a specific dietary origin (1); of the three major mood-related neurotransmitters, serotonin is derived from the amino acid tryptophan and dopamine and norepinephrine from the amino acid phenylalanine *(Table 14.1)*. In addition, the process of creating neurotransmitters requires numerous vitamins and minerals. Any dietary change that limits these nutrients can change nervous system function.

Calorie Deficiency

Low-calorie diets reduce the total volume of amino acids available for metabolic use (2–4) and can render the restrictive eater susceptible to vitamin deficiencies, which have been implicated in the development of numerous nervous system disorders.

Figure 14.1
Dietary Influences on
Absorption Across the
Blood-Brain Barrier

Normal Diet					Low-Calorie/Protein Avoidant Diet				Aspartame Effect				
									Increased production of phenylalanine changes precursor and neurotransmitter ratios.				
Precursors are absorbed in proportion to each other.					Fewer precursors available for absorption.								
Blood				CSF	Blood		CSF		Blood				CSF
CHO	PHE	TRP		TRP	CHO PHE		PHE		PHE	PHE	PHE		PHE
PHE	CHO	TRP		TRP		TRP	TRP		PHE	CHO	TRP		TRP
TRP	PHE	CHO		CHO					PHE	PHE	PHE		PHE
PHE	TRP	CHO		CHO					PHE	TRP	CHO		CHO
CHO	TRP	PHE		PHE	CHO	PHE	PHE		PHE	PHE	PHE		PHE
TRP	PHE	CHO		CHO	TRP		TRP		TRP	PHE	CHO		CHO
CHO	PHE	TRP		TRP					PHE	PHE	PHE		PHE
PHE	CHO	TRP		TRP					PHE	CHO	TRP		TRP
TRP	PHE	CHO		CHO					PHE	PHE	PHE		PHE
PHE	TRP	CHO		CHO					PHE	TRP	CHO		CHO
CHO	TRP	PHE		PHE	CHO	PHE	PHE		PHE	PHE	PHE		PHE
TRP	PHE	CHO		CHO					TRP	PHE	CHO		CHO
CHO	PHE	TRP		TRP	CHO PHE TRP		TRP		PHE	PHE	PHE		PHE
PHE	CHO	TRP		TRP					PHE	CHO	TRP		TRP
TRP	PHE	CHO		CHO					PHE	PHE	PHE		PHE
PHE	TRP	CHO		CHO					PHE	TRP	CHO		CHO
CHO	TRP	PHE		PHE	CHO	PHE	PHE		PHE	PHE	PHE		PHE
TRP	PHE	CHO		CHO	TRP		TRP		TRP	PHE	CHO		CHO
CHO	PHE	TRP		TRP					PHE	PHE	PHE		PHE
PHE	CHO	TRP		TRP					PHE	CHO	TRP		TRP
TRP	PHE	CHO		CHO	PHE CHO		CHO		TRP	PHE	PHE		PHE
PHE	TRP	CHO		CHO	TRP		TRP		PHE	TRP	CHO		CHO
CHO	TRP	PHE		PHE					PHE	PHE	PHE		PHE
TRP	PHE	CHO		CHO					TRP	PHE	CHO		CHO

Blood-Brain
Barrier

CHO = Carbohydrate
CSF = Cerebrospinal Fluid
PHE = Phenylalanine
TRP = Tryptophan

Individuals who frequently fast or diet have a heightened uptake response to intravenous tryptophan (5), suggesting that the brain is programmed to maintain tryptophan and other neurotransmitters at functional levels and that uptake from the blood is adjusted as required. Regular exposure to neurotransmitters also appears to maintain neuroreceptor function. In one study, individuals consuming a diet low in tryptophan had receptors that were less sensitive to circulating serotonin (6). In other words, the nervous system, like the musculoskeletal system, needs a regular "training regimen" to maintain the "fitness level" required for everyday activities. A nervous system deprived of calories and amino acids is quite literally out of shape and unable to respond normally, even when a normal diet is resumed.

Table 14.2 lists the major dietary sources of tryptophan and phenylalanine, which are important to nervous system function. Many of these are foods that dieters and eating disordered individuals typically avoid (cheeses, dairy products, meats, seeds, and nuts) because of their fat content. A typical low-calorie diet, because of its low nutrient volume and its tendency to restrict crucial dietary components, does not appear to provide adequate levels of neurotransmitter precursors or the coenzymes and cofactors necessary for their manufacture.

Tryptophan: Serotonin Precursor

Foods with 50–100 mg of tryptophan per exchange serving°	Foods with >100 mg of tryptophan per exchange serving
Cheeses: blue, brick, Brie, Camembert, cheddar, Monterey, Muenster	Almonds
	Beef
	Brazil nuts
	Canadian bacon
Egg	Cashew nuts
Eggnog	Cheeses: Colby, Gruyere, Swiss, cottage
Fortified oat flakes	
Fruitcake	
GrapeNuts® and GrapeNuts Flakes®	Chicken, light and dark meat
	Duck
Ham	Goose
Ice cream, soft and hard	Hot cocoa
Life® cereal	Lima beans
Mixed nuts	Milk
Peanuts	Pheasant
Pecans	Sesame seeds
Pine nuts	Turkey breast
Pistachio nuts	
Pork	
Sunflower seeds	
Safflower seeds	
Soybeans	
Walnuts	
Wheat germ	
Yogurt	

Phenylalanine: Norepinephrine/Dopamine Precursor

Foods with 100–199 mg phenylalanine per exchange serving	Foods with >200–299 mg phenylalanine per exchange serving	Foods with >300 mg phenylalanine per exchange serving
Bacon	Brazil nuts	Almonds
Cheese: Parmesan	Cashew nuts	Cheeses, most
Corn	Hickory nuts	Chicken, light/dark
Hazelnuts	Kidney beans	Duck
Ham	Lima beans	Eggs
Lentils	Pine nuts	Goose
Navy beans	Pork	Milk
Spinach	Safflower seeds	Peanuts
	Sesame seeds	Pistachio nuts
		Pumpkin seeds
		Soybeans
		Sunflower seeds
		Turkey
		Walnuts
		Yogurt

°Typical serving size as described by the American Diabetes Association Exchange System.

Source: Pennington JAT. *Bowes and Church's Food Values of Portions Commonly Used.* 16th ed. Philadelphia, Penn: JB Lippincott; 1994.

Table 14.2
Eating for a
Healthy Brain

Nutrient	DRIs	Best Food Sources
CNS Development and Structural Maintenance		
Folic acid	400 mcg	Dark greens, dried legumes, kidneys, and liver
Omega 3 fatty acids	°°°	Salmon, mackerel, tuna, sardines, and flaxseed, canola, soy, and walnut oils
Neurotransmitter Production and Maintenance		
Tryptophan	°°°	Cheeses, eggs, meat, milk, nuts, seeds, and yogurt
Phenylalanine	°°°	Cheeses, eggs, meat, milk, nuts, seeds, and yogurt
Choline	°°°	Egg yolks, legumes, and organ meat
Folic acid	400 mcg	Dark greens, dried legumes, kidneys, and liver
Nerve Impulse Transmission		
Iron	15 mg	Dark greens, dried apricots, dried legumes, egg yolks, enriched and whole-grain cereals, kidneys, liver, molasses, potatoes, prunes, raisins, and red meats
Calcium	1,000 mg	Canned salmon/sardines with bones, fortified citrus juice, corn tortillas, dairy products, dark greens, and dried lentils
Magnesium	310 mg	Almonds, cashew, raw leafy green vegetables, seeds, soybeans, and whole grains
Zinc	12 mg	Eggs, liver, meat, milk, poultry, seafood, and whole grains
Manganese	°°°	Fruits, instant coffee, nuts, tea, vegetables, and whole grains
Antioxidants		
Beta carotene	800 mg RE	Dark greens, orange and yellow fruits and vegetables
Vitamin C	60 mg	Citrus fruits, dark greens, green pepper, melon, potatoes, strawberries, and tomatoes
Vitamin E	8 mg	Dried legumes, leafy green vegetables, liver, margarine, vegetable oils, wheat germ, and whole grains
Selenium	55 mcg	Brazil nuts, chicken, egg yolks, garlic, meat, milk, and whole grains
Glutathione	°°°	Avocados, asparagus, grapefruit, okra, oranges, peaches, strawberries, watermelon, and white potatoes

Note: The Dietary Reference Intakes listed are for females between 19 and 30 years of age. These values may vary for men and for younger and older individuals.

Source: Pennington JAT. *Bowes and Church's Food Values of Portions Commonly Used.* 16th ed. Philadelphia, Penn: JB Lippincott; 1994.

Women appear to be more vulnerable to the effect of low dietary tryptophan than men (3). A low-calorie diet administered to a mixed-gender group with proportionately similar caloric levels lowered blood tryptophan levels more significantly in women than in men. Deficiency diseases are usually thought of as third-world problems. However, chronic dieting could very well be creating a whole host of gender-specific deficiency syndromes. Since most deficiencies are identified when they produce *physical* but not *mental* symptoms, the impact of dieting on the overall physical and mental health of participating individuals may not be fully recognized and understood.

Dieting may be an important first step toward the development of an eating disorder in many unwitting individuals. Women, who are more likely to follow weight loss diets and to restrict food as a chronic behavior, are also more likely to suffer from depression. In fact, the rate of depression is twice as high in women (26 percent) as in men (13 percent) (7). Could dietary habits be a major contributor to this difference? Depression is clearly a multifactorial disorder, but dietary habits should not be overlooked as a significant contribution to its development.

Acetylcholine is a neurotransmitter with significant functions in learning and memory retention (8). While choline deficiency has not been directly correlated with eating disorders, it makes sense that some of the memory deficits seen in severe anorexia nervosa may be at least partially due to choosing foods that do not provide adequate choline. Choline is also important in folate metabolism, and choline deficiency has been found to be associated with lower serum folate concentrations (9), another potential issue in eating disorders.

Fat

Though too much dietary fat is generally believed to be detrimental to health, the harmful effects of too little fat have only recently gained attention in industrial countries. Nerve and brain cells are lined with a lipid layer within which sit the neurotransmitter receptors. It is essential to maintain enough dietary fat to keep these cell linings intact. Without these lipid linings, neurotransmitters have nowhere to bind and message transmission can be disrupted. Until recently, the only way to evaluate dietary impact on nervous system function was an invasive procedure. For this reason, studies documenting diet-induced morphological changes were not feasible. However, studies with newer techniques, such as the positron-emission tomography (PET) scan, are revealing that the changes in behavior, mood, and biochemistry that diet induces are accompanied by changes in CNS morphology as well. Individuals with anorexia do not respond well to antidepressant medication during the recovery phase of their disease, yet in a normal weight range they can avoid relapse on the same medication (10).

Recent PET scan studies have documented significant irreversible morphological changes in brain tissue (11) in anorexic individuals when a less than ideal body weight has been maintained for an extended time. Not only do these findings implicate restrictive eating as a potential cause for eating disorders, but they also underscore the importance of early intervention in a restrictive eating pattern to restore normal CNS function and avoid permanent loss of the ability to fully recover.

Essential fatty acids (linoleic acid and linolenic acid) are the precursors necessary for maintenance of membrane linings. Severe caloric and fat restriction disrupts membrane synthesis and membrane maintenance by reducing the availability of necessary dietary building blocks. Omega-3 (n-3) fatty acids, already known for their ability to reduce cardiovascular risk, are also thought to be important for brain function, as they contain significant amounts of both linoleic and linolenic acid. These fatty acids are essential for proper development of the human brain and nervous system, and are of particular importance to the developing fetus (12).

These fatty acids are also important in the learning process. As new information is gathered by the brain, nerve cells create connections between each other for more rapid communication of learned information in the future. These new connections are housed in membranes made in large part of n-3 fatty acids (13). Scientists on the forefront of brain nutrition research have found that children who were breast-fed as infants score significantly higher on IQ tests than do those who were bottle-fed. Noting that breast milk naturally contains a significant amount of long-chain n-3 fatty acids and that American infant formulas lack this nutrient, they propose that one explanation for differences in intelligence is a developmentally based biochemical difference in the ability to obtain and retain information in the brain cells (14).

Like muscle tissue, nerve membranes are dynamic tissues, constantly breaking down, repairing, and rebuilding as part of their normal maintenance routine. As with muscle, a deficiency in the building blocks necessary for structural maintenance and function depletes functional tissue and impairs function.

Eating disordered individuals often report limiting their fat intake to 2 to 3 grams a day, hardly enough to provide even minimal levels of essential fatty acids. These individuals also often experience short-term memory loss, and psychiatrists report that they often experience very little change in mood or behavior on high doses of antidepressants (15), suggesting that even if neurotransmitter balance has been restored, without an intact nerve membrane, the neurotransmitters cannot function.

Epidemiologic studies have correlated extremes in lipid concentrations (high and low) with a variety of mental disorders, including unipolar depression, bipolar depression, schizoaffective disorders, hostility, and aggression (16-30). Controlled laboratory studies have strengthened this assertion. In one study, hypertriglyceridemia and low high-density lipoprotein (HDL) levels were shown to be the sole causative factors in mild to serious depression. When triglyceride levels were lowered and other potential causative factors were accounted for, symptoms of depression significantly decreased (31). Scientists suggest that high triglycerides may act on the brain in a similar fashion as they do on the heart, decreasing cerebral perfusion and oxygenation and creating atherosclerotic lesions that alter basic functions (31).

Factors that can exacerbate hypertriglyceridemia include

- consumption of a large amount of calories in one bolus,
- consumption of a large volume of sugar in one bolus,
- consumption of a disproportionate amount of calories as alcohol, and
- too little exercise.

These behaviors are common to bulimia and binge eating disorder. In addition to the guilt and shame that binge eating is likely to produce, the lipid studies cited provide some evidence that these behaviors may also be promoting biochemical activities that further exacerbate depression and anxiety and accelerate the binge eating cycle. It is important to help clients with bingeing behaviors to understand both the short-term and long-term impact of their behavior on their disease process and to help develop coping skills that provide superior relief using behaviors other than eating.

Many popular low-fat foods are also high in sugar. In some cases the low-fat label is misleading, as the percentage of fat is low only because the carbohydrate content is high. Sugar is often added to increase palatability. It is important to explain that these foods are to be used in moderation as part of a balanced diet, and that there are upper limits of consumption that are important for overall health.

Again, the important word in dietary recommendations is *balance*. While fat moderation is important for cardiovascular health, recommendations to reduce fat should be accompanied with lower limits. Without such lower limits, individuals without a nutrition background limit their intake to less than 10 grams a day. Current recommendations of 30 percent of calories as fat with 10 percent of calories as saturated fat are reasonable for healthy mental functioning. A bottom limit of 20-25 percent of calories as fat, especially for individuals with a history of depression, anxiety, or eating disorders, while not yet studied in vitro, appears to be appropriate, given the number of published studies documenting a correlation between lipid levels and mental health.

Carbohydrates

A diet that eliminates food groups (eg, a low-calorie diet or a diet restrictive in certain food types) can change dietary proportions and blood amino acid concentrations. A large amount of carbohydrate ingested in a short period of time quickly increases blood glucose concentrations, which in turn stimulates insulin release. Insulin, a storage hormone, is known mainly for its impact on blood glucose. However, it also facilitates the uptake of other blood components that can be used to manufacture glucose and glycogen. Though branched-chain amino acids (BCAAs) are removed from circulation in the presence of insulin, tryptophan and phenylalanine, aromatic amino acids, are not. As BCAAs leave the circulation, it becomes easier for the aromatic amino acids to cross the blood-brain barrier and be used for neurotransmitter synthesis.

This "carbohydrate effect" is hypothesized to be one of the main reasons carbohydrate cravings are so prominent in depression-related disorders, such as bulimia and seasonal affective disorder (32) *(Figure 14.2)*. The end result of increased neurotransmitter production would be an increase in all the sensations related to that neurotransmitter. In the case of carbohydrates, the increased sense of calm that has been documented to occur with their consumption has been attributed to the end result of increased brain serotonin (33). This mechanism may not apply to all carbohydrate cravers, but is important to consider as a potential trigger.

Vegetarian Diets

While most vegetarian diets are a healthy alternative to meat-containing diets, the type of vegetarian diet adopted in an eating disorder may be both amino-acid-

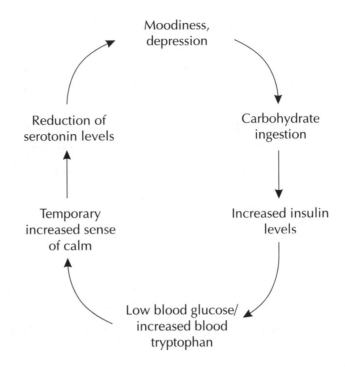

Figure 14.2
The Proposed Effect of Carbohydrate-Dense Food Boluses on Binge Cycling

and fat-deficient. Rather than working to find a balance in their eating habits, eating disordered vegetarians tend to view meat elimination as part of the search for the "perfect" food. Anything that doesn't contribute to meeting this goal is eliminated from the diet. Because of their fat content, vegetarian sources of essential amino acids and essential fatty acids are often completely eliminated. With all meat and dairy products excluded and other fats severely restricted, it is doubtful that enough essential compounds are present for normal brain functioning.

MICRONUTRIENTS Numerous vitamins and minerals come into play in the synthesis and metabolism of neurotransmitters and fatty acids. Some of the best-known include the B vitamins, antioxidants, zinc, iron, magnesium, manganese, and selenium.

B Vitamins B vitamins have long been known to have an impact on mental health. In fact, one community-based study found that simply providing a daily vitamin supplement over a year's time improved mood in a significant portion of the population; this improvement was correlated with higher serum levels of riboflavin, pyridoxine, and thiamin (34). While these findings suggest that vitamin supplementation may help accelerate recovery from an eating disorder, they need to be interpreted with caution. Because typical fad and low-calorie diets often eliminate entire food categories, focus on a narrow range of "acceptable" foods, and decrease total nutrient intake to levels below what is necessary for normal mental functioning, the most important long-term intervention in a nutritionally deficient individual is to increase the variety of foods and food groups eaten. The theme of balance should predominate.

Folic acid appears to be of critical importance in food-related behaviors and neurotransmitter function. In one study, mice on a folate-deficient diet for 5 weeks spilled three times food than control mice fed a supplemented diet. This behavior was postulated to stem from changes in serotoninergic and dopaminergic functioning (35). This finding may have some relevance to eating disorders, as food spilling is often considered to be an intentional behavioral ritual in humans. The nutrition therapist can be an important resource in helping the treatment team determine whether food-related behaviors are pharmacological, nutritional, or behavioral in origin, and which intervention will best address the observed behavior.

As was learned with neurotransmitters, the *balance* between neurotransmitter concentrations, not the concentration of a single neurotransmitter, is what controls nerve transmission. This principle tends to recur throughout the body's systems, and prudent dietary advice should honor, rather than attempt to manipulate, this balance. Inadequate intake of nutrients as well as megadoses of nutrients and supplements can disrupt delicate biochemical ranges, tend to promote the idea of a "magic" solution for a complex problem, discourage the reintroduction of a variety of foods, and can maintain social isolation. The ultimate goal should be to obtain all necessary vitamins and minerals from a variety of foods and food groups.

As with other vitamins, folate deficiency can cause altered taste, severe weight loss, diarrhea, poor appetite, and mood changes (36). It has also been correlated with lowered brain serotonin in rats. There is a high incidence of folate deficiency in depressed individuals, and there are indications that some depressed individuals respond to folate supplementation (37).

Antioxidants

Like the B vitamins, antioxidants may be important to brain function. The brain derives almost all of its energy from glucose, making it a "high-oxidizing" organ and creating free radicals that can do damage. A diet high in antioxidants may help improve brain function by decreasing oxidative damage to brain tissue. One antioxidant that has been consumed less because of the low-fat focus of the last decade is vitamin E. Intake of this vitamin, which is found in vegetable oils and margarine, is deficient in most Americans. This vitamin has been linked to proper CNS function. In one study, lack of antioxidant protection was hypothesized to be a cause of damage to serotonergic neurons (38). Dopamine release appears to increase with serotonergic damage (38,39). In cholinergic neurons, vitamin E deficiency decreased synapse-to-neuron ratio (40).

The effects of vitamin E are not isolated to the brain. Lack of nonadrenergic, noncholinergic inhibitory junction potentials tripled in vitamin E-deficient animals compared with controls, and cholinergic junction potentials were absent in 83 percent of vitamin E-deficient animals (vs 8 percent of controls). Neurotransmitter release could not even be elicited in the deficient animals (41). Compromised gut function (eg, constipation and bloating) is one of the medical symptoms most commonly found in eating disordered individuals. This study suggests that at least part of the compromised gut motility seen in eating disorders may result from nutrition-related atrophy of the nerves that are needed to stimulate contractions. While dietary bulk should be encouraged, these findings regarding vitamin E suggest that bowel regularity is a complex issue and that attention to overall nervous system nourishment may be the core intervention to effect.

Vitamin C may have important antioxidant functions in the CNS as well. In one study of the elderly, cognitive function was poorest in subjects whose diets were deficient in vitamin C (42). It is important not to assume that, because eating disordered individuals tend to favor fruits and vegetables, such a syndrome would not be found. Individuals with bulimia often eat large amounts of these foods but do not keep them ingested long enough to absorb the nutrients they provide. Binge eaters should also not be forgotten when considering micronutrient malnutrition. Many times the foods eaten by a binge eater are high in caloric density and low in nutrient content. The quality as well as quantity of each individual's diet needs to be considered in order to assess the appropriate individualized dietary recommendations.

Zinc

In terms of its potential impact on eating disorders, zinc is one of the better studied minerals. Three hundred enzymes are known to require zinc for their activities (43), including DNA synthesis, cell division, and protein synthesis. These functions are often compromised in eating disorders; inadequate intake and low zinc levels are thought to be at least partially responsible for the poor appetite, mental lethargy, and preference for carbohydrates (44,45) often seen in anorexia.

Iron

Iron deficiency has been implicated in altered cognitive process (ie, poor visual attention and concept acquisition) in children. One study found these alterations resolved after 4 months of iron supplementation (46). However, such damage in infants has been found to be irreversible.

Magnesium

Numerous conditions often seen in eating disorders have also been attributed to magnesium deficiency (47). They include

- intestinal hypoabsorption,
- reduced bone uptake and mobilization,
- hyperadrenoglucocorticism (dexamethasone nonsuppression) by decreased adaptability to stress,
- insulin resistance,
- adrenergic hyporeceptivity,
- mood disturbances, and
- altered mental performance through accelerated hippocampal aging.

Low blood magnesium in mice has been demonstrated to increase catecholamine production (48). In a population of cardiac patients, those with low magnesium were more likely to be neurotic or to exhibit anxiety states compatible with a psychological disorder (49). These data strongly suggest that magnesium deficiency decreases an individual's ability to handle stress and may play a part in the anxiety commonly seen across the spectrum of eating disorders. Magnesium intake is marginal in well-nourished individuals of any age (49); the stress of an eating disorder likely only exacerbates susceptibility to the symptoms listed above.

Manganese

A lesser known mineral, manganese, has also been studied for its impact on behavior. In a population of psychiatric patients, more "disturbed and excitable" individuals were more likely to have low blood manganese levels (50).

Selenium

Selenium is an important cofactor in antioxidant processes. Selenium deficiency appears to be of particular importance in the substantia nigra and striatum of the brain, where low levels for even a short period of time increase oxidative activity (51). In the hippocampus, a low-selenium diet has been demonstrated to increase dopamine turnover, which in turn increases brain oxidative activity (52). Selenium deficiency may also be related to low serum T3 levels (53), which are commonly found in eating disorders.

NUTRITION AND COGNITION

Any dietitian who has worked with eating disordered individuals knows the frustration of spending hours of counseling time answering questions on seemingly basic nutrition and exercise concepts, only to have the client ask the same questions again in the next session. Equally frustrating is the client who does not remember a specific piece of information, then blames her dietitian for the oversight. Though much of this behavior is manipulative, it is important to consider the potential dietary influences on memory and cognition as well, and adjust a treatment plan for a client who appears to have true memory deficits.

These findings do not necessarily suggest that individualized supplementation of vitamins and minerals is appropriate. At this writing, specific nutritional causes of and cures for depression have not been identified. It is more important to gain from this reading an understanding of the complexity of the nervous system and its dependence on a fine balance of interactions between numerous nutrients and substrates. Any extreme dietary modification is likely to upset this balance and create a deficiency or a change in nutrient proportions that could modify cognition, sensation, and response to stimulus.

Some practitioners use prenatal vitamins as part of their refeeding protocol in hopes of accelerating the refeeding process and response to psychiatric and psychological interventions. While at this writing this practice has not been documented to be effective, it likely does not hurt the client and is a reasonable intervention. The most appropriate nutritional recommendation for recovery is achieving a variety of nutrients from all food groups: the paradigm already in use in the form of the Food Guide Pyramid. Vitamin and mineral supplementation can be a useful adjunct to this goal, but should never be a substitute for balanced eating.

NONNUTRITIVE DIETARY COMPONENTS

Aspartame

It has been repeatedly documented that aspartame does not cross the blood-brain barrier. This finding has led to the assumption that aspartame does not affect the brain, the nervous system, or behavior. However, a recent study suggests that aspartame may indeed have adverse effects in some individuals. Knowing that aspartame increases blood levels of tryptophan, researchers designed a study to evaluate whether this change in blood amino acids had any impact on a population thought to be specifically vulnerable to changes in neurotransmitter concentration: individuals with a history of mood disorders. The study was initially designed to compare a response to a dose of 30 mg/kg/day in 40 individuals with diagnosed unipolar depression and 40 who had no psychiatric history. The response to the aspartame challenge in the depressed subjects was so severe that the government halted the study after 13 individuals had received their test dose out of concern for subject safety (54).

Aspartame may have its impact precisely because it doesn't cross the blood-brain barrier. It alters blood amino acid concentrations, which increases blood levels of phenylalanine and in turn increases the amount of phenylalanine that is absorbed into the cerebral spinal fluid. The disruption in neurotransmitter balance in the CSF, not the physical presence of aspartame, may be the crucial factor. Only when the susceptible population was isolated in the above study was this effect visible.

Just as phenylalanine is not appropriate for individuals with phenylketonuria, so it may not be appropriate for individuals with neuropsychiatric systems that are especially sensitive to changes in neurotransmitter ratios. Studies designed to look at healthy populations would not detect these subtleties. However, future studies that isolate susceptible populations for comparison may elucidate a major contributing force in the development of depression.

Caffeine

Caffeine affects the CNS in numerous ways. Like a high-carbohydrate diet, it stimulates insulin release and changes blood amino acid concentrations to favor tryptophan absorption. Caffeine is a stimulant that alters CNS function much as a psychological stressor might; it disrupts sleep patterns, decreases appetite and intake, and depletes neurotransmitter substrates.

Moderate caffeine intake (1 to 2 cups of coffee a day) is thought by most experts to be acceptable. However, eating disordered individuals have a tendency to consume caffeine throughout the day, often in lieu of food and often in the form of diet cola, which together with aspartame may create a "double-whammy" for the brain.

The more sophisticated nutritional science becomes, the more sophisticated the old-fashioned "well-rounded diet" appears to be. It encourages variety and promotes balance: a balance of neurochemicals, a balance of amino acids, a balance of fats, and a balance of vitamins and minerals. Our bodies are too finely tuned for us to assume that restricting even one dietary component is a practice without adverse consequence.

In a country where diseases of overconsumption abound, nutrition professionals are often not trained to recognize or educate against the dangers of malnutrition. It is important to remember that the potential for dietary deficiency exists in every client, regardless of weight. Evidence is accumulating that the adoption of restrictive food practices for weight control can be detrimental and may actually work against the intended goal of better health.

In the past decade, the focus on cardiovascular health may have encouraged dietary practices that have been converted into extreme practices that limit macronutrients and micronutrients. While a heart-healthy diet, practiced in moderation, is also "brain healthy," extreme dietary practices can negatively affect CNS function. It is important to present information without transmitting messages that may encourage avoidance of essential dietary components.

As more is known about nutrition and brain function, a "heart- and brain-healthy" dietary recommendation might emerge. Based on what is currently known, that diet might look similar to the one proposed in *Box 14.1.*

BALANCE—A NOT-SO-OLD-FASHIONED CONCEPT

- 40–50% carbohydrate, mainly complex
- 12–20% protein, no less than 0.8 grams per kilogram of ideal body weight
- 25–30% fat, no less than 40–45 grams fat per day, emphasis on fat sources high in n-3 fatty acids
- Distribution of food groups consistent with the Food Guide Pyramid

If dietary restrictions for other medical conditions require intakes below the lower recommended level in any category, caloric intake of less than 1,600 calories a day should be used only on the advice of a registered dietitian. Under these conditions, use of a multivitamin supplement is strongly recommended.

**Box 14.1
Proposed Heart and Brain Healthy Dietary Recommendations**

SUMMARY

- Dietary habits can alter the total amount of metabolites available for absorption into the cerebrospinal fluid by altering blood metabolite proportions and absorption across the blood-brain barrier.

- Total caloric deficiency and restriction of a macronutrient group can adversely affect both cognition and mood.

- Lack of dietary variety can create deficiencies in micronutrients, many of which are crucial for healthy CNS function.

- Nonnutritive substances such as caffeine and aspartame, in excess, may negatively affect CNS function.

- Current dietary recommendations, provided they are augmented with lower limits of healthy intake, can reduce chronic diseases (ie, cardiovascular disease, cancer, and diabetes) and promote optimal mental health.

REFERENCES

1. Somer E. *Food & Mood: The Complete Guide to Eating Well and Feeling Your Best.* New York: Henry Holt and Company, Inc; 1995.

2. Hirose T. Effects of nutritional status on contents of tryptophan, serotonin and 5-hydroxyindoleacetic acid in rat brain. *Nippon Eiseigaku Azsshi.* 1992;47(2): 627–633.

3. Walsh AE, Oldman AD, Franklin M, Fariburn CG, Cowen PJ. Dieting decreases plasma tryptophan and increases the prolactin response to d-fenfluramine in women but not men. *J Affect Disord.* 1995;33(2):89–97.

4. Anderson IM, Parry-Billings M, Newsholme EA, Fairburn CG, Cowen PJ. Dieting reduces plasma tryptophan and alters brain 5-HT function in women. *Psychol Med.* 1990;20(4):785-791.

5. Goodwin GM, Fairburn CG, Cowen PJ. Dieting changes serotonergic function in women, not men: implications for the etiology of anorexia nervosa. *Psychol Med.* 1987;17:839–842.

6.. Goodwin GM, Cowen PJ, Fairburn CG, Parry-Billings M, Calder PC, Newsholme EA. Plasma concentrations of tryptophan and dieting. *Br Med J.* 1990;300: 1499–1500.

7. Salmans S. *Depression: Questions You Have . . . Answers You Need.* Allentown, Pa: People's Medical Society; 1995.

8. Moriyama T, Uezu K, Matsumoto Y, Chung SY, Uezu E, Miyagi S, Uza M, Masuda Y, Kokubu T, Tanaka T, Yamamoto S. Effects of dietary phosphatidylcholine on memory in memory-deficient mice with low brain acetylcholine concentration. *Life Sci.* 1996;58(6):PL111-PL118.

9. Varela Moreiras G, Ragel C, Perez de Miguelsanz J. Choline deficiency and methotrexate treatment induces marked but reversible changes in hepatic folate concentrations, serum homocysteine and DNA methylation rates in rats. *J Am Coll Nutr.* 1995;14(5):480–485.

10. 7-Lambe EK, Katzman DK, Mikulis DJ, Kenedy SH, Zipursky DB. Cerebral gray matter volume dificits after weight recovery from anorexia nervosa. *Arch Gen Psychiatry.* 1997; 54(6):537–542.

11. Katzman DK, Zipursky RB, Lambe EK, Mikulis DJ. A longitudinal magnetic reso-

nance imaging study of brain changes in adolescents with anorexia nervosa. *Arch Pediatr Adolesc Med.* 1997;151(8):793–797.

12. Connor WE, Neuringer M. The effects of n-3 fatty acid deficiency and repletion upon the fatty acid composition and function of the brain and retina. *Prog Clin Biol Res.* 1988;282:275–294.

13. Yoshida S. New infrared spectroscopic technique as a tool to reveal roles of unsaturated fatty acids in diseases and synaptic functions. *Obes Res.* 1995; 3(Suppl 5): 761S-767S.

14. de Andraca I, Uauy R. Breastfeeding for optimal mental development: the alpha and the omega in human milk. *World Rev Nutr Diet.* 1995;78:1–27.

15. Walsh BT, Devlin MJ. The pharmacologic treatment of eating disorders. *Psychiatr Clin North Am.* 1992;15(1):149–160.

16. Bajwa WK, Asnis GM, Sanderson WC, Irfan A, van Praag HM. High cholesterol levels in patients with panic disorder. *Am J Psychiatry.* 1992;149(3): 376–378.

17. Engstrom G, Alsen M, Regnell G, Traskman-Bendz L. Serum lipids in suicide attempters. *Suicide Life Threat Behav.* 1995;25(3):393–400.

18. Fava M, Abraham M, Pava J, Shuster J, Rosenbaum J. Cardiovascular risk factors in depression: the role of anxiety and anger. *Psychosomatics.* 1996;37(1):31–37.

19. Freedman DS, Byers T, Barrett DH, Stroup NE, Eaker E, Monroe-Blum H. Plasma lipid levels and psychologic characteristics in men. *Am J Epidemiol.* 1995;141(6): 507–517.

20. Weidner G, Connor SL, Hollis JF, Connor WE. Improvements in hostility and depression in relation to dietary change and cholesterol lowering: the Family Heart Study. *Ann Intern Med.* 1992;117(10):820–823.

21. Sullivan PF, Joyce PR, Bulik CM, Mulder RT, Oakley-Browne M. Total cholesterol and suicidality in depression. *Biol Psychiatry.* 1994;36(7):472–477.

22. Morgan RE, Palinka LA, Barrett-Connor EL, Wingard DL. Plasma cholesterol and depressive symptoms in older men. *Lancet.* 1993;341(8837):75–79.

23. Modai I, Valevski A, Dror S, Weizman A. Serum cholesterol levels and suicidal tendencies in psychiatric inpatients. *J Clin Psychiatry.* 1994;55(6): 252–254.

24. Maes M, Delanghe J, Meltzer HY, Scharpe S, D'Hondt P, Cosyns P. Lower degree of esterification of serum cholesterol in depression: relevance for depression and suicide research. *Acta Psychiatr Scand.* 1994;90(4):252–258.

25. Lindberg G, Larsson G, Setterlind S, Rastam L. Serum lipids and mood in working men and women in Sweden. *J Epidemiol Community Health.* 1994;48(4):360–363.

26. Kaplan JR, Shively CA, Fontenot MB, Morgan TM, Howell SM, Manuck SB, Muldoon MF, Mann JJ. Demonstration of an association among dietary cholesterol, central serotonergic activity, and social behavior in monkeys. *Psychosom Med.* 1994;56(6):479–484.

27. Caddedu G, Fioravanti P, Antonicelli R, Gsasparrini PM, Gaetti R. Relationship between cholesterol levels and depression in the elderly. *Minerva Med.* 1995; 86(6):251–256.

28. Glueck CJ, Kuller FE, Hamer T, Rodriguez R, Sosa F, Sieve-Smith L, Morrison JA. Hypocholesterolemia, hypertriglyceridemia, suicide, and suicide ideation in children hospitalized for psychiatric diseases. *Pediatr Res.* 1994;35(5):602–610.

29. Golier JA, Marzuk PM, Leon AC, Weiner C, Tardiff K. Low serum cholesterol level and attempted suicide. *Am J Psychiatry.* 1995;152(3):419–423.

30. Glueck CJ, Tieger M, Kunkel R, Hamer T, Tracy T, Speirs J. Hypocholesterolemia and affective disorders. *Am J Med Sci.* 1994;308(4):218–225.

31. Glueck CJ, Tieger M, Kunkel R, Tracy T, Speirs J, Streicher P, Illig E. Improvement

in symptoms of depression and in an index of life stressors accompany treatment of severe hypertriglyceridemia. *Biol Psychiatry.* 1993; 34(4):240–252.

32. Wurtman JJ. Relationship between carbohydrate intake and disorders of mood. *Drugs.* 1990;39(Suppl 3): 49–52.

33. Sayegh R, Schiff I, Wurtman J, Spiers P, McDermott J, Wurtman R. The effect of a carbohydrate-rich beverage on mood, appetite, and cognitive function in women with premenstrual syndrome. *Obstet Gynecol.* 1995;86(4 Pt 1):520–528.

34. Benton D, Haller J, Fordy J. Vitamin supplementation for 1 year improves mood. *Neuropsychobiology.* 1995;32(2):98–105.

35. Gospe SM Jr., Gietzen DW, Summers PJ, Lunetta JM, Miller JW, Selhub J, Ellis WG, Clifford AJ. Behavioral and neurochemical changes in folate-deficient mice. *Physiol Behav.* 1995;58(5):935–941.

36. Stolzenberg R. Possible folate deficiency with postsurgical infection. *Nutr Clin Pract.* 1994;9(6):247–250.

37. Young SN. The use of diet and dietary components in the study of factors controlling affect in humans: a review. *J Psychiatry Neurosci.* 1993;18(5): 235–244.

38. Castano A, Venero JL, Cano J, Machado A. Changes in the turnover of monoamines in prefrontal cortex of rats fed on vitamin E-deficient diet. *J Neurochem.* 1992; 58(5):1889–1895.

39. Castano A, Herrera AJ, Cano J, Machado A. Effects of a short period of vitamin E-deficient diet in the turnover of different neurotransmitters in substantia nigra and striatum of the rat. *Neuroscience.* 1993;53(1):179–185.

40. Fattoretti P, Bertoni-Freddari C, Caselli U, Paoloni R. The effect of vitamain E deficiency on the plasticity of cholinergic synapses: a computer-assisted morphometric study. *Boll Soc Ital Biol Sper.* 1995;71(5–6):119–124.

41. Hoyle CH, Ralevic V, Lincoln J, Knight GE, Goss-Sampson MA, Milla PJ, Burnstock G. Effects of vitamin E deficiency on autonomic neuroeffector mechanisms in the rat caecum. *J Physiolo Lond.* 1995;487(Pt 3):773–786.

42. Gale CR, Martyn CN, Cooper C. Cognitive impairment and mortality in a cohort of elderly people. *BMJ.* 1996;312(7031):608-611.

43. Prasad AS. Zinc: an overview. *Nutrition.* 1995;11(1 Suppl):93–99.

44. Lask B, Fosson A, Rolfe U, Thomas S. Zinc deficiency and childhood-onset anorexia nervosa. *J Clin Psychiatry.* 1993;54(2):63–66.

45. Rains TM, Shay NF. Zinc status specifically changes preferences for carbohydrate and protein in rats selecting from separate carbohydrate-, protein-, and fat-containing diets. *J Nutr.* 1995;125(11):2874–2879.

46. Soewondo S. The effect of iron deficiency and mental stimulation on Indonesian children's cognitive performance and development. *Kobe J Med Sci.* 1995:41(1–2):1–17.

47. Durlach J, Durlach V, Bac P, Rayssiguier Y, Bara M, Guiet-Bara A. Magnesium and aging. II. Clinical data: aetiological mechanisms and pathophysiological consequences of magnesium deficit in the elderly. *Magnes Res.* 1993;6(4):379–394.

48. Henrotte JG, Aymard N, Leyris A, Monier C, Frances H, Boulu R. Brain weight and noradrenaline content in mice selected for low and high blood magnesium. *Magnes Res.* 1993:6(1): 21–24.

49. Tanabe K, Noda K, Ozasa A, Mikawa T, Murayama M, Sugai J. The relation of physical and mental stress to magnesium deficiency in patients with variant angina. *J Cardiol.* 1992;22(2–3):349–355.

50. Kirov GK, Birch NJ, Steadman P, Ramsey RG. Plasma magnesium levels in a population of psychiatric patients: correlations with symptoms. *Neuropsychobiology.* 1994;30(2–3):73–78.

51. Castano A, Cano J, Machado A. Low selenium diet affects monoamine turnover differentially in substantia nigra and striatum. *J Neurochem.* 1993; 61(4):1302–1307.

52. Castano A, Ayala A, Rodriguez-Gomez JA, de la Cruz CP, Revilla E, Cano J, Machado A. Increase in dopamine turnover and tyrosine hydroxylase enzyme in hippocampus of rats fed on low selenium diet. *J Neurosci Res.* 42(5):684–691.

53. Eder K, Kralik A, Kirchgessner M. Effect on metabolism of thyroid hormones in deficient to subtoxic selenium supply levels. *Z Ernahrungswiss.* 1995;34(4):277–283.

54. Walton RG, Hudak R, Green-Waite RJ. Adverse reactions to aspartame: double-blind challenge in patients from a vulnerable population. *Biol Psychiatry.* 1993; 34(1–2):13017.

CHAPTER 15

Outpatient Nutrition Therapy for Eating Disorders

DIANE KEDDY, M.S., R.D.

Contacting a nutrition therapist for an appointment can be extremely anxiety producing for a person with an eating disorder. Many clients receive a referral from their psychotherapist or physician and then wait days or weeks before contacting the nutrition therapist for an appointment. Eating-disorder clients may fear the nutrition therapist more than any other team member, as he is perceived as the person who may take away control over food or weight. Consequently, the nutrition therapist must establish trust and rapport with the client if treatment is to be successful.

INITIAL CLIENT CONTACT

The trust-building process begins in the initial phone contact with the client. During this conversation, the nutrition therapist should explain exactly what the client can expect from the initial appointment. This includes a description of the detailed history taking and eating disorder evaluation, as well as the reassurance that there will be no weigh-in during the first appointment. It is also important to stress that nutrition therapy will proceed at a speed that is emotionally comfortable for the client and that the client will set the pace. The nutrition therapist should clarify that nutrition therapy is not a diet, but a process of learning how to eat normally again and to establish a nonemotional relationship with food. A client with anorexia or bulimia also needs reassurance that she will not be asked to eat anything she is uncomfortable eating. Addressing the client's fears before the first meeting helps make that meeting much more productive.

The first appointment is typically devoted to establishing the boundaries of the relationship and beginning to build rapport. Clients who are minors should be told that what they say will remain confidential unless the information revealed could be life threatening. For example, if a client said he wanted to hurt himself or felt suicidal, his parents would need to be told. If he admitted that he was vomiting or taking laxatives or diet pills, confidentiality would be maintained. The team approach should also be explained; clients need to understand that treatment team members share information because they work together to provide help. If the client is not yet working with a psychotherapist or is not being followed by a physician, referrals can be provided at the end of the appointment, when some rapport has been established.

Many eating disorder clients feel embarrassment and shame about their eating behaviors. It is important to reassure the client that whatever she says is acceptable and will not be used against her, and to remember that these clients need frequent reassurance and ongoing nurturing during their journey into recovery.

It is helpful for the nutrition therapist to tell clients that she has no intention of making them fat, and that her goal is for them to have the least possible body fat consistent with good health. A second technique is to provide the scientific rationale behind recommendations. A portion of every session should include information about metabolism, physiology, and the nutritional needs of the body. Providing the client with the rationale behind recommendations helps increase the nutrition therapist's credibility, making it easier for the client to trust the treatment plan and the nutrition therapist.

THE FIRST APPOINTMENT

The Assessment

Performing a comprehensive nutrition and eating disorder assessment consists of taking medical, eating disorder, weight, and diet histories, as well as obtaining current medical, physiological, and nutritional data *(Box 15.1)*. When anorexia is the diagnosis, it is important to obtain an accurate height, as clients frequently underreport height to lower the target weight range. The first weight for anxious clients is usually best measured in the second appointment, when trust and rapport have begun to be established. A client with anorexia can be weighed at the end of the first appointment if she appears relaxed and is completely willing. Any client weighing less than 75 percent of ideal body weight (IBW) should be immediately referred to an inpatient treatment program for eating disorders, as her weight is too low for outpatient treatment. Individuals with binge eating disorder do not need to be weighed unless they insist, at which point they can be weighed backwards and should not be told their weight. A weight history is also important, as explained in Box 15.1.

The client should be asked to write down or bring in all medicines he is taking (prescription and over-the-counter), including any products from health food or vitamin stores. Quite often clients use herbal products that act as stimulants, diuretics, or laxatives; it is important to have the client agree to stop using these

**Box 15.1
Eating Disorders
Assessment Format**

Subjective and Objective Data: Age, height (measure client if anorexic), weight (actual or per client), IBW (Robinson formula (1)), low weight (number and date), high weight (number and date), usual weight (5–pound range), target weight (per client)

Medications: Antidepressants, antianxiety medications, hormones, "prn" medications, vitamins, minerals, herbs or nutritional supplements, anything mail order or from health food store

Medical History: Chronic medical conditions, frequent MD visits, past hospitalizations or surgical procedures, pregnancies, allergies; family medical history

Physical Symptoms: Hair loss, dry skin, dry hair, dizziness, fatigue, fainting, headaches, hypoglycemic symptoms, sleep disturbance, esophageal reflux, stomach aches, constipation, diarrhea, abdominal bloating or distention, cold intolerance, cyanotic fingers or toes, amenorrhea or oligomenorrhea, joint pain, shortness of breath, hypercholesterolemia, hypertension, hyperglycemia, anemia, abnormal laboratory data (eg, hypothyroid, leukopenia, thrombocytopenia)

Exercise: Current activity level, current exercise level, history of athletics, history of compulsive exercise, attitude towards exercise

Eating Disorder and Weight History: Weight in elementary school, perception of body at that time. Weight at puberty and beginning of high school, eating habits at that time. Eating habits of family and attitudes towards client's weight and eating (was client's food controlled?) Weight and dieting habits of parents and siblings. Ethnic background. Weight of extended family members. Age at which abnormal eating patterns or body hatred developed. Food intake patterns at that time. Weight range in high school. Purging behavior, commercial diets, diuretics, cigarettes, illegal drugs, compulsive exercise? Weight history until present. Current and past binge eating behavior, restricting, or purging behavior. Current nutritional and weight goals.

Diet History: Typical 24-hour intake, including fluids and timing of meals and snacks. "Good day" and "bad day" with food. Binge and purge food. Binge and purge triggers. Use of caffeine, gum, candy, fluids, or cigarettes to suppress appetite. Safe foods. Food allergies.

products. It is also important to be aware of the side effects of the medicines eating disorder clients frequently take, as the symptoms they produce may be blamed for the client's food plan or weight gain. For example, Prozac (Eli Lilly, Indianapolis), Luvox (Solvay, Marietta, Ga), or Zoloft (Pfizer, New York) can cause drowsiness during the day, and the client may attribute this side effect to the fact that he is eating more food or gaining weight.

Obtaining a comprehensive medical history as well as current physical symptoms helps to determine the effects the eating disorder has had on the body's ability to function and the level of compromise that exists. Obtaining laboratory data most sensitive to malnutrition in young people is essential. A complete blood count and chemistry profile frequently show completely normal lab results, as the young person's body is resilient and can compensate for prolonged malnutrition. The most sensitive tests include a C-3 complement level (a factor in the immune cascade) to measure protein status and serum ferritin, transferrin, and iron levels to accurately assess current iron status and the storage of iron in the body. The more traditional tests to measure protein and iron status (albumin, hemoglobin, and hematocrit) are usually normal in eating disordered clients and can be misleading about the degree of malnutrition present. Seeing normal nonsensitive laboratory data also serves to reinforce the client in her denial about her eating disorder. More sensitive laboratory tests can help to prove that harm is being done. Taking an inventory of likely physical symptoms of the eating disorder also helps demonstrate the daily consequences for the client's body and overall well-being.

Level of Exercise

Another important medical issue to be assessed is exercise. Most eating-disordered clients have disordered exercise patterns. It is important to assess daily activity level, as well as the frequency of aerobic and isometric exercise (eg, sit-ups, jumping jacks, and crunches). In addition, an evaluation of common household tasks and daily activities can reveal behaviors which the client may not categorize as exercise, but which contribute significantly to her metabolic rate.

Hyperkinesis (moving almost constantly) is a common phenomenon in anorexia, and may be a consequence of the desire to expend unwanted calories, as well as of starvation (2). Whatever the cause, it can require some clients with anorexia to consume 3,000 calories a day or more to consistently gain weight. Bed rest may be required for hyperkinetic individuals to gain weight in an outpatient setting. Time spent in aerobic exercise needs to be balanced against daily caloric intake. If a client is exercising compulsively (more than 1 hour a day), the nutrition therapist should negotiate the amount of exercise allowed based on the calorie level the client is willing to consume. It is unrealistic to expect a client to stop exercising entirely unless this is a medical necessity. Total inactivity can increase anxiety and unwillingness to eat out of fear of weight gain. A moderate amount of isometric exercises (eg, sit-ups, leg-lifts, or light weightlifting) may be successfully substituted for time previously spent on aerobic exercise.

With teenagers and college students, physical education classes and team sports are important to address. If the client's weight is less than 80 percent of IBW, the physician may require her to be excused from physical education and team sports until she reaches a minimum of 80 percent of IBW. Participation in team sports can be an effective incentive to gain and maintain a healthy weight.

History of the Eating Disorder

A significant amount of time should be spent obtaining the history of the eating disorder. Weight and body perception in elementary school are important to discuss. Many clients report starting to diet or compulsively eat around puberty. It is important to explore the events that led up to the dieting or compulsive eating. Quite often clients reveal their parents had taken them to a physican because of their weight or put them on a diet for weight loss. It is essential to determine the degree to which the parents controlled the client's food. Was she denied seconds at meals, desserts, or snacks? Was food kept away from her but given to her thinner siblings? When and why did she begin to sneak, steal, or hide food?

A person who had his food controlled as a child is likely to have an emotional relationship with food as an adult. Keep in mind that this may be an embarrassing subject for the client, so probe cautiously and with empathy. Determining the weights, dieting behaviors, and food attitudes of the parents and siblings is essential. It is quite common for one or both parents to be compulsive about food, dieting, or exercise (3). Many mothers of those with eating disorders are chronic dieters or suffer from binge eating disorder themselves.

Ethnic background should be determined, as people with different backgrounds are likely to have different body types and therefore different healthy weight ranges than traditional formulas will account for (4,5). This factor will be important when determining the client's target weight range, as will the weights of extended family members (does there appear to be a tendency toward obesity in the family?).

The next area to be explored is the initial eating disorder behaviors and the age at which body dissatisfaction or hatred developed. A history of eating disorder behaviors (ie, restricting, bingeing, vomiting, use of laxatives, diuretics, diet pills, alcohol, illegal drugs, or cigarettes, and compulsive exercise) until the present time, as well as a weight history to date, provides important information. Current goals regarding weight and eating behaviors, followed by a description of a typical day of eating, also help to determine what interventions will eventually need to be implemented. A detailed diet history, including fear foods, safe foods, binge foods, and purge foods, is important, as are binge and purge triggers (ie, particular foods or emotions). Most eating disordered clients binge on foods that are high in starch, sugar, or fat; this may indicate abnormally low levels of serotonin in the brain. The use of appetite-suppressing agents (eg, caffeine, gum, candy, cigarettes, and sodas) is also important to know about and eventually to discourage.

If the client appears overwhelmed when asked to describe a typical day with food, she can be asked what she ate today and yesterday, or what she eats on a "good" or "bad" day with food. Most clients consider a "good" day with food to be one in which they consumed less than 1,200 calories, and a "bad" day to involve loss of control over their eating (which may or may not be true overeating). The nutrition therapist must appear nonjudgmental and empathetic when inquiring about bingeing or overeating, as most clients will feel shame when describing these episodes. It is important to quantify the foods and calories consumed during a "binge" and avoided during "restricting," as these definitions vary from individual to individual.

ESTABLISHING THE FOOD AND TREATMENT PLANS

Information obtained during the eating disorder and nutrition assessment is used during the formulation of the food and treatment plans. In establishing the initial caloric level, the average daily caloric intake at the time of evaluation is an important consideration. Most individuals with anorexia consume anywhere from 500 calories to 1000 calories a day before treatment. If the nutrition therapist were to design an initial plan of 2200 calories, the client would probably never return for follow-up, as the thought of doubling or tripling her caloric intake would be terrifying and completely unachievable in her mind. Setting the caloric goals too high can promote a feeling of failure and result in the client's ending nutrition therapy.

When determining the initial calorie level for someone with anorexia, the nutrition therapist should explain that consuming less than 1,200 calories is likely to not maintain basal metabolic rate. Every client should receive a detailed explanation of his or her metabolic needs, starting with the calculation for basal metabolic rate and finishing with the total energy expenditure at various activity levels appropriate to the individual's lifestyle. The client should then pick a calorie level that is a comfortable starting point.

Allowing the client with anorexia to choose her own initial calorie level can greatly enhance compliance with the food plan. It also allows her to take a healthy first step with her nutrition. If she chooses less than 1,200 calories a day, she should be reminded about the physical consequences of eating less than 1,200 calories. Using the physical symptoms she has reported during the assessment phase of our session helps to reinforce the personal application of these concepts. Most clients can be gently persuaded to try 1,200 calories, with the agreement that it is just a starting point and that any calorie level achieved is acceptable.

For nutrient distribution, a 60 percent carbohydrate, 20 percent protein, and 20 percent fat plan, using the *Exchange Lists for Meal Planning* (6) to provide structure and portion guidelines, seems to work for most clients. However, about half of clients with anorexia are not emotionally capable of initially consuming 20 percent fat in an outpatient setting, and the nutrition therapist may have to settle for 10–15 percent fat as an initial goal (*Box 15.2*). The nutrition therapist should not initially focus on variety of food choices, but rather tell clients that they can consume the same foods every day if this allows them to meet their calorie and protein goals.

1,200 Calories (64% Carbohydrate, 22% Protein, 14% Fat)		
Breakfast	Lunch	Dinner
1 bread	2 bread	2 bread
½ 1% milk	2 very lean protein	2 very lean protein
1 fruit	1 fruit	1 1% milk
	1 vegetable	1 vegetable
Snack	Snack	Snack
1 bread	1½ juice	1 bread

**Box 15.2
Sample Initial Food Plan for Client with Anorexia Nervosa**

Flexibility is important when establishing the initial treatment plan. Each client is an individual with his or her own emotional capabilities. To provide successful outpatient nutrition therapy, the nutrition therapist must work at an emotional pace reflective of these capabilities. In severe cases, when a client is consuming only one or two foods a day, using the *Exchange Lists* may be postponed until he or she has developed a tolerance for making more food choices. Some clients feel so overwhelmed with making choices that they may benefit from a specific daily menu provided by the nutrition therapist during the first few weeks of treatment.

With bulimia, the initial calorie goal can often be higher than for anorexia. The caloric need for the client's goal weight can be calculated and presented with the same discussion about the importance of adequate intake to maintain metabolism and basic physiologic function. It is important to explain that purging does not eliminate all calories consumed, and that an average of 1,000 calories per 3,000-calorie binge is absorbed into the body (7). This information can be used to demonstrate that if the client follows her food plan, she will be consuming fewer calories in a day than if she was bingeing and purging. With bulimia, clients can also initially choose their own calorie level. However, clients should be warned about the importance of adequate calorie, carbohydrate, and fat intake to prevent binge urges and carbohydrate cravings resulting from dietary restriction.

With an explanation of the important influence of diet on serotonin levels, most clients are willing to try to consume 1,600 to 2,200 calories a day. Walter Kaye's formula (26 calories per kilogram of target weight for a sedentary client, and 30 calories per kilogram of target weight for a client who exercises three days a week or more) appears to be appropriate for calculating caloric need (8). For example, a target weight of 63.64 kg (140 pounds) for a sedentary client would require an initial goal of 1,650 calories, but if the client is physically active, 1,900 calories (30 kcal/kg) would be more appropriate.

Appropriate nutrient distribution is even more critical with bulimia because of the influence of nutrients on brain chemistry (9). An initial distribution of 60 percent carbohydrate, 20 percent protein, and 20 percent fat, using the *Exchange Lists for Meal Planning (Box 15.3)*, is a reasonable goal. Because this amount of fat can seem extreme to the individual who has been avoiding fat, it is important to stress the role of adequate fat in appetite control, satiety, and decreased bingeing. Starting the day with a hearty breakfast is also important for decreasing the likelihood of bingeing later in the day and preventing the metabolic slowdown that accompanies restrictive eating. An afternoon snack of complex carbohydrate and fat can help prevent late afternoon or early evening bingeing, as will having fat at breakfast and lunch.

Some bulimia clients may need help identifying starches and items on the bread exchange list that are nontrigger foods for them. In extreme cases, when a client says, "I binge on everything," only a few starch choices may initially be tolerated. Quite often starchy vegetables are safer than bread products, cereal, or

**Box 15.3
Sample Food Plan
for Client with
Bulimia Nervosa**

1,900 Calories (60% Carbohydrate, 20% Protein, 20% Fat)

Breakfast	Lunch	Dinner
3 bread	2 bread	3 bread
1 fat	2 lean protein	3 lean protein
2 fruit	1 fat	1 fat
	1 vegetable	2 vegetable
	2 fruit	

Snack	Snack	Snack
2 bread	2 bread	Approximately 220 calories
1 fat	1 fat	(equivalent to 2 bread
		exchanges, 3 grams fat, and
		1 ounce lean protein), eg,
		low-fat muffin or low-fat
		yogurt.

NOTE: Very lean protein contains 1 gram fat per exchange.

pastas, and may need to be consumed at each meal until the client feels less triggered by other starches. Again, flexibility and individualization are important.

Structured food plans do not seem to work as well with binge eating disorder. Most clients with this diagnosis had their food controlled or restricted as children, and a structured food plan is seen as another diet or punishment. The nutrition therapist is likely to be seen as another person controlling food. Care to avoid a stance that is too authoritative should be taken; otherwise, the client will rebel against or become angry at the nutrition therapist, and terminate treatment. These clients should be advised when they call for an appointment that dieting is not the goal of the nutrition therapist. Instead, work focuses on normalizing food behaviors and eating in a nonemotional manner. This process can take takes at least one year to achieve, and during this time the client will gradually move toward a weight that is supported with a healthy amount of food.

In setting nutrition goals, two or three areas of work are addressed in each appointment. For example, many clients have learned to skip breakfast, so one initial goal might be to have breakfast by 10 AM three days a week. A second goal might be to have lunch by 1 PM instead of 3 PM during the week. Many chronic dieters delay eating until the late afternoon, and then begin graze eating, followed by bingeing at night. Teaching the client to feed his body throughout the day when he is hungry is essential.

An important tool to use when working with binge eating disorder is a food, hunger, and emotions record. The client records the time of each food eaten, as well as her perceived hunger and fullness before and after each episode of eating. She is also asked to record any emotions she experiences during each episode (see *Box 15.4*). Because many clients feel embarrassment or shame when recording

**Box 15.4
Sample Food, Hunger,
and Emotions Record**

Time	Foods Eaten	Hunger Level*	Emotions
7:30 AM	Bowl of cereal 1 piece fruit	3	OK
1:00 PM	Hamburger Large fries Diet soda	8	Anxious to eat, very hungry
4:00 PM	2 brownies	2	Stressed at work
7:30 PM	3 soft chicken tacos	2	Happy to be home, ate too much
10:00 PM	Large bowl of ice cream	2	Bored

*Using a scale of 1–10, with 10 being maximum.

their foods, it should be stressed that whatever they write is acceptable. The purpose is not to judge, but to collect scientific data. The keeping of the food record, not what is eaten, is the initial measure of success. It is important to educate clients that the biggest predictor of success with losing weight and sustaining weight loss is self-monitoring, which translates into keeping food records. It may take some clients weeks or months before they feel safe enough to write down their foods; during this time patience, nurturing, and nonjudgmental language are crucial. Once the client begins keeping regular records, the nutrition therapist can then begin to analyze her eating and binge cycles, as well as her relationship with food. Exercises that promote normalization of hunger and satiety cues and responses (also called "hunger work") can take place at this time (10), and eventually the client can begin to normalize her relationship with food.

Exercise is an equally important component of the therapy process, but if there is a history of self-punishment with exercise or an association between exercise and dieting or starvation, clients may resist a nurturing activity program. Waiting to work on exercise until after the client has had some success with nonemotional eating tends to make the client more open to trying what the nutrition therapist suggests. Consequently, exercise discussions can be delayed for several months, unless the client wishes to begin sooner. Again, it is important to assess where each client is at emotionally before determining what goals to set at each session.

Once the client is willing to try exercise, it is important to start slowly. Possible activities include walking, house cleaning, gardening, playing ball with a child, or walking a dog. Referring clients to a local health club or gym is usually counterproductive. An outdoor activity with a partner might be a more acceptable option. Working with a personal trainer familiar with the proper treatment of eating disorders can be a good choice for some clients.

Once the food plan or nutrition program has been established, a personalized, written goal sheet outlining the remainder of the treatment plan can be provided. All clients should be asked to do their best to keep some type of food record, which can be individualized based on diagnosis (ie, with anorexia, keep a food record; with binge eating disorder and bulimia, keep a food, hunger, and emotions record). Because anorexia tends to include obsessions about record keeping, clients with this diagnosis should limit their records to the food eaten and the time it is consumed. If bingeing or purging is present with anorexia, it is also important to record feelings before each binge or purge episode. Obsessive counting of calories or fat grams can be reframed as a positive behavior by keeping track of calories, protein, or fat, with the objective of meeting the established goal for each nutrient. Of course, the eventual goal is to consume adequate nutrition without obsessive counting, but this may take a long time to achieve, particularly in clients with concomitant obsessive compulsive disorder.

CREATING A GOAL SHEET

A useful second goal to set with anorexia and bulimia clients is the completion of Reiff and Reiff's "Beliefs About Food, Hunger, and Weight" questionnaire (11, p 151). The client's responses can be reviewed in a subsequent appointment, providing another opportunity for education about physiology, metabolism, and proper nutrition. Clients with binge eating disorder may benefit from reading Tribole and Resch's *Intuitive Eating* (12). This book is useful on all three eating disorders, but if other assignments are given, including it as an initial goal may overwhelm the client. Depending on the client's attitude toward reading, it might also be useful to give her a reading list of self-help books. All clients should be given a folder containing nutrition and physiology handouts pertinent to their diagnosis, along with the request that they read all the materials provided.

A third goal involves vitamin and mineral supplementation. A multivitamin with extra iron and calcium is recommended for individuals with anorexia and bulimia. A client who has trouble swallowing pills or complains of gastrointestinal upset from vitamins might better tolerate the chewable multivitamin and mineral formulas available over the counter. An additional 500–800 mg/day of calcium should be recommended if the client does not consume dairy products. The goal is for the client to consume a total of 1,200 mg/day of calcium. For clients with binge eating disorder, the RDA for calcium intake is the goal and supplemental calcium is recommended only as needed. Similarly, supplemental iron in conjunction with a stool softener is recommended if the client has iron deficiency anemia. It is especially important to monitor iron status (through laboratory data) and the potential need for iron supplementation in clients who are lactovegetarian or vegan. Postmenopausal women should be assessed for the need to take supplemental iron, as it may be atherogenic (13).

A fourth goal with anorexia and bulimia clients involves decreasing compulsive exercise. Exercise should be negotiated based on what the client is willing to try to consume in calories. Time spent should be decreased initially by 50 percent, with an eventual goal of 30 minutes to 1 hour maximum a day. The goals for aerobic and anaerobic activity can be written on the client's goal sheet so that she has it in writing. Most clients like having a goal sheet to follow, and many will pin the sheet up in a place where they can review it each morning.

MAKING MULTI-DISCIPLINARY REFERRALS

When providing outpatient nutrition therapy for eating disorders, the nutrition therapist must work as part of a multidisciplinary team of professionals. The first referral to be made for a client with anorexia or bulimia should be to a physician (family practice or internal medicine) specializing in eating disorders. It is well worth the time to locate such a professional in the community. Most physicians do not have special training in eating disorders, and therefore do not provide comprehensive medical evaluations sensitive to the idiosyncrasies of this population. One way to locate a well-trained physician is to network with other eating disorder professionals.

If a medical specialist is not available in the community, the nutrition therapist should request that the client have an EKG, a complete blood count and chemistry profile, and a serum ferritin, transferrin, iron, and C-3 complement level done by the client's physician. It may be necessary for the nutrition therapist to educate the physician about indicators of malnutrition in eating disordered clients. A sample report that can communicate essential information is provided in *Figure 15.1.*

The second referral, if necessary, should be to a licensed mental health professional trained in eating disorder therapy. A psychotherapist experienced in treating eating disorders with cognitive behavioral therapy is most desirable, as this type of therapy has been found to be the most effective with this population (14). The third referral, as appropriate, may be to a support group for eating disorders, such as ANAD (Anorexia Nervosa and Associated Disorders) on the West Coast, AABA (American Anorexia and Bulimia Association) on the East Coast, or ABA (Anorexics and Bulimics Anonymous) or OA (Overeaters Anonymous). The use of the 12-step model for the treatment of eating disorders is controversial, but can be helpful for some clients. As clients progress in psychotherapy and nutrition therapy, they naturally gravitate away from the 12-step programs. The exception to this rule is those with a dual diagnosis with alcohol or drug addiction. Clients whose anorexia is purely restrictive should not be referred to OA, as the focus of OA is on overeating, which can be counterproductive.

PROVIDING FAMILY COUNSELING

The families of clients are also in need of education and support during the treatment process. Adolescent clients should be seen alone for the first portion of the initial session; then the parent or parents can be invited to join the session. The client should be told ahead of time what will be discussed with the parent, and should be asked if there are any issues that she would like to be addressed. The

EATING DISORDER EVALUATION

Name: _____ Date: _____ Referred by:_____

Physician:_____ Psychotherapist:_____

Age: _____ Ht: _____ Wt (per pt): _____ IBW: _____

Low wt: _____ High wt: _____ Target wt: _____ Usual wt: _____

Medications:
_____
_____

Medical history:
_____
_____

Physical symptoms:
_____
_____
_____

Exercise:
_____
_____

ED/Wt history:
_____
_____

Diet history:
_____
_____

Safe foods: Binge foods:
_____   _____
_____   _____

Binge triggers: Purge triggers:
_____   _____
_____   _____

ASSESSMENT AND PLAN
_____
_____
_____
_____

SIGNED: _____

Figure 15.1
Sample Report Format

parent needs to be asked to disengage from the child's eating completely. It can be acknowledged that this will be difficult, but it should be stressed that the more the parent(s) disengage, the faster the child will get better. It can help to explain that the child has agreed to work with a professional on improving her nutrition, so the parents will no longer have to assume this stressful responsibility. The majority of parents feel relieved to have this burden lifted, and try to follow the treatment guidelines to the best of their ability.

Specific guidelines regarding food shopping and mealtimes need to be established. The client can be responsible for letting her parent know what she needs from the market each week, or she can be asked to accompany the parent to the market to make her own selections. If a strong power struggle is occurring in the family (common when anorexia is the diagnosis), the parent may be asked to give the client a food allowance each week and allow the child to do her own shopping, with the responsibility of giving the parent the grocery receipts. In the case of clients who are bingeing, it is probably better to have a family member do the shopping.

The client should decide who prepares his food. Most clients want to control their own food and meal preparations, but less resistant clients may be willing to eat their parents' cooking at dinner time. If a child is willing to eat the parent's cooking, the parent should be completely honest about what the food contains and should not attempt to sneak fat into the food. Similarly, the client should decide with the nutrition therapist when and where he can best consume his meals. If the parents want the child at the dinner table, it can usually be negotiated that the child will eventually eat with them but is not required to do so until he feels comfortable.

Most parents expect periodic feedback about how their child is progressing. Parents should be told that, to build trust with their child, the nutrition therapist cannot converse with the parents without her permission. If the nutrition therapist does speak to the parents, the client should know what was said. The only time there should be an exception to this rule is when the client admits to suicidal or homicidal intent.

Sometimes it is necessary to remind parents about the guidelines that were set up in the first appointment, as the nutrition therapist is always the client's advocate in the family system. In general, parents can be reminded that no news is good news, and that they will contacted only if the child is not progressing as expected. However, in the case of an anxious parent, it may be in the client's best interest to obtain her permission to speak to the parents to provide reassurance on a regular basis. Most parents respect boundaries if their fears are allayed by health professionals. Developing a relationship of mutual respect with the parents is essential for a successful treatment outcome.

When working with a client who is married or has a significant other, at some point during the treatment process the partner may need to be included in counseling. Typically this involves giving the partner the opportunity to ask questions about eating disorders. These questions usually include a request for information about how to be supportive. Many clients have trouble communicating with their significant other about food issues and their needs because of their strong feelings of embarrassment and shame. It can help to have the client describe the needs and boundaries she would like respected, and then to present specific guidelines regarding food and weight issues to the couple.

Depending on the situation, the significant other and the client may come together on one or two occasions, normally after the client has been in treatment for a few months and a high level of trust has been established. Just as with an adolescent's family, the nutrition therapist serves as the client's advocate during the session. If a client appears to be in a highly dysfunctional or abusive relationship, their meeting together with the nutrition therapist is not recommended. Instead, they should be encouraged to meet with the psychotherapist.

The frequency of follow-up appointments should be individually determined, based on the client's progress, attitude, and financial limitations. Low-weight clients (<85 percent of IBW) should meet weekly until achieving 85 percent of IBW, and then biweekly after that. If a client is purging multiple times on a daily basis, weekly appointments are recommended until some abstinence from purging is achieved.

PROGRESSION OF NUTRITION THERAPY

It is important to negotiate two issues in the second appointment: weighing the client and determining an initial target weight. Only low-weight clients need to be weighed at every session. The client may need to be frequently reassured that the nutrition therapist is the team member responsible for weighing, and that part of his responsibility includes not allowing the client to get fat. The client should have the choice of whether to be weighed forward or backward and whether to be told her weight. Backward weighing should be encouraged, with information disclosed being limited to whether weight has gone up or down or stayed the same, without providing an exact number. Most clients eventually choose the freedom from obsessing about their weight, but it may take a while before they trust the nutrition therapist to monitor their weight for them. A client's weight can fluctuate 3 to 5 pounds between morning and evening; this needs to be taken into account when assessing weight progress if appointment times vary week to week. A premenstrual state can also promote water retention and weight gain, as will bingeing. It is difficult to obtain an accurate weight on someone who is bingeing and purging on a daily basis, as hydration shifts can cause regular fluctuations of up to 10 pounds.

All clients should be weighed without shoes and any extra clothing (eg, jacket or sweater) or heavy items (eg, keys or pagers) in pockets. With normal-weight clients, weighing more than once every 2 weeks should be discouraged. The client needs to be given as much control as possible over being weighed, as this is an extremely anxiety-producing event.

Initial Target Weight   Negotiating an initial target weight requires the nutrition therapist to be persuasive, reassuring, and patient. The subject should be at least broached in the second appointment, with the nutrition therapist providing her input. It may take the client several more sessions before she agrees with the nutrition therapist's assessment. With bulimia, the discussion should include the explanation that the client's present weight is a purging weight, not a true weight. Once she stops purging, short-term rehydration of up to 5 pounds is highly likely and normal. After a few days of abstinence, the client may begin retaining extra water weight, which is likely to diurese as recovery progresses.

Most clients initially retain 3 to 5 pounds of water, and up to 10 pounds if they have also been abusing laxatives. This extra water retention can last from 4 to 8 weeks, and seems to correlate with the length of time the person has been purging (the longer the duration of bulimia, the longer the period of water retention). Clients generally find this news very distressing, and many cry. The nutrition therapist can promote trust in the process by reassuring the client that the weight gain (except for the 5 pounds from rehydration) is temporary and a survival mechanism for the body.

A technique to help the client through this initial stage is to ask if he is willing to gain 10 pounds in exchange for abstaining from disordered behaviors. When put in this context, most clients agree to try to tolerate the weight gain, especially if the nutrition therapist reassures them that she will not allow the weight gain to get out of control. Most individuals with bulimia keep their weight artificially low by purging and have no idea what their natural weight really is. An important function of the nutrition therapist is to help the client establish his natural, non-restricted weight range. Many clients will not accept this weight range initially, but the client's nutritional goals should be determined using these data. If the client is unwilling to accept his natural set-point weight, the nutrition therapist should seek the help of the psychotherapist in confronting the client's resistance. Continuous education about the importance of accepting the nonrestricted weight is crucial for the client's success at abstaining from bulimia.

Clients with binge eating disorder or obesity also need education about their natural weight. Most clients with these disorders are more open to the concept of nonrestricted weight, but many also suffer from body image distortion. Many individuals who have lost significant amounts of weight continue to see themselves as fat, even if they are nearing a healthy weight. In particular, adults who were overweight as children continue to see themselves as fat no matter what their weight, while individuals who developed their weight problem later in life seem to have a more realistic perception of their body image. Women who had anorexia as teens and then developed compulsive eating as adults also seem to have body image distortion no matter what their current weight. The nutrition therapist can help overweight clients set realistic weight goals for themselves, as well as reinforce that losing as little as 10 percent of body weight can have significant health benefits. Most clients with anorexia are willing to consider returning to their pre-illness weight, as long as that was a normal weight. Approximately 50 percent of anorexic individuals are overweight at the onset of their eating disorder. An exercise that discusses set-point weight helps to address body image issues.

The rate of weight gain also needs to be negotiated with the client. An *average* weight gain of 1 to 2 pounds a week is reasonable, with the explanation that the body will gain weight in jumps (eg, the client may gain 2 pounds one week and nothing the next). If the client is not gaining each week, her activity level may need to be restricted. Some hyperkinetic clients may need bed rest for 1 to 2 weeks followed by a sedentary lifestyle before consistent weight gain occurs. Any client who is less than 80 percent of IBW should not participate in any physical education or sports. Those who are between 80 percent and 85 percent of IBW should have their activity level carefully monitored by the nutrition therapist, and should probably not exceed 30 minutes of aerobic exercise a day. All eating disordered clients should be cleared by a physician before beginning or continuing any exercise program. Continuing to participate in sports or an exercise program should always be contingent on maintaining an adequate weight and healthy eating patterns.

PROTOCOL FOR FOLLOW-UP APPOINTMENTS

During follow-up sessions, the client's food record should be analyzed for consumption of calories, protein, and fat. It can be educational to perform this analysis using a calculator while speaking to the client, who can also describe how her experiences with food and eating have been going. The nutrition therapist can also inquire about medications she should be taking, how she feels physically, how she feels about her therapy, and how things are going at home. It is important to get an overall picture of the client's functioning level at each session, as all of these issues will affect her eating.

The client should also be asked during each follow-up appointment about any episodes of bingeing or purging. She may be too embarrassed to volunteer this information, so gentle encouragement may be needed. For clients with a history of alcohol or drug use, it is important to also inquire about current use, as it is not uncommon for clients to relapse with alcohol or drugs when they are working with food issues. If the client is in the process of gaining weight, she should be asked at each appointment about her feelings about her body. It is important to work on body image issues and to confront distortions each time they are raised.

During the session, it may become apparent that a family or work problem is making it more difficult for the client to follow her food or nutrition program. When this occurs, the client should be encouraged to raise the issue with her psychotherapist. The nutrition therapist should also contact the psychotherapist with the information (after obtaining a signed release of information from the client). The nutrition therapist must be in close communication with the psychotherapist as non-food-related issues arise so they can be referred to the psychotherapist.

For example, a client with compulsive eating may report that her husband is being critical of her eating or weight, and that she binges after they have a confrontation. The psychotherapist needs to know this so he can address it with the client. The nutrition therapist should expect the same type of feedback from the psychotherapist, with the psychotherapist referring food- and weight-related issues to the nutrition therapist as they arise.

After the food record has been analyzed, the average intake for each nutrient can be determined and feedback provided on how the client did in meeting his goals. Most clients do better with general feedback, or framing the range of calories consumed. If under- or overeating is occurring consistently, the food record can be used to determine the problem areas and new goals can be set with the client that incorporate a solution. With bulimia, the frequency of bingeing and purging episodes and the triggers for each occurrence need to be addressed. It is important to help the client determine his physical binge or purge triggers (ie, getting too hungry, keeping trigger foods in the house), and then to problem solve and set new goals incorporating the possible solution. The frequency and duration of exercise should also be addressed, and any difficulties the client may be having should be processed. New exercise goals should be set as needed.

Education about physiology, metabolism, and nutrition should be provided in each session, as eating disordered individuals frequently have knowledge in these areas but their cognitive distortions and delusions prevent them from applying this information to themselves. It is the job of the nutrition therapist to process such distortions with each client, explaining why a particular scientific fact *does* apply to her. Many clients believe that what the nutrition therapist says is true, but also believe that their bodies are different from others and thus the information does not apply to them. The nutrition therapist should look for opportunities to show the client that her body responded as predicted to help correct this dysfunctional belief system.

PROGRESSION OF CALORIES FOR CLIENTS WITH ANOREXIA

Most anorexia clients will need to consume 50 kcal/kg body weight before they will consistently gain weight. Once the client can consume her initial goal of 1,200 calories, weekly calorie increases of 200–300 calories should be prescribed until the client reaches her target weight. Clients who are hyperkinetic or very anxious may need to consume as high as 80–90 kcal/kg body weight before reaching their goal weight (2).

If the client is having trouble with protein intake, a powdered supplement added to milk can be used. If the client dislikes milk or is legitimately vegan, a soy-based protein supplement (available at health food stores) may be used. The importance of consuming an adequate protein intake should be stressed to the client, with the nutrition therapist providing education about the numerous functions of protein in the body. Clients who are vegan should be instructed to obtain soy-based protein sources from a local health food store. When working with this population, the nutrition therapist must be well informed about available vegan protein sources. Once protein needs can be consistently met, the variety of protein choices should be increased at a pace that is emotionally comfortable for the client.

When the client complains of excessive fullness, he should be encouraged to report these symptoms to his physician, who might consider prescribing cisapride. Delayed gastric emptying is usually seen with anorexia and results in a persistent fullness that makes it difficult to adhere to meal plans. Cisapride normalizes gastric emptying by increasing gastric motility, serving to decrease excessive fullness as well as help with constipation. Many clients express fear that cisapride will make them excessively hungry and lead to excessive weight gain; it is essential to reassure the client that this will not happen. The nutrition therapist should explain that cisapride does not cause excessive hunger, but rather helps to normalize hunger and gastrointestinal function. Similarly, constipation is a frequent complaint of these clients, and may be addressed using a psyllium-containing fiber supplement.

Once the client reaches 85 percent of ideal body weight, she should be encouraged to take more risks with food, especially fat. At this time she can be encouraged to gradually increase the fat in her diet to 20 percent of calories, using foods she is comfortable with to meet this goal. Many clients insist on avoiding animal fats because of their association with coronary artery disease. Sources of fat that are usually well tolerated include nuts, peanut butter, vegetable oil, and, to a lesser extent, low-fat salad dressings and cream cheese. Another option is to encourage the client to begin using all low-fat dairy products, including milk, cottage cheese, and yogurt. Some clients tolerate reduced-fat cheeses, but most are deathly afraid of cheese unless it is fat-free. Another way to increase fat intake is to encourage the client to begin choosing combination foods.

TOPICS TO BE COVERED DURING TREATMENT

Once a client's weight is approaching her set-point and her nutritional goals are being met on a consistent basis, it is time to begin to address more complex food and weight issues. Clients should be asked to list their fear or risk foods. These are any foods that the client enjoyed before the eating disorder but is now afraid to eat. Most clients with anorexia have a long list of fear foods that are high in fat and sugar, as well as beef, processed meats, pork, veal, and chicken.

Restaurant foods are also risky, as clients do not know what the foods contain and fear the fat content. Clients could be asked to choose one or two risk foods to try between each appointment. It is important to reassure them that eating one food item, regardless of the caloric or fat content, will not cause weight gain. Many clients find eating risk foods easier if they go to a restaurant with a friend who eats normally. Eating risk foods in a restaurant setting is attractive for these clients, as they fear losing control over their eating if left home alone with a large quantity of risk food.

Ideally, the nutrition therapist should accompany the client on at least one restaurant outing as a nutrition therapy session, so that eating behaviors and food rituals can be observed and then processed in future sessions. Another option is to have a meal in the nutrition therapist's office, which is less time consuming and still affords the opportunity of direct observation. Most anorexia clients have distinct food rituals; these merit specific feedback regarding normalizing eating and gradually decreasing these rituals.

Anorexia with concomitant obsessive compulsive disorder will likely include rituals involving counting, sorting or organizing food, or eating in a peculiar manner. In these cases, the nutrition therapist should communicate with the psychotherapist to determine who will address these food rituals, as the psychotherapist may prefer to do so. Individuals with bulimia frequently use excessive amounts of condiments on their food (eg, salsa, ketchup, or mustard) or eat strange combinations of foods; they should also be counseled to gradually normalize these behaviors.

Other topics that should be covered include social eating (ie, eating with others, at restaurants or parties), surviving the holidays, dealing with periods of increased stress, and body image. Most eating disordered individuals fear losing control with food in a social setting, and for this reason social events are completely avoided. For teenagers or young adults, the fear of social eating serves to isolate them from their peers, and may contribute to delayed social development. When eating at home begins to feel comfortable, the nutrition therapist should assign the task of having a meal with a trusted friend or family member. Some individuals are willing to try a restaurant meal with a friend, while others may need the safety of home for a while longer. In either case, the fears should be processed in a session before the meal, and guidance should be offered as needed.

The next step should be experiencing a restaurant meal, preferably with the nutrition therapist or a trusted peer. Nutrition therapy is best continued until the client is comfortable eating all types of ethnic foods and in a variety of restaurant settings (including fast food). Eating in a party atmosphere, including weddings, brunches, and buffets, should also be undertaken when the client feels ready and has had prior successes with social eating. The nutrition therapist will need to help the client relearn what normal eating is like in these environments, emphasizing that normal eating allows the client to eat any food without guilt or fear of weight gain.

Periods of Increased Stress

Between the middle of October and the middle of January, clients tend to exhibit increased anxiety, depression, and food preoccupation related to the holidays and possibly seasonal affective disorder. Halloween marks the beginning of a 3–month struggle involving holiday parties, a constant barrage of holiday food, and family gatherings that combine food and emotional issues. One client said every holiday season she felt that for 3 months she was a prisoner of food. This time of year is one of the busiest in eating disorder practices, as many clients request extra sessions to help them cope.

The nutrition therapist should help the client to plan a strategy for each holiday, including planning meals for the day and finding support to aid in maintaining recovery. The client will also need structure for dealing with holiday parties and get-togethers that are likely to involve binge or trigger foods in abundant supply. Many clients' behaviors are triggered by family issues, and they may need to be encouraged to have additional sessions with their psychotherapist or to attend additional support group meetings. Similarly, when clients are under increased stress for other reasons (eg, exams, relationship dysfunction, or school pressures), they need the same type of structure and support to help maintain recovery. Problem areas that need to be addressed include skipping meals or snacks, delaying meals leading to increased hunger and subsequent overeating or bingeing, and over- or underexercising. It is important to help the client identify when his recovery with food or exercise is slipping, and to help prevent relapse or further regression that could lead to relapse.

The most difficult treatment issue to work with is body image distortion. Most clients see their body accurately only at the very end of treatment or not at all. Many say that no matter what their weight, they still see themselves as too large or fat. Those who are successful at maintaining long-term recovery say they accept that they have body image distortion, and they choose to move on with their lives.

Clients with early diagnosis and treatment seem to have little to no distortion, and normal body perceptions can return over time. For these individuals, body image exercises using magazines or body tracings may prove useful. However, body image distortion seems to persist in clients with longer-term dysfunction, and they may need to accept they have a distortion to move on in recovery. Typically these clients do not respond well to body image exercises, and frequently even see normal-size women other than themselves as fat.

PROTOCOL FOR DISCHARGE AND INDICATORS OF RELAPSE

Most clients need nutrition therapy somewhere between 6 months and 2 years. For those with long-term (eg, more than 5 years) eating disorders or a concomitant diagnosis of multiple personality disorder, obsessive compulsive disorder, post-traumatic stress disorder, or other chronic conditions, nutrition therapy may last 3 to 5 years or longer. This type of client typically experiences stable eating cycles, followed by decompensation in general functioning, necessitating the return to nutrition therapy.

When asked about ending nutrition therapy, the nutrition therapist can share discharge criteria with the client *(Box 15.5)*. During the closing session, the client's progress should be reviewed and indicators of relapse discussed. Once again, these indicators are individualized based on the client's treatment course. The client can be asked what she believes her personal indicators to be, and the discussion can proceed from there. General warning flags include

- skipping meals,
- restricting calories, protein, or fat,

**Box 15.5
Sample Criteria for
Discharge from
Outpatient Treatment
(may be individualized)**

- A healthy weight range has been achieved.
- Any food can be eaten without feelings of worry or guilt.
- Clients with anorexia will be able to
    —maintain goal weight for approximately 2 months,
    —eat a variety of age-appropriate foods,
    —try all fear foods.
- Clients with bulimia will be able to
    —achieve a minimum of 3 months of abstinence,
    —maintain a healthy weight,
    —be able to eat all their fear foods.
- Clients with binge eating disorder will be able to
    —normalize their relationship with food (usually requires at least 1 year of nutrition therapy).

NOTE: Each client's criteria for discharge are individual, and should be consistent with the behavioral goals developed by the client's psychotherapist.

- avoiding social situations because of anxiety around eating,
- increasing weighing or focus on weight,
- gaining or losing more than 5 pounds in 1 week,
- avoiding fear foods,
- getting too hungry,
- eating frequently for emotional reasons, and
- going for long periods of time without eating.

Most clients are invested enough in recovery that they will call immediately if any of these behaviors begin to occur. At this time a "tune-up" session can be recommended, which involves an assessment of the client's current eating situation and a structured plan to get back on track. Other situations that may necessitate a "tune-up" include pregnancy, marriage, divorce, breakup of a significant relationship, starting a new job, death of a parent, or any other significant life stressor. Quite often the client's psychotherapist will refer her back to nutrition therapy at this time. It is important to affirm the client's asking for help to get back on track. Most clients will need only 1 or 2 months of nutrition therapy to get back on track, with intermittent follow-up as needed. Some individuals may need nutrition "tune-ups" throughout their life.

Another population that seems to be emerging for treatment is the children of women with eating disorders. Nutrition therapists who have worked in the field for several years eventually begin to see the children of former clients. In order to prevent abnormal eating disorder behaviors from being passed down, women with children should be counseled on how to appropriately feed and monitor their children's eating and weight. New mothers should be given printed information on infant feeding guidelines, and counseled as issues with their children's eating arise. Mothers can also benefit from reading Ellyn Satter's *Child of Mine: Feeding with Love and Good Sense* (15) and *How to Get Your Kid to Eat, But Not Too Much* (16).

One sign of recovery from an eating disorder is willingness to change. Most clients experience some fear and ambivalence about giving up their eating disorder, which is normal. These feelings should be processed periodically so they can be addressed on an ongoing basis. If a client stops gaining or losing weight or cannot refrain from bingeing or purging, the nutrition therapist and the client should examine where the resistance is coming from and assess the client's ability to change. For some individuals, having professional permission to stabilize their weight or behavior for a while will provide the impetus to continue moving forward in treatment. Allowing the client to feel more in control is a useful tool that should be used as needed throughout treatment.

DEALING WITH RESISTANCE OR LACK OF PROGRESS

For a client who is completely resistant or oppositional, or who remains firmly entrenched in denial, other treatment options need to be considered. If weight loss progresses to less than 75 percent of ideal body weight (IBW) or other destabilizing factors develop, the client should be referred for inpatient hospitalization. When weight drops below 80 percent of IBW, medical instability can develop and the client should not be allowed to do any aerobic exercise or sports. When working with a client with anorexia who drops below 80 percent of IBW, a contract for weight gain should be considered. The nutrition therapist should confer with the client's psychotherapist and physician to formulate the guidelines of the weight gain contract. A reasonable expectation for weight gain for an outpatient is 1 to 2 pounds a week. The client's medical status and the recommendations of the psychotherapist and physician should be considered when setting the weekly weight goal. It is also important to confer with the client's family, answer any questions they may have, and obtain their support for the new treatment plan. If the family is resistant or in denial about the severity of the problem, it may be necessary to have a family meeting with the psychotherapist present to confront the family.

Consequences of not meeting the weekly weight goal need to be established, and should consist of restriction of activities or events the client perceives as desirable. Examples of such activities include continuing to work at a part-time job, engaging in extracurricular activities such as drama or music, and, in severe cases, participation in school. The nutrition therapist should prepare a weight gain graph, drawn in such a way that the client is responsible for an average gain of 1 to 2 pounds a week until she reaches 80 percent of IBW. It is important for the graph to be drawn in this manner, as the client will naturally lose or gain weight in uneven increments. For example, she might gain 1.5 pounds one week and only 0.5 pounds the next week, meeting the goal of averaging a gain of 1 pound a week. If the client does not meet her weight goal, the agreed-upon activities need to be restricted until she resumes meeting her goal. In most cases, the client should be informed that if she drops to less than 75 percent of IBW, she will need to be hospitalized for her own safety.

It is very important for the nutrition therapist not to be seen as threatening or controlling during this situation. Clients can be told that if they are unable to ensure their own health and well-being, the treatment team will take over this function for them until they are able to resume doing so. Most clients respond well to care and nurturing in this situation, as long as frequent reassurance is provided that they will not become fat or overweight. For clients with concomitant borderline personality disorder or oppositional defiant disorder, it is probably better not to give them a weight ultimatum for hospitalization, as they may intentionally lose weight to provoke the treatment team. In these cases it is better to determine the hospitalization weight with the other team members and to give the client general medical guidelines for hospitalization, rather than specific weight criteria.

Treatment Boosters   When working with bulimia clients who are not progressing, evaluating their need for medication and increasing their support system are two treatment boosters that can be used. The psychotherapist of a client who continues to binge and purge after 2 to 3 months of nutrition therapy should be consulted regarding the need for medication and a referral to a qualified psychiatrist. Very few bulimia clients can abstain without the assistance of a selective serotonin reuptake inhibitor (SSRI). Examples of medicines in this category frequently used to treat bingeing and purging include Prozac, Zoloft, Luvox, Paxil (Smith Kline Beecham, Philadelphia), and Serzone (Bristol-Myers Squibb). If the bulimia client is already on medication, the nutrition therapist should contact the psychiatrist with her concerns and refer the client back to the psychiatrist for an increase in medication as appropriate. One category of clients who may not need medication are teenagers with early diagnosis (less than 6 months of eating disorder thoughts or behaviors) and the absence of depression.

The other area to address is the client's support system. Those having trouble should be encouraged to attend as many support group meetings as possible each week, including 12-step meetings if they find them helpful. Obtaining a sponsor through a 12-step program can be useful, especially for individuals with a long history of bulimia. Another option is to ask the client to consider seeing her psychotherapist twice a week, especially if she is bingeing and purging several times each day. The nutrition therapist should see the client weekly until her bingeing and purging decrease to a maximum of twice a day. Clients in this situation should be encouraged to have one therapeutic contact a day, whether it be with their psychotherapist, nutrition therapist, support group, or a friend or sponsor in recovery.

For individuals struggling with binge eating disorder, the same recommendations apply. Using an SSRI and increasing the support system should both be considered. Another option that may be appropriate in certain cases is recommending a break from nutrition therapy. This is most useful for individuals who are struggling with heavy emotional issues (eg, divorce, rape, sexual abuse, physical abuse, or other trauma) that are triggering their eating. In this situation, the client's psychotherapist should be consulted. If he is in agreement, more intensive work with the psychotherapist (eg, two sessions a week) can be the treatment focus until the client reaches a more stable emotional state. At that time the psychotherapist will refer her back to resume nutrition therapy. This gives the client permission to deal with one issue at a time, and decreases the likelihood of her feeling like a failure when she has difficulty meeting any nutritional goals.

Some clients who are less perfectionist or self-critical may choose to continue nutrition therapy for the added support, and may be able to continue coming without feeling like a failure. The nutrition therapist's responsibility is to assess what is best for the client, given her emotional state and functioning level. If the team (including the client) agrees that it is best for the client to take a break from nutrition therapy, the nutrition therapist should be careful not to make the client feel rejected or abandoned. (See Chapter 16.)

MAKING A REFERRAL TO INPATIENT HOSPITALIZATION

If it becomes necessary to refer a client for inpatient treatment, the psychotherapist should be contacted. The psychotherapist will normally check the client's hospitalization benefits and confer with the family to obtain their support. If the family is resistant, the nutrition therapist may need to call them or meet with them in person. She should convey her medical and nutritional concerns, explaining the typical hospital course of treatment and the benefits of hospitalization from a nutrition and weight perspective. The physician and psychotherapist should also give the family information from their perspectives. If the family still refuses to hospitalize the client, it may be necessary for the nutrition therapist to terminate nutrition therapy, stating that it is not ethical for her to continue treating the client in an outpatient setting.

The choice of the treatment program will be dictated mainly by the insurance benefits. In lieu of inpatient treatment, some insurance companies may authorize a day treatment program, where the client participates in treatment from 7 AM to 7 PM for 4 or 5 days a week. Once the client is admitted to a program, the outpatient nutrition therapist should contact the nutrition therapist at the treatment program to facilitate the transfer of care. Similarly, once the client is discharged back to outpatient treatment, the outpatient nutrition therapist should speak with the inpatient nutrition therapist regarding treatment concerns and obtain a copy of the client's discharge food plan.

Most clients will be discharged below their target weights because of insurance limitations. This means that the client may leave the inpatient program with a food plan of 3,000 calories a day or more for weight gain. However, many clients will be resistant to gaining weight once they leave the hospital. An initial compromise is to have the client agree to maintain his discharge weight, with the outpatient nutrition therapist adjusting the calories for weight maintenance. Over time, as the client becomes emotionally comfortable with his new weight, the nutrition therapist can facilitate continued weight gain up to the target weight. If the client immediately begins losing weight after discharge, he may need to be readmitted for further intensive treatment.

SUMMARY

- **Developing trust with the client is essential for successful progress in nutrition therapy.**

- **An important component of medical nutritional therapy is helping the client make the connection between her food choices and negative physical consequences she is experiencing.**

- **Goals of nutrition therapy include working toward appropriate food choices, as well as related behaviors, including rigidity, compulsions, and rituals involving food and exercise.**

- **While some cognitive behavioral techniques can facilitate nutrition therapy, it is essential to work with an interdisciplinary team and to make referrals when an issue arises that is beyond the scope of nutrition therapy.**

REFERENCES

1. Robinson JD, Lupklewica SM, Palenik L, Lopez LM, Ariet M. Determination of ideal body weight for drug dosage calculations. *Am J Hosp Pharm.* 1983;40: 1016–1019.

2. Kron L, Katz JL, Gorzynski G, Weiner H. Hyperactivity in anorexia nervosa: a fundamental clinical feature. *Compr Psychiatry.* 1978;19(5):433–440.

3. Stein A, Woolley H, Cooper SD, Fairburn CG. An observational study of mothers with eating disorders and their infants. *J Child Psychol Psychiatry.* 1994;35(4): 733–748.

4. Gasperino J. Ethnic differences in body compostion and their relation to health and disease in women. *Ethn Health.* 1996;1(4):337–347.

5. Goran MI, Gower BA, Treuth M, Nagy TR. Prediction of intra-abdominal and subcutaneous abdominal adipose tissue in healthy pre-pubertal children. *Int J Obes Relat Metab Disord.* 1998;22(6):549–558.

6. *Exchange Lists for Meal Planning.* Chicago, Ill: The American Dietetic Association; 1995.

7. Kaye WH, Weltzin TE, Hsu LK, McConaha CW, Bolton B. Amount of calories retained after binge eating and vomiting. *Am J Psychiatry.* 1993;150(6):969–971.

8. Weltzin TE, Fernstrom MH, Hansen D, McConane C, Kaye WH. Abnormal caloric requirements for weight maintenance in patients with anorexia and bulimia nervosa. *Am J Psychiatry.* 1991;148:1675–1682.

9. Wurtman RJ, Wurtman JJ. Brain serotonin, carbohydrate-craving, obesity, and depression. *Obes Res.* 1995;3(Suppl 4):477S-480S.

10. Kratina K, King NL, Hayes D. *Moving Away from Diets: New Ways to Heal Eating Problems and Exercise Resistance.* Lake Dallas, Tex: Helm Publishing; 1996.

11. Reiff KKL, Reiff DW. *Eating Disorders: Nutrition Therapy in the Recovery Process.* Mercer Island, Wash: Life Enterprises; 1997.

12. Tribole E, Resch E. *Intuitive Eating.* New York, NY: St Martin's Press; 1995.

13. Berge LN, Bonaa KH, Nodoy A. Serum ferritin, sex hormones, and cardiovascular risk factors in healthy women. *Arterioscler Thromb.* 1994;14(6):857–861.

14. Wilson GT, Fairburn CG. Cognitive treatments for eating disorders. *J Consult Clin Psychol.* 1993;61(2):261–269.

15. Satter EM. *Child of Mine: Feeding with Love and Good Sense.* Palo Alto, Calif: Bull Publishing; 1991.

16. Satter EM. *How to Get Your Kid to Eat . . . But Not Too Much.* Palo Alto, Calif: Bull Publishing; 1987.

CHAPTER 16

Development of Psychotherapeutic Techniques to Facilitate Successful Change

SONDRA KRONBERG, M.A., R.D.

While eating disorder behaviors are ultimately destructive, they are initially clever adaptations for emotional survival. They suppress painful feelings of shame, guilt, worthlessness, anger, and fear resulting from past abuse, trauma, chaotic surroundings, excessive need for control, or perfectionism. Eating disorders serve as a vehicle for expressing or coping with uncomfortable circumstances and feelings. The eating disorder is a veil that conceals the client's lack of self-worth and filters her perceptions of her life and world. It may be an outlet for feelings, needs, or hungers that the client is unaware of or unwilling to embrace. The client with anorexia nervosa says, "I can't take it in. I can't take in food, or life, or people. I am not good enough." The individual with bulimia nervosa says, "I will dare to take it in, but then I have to get rid of it. I feel shameful and guilty. I am not entitled to keeping it." The binge eater says, "I want more. I can't get enough. Nothing can fill me up. I can't say no to people or to food." The eating disorder behavior and identity give definition, value, control, and substance to clients struggling with an inner sense of worthlessness. It becomes a voice, a container for feelings, an escape, and a confidante.

The nutrition therapist listens to the messages and deciphers the codes to help his client understand how the eating disorder functions in her life. For example, a client who wants to come home from college but is unable to communicate that with words may become so medically compromised that her parents, psychotherapist, and nutrition therapist will insist that it is no longer safe for her to stay in school. Her eating disorder is the language this individual uses to communicate what she cannot express with words.

Successful treatment of eating disorders requires specialized counseling skills and the incorporation of processes that address the psychological components of eating. The emotional and behavioral entanglements revolving around food, weight, and body image dissatisfaction require that the nutrition therapist develop a long-term relationship with the client to facilitate positive changes. Using the therapeutic process, the nutrition therapist and psychotherapist enable the client to

THE ROLE OF THE NUTRITION THERAPIST IN TREATMENT

- become aware of her behaviors, thoughts, feelings, and/or needs,
- understand the purpose the eating disorder serves,
- find alternative ways to express those feelings or meet those needs,
- take action to change the behavior, and
- develop the courage to cope with the consequences of the change.

The ultimate goal of treatment to develop of a new sense of self that leaves behind the self that was dependent on the eating disorder for identity.

The successful approach of the nutrition therapist depends less on imparting nutritional information and more on forming a relationship for conveying this information. The nutrition therapist helps the client develop a positive self-image that will ultimately heal her. The client becomes a part of the treatment, rather than an object to be treated.

The nutrition therapist's words, movements, and reactions all influence treatment. The nutrition therapist must become aware of what is being communicated with the client, even when words are not used. What does one client say about missing an appointment? Why does another client make the nutrition therapist uncomfortable?

Psychotherapeutic techniques are not taught to dietitians in school. The traditional role of the registered dietitian in the medical model is to provide information to the client and to devise and implement a plan that fixes a nutrition problem. Conveying information on the biochemistry of foods and the physiology of the body and constructing a treatment plan alone will not change the eating disorder. Delivering this information in a therapeutic environment supported by a positive framework and a sense of hope, however, can be very effective.

Nutrition therapists must develop their own strong psychotherapeutic network and therapeutic alliances. Through practice, professional supervision, and self-examination, they can learn how to engage clients, sharpen their own communication skills, and deepen their inquiry into clients' issues. Nutrition therapists must learn to accept and express their own feelings, strengths, and deficits so that they can explore and empathize with their clients' feelings in an accepting and nonjudgmental manner.

Healing occurs when connections to people, places, and life itself replace the dysfunctional relationship with food. Helping a client to give up a symptom, thought, or action that has brought security, control, structure, and comfort must be done in a gentle and caring way over time. Though respectful of the way in which the eating disorder gives format, identity, and power to the client, the nutrition therapist helps the client develop relationships that offer positive replacements for the eating disorder.

All professionals treating eating disordered clients address the behavioral, emotional, and physiological components of the disordered thoughts and actions and their consequences. Chapter 15 outlined how to manage the physiological components in outpatient treatment. This chapter explains how to develop and refine the skills necessary for addressing the emotional and behavioral dimensions of these disorders.

THE THERAPEUTIC PROCESS

Individuals with eating disorders often have not experienced healthy relationships. The therapeutic process provides an opportunity to experience such a relationship. Communication, a critical medium for the development of any relationship, is nourished by an environment of acceptance, trust, and safety. It is the vehicle through which connection, change, and worth are established.

The therapeutic process enables the nutrition therapist to safely explore the client's needs, hungers, violations, and past hurts. Understanding one's needs is empowering, for it is the lack of awareness or denial that often leads to the eating disorder. Through the therapeutic relationship, the client learns to manage relationships, foods, and himself by learning to speak up, back away, assert a boundary, or ask for help. Learning these skills helps him to better navigate relationships, to make choices, and to learn to trust himself around people and food. Ultimately, therapeutic work leads the client to a deeper connection with his own inner experience. As he is listened to, he eventually learns to listen and trust his internal cues. This allows him to disconnect from external cues and distorted thoughts that have immobilized his being.

The therapeutic process guides clients through periods of engagement, exploration, grieving, integration, acceptance, maintenance, and termination. This process of change and recovery occurs over an extended period of time. Paralleling the flow of the overall treatment, the flow of each session includes combinations of change, trust building, awareness development, active listening, exploration, reflection, feedback/direction, goal setting/agreements, minimizing sabotage/fear of success, support, progress, maintenance of change, relapse prevention, and closure/termination.

Change

According to Prochaska (1), permanent change occurs as a process, in predictable stages or steps that usually take place over an extended period in a supportive environment. In eating disorder treatment, change occurs through awareness, self-observation, contemplation of alternatives, production of an environment that encourages new behaviors, and support and maintenance of those behaviors. While progress takes place in all the stages, changes in awareness, self-observation, self-image, emotions, and thinking occur before the new behaviors *(Box 16.1)*. Visible, tangible change takes place after the risk of action has been taken.

The therapeutic process and communication are essential instruments for producing change. The nutrition therapist and client should spend time becoming aware of the function and purpose of the eating disorder. When the needs behind the eating disorder are uncovered, alternative ways to meet those needs can be developed. Treatment requires patience, creativity, and competence to enable a client to give up a support system around which she has developed her identity.

Trust Building

Successful communication and change depend on the nutrition therapist's ability to create a safe place and to develop trust. The client's success depends upon his willingness to explore, to learn how to trust and express his feelings, and to take some risks within the safety of the relationship and eventually in the world. Coming to the nutrition therapist's office may be more frightening than visiting any other professionals' offices. The client fears the confrontation about his food and is anxious about the attempts that will be made to alter his food choices and weight.

The nutrition therapist must understand that, to the client, the eating disorder has functioned almost like a life preserver. Threatening to take it away, or giving the client the idea that this will happen, may scare her away. The eating disorder needs to be treated with respect. Despite any pain and suffering it inflicts in the present, it is also a source of comfort, protection, intimacy, and salvation. The idea of leaving it or getting rid of it is like getting rid of a best friend. It is critical to allow the client these feelings and to recognize how valuable the eating disorder has been. It is also important to acknowledge that a part of the client doesn't want to give the eating disorder up, and that it is okay to have those feelings for now. The goal is to strengthen the part that does want to get better by teaching the client the tools she needs to do so.

Box 16.1
Progress vs Relapse

<u>Progress</u>
Takes place in all stages.
Moving from stage to stage is also progress.
Invisible changes take place in the first three stages (eg, changes in awareness, emotions, self-image, and thinking).
Visible changes take place in the last three stages.

<u>Recycle/Relapse</u>
Progress is not linear.
Relapse is the rule, not the exception.
It is not uncommon to "spiral" through the stages 3 or 4 times before exiting.
Complications should be expected.
Distress and social pressure precipitate relapse.
Guilt and self-blame exacerbate the relapse.

The eating disorder client carries a myriad of uncommunicated thoughts and feelings, including any combination of the following:

- not feeling worthy of the therapist's time,
- feeling ashamed of the presenting behavior,
- fearing abandonment, abuse, or rejection, and/or
- not thinking there is a problem (denial) (2-5).

A variety of distorted thinking modes support these thoughts and feelings. There are often strongly developed feelings of worthlessness and a repertoire of self-loathing thoughts and behaviors. The eating disordered client is incredibly self-judgmental and overly sensitive to the surrounding environment.

The client's perception of the nutrition therapist and the subsequent barrier building will begin long before the actual session. The therapist's voice, how she answers the phone, and where her office is located will all be evaluated. Once the client is at the office, she will judge the furniture and the nutrition therapist's hair, clothing, body language, and weight. She will probably experience transference, likening the nutrition therapist to someone else in her life. Each of these thoughts or feelings will be a potential reason for not trusting the nutrition therapist in a therapeutic relationship. What the client is really thinking is, "Can I trust this person? Will I be understood? Can I let anyone get close to me?" The nutrition therapist needs to be aware of how the client's conscious and unconscious feelings will affect the sessions and the relationship.

From the initial moment of connection, the nutrition therapist will have an impact on the client and vice versa. Early sessions are an opportunity for the client to find fault. They are also the nutrition therapist's opportunity to show acceptance, to foster trust, and to provide hope. The client may push or provoke to prove to himself that the nutrition therapist is not to be trusted or that he himself is again unworthy. Food is nothing more than the medium through which this takes place. This testing period is emotionally stressful, creating uncomfortable feelings for both participants. Practice and professional supervision will develop skills that enable the nutrition therapist to manage personal feelings in a manner that support the client's progress.

The eating disordered client requires unconditional acceptance of her behavior, as well as of her potential for growth. Many of these clients have been in relationships in which they have been overly controlled, neglected, abandoned, or abused (emotionally, sexually, or physically). They may fear relationships, lean toward isolation, or have an obsessive relationship with food or its absence. The prospect of relating to people presents the potential for hurt and the fear of reliving past patterns of abuse.

The client needs to know that the nutrition therapist is aware of her fear. The courage needed to call and come in needs to be acknowledged. From there, she needs to be listened to. The nutrition therapist's focus, silence, words, and demeanor are important. The nutrition therapist fosters trust by listening carefully to everything that is said without judgment or ridicule. Actions of the nutrition therapist that promote the development of trust include

- beginning and ending appointments on time,
- making as few changes as possible in the appointment schedule,
- informing clients far in advance of any vacations or off-time,
- setting firm limits and boundaries for both the client and oneself,
- adhering to these limits and boundaries,
- keeping one's word,
- telling the truth,
- modeling integrity,
- being consistent,
- admitting mistakes or uncertainties,
- respecting the client's self-knowledge,
- maintaining confidentiality,
- listening,
- following through with rules, and
- exhibiting patience.

These behaviors not only earn trust, but also teach the client to be trustworthy. Eventually the client will learn to trust herself. This process may be long and fragile. It will continue throughout treatment. It will be constantly tested. It may ebb and flow according to other traumas and betrayals perceived or encountered during treatment. If a client was referred by a psychotherapist, physician, or someone else who earned her trust, the nutrition therapist can ride on that trust for a while, but he must work quickly to earn his own. A client who presents for treatment under less cooperative circumstances will be more reluctant to trust her treatment team.

Once in the session, what the nutrition therapist says, how she says it, how she appears, smells, even laughs, will all become part of treatment. This is the time to engage the client. It is the time for the nutrition therapist to listen to where the client has been, hear about the struggles, observe reactions, give a forum to frustrations, and allow her to talk freely about whatever she needs to talk about.

The nutrition therapist must clearly identify that the first stage of treatment is about awareness—the first step in all permanent change. Developing the client's awareness allows the nutrition therapist and client to observe how foods, circumstances, and other people affect the client. The nutrition therapist should be clear that the client will be met where she is and move at a pace comfortable to her. For example, the nutrition therapist can make the client a partner in treat-

Awareness Development

ment by saying, "You are the expert on you, I am the expert on food, eating, and the eating disorder, and your psychotherapist is the expert on feelings, emotions, and the eating disorder. We will all work together on this as a team." This engages the client by making her a member of the team.

Creating value is another major goal of treatment. The client needs to understand that therapy is not about being "fixed" or controlled. Instead, the team works toward mutually agreed-on goals. "Fixing" would not teach the client to take responsibility for himself. The treatment sessions would become a battleground for control through which the client could be lost. Engaging and directing the client by asking how he feels about things or what things mean to him deepens the client's self-awareness, which serves to deepen the therapist-client connection.

The therapeutic process uses open-ended questions (not "Did you like that?" but "What was that like?") The difference in wording is slight, but the possible responses are dramatically different. The first question can be answered "Yes" or "No". The other needs thought, words, and sentences. Open-ended questions engage the client and encourage her to go deeper. Finding out where the client is and how she feels about being there will help the nutrition therapist gauge how to continue. Examples include

- What made you want to see a nutrition therapist?
- What were you hoping I would tell you?
- What events in the past influence your behavior today?
- How did you feel when you got here today?
- How do you feel now?

Exploring where the client is is imperative not just at the first session, but throughout the recovery process. Asking the client to gauge what she is feeling models a skill she may later be able to use herself. Eventually the client's feelings will provide information on how she should proceed through certain situations, and not represent something she should suppress, avoid, or fear.

Active Listening   Of equal importance to the question asked is the response. Active listening is a skill which is important in all stages of the process, particularly in engagement and exploration. The client needs to know that her words were heard and their meaning understood. The nutrition therapist should show concern and interest, not judgment, disappointment, or disapproval. He should listen actively. Nonjudgmental listening is neither positive nor negative. It merely acknowledges that information has been heard, without judging the information as shocking, mundane, or exciting. Clients will watch closely for signs of approval or disapproval because they are used to being judged or judging themselves. Emotions and actions are not good or bad, right or wrong, healthy or unhealthy. They are simply emotions and actions, and they need an accepting audience.

Clients will say that no one understands or listens to them. They feel shamed by their behaviors and believe they are the only ones who behave like this. It helps them to know that nothing they could share will shock the nutrition therapist. The greater the nutrition therapist's awareness and acceptance of eating disordered thinking and behaviors, the more comfortable clients will feel disclosing thoughts, feelings, and behaviors in the session.

Clients need to know that the nutrition therapist understands what no one else has. They need to know that they count. They need to know that what they say and who they are has value. The nutrition therapist should use her voice, eyes, and body language to communicate that she has heard the client.

Acceptance of the client and her actions allows analysis of what the actions mean to her.

- What does it mean when you lose or gain weight?
- How does it feel when you eat two extra graham crackers?
- What does it mean when someone tells you that you look healthier?

The nutrition therapist should let the client express the thoughts behind her behavior and share her concerns. He should not place a negative or positive value on the information that is shared. He should address the client's concerns and not minimize her feelings. He should be interested in what the client has to say and flexible enough to focus on her agenda.

People with eating disorders have experienced years of feeling devalued. The nutrition therapist should not recreate these feelings in the session by placing another agenda ahead of the client's, or by suggesting that anyone else's feelings are more important or valuable than the client's. The nutrition therapist should continually support information with data, articles, examples, and handouts, but should not disregard the client's beliefs or perspective. He should search for meaning in whatever information the client shares by asking questions that promote exploration:

- How did that make you feel?
- What messages were you giving yourself?
- What happens when you eat 12 slices of pizza?

Again, open-ended questions, coupled with active listening in a safe environment, will help the client to look inward and become aware of the feelings the eating disorder has been covering.

The nutrition therapist's own values and feelings (eg, sadness, frustration, anger, or discouragement) will naturally be challenged by topics discussed in the session. This phenomenon is called *countertransference*. The nutrition therapist should learn to recognize these feelings and use them as a gauge. Feelings that arise in session provide useful information. For the client, these feelings should be processed in session; for the nutrition therapist, they can be discussed in supervision.

Exploration   Exploration is about introspection and discovery. It is the process by which the client discovers the purpose of the eating disorder through such questions as

- How does it help you function?
- When do you need it?
- How do you use it to protect yourself?
- What are the benefits?

During exploration the nutrition therapist helps the client uncover feelings, expose needs, and unveil past hurts. This must be done gently, entering only when, where, and at the speed the client is willing to go.

Exploration techniques provide the opportunity to connect the eating disordered behavior to life circumstances and feelings. It may connect purging to shame, restricting to feelings of worthlessness, overeating to a fear of intimacy, and bingeing to a sense of deprivation. The quest to identify situations and feelings that require the coping mechanism of the eating disorder will include questions like these:

- How did you feel when your sister did that?
- What were you telling yourself when you got the job interview?
- Can you remember what you were feeling when no one asked you to go?

The first line of questioning provides the opportunity to explore the circumstance. The next step is to connect the circumstance or feeling to the eating disordered behavior:

- So how did your friend's comment affect your restricting?
- How do you think weighing yourself more often this week was connected to your new relationship?
- How did what happened affect your eating?
- How was what you were feeling connected to your need to purge?

In early stages, clients will have difficulty acknowledging emotions and expressing feelings. Words are often scary and threatening. The nutrition therapist needs to be creative when exploring the connection between eating disordered behaviors and the client's emotions. It is important to develop a repertoire of ways to interpret the metaphors and repave the path of expression.

Exploration techniques vary, and range from provocation to empathy. A mix of humor, confrontation, sarcasm, imitating, modeling, and silence can be effectively integrated to facilitate exploration and discovery. Creative exercises that incorporate various modes of expression promote this process. Examples include guided imagery, journal writing, dance and movement exercises, music, role-playing, art projects, writing assignments, and food play. Each offers an opportunity to express hidden messages that have eluded verbal expression. Through these activities, connections between behaviors and feelings evolve. Eventually the treatment team guides the client toward more direct expression through verbal communication.

An important goal of treatment is to teach clients to effectively communicate their thoughts and feelings to have their needs met. The nutrition therapist's reflection of messages that are heard, seen, or experienced in the exploration process helps communication in the session and models for the client ways to communicate in the world. It clears up miscommunications and lessens the damage incurred by uncommunicated assumptions. It also provides a soft summary of what has been heard and connects feelings to actions. For example, the nutrition therapist might say

Reflection

- I'm hearing that you were able to say no to your son and not feel guilty.
- It sounds as if you were very angry when your father didn't call you.
- What I'm hearing is that you were confused about what we had talked about last week.

Eating disordered clients assume others view them negatively. Reflection provides a means of testing that assumption. It ensures that the client has been heard correctly and allows her to clarify if necessary. It allows the client to express feelings that make her uncomfortable, such as loneliness and anger, and it allows the nutrition therapist to note the absence of appropriate feelings. It encourages the client to indicate when she has not been heard correctly. It allows the nutrition therapist to clarify the client's negative responses and to cast her behavior in a more positive light *(Box 16.2)*.

Through reflection, the nutrition therapist helps the client begin to see herself in a more positive light. When the client's anger is appropriate, it can be understood as evidence of the client's increasing ability to express how she is feeling.

Up to this point, the focus has been on recognizing circumstances, the resulting painful thoughts and feelings, and the disordered eating behaviors that develop out of those thoughts and feelings. Once this has been accomplished, the focus changes to altering some of these behaviors. The goals of recovery are to separate thoughts and feelings from food, weight, and body image behaviors and to find healthier ways of expressing and coping with feelings.

Feedback and Direction

One of the most successful techniques for treating eating disorders is *cognitive behavioral therapy* (CBT) (6). In addition to increasing awareness of behaviors

Cognitive Behavioral Therapy

Box 16.2
CASE STUDY
The Use of Reflection

In one session Barbara related how a friend had called to cancel plans right before an evening they had planned long ago. She said that when the friend gave her the news, she responded, "No problem. We can do it another day." Barbara ended up staying home and bingeing. In the session, she reported this incident without signs of anger, frustration, sadness, or disappointment. In fact, she told the story with a smile on her face. A focus of treatment to this point had been that Barbara's inability to handle anger and her continual suppression of her feelings repeatedly led her to eating and bingeing.

At this point, reflection was used to heighten awareness of the conflict between what Barbara had heard and how she had responded.

NUTRITION THERAPIST: How did that feel when your friend cancelled so late?

BARBARA: Okay.

NUTRITION THERAPIST: Okay, huh? I'm hearing that you ended up bingeing and noticing that you are telling me this story with a smile on your face. Can you tell me about this? I get the sense that you are not so okay with this. Let's go back there. Was it really okay? I'm thinking about the last time you felt she disregarded your feelings. Can you remember that? What were you feeling? Would it be okay for you to be angry, sad, or disappointed with her?

By continually connecting Barbara's eating with her inability to acknowledge or express her feelings, the nutrition therapist pointed out the inconsistency between what she felt and how she was describing it. In addition, the nutrition therapist validated those appropriate feelings of sadness, anger, and disappointment. Expressing those feelings would be a healthy, positive response that would decrease the need to binge.

and their functions, CBT supports the process of change by increasing awareness of the thoughts that precede the behaviors.

In eating-disordered clients, negative thoughts prompt negative feelings, which foster negative behaviors, which eventually reinforce a negative belief system and ultimately support a negative identity *(Figure 16.1)*. Recognizing the earliest disordered thought and changing it to a positive, more constructive thought will change the ensuing behavior. Examples of tools that support this treatment technique include positive self-talk exercises, positive affirmations, handouts that expose the client to positive and motivating thoughts about life and people, and books that reinforce self-empowerment. These tools feed positive thinking and feeling. Handouts and books serve both as reinforcements of positive thoughts between appointments and as objects that represent the nutrition therapist's presence and support in the client's life on a daily basis.

In session, the nutrition therapist models positive thinking by emphasizing the client's success and deemphasizing perceived failures. Thoughts that precipitated the eating disordered behavior are replaced with more constructive thoughts. CBT concepts help the client to create new thoughts, which increase his ability to create new behaviors. Sessions provide the environment for these new thoughts to develop. For example, the nutrition therapist might ask:

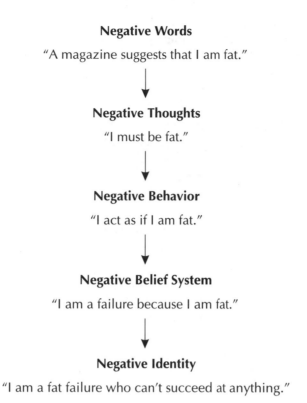

Negative Words

"A magazine suggests that I am fat."

↓

Negative Thoughts

"I must be fat."

↓

Negative Behavior

"I act as if I am fat."

↓

Negative Belief System

"I am a failure because I am fat."

↓

Negative Identity

"I am a fat failure who can't succeed at anything."

Figure 16.1
The Consequences of Negative Thoughts

- What was it you were telling yourself?
- Can you focus on the thought or feeling you had before you began purging?
- What were you telling yourself about that graham cracker?
- Were there any rules or messages you were hearing?

The client may need help identifying specific negative thoughts. The nutrition therapist might prompt, "Let's go through the day together." Self-monitoring tools as journal writing and lists of rules, messages, and thoughts identified outside the session can help to make the client's thoughts more accessible during the session:

- I was wondering if you would be willing to write down your thoughts the next time you want to purge?
- Would you be willing to keep an ongoing list of the rules that your eating disorder requires you to follow as you hear them this week?

Once the thought that triggers the behavior has been identified, the team works to create new thoughts and encourage new behaviors. It is at this stage that negative thought patterns, attitudes, and errors in thinking are challenged. Trust and willingness to change allow for active challenge of distorted thoughts through CBT. Recovery requires continued practice in identifying errors in thinking and using a positive frame for constructing new thoughts *(Box 16.3)*.

**Box 16.3
Errors in Thinking
and Attitudes That
Perpetuate Eating
Disorders**

All-or-none reasoning
There are no intermediate states. Frequently used words include "control" and "chaos", "binge" and "starve", "thin" and "fat", and "everything" and "nothing".

Personalization
Self-worth depends on what others think. Everything that happens in the world reflects one's personal failures and others' disapproval.

Overgeneralization
If something turns out badly once, it will always turn out badly.

Magical or superstitious thinking
When some thing or state is acquired, everything will be perfect.

Catastrophizing/magnification
The outcome or potential outcome is thought of as the worst of all possible consequences to validate negative feelings.

Abstraction
The individual focuses on a single aspect of a situation, even though the whole picture may be quite different.

Perfectionistic thinking
Rigid thinking prevents deviation from a task or behavior because of (often unfounded) fear of negative consequences.

**Brief Solution-
Focused Therapy**

An approach that is usually coupled with CBT is *solution-focused behavioral therapy* (SBT) (7). This increasingly popular form of therapy has long been an effective tool for nutrition therapists treating eating disorders. It does not investigate the reasons and feelings behind actions, but rather explores solutions. The goal is to help the client to find different solutions and ways to diminish the need for the behavior.

This technique encourages the client to create an ideal solution: a magical or ideal day, situation, or behavior. From there, she is asked to gauge where she is in relation to the ideal, on a scale from 1 to 10. The client is encouraged to create solutions that help her to get closer to that ideal or improve the outcome. Typical questions include:

- What would the ideal dinner with your husband be like?
- On a scale from 1 to 10, where would last night's dinner be?
- What would have to happen for you to get closer to the ideal dinner, closer to a 10?

If the nutrition therapist asks questions that generate client introspection or proposes possible solutions in a neutral context, it opens the door to alternatives:

- What would you like to happen?
- What would happen if you didn't go to the candy store?

- What would have to happen for you to get through the day without exercising?
- What would you be willing to do to prevent, delay, or minimize your binge-ing after lunch?

The idea is to create solutions and help the client to incorporate them. Questions are aimed at getting the client to provide the solutions. If the client cannot create the solutions, the nutrition therapist can make suggestions through questions:

- Would it be more relaxing if you played soft music while you were eating with your husband tonight?
- I'm wondering what would happen if you wrote in your journal instead of going to the refrigerator?
- Would you be willing to eat more of your food earlier in the day so that you would not be so hungry at night?
- Do you think if you were able to make a phone call at that time, you might be able to take better care of yourself? How does that sound to you?

The nutrition therapist should not tell the client what to do, but provide her with as much information as necessary to back up the suggestions. For example, information on blood sugar, metabolism, and the binge/purge cycle would all support the suggestion that eating earlier would decrease the tendency to overeat at night.

Goal Setting and Agreements

Exercises using CBT or SBT gradually move the client from awareness and exploration toward action. The point in treatment at which action takes place depends on the client's willingness to take risks in the environment of trust, safety, and support that has been created. Those who are willing to risk will be able to challenge old thoughts, beliefs, and behaviors through negotiated goals. Sessions help to determine what the risks will be, as well as when, how, and with whom the risks will be taken. The ultimate goal of these challenges is for the client to develop a healthy relationship with food, weight, body, self, and others.

Interim goals are tiny steps along the way. These include changing the quantity, quality, and variety of food the client eats, as well as changing what, where, when, how, and with whom the client eats. Fostering the process of making, supporting, and maintaining these changes requires a wealth of information, alternatives, and tools, including alternative behaviors, shared eating activities, calming techniques, buffering skills, cognitive behavioral dialogues, guided imageries, self-care techniques, support groups, and constant reinforcement of the physiological, metabolic and food facts that have been distorted by the eating disorder.

It is important to impress upon the client that her growth and progress will be different from anyone else's. Not all tools will work for her, and she will need to practice with all the tools to determine which best develop her skills. With time, she will become better at assessing which tools to use in which situations. The more a behavior is practiced, the more skilled the client will become. The goal is to learn to be persistent, patient, and self-compassionate.

During treatment, the nutrition therapist must deliver and model the qualities she is asking of the client. She needs to continuously affirm that there is hope and that she will not give up on the client or his recovery. Actions and demeanor, as well as words, will communicate this. Healing takes place out of self-compassion and not out of self-loathing. Clients are prone to all-or-none thinking, and often give up if they slip or fall because of fear of failure or unwillingness to risk success. The nutrition therapist's commitment, compassion, and understanding, as well as her strength and determination, provide a model to follow.

Moving into action is a crucial part of recovery, like a fork in the road. It requires active decisions and effort. The client will need guidance onto a different path and into a new way of handling old situations. A strong therapeutic relationship and caring are what will push her forward, if she is ready. However, all the caring in the world will not help if the client is not ready. It is not the nutrition therapist's responsibility to make the client change. She has to be willing to work on changing herself, to move from the fork in the road. Standing in place or retreating down the old path cannot be prevented if the client chooses to do so. Many clients may never be ready, no matter how hard the *nutrition therapist* works. Recognizing this and setting professional limits are necessary for the nutrition therapist's self-care.

In negotiating change with the client, the nutrition therapist needs to work out agreements with the client about what he is willing to strive for between sessions. The client should be asked for suggestions and solutions:

- What do you think you would like to see happen this week?
- What are you willing to do this week?

The goals should be achievable and match what the client is willing or ready to agree to doing. The nutrition therapist should not set the client up for failure or let him set himself up for failure by setting unachievable goals, which will reconfirm to him that he is worthless. The nutrition therapist should avoid tendencies to try to "fix" the client, to get the job done quickly, or to do the work for him.

The nutrition therapist should be leery of the words "I'll try." These usually signal that the goal that has been set up is too risky or that the client is not prepared for it. The two answers that follow the nutrition therapist's question in this scenario show the difference:

NT: It sounds as if you recognize how important it has been for you to monitor your feelings. Are you willing to resume writing in your journal this week?

1:    Yes, I can do that.

2:    I'll try.

If the first response is clear and accompanied by a confident manner, it suggests that both the nutrition therapist and the client are comfortable with the goal. The second response suggests that further questioning is needed:

- It sounds as if you are uncertain whether you will be able to resume your writing. What is in the way of that happening?
- What are your concerns or what is your unwillingness about?

The client might respond, "Well, I really don't like the book I have and I don't have money to buy a new one." The goal could then be adjusted to remove some of these barriers or to discover what the real resistance is. If stated barriers are not cleared or true barriers are not uncovered, the client will not write. "I'll try" is a way for most clients to say "No" without a confrontation.

Each client needs to be treated individually. Agreements should be simple, clear, and few. Each goal should be broken into small steps that lead to its completion. Techniques should be chosen that will help this particular client comply. Agreements can be made to simply observe something or to take action. The client will need help to think through what has to happen to achieve the goal. What thoughts, behaviors, and actions need to be considered? The nutrition therapist should attempt to uncover thoughts that might get in the way of the goal. CBT will promote changing a thought or creating a new image to help the client change her behavior.

Through treatment, the client will become willing to take small risks, to fall, and to learn from the fall. She becomes willing to experiment with behaviors that have been difficult for her. It is important to take small and realistic risks. The nutrition therapist directs the client toward changes in food choices. The psychotherapist works with similar goals in other aspects of the client's life. For example, when the psychotherapist is working with a client who can't ask for what she needs from her husband, the nutrition therapist can work with the client on asking for some special food or preparation in a restaurant. Taking a risk in either area fosters growth in both.

Minimizing Sabotage/Fear of Success

Roadblocks often develop—situations, thoughts, and behaviors that keep clients stuck or set them back. The nutrition therapist should anticipate sabotage. She should help clients think through the week ahead, plan ahead, and learn how to take care of themselves. Clients should look at the coming week to identify places, people, thoughts, behaviors, or circumstances that might be barriers to completing goals, and should help clients be specific in defining how to break through barriers. She should discuss solutions with them, encourage safe risks. She should ask, "So what's happening this week that will get in the way of you taking care of yourself?" It is important to be specific, to get into details.

Clients will have difficulties with certain occasions. Anniversaries of deaths and past traumas will trigger uncomfortable feelings, and the nutrition therapist should discuss these with the clients. She should also be aware of the impact of certain vacations and holidays, particularly the gift-giving and food-consuming holidays. The nutrition therapist and client should together process other special occasions, particularly weddings and proms, where there are a conglomerate of emotional elements, including wearing special clothes, exposing more of the body, being exposed to an abundance of food, and dealing with feelings about acceptance, rejection, visibility, exclusion. The nutrition therapist should help the client learn how to anticipate, think through, and solve problems, cope with feelings, and get needs meet.

The nutrition therapist should also watch for ambivalence about success on the part of the client. Fear of success produces many side effects that the client must deal with to move forward. It may be one thing to desire to change and struggle to do so, but the actual achievement of progress may be scary. Succeeding means giving up the identity of the eating disorder, or at least parts of it. Clients fear this because they don't know what to expect. "Who am I? Will there be anything there? What will I become?" The known, the eating disorder, although painful, is consciously or unconsciously perceived as more desirable than the unknown of success.

Success is also difficult because most clients feel they are not entitled to anything good. They are unable to give to themselves and uncomfortable with the unfamiliarity of positive feelings. Finally, succeeding is arduous. As eating disordered behaviors are discontinued, the painful or submerged feelings they covered up begin to surface. Clients often choose the comfort of the eating disorder over the uncomfortable, unknown territory of success. (See *Box 16.4.*)

Support   Eating-disordered clients have learned to isolate, to count only on themselves, and not to depend on others. Learning to trust and letting the nutrition therapist and others into their lives is an important part of recovery. Clients must learn to connect and to get help from others in recovery and in life. They need to acknowledge their need for help and support. They need to learn how to move from isolation, deprivation, and perfectionism into connectedness and being alive. They

---

Box 16.4
CASE STUDY
Developing Trust
in Relationships

Joann was an obese client who was attempting to lose weight. She had an underlying fear that if she lost the weight, she would be forced into an intimate romantic relationship. Although she presented with the conscious desire to lose weight, therapy helped her to identify that she subconsciously resisted herself and the nutrition therapist because she was afraid of being hurt in any kind of close relationship. Joann's therapy focused on resolving her fear of intimacy. Assignments involved examining relationships and getting her needs met without using food. She was encouraged to explore the connection between foods and her needs with her nutrition therapist while working slowly on small steps and small successes with her food and eating behaviors. Throughout the process, her commitment to her therapeutic relationship and other relationships was acknowledged. Joann was asked to take daily note of even small things she succeeded at and record those marks of progress in her journal. This process prepared her for success by getting her more comfortable with praising herself, her positive feelings, and her small steps forward.

need to discover the strength, support, and recognition of belonging to a group. They need to be able to give and receive.

Nutrition therapy helps clients develop significant supports that nurture their well-being and facilitate a healthy relationship with the nutrition therapist. (The nutrition therapist should be conscious of her own boundaries so she does not overburden herself in the process.) Clients need to discover supports that cushion their ups and downs and build a sense of positive self-worth. Each new challenge requires different supports. The nutrition therapist should tailor her supports to the needs and ability of the client at the time. Examples of supports include offering group therapy and support groups, checking voicemail frequently for messages from clients, allowing clients to fax their journals to the office, scheduling more frequent visits, replaying tapes of sessions, and enrolling other key support people.

Progress

The nutrition therapist should promote all work as progress and an opportunity to learn more, not simply a matter of whether the task was completed or not. She should continually teach the client to create new thoughts and behaviors to replace the eating disordered distortions and to manage the actions that result. Though initial work will focus on the client's relationship with food, that relationship is actually a metaphor for how she deals with life. She is learning to negotiate life and its difficulties. This process is ultimately about self-care; the skills need ongoing development. Practice is what makes them work.

It is important that the nutrition therapist continually impress upon the client that change does not take place overnight. Old behavior has been reinforced over many years, and creating new thoughts and behaviors takes time, compassion, patience, practice, and repetition. It is a long process with many ups and downs. Many feelings will be aroused in both the client and the nutrition therapist, including frustration, disappointment, hopelessness, incompetence, empowerment, fear, success, failure, dependency, inadequacy, and anger. These are intense feelings, and may have led to the abandonment of therapy in the past.

Helping the client learn to tolerate these feelings is part of the process. Feelings have a beginning, a middle, and an end. Learning to ride out an intense feeling is an important skill that therapy facilitates. With time, the client will learn to embrace her feelings and understand that they are her guides. Incorporating new thoughts and behaviors will promote change; reinforcing and supporting this change will help the client to leave the old behavior behind.

Maintenance of Change

Equally important to making changes is maintaining them. As treatment continues and progress is made, a big part of the work will be to help the client adjust to the consequences of the changed behaviors. This is a difficult but crucial part of recovery. The client may have difficulty tolerating changes that occur as emotional and physical needs begin to be met. Even positive feelings will be a part of this process.

Clients often express discomfort with positive feelings. They are uncomfortable feeling happy or fulfilled and often frightened about success. Up to this point they have devalued themselves and are often incapable of letting in positive feelings. They need to learn to use positive and negative feelings as guides. They need to understand that embracing their feelings, needs, and hungers and working through the consequences is an ongoing process that requires constant work. This self-examination needs to be productive and self-compassionate:

- What am I frightened about?
- What can I do to change the situation?
- Who can I talk to about it?
- What can I do to feel better?
- How can I take care of myself?
- What am I hungry for?
- Do I want something hot or cold?
- Do I want to eat by myself?
- When do I want to eat?
- Where will I find what I want?
- How will I know if I'm satisfied?

The nutrition therapist's function is to help the client learn to allow positive thoughts to flourish and to help the client tolerate a full range of feelings. She fosters a move away from perfectionist, all-or-none, black-and-white thinking and encourages adventuring into the gray middle. Each day is a new day, and each meal is a new meal. Though the sun does not shine every day, there is something positive to be found in each day. Teaching the client to accept where he is and to learn from whatever that day brings is a big part of recovery.

Relapse Prevention   Relapse, or recycling, is always part of the process. Along the path to recovery, relapses identify areas that the client may have trouble with, areas that need to be explored. The client is reminding herself and the nutrition therapist that success frightens her. Each setback communicates that something not yet identified is still painful.

When a client's symptoms resurface or she is unable to achieve his goals, this is a message that needs to be addressed. The nutrition therapist might ask:

- What do you think was happening?
- What were you feeling?
- What happened that day?

When something causes the client pain, anxiety, or fear, the resulting bingeing enables the client and nutrition therapist to pinpoint the cause and work on ways to handle it.

Sometimes a client's unwillingness or inability to look at her feelings keeps her immersed in her eating disordered behaviors. She may strongly resist doing any work on food or food-related behaviors because she badly needs them to survive. It is important for the nutrition therapist to recognize this and to allow the client to take a break from challenging issues. This may mean that the nutrition therapist will see the client less often for a time, or that sessions will be suspended until the treatment team (the client included) determines that it is appropriate to resume them. The client must view any break as part of the process, rather than failure or rejection by the nutrition therapist. It is an opportunity to let things settle and perhaps concentrate on emotional issues before addressing food issues.

Clients can still be seen during this period, with a focus on communication and support. They usually welcome the support, even though they are not "producing results." The result is often a shortened "down time" and reduced likelihood of the client's perceiving herself as a failure. If a client is uncomfortable with sessions in which she is unable to work directly on her food behaviors, it may be helpful to make an appointment for a specified time 4 to 6 weeks in the future. This keeps the client and nutrition therapist connected. From there, appointments can be scheduled every 4 to 6 weeks until the client expresses, or the treatment team observes, that she is ready to resume work.

Closure/Termination

Clients are loaned to therapists. Treatment is a mutual process. Every client learns from her nutrition therapist, but does her own teaching as well. As clients change, so do nutrition therapists change. The goal of treatment is to teach clients self-care, to manage hunger and to feed themselves physically, emotionally, and spiritually, to connect with their inner strength. Both the client and the nutrition therapist are rewarded by this transformation.

The client begins treatment dependent on her nutrition therapist. During treatment, she learns how to be independent; she moves on to function in and be part of a larger world. The process is similar to raising a child, then watching the child develop and go out into the world. Both the child and the parent have ambivalent feelings. There is a sense of both joy and loss.

Clients experience varying degrees of anxiety about the loss of their therapeutic relationship. Some even choose to hold on to some aspect of their eating disorder as a way of remaining in need of help and staying in treatment. There is often fear of getting better for fear that the relationship will be lost.

This fear should be discussed several times during treatment. It is important at the time of closure to assure the client that this is not the end of the relationship, but the beginning of a new phase. When it is time for the client to end treatment, the nutrition therapist should discuss with the client the possibility of seeing him less and less frequently. This helps decrease the client's sense of dependence, lessen his sense of loss, and assure him of his capabilities and stability.

One technique for closure is to set up a series of two or three closing sessions once a mutual decision has been reached that it is time for the client to fly on her own. In the sessions, the nutrition therapist and client should review progress made, strengths, weaknesses, tools, and current life circumstances. They should acknowledge growth that has occurred, potential challenges, and confidence that the client will succeed. The nutrition therapist should assure the client that she can schedule an appointment when necessary, but remind her that she now has the tools she needs for problem solving. The client should also be reminded that there will be ups and downs, and that she knows how to work through both.

Closure and termination will be less complete for clients who are frustrated with themselves or with the nutrition therapist, frightened that they are getting better, or discouraged that they are not getting better. Some may just not show up or cancel appointments and not reschedule them. It is important for the nutrition therapist to call and encourage them to come in and talk about what is happening face to face. A client may be angry at the nutrition therapist for her lack of success or avoid the therapist because she doesn't want to succeed. In either case, she should be encouraged to come in. In that session, the nutrition therapist should help the client identify her need to leave and share any negative emotions she was unwilling to verbalize or found easier to cope with through not coming to appointments. There are several approaches the nutrition therapist could take:

- Perhaps something you want/need isn't happening here.
- I'm wondering if I disappointed you.
- I'm wondering how long you've wanted to leave and why you didn't say anything.
- What has given you the courage to leave now?
- Where else do you leave when you feel disappointed, angry, frustrated, etc. . . ?
- Is there any other way you could handle that feeling?
- Would you like me to help you to stay or help you to leave?

Even in the process of leaving, the goal is to explore, reflect, and then plan the action. If the client still wants to leave, the nutrition therapist should close as with any other client, outlining the progress thus far and the potential seen. He should ask if the client would like to be referred to someone else, and leave the door open to return if she ever chooses to do so.

If the client will not come to a closure session, phone sessions or letters are other options. Completion models responsibility in relationships and the importance of communicating what is happening. It is an important part of the therapeutic process because it teaches clients to face uncomfortable emotions, instead of simply running away.

RECOVERY Recovery is the ongoing process of creating value in one's life. Throughout treatment, the nutrition therapist will work with the client to change her thinking processes and replace eating disordered behaviors and thoughts with healthy behaviors and thoughts. The nutrition therapist needs to help the client establish value in life beyond the eating disorder, to shift the value from her eating disorder to herself and constructively deal with the uncomfortable feelings that the eating disorder was masking. This can be difficult and painful.

Through the process of mirroring and discovery, the treatment team works to help the client see herself through different eyes. The nutrition therapist reflects a nurturing, accepting view of the client and teaches skills the client will eventually master. Eventually the client becomes increasingly willing to take risks and to experiment with experiences that are difficult, and is no longer willing or able to hide from herself or her feelings. The nutrition therapist continues to direct the client toward making changes in her foods, as well as finding other ways to cope with her feelings.

The client actively works at breaking rules and patterns she previously considered untouchable. She expands her circle of foods, her relationships in the world, and her life. All actions are learning experiences and deserve applause. Uncompleted goals are never failures. Every action provides information. Inability to complete a task suggests that the need for the original behavior requires reexamination. More achievable solutions can then be created, strengthening the overall concept of nonjudgment and acceptance. Helping the client accept who she is and where she is is essential to moving forward.

SUMMARY

- Eating disorders serve a purpose in the client's life. The eating disorder is a medium for expression and a mechanism for coping. Recovery from an eating disorder requires that the client become aware of the connection between the eating disordered behaviors and her feelings, learn to acknowledge and express these feelings, and finally cope with the consequences of expressing how she feels and what she needs.

- The nutrition therapist must learn to listen to the language of the eating disorder, to effectively decipher the code and reflect the underlying message back to the client in a safe and trusting environment.

- The nutrition therapist must develop specialized counseling skills that foster a long-term relationship and facilitate positive change through the incorporation of the therapeutic process.

- The nutrition therapist guides the client through the process of change from awareness to alternative actions and finally to the elimination of the eating disordered behavior. Changes include taking risks to replace distorted beliefs and behaviors with healthier ones. The nutrition therapist should not do the work for the client, but rather guide her through the work.

- Changes in behavior result when the client recognizes the purpose of the eating disorder and is able to find new ways to satisfy her needs.

- Closure is an important part of the treatment plan, and it is important to prepare the client to view it as a part of recovery.

REFERENCES

1. Prochaska W. *Changing for Good.* New York: Avon Books; 1995.
2. Masheb BM, Grilo CM, Brondido E. Shame and its psychopathologic correlates in two women's health problems: binge eating disorder and vulvodynia. *Eat Weight Disord.* 1999;4(4):187–193.
3. Burney J, Irwin HJ. Shame and guilt in eating disorder symptomatology. *J Clin Psychol.* 2000;56(1):51–61.
4. Rorty M, Yager J. Histories of childhood trauma and complex post-sequelae in women with eating disorders. *Psychiatr Clin North Am.* 1996;19(4):773–791.
5. Patton CJ. Fear of abandonment and binge eating: a subliminal psychodynamic activation investigation. *J Nerv Ment Dis.* 1992;180(9):484–490.
6. Wilson GT, Fairburn CG. Cognitive treatments for eating disorders. *J Consult Clin Psychol.* 1993;61(2):261–269.
7. Chandler MC, Mason WH. Solution-focused therapy: an alternative approach to addictions nursing. *Perspect Psychiatr Care.* 1995;31(1):8–13.

CHAPTER 17

Developing Proficiency as a Nutrition Therapist

MONIKA M. WOOLSEY, M.S., R.D.

$\mathbf{A}$s the preceding chapters have detailed, eating disorders are a biopsycho-cultural phenomenon. Effective treatment is not possible without a multi-disciplinary team. The most effective teams are those in which each specialist has a working understanding of the areas in which he or she is not directly practicing and the way each team member's work affects the work of other team members.

For nutrition therapists, this means gaining knowledge and skills in areas not traditionally included in their undergraduate, internship, or even postgraduate training. Being viewed by the client as the team member with all the answers to eating problems yet not having concrete training in eating disorders treatment can be intimidating and frustrating. The increasing incidence of eating disorders and the recognition that many instances of obesity are actually manifestations of binge eating disorder (1) increase the need that nutrition therapists have the knowledge and skills to adequately care for clients who seek them out for help.

Educational institutions and internship programs are working to upgrade their curricula to meet this need. Unfortunately, however, at this time the vast majority of nutrition therapists have been trained in the medical model of treatment and lack the mental health training and counseling skills to feel confident working with disordered eating and eating disorders. This chapter describes the attributes of an effective nutrition therapist and current options for gaining knowledge and experience in the specialty of eating disorder therapy.

THE PERSONALITY OF A NUTRITION THERAPIST

The medical model in which most dietetics professionals have been trained seeks to provide a concrete solution for every problem. Dietetics education has focused on finding appropriate diets for various diseases. This approach is appropriate in many cases, but the rate of recidivism in obesity treatment and the poor success rate for treating anorexia nervosa and bulimia nervosa suggest that it does not work in a significant number of eating disordered clients.

In an attempt to improve success with such clients, the nutrition profession has been moving toward a new paradigm, the empowerment approach. The case illustrations in this book illustrate that approach in action. While some practitioners may embrace this approach and likely incorporated it intuitively as they matured in their profession, others may feel uncomfortable with it. It is important to recognize that empowerment work requires the desire and ability to listen and to work with an interdisciplinary team.

Learning/ Communication Style

A logical/mathematical learning style can be a strength in dietetics education, as it facilitates mastering the hard sciences. Most teachers tend to teach using the learning style that works for them. However, recent advances in education theory suggest that learning success depends on the ability of the teacher to understand and adapt to the style that works for the learner. *Table 17.1* summarizes the seven basic learning styles, or intelligences, described by Howard Gardner (2).

Eating disordered clients do not always relate to the world in a logical/mathematical way. In fact, numbers, charts, and graphs, the tools often used in nutrition education, may confuse them and create anxiety. Individuals with eating disorders often respond better to expressive and experiential work (journaling, art therapy, dance therapy, real-life experiences, and role playing) than to traditional dietetics interventions. To be effective, the nutrition therapist needs to be fluent with all of these learning tools.

What can be most disconcerting about moving out of the nutrition education/medical model into the nutrition therapy/empowerment model is that it becomes more difficult to measure success. The new model does not view weight gain or loss as the primary indicator of success; improved self-esteem and relief from depression are the more important parameters. Chapter 11 describes some resources for incorporating the empowerment model into one's counseling style.

Even when they understand various learning styles, practitioners should evaluate their own learning style and decide if it is compatible with the demands of disordered eating work. This type of work is highly emotional, and can exhaust the person who needs to modify her personality to perform her work. Individuals who find disordered eating work stressful should limit their exposure to it or refer clients to disordered eating specialists, as a client's experience with his nutrition therapist can greatly affect his recovery.

Preferred Teaching Style

The empowerment approach requires more listening and less talking on the part of the practitioner than the traditional approach. It requires the ability to listen

Intelligence	Core Components	Sample Teaching Tools	**Table 17.1**
Logical-mathematical	Sensitivity to, and capacity to discern, logical or numerical patterns; ability to handle long chains of reasoning	Calorie/fat gram charts Body composition readings Label reading class	**The Seven Intelligences**
Linguistic	Sensitivity to sounds, rhythms, and meanings of words; sensitivity to different functions of language	Journaling exercises Essay-type assessments Word finds/crossword puzzles Memorization anagrams	
Musical	Ability to produce and appreciate rhythm, pitch, and timbre; appreciation of forms of musical expressiveness	Nutrition-related jingles Music played during session or meals Dance therapy	
Spatial	Capacity to perceive visual-spatial world accurately and to perform transformations on one's initial perceptions	Food models Science experiments Cooking classes Food exposure therapy	
Bodily-kinesthetic	Ability to control one's body movements and to handle objects skillfully	Dance therapy Role playing Cooking classes Scavenger hunts	
Interpersonal	Capacity to discern and respond appropriately to moods, temperaments, motivations, and desires of other people	Individual counseling Group counseling Peer support groups	
Intrapersonal	Access to one's feelings and ability to discriminate accurately among them and draw upon self-knowledge to guide behavior; knowledge of one's own strengths, weaknesses, desires, and intelligences	Independent study modules All of the above without a facilitator Self-guided grocery tours Internet Web sites	

Source: Adapted from Gardner (2).

empathetically to tragic stories, irrational thinking, and emotional outbursts, as well as nutrition and exercise histories. Disordered eating work is likely to be stressful for the practitioner who prefers teaching/instructing over facilitating/listening. The aspiring practitioner would be wise to observe nutrition therapy in action with a seasoned counselor in both individual sessions and group settings, and perhaps to attend several multidisciplinary supervision meetings. Her emotional response to these experiences would likely be a good indicator of the impact, positive or negative, nutrition therapy work would have on her.

Team Work

Eating disorders work requires frequent communication with a number of professionals, each with their own learning styles, perspectives, and knowledge. A difficult client may require more team member contact than actual session time.

Interventions are often made by team consensus, requiring that members often relinquish personal opinion for the sake of team unity and client recovery. There is no one "right" intervention or approach to treatment. A level of comfort with the team style is crucial, as working independently within a team setting can disrupt both colleague and client trust and sabotage client progress. One of the most important jobs of the treatment team is to model healthy family/group functioning. Every interaction between team members is an opportunity to demonstrate how healthy communities make decisions and resolve conflicting opinions. Therefore, a crucial characteristic of the competent nutrition therapist is the ability to follow through with an intervention developed through team consensus, even if it does not completely agree with her personal opinion.

Personal History

Prospective nutrition therapists must honestly evaluate their personal and family history and reasons for entering the profession before choosing disordered eating as a specialty. If personal issues are not resolved (or at least stabilized) before the individual enters nutrition therapy work, they can be triggered in the course of client work and impair client progress.

Family History

An individual's family dynamics (eg, codependency, caretaking, and victimization) are likely to be reenacted in other environments, including work. The effective nutrition therapist recognizes this and actively works to avoid bringing unrelated issues into her team and client relationships. Failure to recognize these issues can distract the practitioner and increase the possibility of transference and countertransference.

While many nutrition therapists chose their career after a loved one's illness stimulated an interest in nutrition, this motive can impair effectiveness in counseling. Such individuals may try to "fix" clients, become upset when clients cannot change behaviors, and fail to maintain professional boundaries. These behaviors can transfer responsibility for the disease from the client to the nutrition therapist, prolong the illness, and lead to practitioner burnout. While personal or family issues can be important motivators for a career choice, they need to be separated from professional activities. The client needs to be viewed as a unique individual, free from any tendency to remind the practitioner of another.

Eating History

"But how would you know? You've never been there!" Every nutrition therapist has heard those words, but personal experience with disordered eating is not necessary to be effective. Everyone has eating habits that are not purely physiological. Therefore, every nutrition therapist has experience with the more general issues that need to be addressed in counseling. What is most important is whether the practitioner's issues have been resolved before she exposes herself to the rigors of treating eating disorders. A practitioner who has not resolved her food issues may find it difficult to discuss certain topics and to model the behaviors the client needs to learn. *Box 17.1* presents some questions for introspection that

MY FOOD BEHAVIORS

Do I practice nonrestrained eating?

Does it take me significantly more or less time to eat a meal than most other people? Does this change when I am eating alone?

Do I receive pleasure from the food that I eat, enjoying its texture, aroma, color, and taste?

Do I enjoy a variety of foods (including fats, dairy, and protein) without guilt or shame?

Can I try new or exotic foods (eg, tropical fruits, ethnic foods, mixed dishes in which nutritional makeup or fat content is not obvious) without fear?

Do I enjoy all the sensory aspects of food (eg, touching/smelling produce when shopping, aromas of sautéed and grilled foods, visual appeal of a variety of foods in a meal)?

Do I frequently overeat or undereat from emotional stress? If I do so, can I acknowledge this without guilt or shame?

Do I think about the caloric content of each food as I eat it? Are there certain foods (eg, cheesecake) that receive caloric scrutiny while others do not?

Are others uncomfortable eating around me?

Can I talk about food all day long and then go home and eat normally, without food preoccupation?

MY BODY IMAGE

Am I comfortable with my body the way it is now? Do I like my body?

Do I think of all of my various body parts in a positive way? Or do I have body parts I do not like/wish were different?

Do I accept a variety of body sizes and shapes as being (potentially) healthy, depending on one's physical fitness and nutritional intake?

Do I diet to lose weight even though my weight is in a medically healthy range and peers affirm that my appearance is fine?

How do I feel about my own weight?

How do I feel when I see a very large person? A very thin person?

MY COMFORT IN COUNSELING SITUATIONS

Can I listen to another's struggle with food and behaviors without relating it to myself? Without talking about my own struggles?

Can I be nonjudgmental at all times?

Can I accept that my clients may have different values than I do?

Can I accept that a client may choose not to get well?

Am I willing to take courses and get supervision in counseling?

Can I listen to a client without having to change him/her?

Can I put myself in someone else's position and imagine what his/her life would be like?

Can I be patient if people don't do what I want them to do?

Am I able to be flexible and change course when something isn't working?

Am I comfortable with other people's pain? Can I tolerate it without having to make it stop? If someone tells me something sad, can I listen without changing the subject or telling him/her it will be all right?

Box 17.1
Nutrition Therapist Self-Evaluation: Am I Ready to Counsel Others?

can help an aspiring practitioner evaluate the possibility that her professional choice may be driven by personal issues that could influence her work.

A few "no" answers does not necessarily indicate that nutrition therapy is an inappropriate career choice. The questions are intended to provoke introspection and provide insight into areas of personal growth that, when honestly addressed through peer support, counseling, or professional supervision, can improve chances of career satisfaction and client benefit.

Reasons for Entering the Profession

While a love of science can be useful in the technical aspect of the profession, it needs to be blended with a desire to help people. At the same time, if the desire to help is founded in codependency (wanting to "fix" people or basing one's self-esteem on the behavior of others), it may not be healthy. A balance between scientific knowledge and empathy is the best goal.

Because a primary symptom of eating disorders is a preoccupation with food, eating disordered individuals are sometimes drawn to the nutrition profession. While many practitioners use their personal experience with eating disorders to great advantage in helping others, this success can come only after a challenging journey of personal growth.

In working with disordered eating clients, nutrition therapists must talk regularly about food, body image, and weight. Clients ask how much practitioners weigh, how many calories they consume, and why they choose the foods they do. This kind of questioning can be stressful for the nutrition therapist and create an excessive awareness of food and body. This should be thoughtfully considered by individuals considering whether to specialize in disordered eating work.

EDUCATIONAL REQUIREMENTS

A core dietetics curriculum will provide the foundation for training in disordered eating therapy. However, helpful courses in the social sciences may not fit into the traditional course plan for a dietetics major. Should a student have the time and desire to pursue extra coursework as electives, useful courses include endocrinology and neuroendocrinology; pharmacology and psychopharmacology; exercise science; introductory, developmental, and abnormal psychology; family systems; counseling; spirituality; and feminist theory.

Some specialists have double majors in nutrition and psychology. Others specialized in nutrition in their undergraduate years and in psychology, social work, or counseling during graduate work. As many counseling jobs require a master's degree in therapy, this route may be most appropriate for the individual who wishes to provide individual counseling. The decision should be made after consulting with professionals in the state of residency regarding degree, licensure, and credentialing requirements.

While certification is not necessary to practice eating disorders treatment, the International Association of Eating Disorders Professionals (IAEDP) offers a certification course and examination. IAEDP and other organizations that offer seminars, workshops, newsletters, and opportunities for professional advancement are listed in the appendix. Many private treatment centers have professional mailing lists and offer professional seminars and workshops as well. The most comprehensive, up-to-date list of treatment centers around the world is listed on the Something Fishy Web site, www.something-fishy.org.

ONGOING SUPPORT AND EDUCATION

One of the most rapidly growing sources of information on eating disorders is the Internet. In addition, practitioners who have challenging questions can take advantage of several listserves for dietetics and eating disorders professionals. These online resources are listed in the appendix, and can be accessed from any computer that has Internet access.

Another important source of education, support, and insight is supervision. Supervision involves meeting regularly with an experienced specialist to discuss one's caseload. Its purpose is to maintain perspective in one's counseling by getting a second opinion. Because eating disorders work involves the emotions, the practitioner's feelings can be triggered in the process of helping a client. Many times these emotions can leave the practitioner exhausted and feeling that she has failed to benefit the client. Supervision allows the nutrition therapist to sort through these feelings, understand how they were elicited, and develop a counseling style that minimizes negative interactions. At times it can validate the practitioner's actions by providing an understanding of the client's anger or dysfunctional behavior that the traditional medical model treatment does not provide.

Because supervision requires time on the part of the supervisor, the standard practice is to pay her for her time at a rate equivalent to her normal counseling rate. The Nutrition Entrepeneurs practice group of the American Dietetic Association has a mentoring program that provides assistance in locating supervision providers; this program can be reached through the Nutrition Entrepeneurs Web site at www.nutritionentrepeneurs.org.

Supervision groups can be interdisciplinary or specialized, and can be a source of support outside of the intensity of the counseling climate. The appendix lists active supervision groups that responded to a survey at the time of this writing.

Numerous publications designed to provide ongoing professional education have also become available. A complete list of useful journals, books, and other publications is provided in the appendix. In addition, nonprofit organizations and private treatment centers often publish newsletters, brochures, and books with useful information. A regularly updated list of treatment centers that might have such information can be found at www.something-fishy.org.

SUMMARY

- Nutrition therapy is a relatively new dietetics specialty that requires knowledge of behavioral science as well as nutrition.

- The nature of counseling and the emotional issues it tends to address require the practitioner to be physically and emotionally health.

- A history of family issues or eating issues does not prevent one from specializing in nutrition therapy. It simply adds a dynamic that must be acknowledged and used in a way that benefits the client.

- A variety of learning styles must be included in nutrition therapy. Relying on nutrition education alone may not result in positive outcomes.

- Education and training are available in a variety of formats and should be pursued, despite the fact that there is currently no certification requirement for disordered eating/nutrition therapy work.

- Supervision is strongly recommended as a means of managing personal reactions to interactions with clients.

REFERENCES
1. de Zwaan M, Mitchell JE, Raymond NC, Spitzer RL. Binge eating disorder: clinical features and treatment of a new diagnosis. *Harv Rev Psychiatry.* 1994;1(6):310-325.
2. Gardner H. *Multiple Intelligences: The Theory in Practice.* New York, NY: Basic Books; 1993.

Additional Resources

Arenson G. *A Substance Called Food: How to Understand, Control, and Recover from Addictive Eating.* New York: McGraw-Hill; 1989.

Berg F. *Health Risks of Weight Loss.* Hettinger, ND: Healthy Weight Network; 1995.

Claude-Pierre P. *The Secret Language of Eating Disorder.* New York: Vintage Books; 1998.

Costin C. *Eating Disorder Sourcebook.* Los Angeles, Calif: Lowell House; 1999.

Friedman S. *When Girls Feel Fat.* New York: HarperCollinsPublishers; 1999.

Gubin K, Themes R. *Healing the Hungry Heart: The Link Between Eating Disorders and Sexual Abuse.* Memphis, Tenn: Medical Services Research Group; 1994.

Hesse-Biber S. *Am I Thin Enough Yet?* Oxford, England: Oxford University Press, Inc; 1996.

Moe B. *Coping with Eating Disorders.* New York: Rosen Publishing Group; 1999.

Sherry C. *Drugs and Eating Disorders.* The Drug Abuse Prevention Library. New York: Rosen Publishing Group; 1994.

Somer E, Snyderman N. *Food & Mood: The Complete Guide to Eating Well and Feeling Your Best.* New York: Henry Holt; 1999.

Woodman M. *Addiction to Perfection: The Still Unravished Bride: A Psychological Study.* Toronto: Inner City Books; 1988.

Woodman M. *The Pregnant Virgin: A Process of Psychological Transformation.* Toronto: Inner City Books; 1985.

Zerbe K. *Body Betrayed: A Deeper Understanding of Women, Eating Disorders and Treatment.* Carlsbad, Calif: Gürze Books; 1995.

GENERAL INFORMATION ON EATING DISORDERS

Abramson E. *Emotional Eating: A Practical Guide to Taking Control.* San Francisco: Jossey-Bass; 1998.

Asada C, Haase J. *Conscious Eating: How to Stop Eating in Response to Everything!* Seattle, Wash: Elton Wolf Publishing; 1997.

GENERAL SELF-HELP

Champion V. *Change Your Relationship with Food: Soar Above the Battlefield.* Tempe, Ariz: Feeding the Heart; 1998.

Cohen MA. *French Toast for Breakfast: Declaring Peace with Emotional Eating.* Carlsbad, Calif: Gürze Books; 1995.

David M. *Nourishing Wisdom: A Mind/Body Approach to Nutrition and Well-Being.* New York: Bell Tower; 1994.

Ebbitt J. *Eating Illness Workbook.* Center City, Minn: Hazelden; 1987.

Elizabeth L. *Inner Harvest: Daily Meditations for Recovery from Eating Disorders.* Center City, Minn: Hazelden; 1990.

Greeson J. *It's Not What You're Eating, It's What's Eating You.* New York: Simon & Schuster; 1993.

Hirschmann J, Munter C. *When Women Stop Hating Their Bodies.* New York: Fawcett; 1996.

Hollis J. *Fat Is a Family Affair.* Center City, Minn: Hazelden; 1990.

Kano S. *Making Peace with Food.* New York: HarperCollinsPublishers; 1989.

Kratina K, King N, Hayes D. *Moving Away from Diets.* Lake Dallas, Tex: Helm Seminars; 1996.

Levine M. *I Wish I Were Thin . . . I Wish I Were Fat: The Real Reasons We Overeat and What We Can Do About It.* Huntington Station, NY: Vanderbilt Press; 1997.

Liebengood J. *Freedom from Eating Disorders.* Lafayette, La: Prescott Press; 1995.

Mallord L. *No More Black Days: Complete Freedom from Depression, Eating Disorders and Compulsive Behaviors.* Los Angeles: White Stone Publishing; 1992.

Omichinski L. *Staying Off the Diet Roller Coaster.* Washington, DC: Advice Zone Publishing, 2000.

Orbach S. *Fat Is a Feminist Issue: A Self-Help Guide for Compulsive Overeaters.* New York: Berkley Publishing Group; 1994.

Ray S. *The Only Diet There Is.* Berkeley, Calif: Celestial Arts; 1995.

Roth G. *Feeding the Hungry Heart.* East Rutherford, NJ: Plume; 1993.

Sheppard K. *Food Addiction: The Body Knows.* Deerfield Beach, Fla: Health Communications; 1993.

Sward S. *You Are More Than What You Weigh.* Denver, Col: Wholesome Publishing; 1995.

Virtue D. *Constant Craving: What Your Food Cravings Mean and How to Overcome Them.* Carlsbad, Calif: Hay House; 1995.

Worth J. *The Toad Within: How to Control Eating Choices.* Dubuque, Iowa: Islewest Publishing; 1995.

ANOREXIA NERVOSA AND BULIMIA (LAY)

Bruch H. *Golden Cage: The Enigma of Anorexia Nervosa.* New York: Vintage Books; 1979.

Bruch H. *Hilde Bruch: Conversations with Anorexics.* New York: Jason Aronson; 1994.

Epling WF, Pierce WD. *Solving the Anorexia Puzzle: A Scientific Approach.* Toronto: Hogrefe & Huber; 1992.

Fodor V. *Desperately Seeking Self: An Inner Guidebook for People with Eating Problems.* Carlsbad, Calif: Gürze Books; 1997.

Hall L, Cohn L. *Bulimia: A Guide to Recovery.* 5th ed. Carlsbad, Calif: Gürze Books; 1999.

Hall L, Ostroff M. *Anorexia Nervosa: A Guide to Recovery.* Carlsbad, Calif: Gürze Books; 1998.

Kolodny N. *When Food's a Foe: How You Can Confront and Conquer Your Eating Disorder.* Boston, Mass: Little, Brown and Company; 1998.

Landau E. *Why Are They Starving Themselves? Understanding Anorexia Nervosa and Bulimia.* Columbus, Ohio: Silver Burdette; 1983.

Lawrence M. *The Anorexic Experience.* Rev ed. London: The Women's Press; 1997.

Rumney A. *Dying to Please: Anorexia Nervosa and Its Cure.* Jefferson, NC: McFarland; 1983.

Sandbek T. *The Deadly Diet: Recovering from Anorexia and Bulimia.* 2nd ed. Oakland, Calif: New Harbinger Publications; 1993.

Schmidt U, Treasure J. *The Clinician's Guide to Getting Better Bit(e) by Bit(e).* East Sussex, England: Psychology Press; 1997.

Siegel M, Brisman J, Weinshel M. *Surviving an Eating Disorder.* New York: Harper-Collins; 1997.

Treasure J. *Anorexia Nervosa: A Survival Guide for Families, Friends and Sufferers.* Mahwah, NJ: Lawrence Erlbaum Assoc; 1997.

COMPULSIVE EATING, BINGE EATING, AND OBESITY (LAY)

"A" J. *Recovery from Compulsive Eating: A Complete Guide to the Twelve-Step Program.* Center City, Minn: Hazelden; 1994.

Alpert J. *I Always Start My Diet on Monday: A Unique Approach to Permanently Conquer Emotional Overeating.* Northfield, Ill: Pearl Publishing; 1997.

Anonymous. *Overeaters Anonymous.* Torrance, Calif: Overeaters Anonymous; 1980.

"B" B. *Compulsive Overeater.* Center City, Minn: Hazelden; 1981.

Bruno B. *Worth Your Weight.* Bethel, Conn: Rutledge Books; 1996.

Fairburn C. *Overcoming Binge Eating.* New York: Guilford Press; 1995.

Foreyt J, Goodrick K. *Living Without Dieting.* New York: Warner Books; 1994.

Johnston A. *Eating in the Light of the Moon.* Carlsbad, Calif: Gürze Books; 2000.

Katherine A. *Anatomy of a Food Addiction.* Carlsbad, Calif: Gürze Books; 1996.

Katz A. *Eating Without Guilt: Overcoming Compulsive Eating.* North Vancouver, BC: Self-Counsel Press; 1991.

"L" E. *Twelve Steps for Overeaters: An Interpretation of the Twelve Steps of Overeaters Anonymous.* Center City, Minn: Hazelden; 1993.

Newman L. *Eating Our Hearts Out.* Freedom, Calif: Crossing Press; 1993.

Saillant F. *Interior Passages: Obesity and Transformation.* Toronto: Second Story Press; 1996.

Simpson C. *Coping with Compulsive Eating.* New York: Rosen Publishing Group; 1997.

Virtue D. *Losing Your Pounds of Pain: Breaking the Link Between Abuse, Stress, and Overeating.* Carlsbad, Calif: Hay House; 1994.

Ward S. *Beyond Feast or Famine: Daily Affirmations for Compulsive Eaters.* Deerfield Beach, Fla: Health Communications; 1990.

BODY IMAGE AND SIZE ACCEPTANCE

Brannon-Quan T, Licavoli L. *Love Your Body: A Guide to Transforming Body-Image.* Kearney, Neb: Esteem Publishing; 1996.

Bryan N. *Thin Is a State of Mind.* Minneapolis, Minn: CompCare Publishers; 1980.

Cash T. *The Body Image Workbook.* Oakland, Calif: MJF; 1997.

Crook M. *Body Image Trap: Understanding and Rejecting Body Image Myths.* North Vancouver, BC: International Self-Counsel Press; 1991.

Dixon M. *Love the Body You Were Born With.* New York: Berkley Putnam Group; 1996.

Edison L, Notkin D. *Women En Large: Images of Fat Nudes.* San Francisco, Calif: Books in Focus; 1994.

Emme, Paisner D. *True Beauty: Positive Attitudes and Practical Tips from the World's Leading Plus-Size Model.* New York: GP Putnam's Sons; 1996.

Hillman C. *Love Your Looks: How to Stop Criticizing and Start Appreciating Your Appearance.* New York: Simon and Schuster; 1996.

Hutchinson M. *Transforming Body Image.* Freedom, Calif: Crossing Press; 1998.

Johnston J. *Appearance Obsession.* Deerfield Beach, Fla: Health Communications; 1994.

Newman L. *SomeBody to Love: A Guide to Loving the Body You Have.* Chicago, Ill: Third Side Press; 1991.

Thone R. *Fat: A Fate Worse Than Death?* New York: Haworth Press; 1997.

FOR YOUNG PEOPLE

Bode J. *Food Fight: A Guide to Eating Disorders for Preteens and Their Parents.* New York: Simon & Schuster; 1997.

Cooke K. *Real Gorgeous: The Truth About Body and Beauty.* New York: WW Norton; 1996.

Folders G, Engelmann J. *Taking Charge of My Mind & Body.* Minneapolis, Minn: Free Spirit Publishing; 1997.

Hall LF. *Perk! The Story of a Teenager with Bulimia.* Carlsbad, Calif: Gürze Books; 1997.

Kammker L. *Exercise Addiction: When Fitness Becomes an Obsession.* New York: Rosen Publishing Group; 1998.

Kubersky R. *Everything You Need to Know About Eating Disorders.* New York: Rosen Publishing Group; 1992.

Ward C. *Compulsive Eating: The Struggle to Feed the Hunger Inside.* New York: Rosen Publishing Group; 1998.

FOR PARENTS AND LOVED ONES

Berg F. *Afraid to Eat: Children & Teens in Weight Crisis.* Hettinger, ND: Healthy Weight Network; 1997.

Costin C. *Your Dieting Daughter . . . Is She Dying for Attention?* New York: Brunner/Mazel; 1997.

Goodman L. *Is Your Child Dying to Be Thin?* Pittsburgh, Pa: Dorrance Publishing Co; 1992.

Hirschmann J, Zaphiropoulos L. *Preventing Childhood Eating Problems.* Carlsbad, Calif: Gürze Books; 1993.

Jablow M. *Parent's Guide to Eating Disorders and Obesity.* New York: Dell Publishing; 1992.

Maine M. *Father Hunger: Fathers, Daughters & Food.* Carlsbad, Calif: Gürze Books; 1991.

Sherman R, Thompson R. *Bulimia: A Guide for Family & Friends.* 2nd ed. San Francisco: Jossey-Bass; 1997.

Waterhouse D. *Like Mother, Like Daughter.* London: Thorsons; 1997.

PERSONAL STORIES, BIOGRAPHY, AND FICTION

Bruch J. *Unlocking the Golden Cage: An Intimate Biography of Hilde Bruch, MD.* Carlsbad, Calif: Gürze Books; 1996.

Foster P, ed. *Minding the Body: Women Writers on Body and Soul.* New York: Anchor Books; 1995.

Hall L. *Full Lives: Women Who Have Freed Themselves from Food and Weight Obsession.* Carlsbad, Calif: Gürze Books; 1993.

Hanauer C. *My Sister's Bones.* New York: Dell; 1996.

Hornbacker M. *Wasted: A Memoir of Anorexia & Bulimia.* New York: HarperPerennial; 1999.

Latimer J. *Beyond the Food Game.* Denver, Col: LivingQuest; 1993.

Levenkron S. *The Best Little Girl in the World.* London: Puffin Books; 1979.

Medoff J. *Hunger Point.* New York: Regan Books; 1997.

Messinger L. *Biting the Hand That Feeds Me: Days of Bingeing and Purging.* Novato, Calif: Arena Press; 1986.

Newman L. *Fat Chance.* London: Livewile; 1994.

O'Neill C, O'Neill D. *Living on the Border of Disorder.* Minneapolis, Minn: Bethany House Publishers; 1992.

Robertson M. *Starving in the Silences: An Exploration of Anorexia Nervosa.* New York: New York University Press; 1992.

Rosen J. *Eve's Apple.* London: Grantz; 1997.

Roth G. *Appetites.* New York: Penguin; 1996.

Schoenfielder L, Wieser B, eds. *Shadow on a Tightrope: Writings by Women on Fat Oppression.* Glasgow: Rotunda; 1983.

Smith C, Runyon B. *Diary of an Eating Disorder: A Mother and Daughter Share Their Healing Journey.* Dallas, Tex: Taylor Publishing; 1998.

PROFESSIONAL TEXTS

Allison D, ed. *Handbook of Assessment Methods for Eating Behaviors and Weight-Related Problems.* Thousand Oaks, Calif: Sage Publications; 1995.

Andersen A, ed. *Males with Eating Disorders.* New York: Brunner/Mazel; 1990.

Bemporad J, Herzog D, eds. *Psychoanalysis and Eating Disorders.* New York: Guilford Press; 1989.

Blackburn G, Kanders B, eds. *Obesity: Pathophysiology, Psychology, and Treatment.* New York: Chapman & Hall; 1994.

Brownell K, Fairburn C, eds. *Eating Disorders and Obesity: A Comprehensive Handbook.* New York: Guilford Press; 1998.

Brownell K, Foreyt J, eds. *Handbook of Eating Disorders.* New York: Basic Books; 1986.

Brownell K, Rodin J, Wilmore J, eds. *Eating, Body Weight, and Performance in Athletes: Disorders of Modern Society.* Malvern, Pa: Lea & Febiger; 1992.

Capaldi E, ed. *Why We Eat What We Eat: The Psychology of Eating.* Washington, DC: American Psychological Association; 1996.

Ciliska D. *Beyond Dieting.* New York: Brunner/Mazel; 1990.

Cooper PJ, Stein A, eds. *Feeding Problems and Eating Disorders in Children and Adolescents.* Philadelphia, Pa: Harwood Academic; 1992.

Crowther J, Tennenbaum D, Hobfoll S, Stephens M. *The Etiology of Bulimia Nervosa: The Individual and Familial Context.* Washington, DC: Hemisphere Publishing Corporation; 1992.

Emmett S, ed. *Theory and Treatment of Anorexia Nervosa and Bulimia: Biomedical, Sociocultural and Psychological Perspectives.* New York: Brunner/Mazel; 1985.

Epling WF, Pierce WD. *Activity Anorexia: Theory, Research, and Treatment.* Mahwah, NJ: Lawrence Erlbaum Associates; 1996.

Fairburn C, Wilson T, eds. *Binge Eating: Nature, Assessment and Treatment.* New York: Guilford Press; 1993.

Fallon P, Katzman M, Wooley S, eds. *Feminist Perspectives on Eating Disorders.* New York: Guilford Press; 1994.

Garner D, Garfield P, eds. *Handbook of Psychotherapy for Anorexia Nervosa and Bulimia.* New York: Guilford Press; 1985.

Garner D, Garfinkel P, eds. *Handbook of Treatment for Eating Disorders.* New York: Guilford Press; 1997.

Halmi K. *Psychobiology and Treatment of Anorexia Nervosa and Bulimia.* Washington, DC: American Psychiatric Press; 1992.

Harper-Giuffre H, MacKenzie K, eds. *Group Psychotherapy for Eating Disorders.* Washington, DC: American Psychiatric Press; 1992.

Hoek H, Treasure J, Katzman M, eds. *Neurobiology in the Treatment of Eating Disorders.* New York: John Wiley; 1998.

Hornyak L, Baker E,eds. *Experiential Therapies for Eating Disorders.* New York: Guilford Press; 1989.

Hsu LKG. *Eating Disorders.* New York: Guilford Press; 1990.

Johnson C, Connors M. *The Etiology & Treatment of Bulimia Nervosa .* 2nd ed. Northvale, NJ: Jason Aronson; 1987.

Johnson C, ed. *Psychodynamic Treatment of Anorexia Nervosa and Bulimia.* New York: Guilford Press; 1991.

Kaplan A, Garfinkel P, eds. *Medical Issues and Eating Disorders.* New York: Brunner/Mazel; 1993.

Lask B, Bryant-Waugh R, eds. *Childhood Onset Anorexia Nervosa and Related Eating Disorders.* Mahwah, NJ: Lawrence Erlbaum Assoc; 1993.

Levens M. *Eating Disorders and Magical Control of the Body: Treatment Through Art Therapy.* London: Routledge; 1995.

Logue A. *Psychology of Eating and Drinking.* 2nd ed. New York: WH Freeman and Company; 1991.

McFarland B. *Brief Therapy and Eating Disorders.* San Francisco, Calif: Jossey-Bass; 1995.

Mitchell J, ed. *Anorexia Nervosa and Bulimia: Diagnosis and Treatment.* Minneapolis, Minn: University of Minnesota Press; 1985.

Palazzoli M, Pomerans A. *Self-Starvation: From Individual to Family Therapy in the Treatment of Anorexia Nervosa.* Northvale, NJ: Jason Aronson; 1996.

Parr R, Castelli W, Clark K, eds. *Evaluation and Management of Eating Disorders: Anorexia, Bulimia, and Obesity.* Champaign, Ill: Life Enhancement Publications; 1988.

Perri M. *Improving the Long-Term Management of Obesity: Theory, Research, and Clinical Guidelines.* New York: John Wiley; 1992.

Piran N, Kaplan A, eds. *A Day Hospital Group Treatment Program for Anorexia Nervosa and Bulimia Nervosa.* New York: Brunner/Mazel; 1990.

Pirke KM, Ploog D, eds. *The Psychobiology of Anorexia Nervosa.* New York: Springer-Verlag; 1984.

Pirke KM, Vandereycken W, Ploog D, eds. *The Psychobiology of Bulimia Nervosa.* New York: Springer-Verlag; 1988.

Powers P, Fernandez R, eds. *Current Treatment of Anorexia Nervosa and Bulimia.* Basel, Switzerland: Karger; 1984.

Reiff D, Lampson-Reiff K. *Eating Disorders: Nutrition Therapy in the Recovery Process.* Gaithersburg, Md: Aspen Publishers; 1992.

Schwartz H, ed. *Bulimia: Psychoanalytic Treatment and Theory.* 2nd ed. Madison, Conn: International Universities Press; 1988.

Schwartz M, Cohn L, eds. *Sexual Abuse and Eating Disorders.* New York: Brunner/Mazel; 1996.

Smolak L, Levine M, Striegel-Moore R, eds. *The Developmental Psychopathology of Eating Disorders.* Mahwah, NJ: Lawrence Erlbaum Associates; 1996.

Steinhausen H, ed. *Eating Disorders in Adolescence: Anorexia and Bulimia Nervosa.* New York: Walter De Gruyter; 1996.

Stierlin H, Weber G. *Unlocking the Family Door: A Systemic Approach to the Understanding and Treatment of Anorexia Nervosa.* New York: Brunner/Mazel; 1989.

Szmuckler G, Dare C, Treasure J. *Handbook of Eating Disorders Theory, Treatment, and Research.* New York: John Wiley; 1995.

Thompson JK, ed. *Body Image, Eating Disorders and Obesity.* Washington, DC: American Psychological Association; 1996.

Thompson R, Sherman R. *Helping Athletes with Eating Disorders.* Champaign, Ill: Human Kinetics Publishers; 1993.

Touyz SW, Beumont PJV, eds. *Eating Disorders: Prevalence and Treatment.* Baltimore: Williams & Wilkins; 1985.

Vandereycken W, Kog E, Vanderlinden J, eds. *The Family Approach to Eating Disorders.* New York: PMA Publishing; 1989.

Vandereycken W, Meermann R. *Anorexia Nervosa: A Clinician's Guide to Treatment.* Hawthorne, NY: Walter De Gruyter; 1984.

Vanderlinden J, Norre J, Vandereycken W. *A Practical Guide to Treatment of Bulimia Nervosa.* New York: Brunner/Mazel; 1989.

Vanderlinden J, Vandereycken W. *Trauma, Dissociation and Impulse Dyscontrol in Eating Disorders.* New York: Brunner/Mazel; 1997.

Vath R. *Counseling Those with Eating Disorders: Resources for Christian Counseling.* Waco, Tex: Word Books Publisher; 1986.

Wadden T, VanItallie, T, eds. *Treatment of the Seriously Obese Patient.* New York: Guilford Press; 1992.

Werne J, ed. *Treating Eating Disorders.* San Francisco, Calif: Jossey-Bass; 1996.

Wilson CP, Hogan C, Mintz I, eds. *Psychodynamic Technique in the Treatment of Eating Disorders.* Northvale, NJ: Jason Aronson, Inc., 1992.

Woolston J. *Eating and Growth Disorders in Infants and Children.* Newbury Park, Calif: Sage Publications; 1992.

Yager J, Gwirtsman H, Edelstein C, eds. *Special Problems in Managing Eating Disorders.* Washington, DC: American Psychiatric Press; 1991.

Yates A. *Compulsive Exercise & Eating Disorders.* New York: Brunner/Mazel; 1991.

SOCIOCULTURAL AND HISTORICAL PERSPECTIVES

Bell R. *Holy Anorexia.* 2nd ed. Chicago, Ill: University of Chicago Press; 1987.

Bloom C, Gitter A, Gutwill S, Kogel L, Zaphiropoulos L. *Eating Problems: A Feminist Psychoanalytic Treatment Model.* New York: Basic Books; 1994.

Bordo S. *Unbearable Weight: Feminism, Western Culture, and the Body.* Berkeley, Calif: University of California Press; 1995.

Brown L, Rothblum E. *Overcoming Fear of Fat.* Binghamton, NY: The Haworth Press; 1989.

Brumberg J. *The Body Project: An Intimate History of American Girls.* New York: Random House; 1998.

Brumberg J. *Fasting Girls: The History of Anorexia Nervosa.* New York: Vintage Books; 1989.

Chernin K. *The Hungry Self: Women, Eating and Identity.* New York: HarperPerennial; 1994.

Chernin K. *Reinventing Eve: Modern Woman in Search of Herself.* New York: HarperPerennial; 1999.

Dolan B, Gitzinger I, eds. *Why Women? Gender Issues and Eating Disorders.* Atlantic Highland, NJ: Athlone Press; 1994.

Fraser L. *Losing It: False Hopes and Fat Profits in the Diet Industry.* New York: Plume Books; 1998.

Gaesser G. *Big Fat Lies.* New York: Fawcett Columbine; 1996.

Gilbert S. *Pathology of Eating: Psychology and Treatment.* London: Routledge; 1986.

Goodman WC. *The Invisible Woman: Confronting Weight Prejudice in America.* Carlsbad, Calif: Gürze Books; 1995.

Gordon R. *Anorexia & Bulimia: Anatomy of a Social Epidemic.* 2nd ed. Williston, Vt: Blackwell Publishers; 1990.

Heywood L. *Dedication to Hunger: The Anorexic Aesthetic in Modern Culture.* Berkeley, Calif: University of California Press; 1996.

Jackson E. *Food and Transformation: Imagery and Symbolism of Eating.* Toronto, Canada: Inner City Books; 1996.

Klein R. *Eat Fat.* New York: Vintage Books; 1996.

MacSween M. *Anorexic Bodies: A Feminist and Sociological Perspective on Anorexia Nervosa.* New York: Routledge; 1996.

Malson H. *The Thin Woman: Feminism, Post-Structuralism, and the Social Psychology of Anorexia Nervosa.* New York: Routledge; 1997.

Meadow R, Weiss L. *Good Girls Don't Eat Dessert: Changing Your Relationship to Food and Sex.* New York: Harmony Books; 1992.

Nasser M. *Culture and Weight Consciousness.* New York: Routledge; 1997.

Ogden J. *Fat Chance: The Myth of Dieting Explained.* New York: Routledge; 1992.

Orbach S. *Fat Is a Feminist Issue.* New York: Putnam Berkley Group; 1988.

Orenstein P. *Schoolgirls: Young Women, Self-Esteem and the Confidence Gap.* 2nd ed. New York: Anchor Books; 2000.

Pipher M. *Reviving Ophelia: Saving the Selves of Adolescent Girls.* New York: Putnam; 1994.

Ryan J. *Little Girls in Pretty Boxes: The Making and Breaking of Elite Gymnasts and Figure Skaters.* New York: Doubleday; 1995.

Schwartz H. *Never Satisfied: A Cultural History of Diets, Fantasies and Fat.* New York: Free Press; 1986.

Silverstein B, Perlick D. *Cost of Competence: Why Inequality Causes Depression, Eating Disorders, and Illness in Women.* Oxford, England: Oxford University Press; 1995.

Thompson B. *A Hunger So Wide and So Deep.* Minneapolis, Minn: University of Minnesota Press; 1994.

Williams G. *Internal Landscapes and Foreign Bodies: Eating Disorders and Other Pathologies.* New York: Routledge; 1997.

Winkler M, Cole L, eds. *The Good Body: Asceticism in Contemporary Culture.* New Haven, Conn: Yale University Press; 1994.

Wolf N. *The Beauty Myth.* New York: Anchor Books; 1991.

NONPROFIT ORGANIZATIONS WITH PROFESSIONAL EDUCATION OPPORTUNITIES

Academy for Eating Disorders (AED)
Montefiore Medical School—Adolescent Medicine
111 East 210th St
Bronx, NY 10467
(718)920-6782
www.acadeatdis.org

American Anorexia/Bulimia Association (AABA)
165 West 46th St, Suite 1108
New York, NY 10036
(212)575-6200
www.aabainc.org

Anorexia and Bulimia Nervosa Association (Australia)
Woodards House, 2nd Floor
47-49 Waymouth Street
Adelaide, South Australia, Australia 5000
(08) 8212 1644

Anorexia and Bulimia Nervosa Foundation of Victoria
    (Australia)
1513 High Street
Glen Iris, Victoria, Australia 3146
(03) 9885 0318

Anorexia Nervosa and Bulimia Association (Canada)
    (ANAB)
767 Bayridge Drive
PO Box 20058
Kingston, Ontario, Canada
K7P 1C0
(613)547-3684
www.ams.queensu.ca/anab

Anorexia Nervosa and Related Eating Disorders, Inc
    (ANRED)
PO Box 5102
Eugene, OR 97405
(541)344-1144
www.anred.com

Asociación Civil de Lucha contra Desórdenes
    Alimentarios (Argentina)
Sector Desórdenes Alimentarios
5600-San Rafael (Mendoza)
República Argentina
54-627-22580/24290/24291 Int 211
aclda@bigfoot.com

Association for the Health Enrichment for Large
    People (AHELP)
PO Drawer C
Radford, VA 24143
(703)731-1778

Australian Capital Territory Anorexia and Bulimia
    Nervosa Support Group (Australia)
PO BOX 773
Woden, Australian Capital Territory, Australia 2606
(02) 6286 3941

Body Image Interest Group (Australia)
Telephone: (08) 9346 8211
Fax: (08) 9346 8008

Bulimia Anorexia Nervosa Group Inc (Australia)
Unit 10; 1 Rupert Street
Subiaco, Western Australia, Australia 6008

Christy Henrich Foundation
PO Box 414287
Kansas City, MO 64141-4287
(816)395-2611
www.falcon.cc.ukansas.edu/~jpresley/christy.html

Council on Size & Weight Discrimination, Inc
PO Box 305
Mt Marion, NY 12456
(914)679-1209

Eating Disorders Association (United Kingdom) (EDA)
First Floor, Wensum House
103 Prince of Wales Road
Norwich, Norfolk, UK
NR1 1DW
(01) 603621414
www.edauk.com

Eating Disorders Association Inc (NSW)
PO Box 811
Castle Hill, New South Wales, Australia, 2154
(02) 9655 1511 or (02) 9634 7642

Eating Disorders Association Resource Centre
    (Australia)
PO Box 138
Wilston, Queensland, Australia 4051
(07) 3352 6900
www.uq.net.au/~zzedainc

Eating Disorders Association of Western Australia
    (Australia)
PO Box 523
Claremont, Western Australia, Australia 6010
(08) 9371 0752

Eating Disorders Awareness & Prevention (EDAP)
603 Stewart St, Suite 803
Seattle, WA 98101
(206)382-3587
www.members.aol.com/edapinc/home.html

Eating Disorders Council of Long Island (EDCLI)
82-14 262nd Street
Floral Park, NY 11004
(718)962-2778
www.edcli.org

Family Resources for Education on Eating Disorders
    (FREED)
9611 Page Avenue
Bethesda, MD 20814-1737
(301)493-4568
www.cpcug.org/user/rpike/freed.html

Gold Coast Eating Disorders Association (Australia)
PO Box 391
Pacific Fair
Broadbeach, Queensland, Australia, 4218

International Association of Eating Disorders
    Professionals (IAEDP)
123 NW 13th Street, Suite 206
Boca Raton, FL 33432-1641
(561)338-6494
www.iaedp.com

ISIS Centre for Women's Action on Eating Issues
    (Australia)
88 O'Keefe Street
Buranda, Queensland, Australia 4120
(07) 3392 2233

Largely Positive
PO Box 17223
Glendale, WI 53217

Largesse: The Network for Size Esteem
PO Box 9404
New Haven, CT 06534
(203)787-1624

Massachusetts Eating Disorders Association, Inc
    (MEDA)
92 Pearl Street
Newton, MA 02158
(617)558-1881
www.medainc.org

National Association to Advance Fat Acceptance, Inc
    (NAAFA)
PO Box 188620
Sacramento, CA 95818
(916)558-688
www.naafa.org

National Association of Anorexia Nervosa & Associated
    Disorders (ANAD)
PO Box 7
Highland Park, IL 60035
(847)831-3438
www.healthtouch.com/level1/leaflets/anad/anad001.htm

National Center for Overcoming Overeating
PO Box 1257
Old Chelsea Station
New York, NY 10113-0920
(212)875-0442
www.OvercomingOvereating.com

National Eating Disorders Organization (NEDO)
    Affiliated with Laureate Eating Disorders Program
(Also administrative office for ANRED)
6655 S Yale Avenue
Tulsa, OK 74136
(918)481-4044
www.laureate.com

National Eating Disorders Screening Program
    (NEDSP)
One Washington Street, Suite 304
Wellesley Hills, MA 02181
(781)239-0071
www.nmisp.org

Overeaters Anonymous Headquarters (OA)
PO Box 44020
Rio Rancho, NM 87174-4020
(505)891-2664
www.overeatersanonymous.org

Quanah Mercredi Society for Eating Disorders
   (Canada)
(403)783-8737
www.excal.net/~sheucher/qms.html

Support and Assistance for Binge-Related Eating and
Associated Disorders (SABRE)
726 Eglin Parkway NE, Suite 3016
Ft Walton Beach, FL 32547

Vitality, Inc, Promoting Wellness and Respect for All
   Shapes & Sizes
91 S Main Street
West Hartford, CT 06107
(860)521-2515
www.tiac.net/users/vtlty/

ONLINE EATING DISORDERS RESOURCES

Web Sites
American Society of Bariatric Physicians
www.sni.net/bariatrics

Concerned Counseling
www.concernedcounseling.com

Eating Disorder Recovery Online
www.edrecovery.com

Eating Disorders Support and Information
www.geocities.com/HotSprings/5395

Lucy Serdell
www.iop.bpmf.ac.uk/home/depts/psychiat/edu/eat.htm

Males and Eating Disorders
www.primenet.com/~danslos/males.html

Mental Health Net: Eating Disorders
www.eatingdisorders.cmhc.com

Mirror-Mirror
www.mirror-mirror.org

Optimal Eating
www.healthyeating.com

Something Fishy
www.something-fishy.com

Listserves
(Note: These are intended for the exchange of professional information, not for resolving personal eating issues.)

American Dietetic Association Listserve (dietetics professionals, all specialties)
dietetics-l@www.eatright.org

Eating Disorders Listserve (eating disorders professionals, all disciplines)
eating-disorders@maelstrom.stjohns.edu

Mudfence Listserve (mainly eating disorders professionals on college campuses, all disciplines)
listproc@mudfence.ce.psu.edu

SCAN Eating Disorders/Disordered Eating (EDDOE) Network (nutrition professionals specializing in disordered eating)
www.nutrifit.org

GROUP SUPERVISION OPPORTUNITIES AVAILABLE TO NUTRITION THERAPISTS

California
27162 Sea Vista Drive
Malibu, CA 90265
Phone: (310)457-9958
e-mail: membership@(800)therapist.com
Contact: Carolyn Costin, MA, MEd, MFCC

New Hampshire
Associates in Psychology
127 Water Street
Exeter, NH 03833
Phone: (603)772-3386
E-mail: www.foodhelp.com
Contact: Marc Wilson, PhD

New Jersey
The Renfrew Center of New Jersey
70 West Allendale Avenue, Suite D
Allendale, NJ 07401
Phone: (201)327-9229
Contact: Nancy Feldman, RD

Pennsylvania
The Renfrew Center
475 Spring Lane
Philadelphia, PA 19128
Phone: (215)482-5353
Contact: Amy Tuttle, MSS, RD
The Pennsylvania Educational Network for Eating
    Disorders
7805 McKnight Road
Pittsburgh, PA 15237
Phone: (412)487-6928
Contact: Anita Sinicrope Maier, MSW

Texas
Dallas ED Peer Supervision Group for RDs, Dallas, TX
Phone: (972)242-9152
E-mail: ChinLai2@aol.com/PanTere@netscape.net
Contact: Pam Chin-Lai, MS, RD/Teresa Pangan,
    PhD, RD

Washington
The Center, Inc
PO Box 700
547 Dayton
Edmonds, WA 98020
E-mail: THECENTERINC@MSN.COM
Phone: (888)771-5166

Wisconsin
Lees Psychological Services/Regional Professionals for
    Size Acceptance
20720 W Watertown Rd, Suite 203
Waukesha, WI 53186
E-mail: LLees10210@aol.com
Phone: (414)798-6878
Contact: Laura Lees